FLIGH

HOWARD HUGHES
Pilot

C. JUCKER
Crew Chief

M. COFFEE
Radio Operator

M. THIBODEAU
Systems Mechanic

T. DUGDALE
Hydraulic Mechanic

J. GLENN
Engine Mechanic

2 Nov

V. LEONARD
Hydraulic Mechanic

A. GEVERINK
Engine Mechanic

H. KAISER
Engine Mechanic

Management

D. ROE

W. BERRY

R. HOPPER

CREW

D. GRANT
Copilot

D. SMITH
Flight Engineer

J. PETRALLI
Flight Engineer

M. GLASER
Engine Mechanic

D. SHIREY
Engine Mechanic

W. NOGGLE
Hydraulic Mechanic

er 1947

V. STORM
Systems Mechanic

J. JACOBSON
Electrical Mechanic

B. JIMINEZ
Electrical Mechanic

Engineering

W. REED

D. EVANS

J. DALLAS

HOWARD HUGHES
and his

FLYING
BOAT

Permission to use the photos in the text has been given to the publisher by Wrather Port Properties, Ltd. and the Summa Corporation.

HOWARD HUGHES
and his
FLYING BOAT

Charles Barton

CHARLES A. BARTON
Captain US Navy, Retired
131 East Street, NE
Vienna, VA 22180-3615

Revised Edition

February 1998

Library of Congress Catalog Card Number: 98-90157
ISBN 978-0-96631-750-3
(Previously ISBN 0-8168-6456-X (pbk.))

Charles A. Barton
Captain US Navy, Retired
131 East Street, N.E., Vienna, VA 22180-3615
Fax: (703) 562-0797, E-mail: Charalbert@msn.com

PRINTED AND BOUND IN THE UNITED STATES OF AMERICA

Foreword

I have read thirteen books regarding Howard Hughes, but of them all "Howard Hughes and His Flying Boat" by Charles Barton handles the flying boat story the best of all. This is not just another Hughes book. It is the definitive story of the flying years of Howard Hughes and of the building of the giant Hughes Flying Boat whose wingspan equals the length of a football field including the end zones.

Initially designated the Hughes Kaiser HK-1, the flying boat later became better known as the "Spruce Goose." But I can tell you, as one who was close to Howard for almost twenty years, including living with him around the world for the last four years of his life, that he would threaten to wash your mouth out with soap if you ever referred to the HFB (Hughes Flying Boat) as the Spruce Goose. It was for this reason that I knew the so called Dummar or Mormon Will was a fraud, because of its provision to provide money for the perpetual upkeep of the "Spruce Goose."

Only the courage and dedication of Howard Hughes and his small development group advanced the flying boat project against the opposition of such as one disgruntled senator who dubbed the boat a "flying lumberyard." Barton's book contains great stories from the people who helped design and maintain the aircraft. They tell what Howard was really like during those critical years. Most of these people have now passed away and it is fitting that this book captures the life of Howard as told by people who knew him well during those very important years of his life and provides a glimpse of aviation at that dramatic time.

Barton records the drama of the senate hearings that Howard faced, beginning in early 1947, that continued until the first flight of the flying boat on November 2, 1947. Howard's responses to this senatorial inquisition, not previously recounted in other books, reveal much about his character. The positive responses he received from the public during this battle with the adversarial members of the Senate committee were very gratifying to Howard. Up until a few months before he died, he spoke to me fondly of the people who aided him during these hearings, particularly of the help he received from publisher "Bill" Hearst.

I always felt that Howard only had three close friends, Sherman Fairchild, the aircraft and camera developer; Robert Gross, the founder of the modern day Lockheed Aircraft Corporation; and Del Webb, the land developer and one-time owner of the New York Yankees. This book includes a brilliant chapter describing in detail the exciting story of the duramold process, initially invented by Sherman Fairchild, but further developed by the Hughes Aircraft Company.

The Hughes Flying Boat is still the biggest aircraft ever built in terms of wing span. In the early 1940s, it was decades ahead of its time. It revolutionized jumbo flying bodies and large lift capability, shaping modern flight. Howard and his engineers and mechanics encountered and dealt with tremendous design and engineering problems, from the testing of new concepts for large-scale hulls and flying control surfaces, to the incorporation of complex power boost systems that gave the pilot the power of 100 men to move the controls. They designed a mammoth fuel and storage supply system to allow long, over water flights.

Howard Hughes and his team accomplished all of this working with "non-essential" materials to build an aircraft of wood that many dismissed as impossible to build. All of this was done within the impractical schedule of wartime. On November 2, 1947, Howard Hughes and a small crew of engineers and mechanics, fired up the eight R-4360 engines, the largest engines then available, and prepared for taxi tests.

Thousands of onlookers were thrilled when the aircraft made an unannounced flight. With Howard Hughes at the controls, the aircraft lifted 70 feet off the water and flew one mile in less than a minute at a top speed of 80 miles per hour before making a perfect landing. The flight vindicated the program and is looked back upon as a great moment in flight history. The Hughes Flying Boat is now appropriately regarded as a true American icon.

When first published, this book was selected as the best non-fiction aviation book of the year by the Aviation/Space Writers Association. The final chapter of this new edition contains the full story of how the Flying Boat was moved from Long Beach, California to McMinneville, Oregon to be honored as the centerpiece of a new world class aviation museum, part of the Michael King Smith Evergreen Aviation Educational Center.

Jack Real

President
Evergreen AirVenture Museum

Table of Contents

Introduction

Early in 1977 when *Popular Mechanics* editor John Linkletter first wrote to me that he had long wanted to publish an article on the Hughes flying boat (published as "Spruce Goose: Pterodactyl of World War II" in November, 1977) the U.S. Navy was actively considering a full flight test program for the 35-year-old airplane. At the start of my research, the Office of the Chief of Naval Information set up an interview with Rear Admiral Carl Seiberlich, then heading the effort to explore possible uses for the flying boat. Through Seiberlich I contacted Hughes's Chief Engineer, Rea E. Hopper, and obtained the crew list for that one-and-only flight of the giant boat.

The crew list was a major breakthrough. The men named on the list had worked for Hughes for many years and had friends who had played various roles in developments at Hughes Aircraft. Some of these friends had flown as flight engineer/mechanics with Hughes. Contacts snowballed.

Because I was a former naval aviator with flying boat experience, the Hughesmen talked more readily than they would have to a journalist without an aviation background. In this way previous walls of secrecy were breached and a treasure trove of information became available.

Other breakthroughs were the discovery of a Hughes Flying Boat file in the records of the War Production Board in the National Archives; a list provided by NASA of former National Advisory Committee for Aeronautics employees who had participated in the design and testing of the flying boat at the Langley Research Center; transcripts of taped interviews with Sherman Fairchild concerning his association with Howard Hughes made available by Theron Rinehart of Fairchild Industries; the assistance of Hughes's Chief of Aerodynamics Carl Babberger who in turn put me in touch with other key engineers; and the cooperation and assistance of Hughes's long-time friend and associate, Glenn Odekirk, of Hughes's Flight Test Engineer Gene Blandford; and of all the others who so generously gave of their time in support of this project.

Thus, as a result of fortunate timing, favorable circumstances, and much foot-slogging research, this book is based on first hand accounts of many who knew and worked for Hughes and on previously unpublished documentary material.

The manuscript for HOWARD HUGHES and his FLYING BOAT has been reviewed for accuracy by Nadine Henley Marshall, the personal secretary to Howard Hughes who rose to become a high-level Summa executive; by Carl Babberger, Hughes's Chief of Aerodynamics; by David Van Storm, long-time Hughes flight engineer/mechanic; by Perry Lieber, Consultant for the Summa Corporation; and by Edward West, Jr., former Hughes F-11 Project Engineer. The responsibility for the book's contents remains that of the author.

Acknowledgements

I am grateful to John Linkletter, editor of *Popular Mechanics*, who some four years ago first asked me to write the story of the Hughes Flying Boat.

Since then, many people have contributed to this account of Howard Hughes and his airplanes. To all of them I owe more than the footnote references indicate.

I am especially grateful to Rea E. Hopper, former Chief Designer and Chief Engineer for Hughes, for his very helpful letter of June 1, 1977 telling me of the background and the incidents connected with the one-and-only flight of the giant flying boat and listing those who were on board.

Marie Tuttle, librarian at the NASA Langley Research Center, provided the initial leads to former Center employees who had contributed to the design and testing of the Hughes flying boat.

John B. Parkinson, former Assistant Chief of the Langley Research Center's Hydrodynamic Division, provided key information on the preliminary design and testing of the flying boat.

Carl Babberger, former Hughes Chief of Aerodynamics, provided key technical information, personal recollections of his association with Hughes, and help in locating other key engineers—contributions that were absolutely central to the development of this book. I am deeply grateful.

Glenn E. ("Odie") Odekirk, Hughes's oldest and closest associate and friend, talked at length during several telephone interviews and gave generously of his time in meeting with me personally in Santa Ana, California. His chance remark that he had recently seen the marine who had rescued Hughes from the flaming crash in Beverly Hills provided the clue that enabled me to locate Captain William L. Durkin, USMC (Ret.) from whom I obtained a first hand account of that famous rescue.

Earl Martyn, one of Hughes's long-time flight engineers, and his wife, the former Bernadine Odekirk, provided first hand stories of Hughes the pilot and intimate glimpses of Hughes the man.

Charles E. ("Gene") Blandford, former flight test engineer for Hughes, was the primary source for my accounts, of "Death on Lake Mead" and "The Ten-thousand-foot Split-S."

Nadine Henley Marshall, former personal secretary to Howard Hughes, reviewed the preliminary manuscript. Her suggestions and personal observations are much appreciated.

Hughes's flight engineer/mechanics Dick Beatie, Bob Martin, Ray Kirkpatrick, and Bill Grant told the story of Hughes's seven-month "disappearance" in the S-43 Sikorsky amphibian.

My special thanks to the ever-helpful David Van Storm, former Hughes flight engineer/mechanic, for inputs from Hughes's flight log books, photographs, personal recollections of working for Hughes, and for his review of and comment on the manuscript.

I am indebted to writer Anthony Brandt for his perceptive comparison of Hughes and Fairchild, and to Theron Rinehart of Fairchild Industries for making the material available.

Many thanks, too, to Edward West, Jr., former Hughes F-11 Project Engineer, who shared the story of his experiences with Hughes during a two day business trip he made to Washington, D.C.

David Grant, Hughes Hydraulic Staff Engineer and "copilot" on the one-and-only flight of the flying boat provided essential first hand information during a series of telephone interviews.

Others who provided valuable help were: Clarence M. Selberg, Hughes Aircraft inspector; Roy Wendahl, Hughes design engineer; Richard B. Murrow, one-time Chief of Aerodynamics; John H. Glenn, powerplant mechanic; Jim Dallas, electrical engineer; Harry Kaiser, powerplant mechanic; Chuck Jucker, crew chief on the Hughes flying boat; Al Geverink, powerplant mechanic; Christopher A. Reising, Jr., electrical engineer; Bill Noggle, hydraulic mechanic; Homer "Dave" Roe, powerplant engineer; Louis Tribbett, engineer who headed Duramold developments for Hughes; Jack Jocobsen, powerplant mechanic; Merle Coffee, Hughes's electrical and electronic supervisor; Don Smith, flight engineer aboard the flying boat; Phil Thibodeau, general mechanic; George Bromley, General Supervisor Plant Engineering Pier E; Don Shirey, powerplant mechanic; Earl Martin, former President Hamilton Standard Propellers; Frank J. Prinz, former technical representative for Hamilton Standard; George W. Haldeman, former FAA engineering test pilot; Clarence L. ("Kelly") Johnson, former Chief Engineer Lockheed Aircraft Corporation; Francis D. Flanagan, former Assistant Chief Counsel for the Senate Special Committee to Investigate the National Defense Program; William P. Rogers, former Chief Counsel for the Senate Special Committee; Senator Claude Pepper, former member of the Senate Special Committee Investigating the National Defense Program; James C. McNamara, who made the famous broadcast of the one-and-only flight; Charles Vickers, former manager of the Port of Long Beach; Don Lopez, Chief Aeronautical Section Air Space Museum, Smithsonian Institution; and Eddie Holohan, Secretary Aero Club of Southern California.

And finally, thanks to John Taylor and Edward Reese of the National Archives, Division of Modern Military History, for locating records concerning the Hughes flying boat and the D-2 and F-11 aircraft.

Capt. Charles Barton, USN (Ret.)

Arlington, Virginia
October 6, 1981

1

Roasting Howard's Goose

IT WAS THE AFTERNOON of August 5, 1947. As usual Howard Hughes wore his "lucky" brown fedora hat and carried no luggage. Only a clutch of manila envelopes under one arm indicated that this was a business trip.

"All set, Earl?" he asked as he walked up to the airplane.

"All set, Howard."

The converted World War II B-23 bomber squatted low on its two main mounts and a tail wheel on the private Culver City, California ramp.[1] As Hughes ducked to enter the aircraft he greeted the two men waiting inside, George Simpson, former FBI man who headed Hughe's guard force, and Fire Chief Earl Llewellyn. Never before had Hughes carried guards with him, but this time he had reason to worry about security.

He made his way between the empty passenger seats to the cockpit and eased into the pilot's seat with practiced familiarity. Earl Martyn, one of Hughes's longtime flight engineers and a nonpilot, followed and belted himself into the copilot's seat. Hughes avoided flying with other pilots, preferring to handle all piloting responsibilities himself.

No one saw them off. A few hours earlier Hughes had telephoned Earl to have the plane ready, so the preflight check and engine run-up had been completed.[2] Soon they were climbing out of the smog-filled Los Angeles basin heading for Washington, D.C. and a dramatic confrontation with the United States Senate.

As the twin-engine plane droned over the arid vastness of the Southwest, Hughes's jaw tightened with anger. At issue in Washington were the unfinished contracts for the Hughes XF-11 photo reconnaissance plane and for his giant wooden eight-engine flying boat.

"I had one percent of the contracts," he thought, "and now I'm getting ninety percent of the investigations." More than sixty other aircraft designs ordered during World War II from such firms as Boeing, Consolidated Vultee, Douglas, Lock-

11

heed, Republic, and Northrop never saw action and they were not being investigated.[3] In all, more than $824,500,000 had been spent on aircraft that never reached the fighting fronts. While the $60 million total for Hughes's two contracts accounted for a small percentage of the nation's unfinished aircraft contracts, Hughes had provoked more controversy and made more enemies than all the other contractors put together.

Hughes was convinced that these hearings of the Senate Committee to Investigate the National Defense Program had less to do with the merits of his aircraft than with the political ambitions of its chairman, Owen Brewster. Brewster, from Maine, had succeeded Harry Truman as the committee's chairman; and for Truman that chairmanship had been a stepping stone to the White House. As a senior Republican Brewster had similar ambitions. In addition, Brewster had close connections with Pan American Airways's Juan Trippe, whose goal of making Pan Am the sole international flag carrier of the United States was being opposed by Hughes, the major stockholder of TWA.

The Committee's public hearings had begun after Congress adjourned that summer. Johnny Meyer, Hughes's press agent and good-time provider, had been an early witness. He had indicated in his testimony that cash and pretty girls had been used to influence military and government officials in Hughes's favor.

The media responded hungrily. As *Time* put it in its August 4 issue, the summer-becalmed tabloids "sailed into the story with shrieks of joy and thankful indignation. They were sure they saw squads of scantily clad models, actresses and whatnots running in and out of New York and Hollywood bars, house parties, night clubs, swimming pools, hotels—hotly pursued by grinning generals and government administrators."[4]

For awhile Hughes had avoided being served a subpoena, but as the hearings had turned into a media circus he decided to attack his attackers. He released a statement to the press charging that Senator Brewster had told him in so many words that if he would agree to merge TWA with Pan American, and would go along with Brewster's community airline bill, there would be no further inquiry into the Hughes contracts.

Having fired this opening salvo, Hughes prepared to follow up his attack by appearing in person at the hearings.

Hughes had been called "an unreasonable perfectionist" and "a playboy"; but most hurtful to him were the derisive references to his giant flying boat. Senator Brewster called it "a flying lumber yard," while others called it "the Spruce Goose." Hughes burned with indignation. He knew a direct public confrontation with his Senate accusers could blunt the accusations and the derision. But full vindication could come only with the successful completion and test flights of both airplanes. As his B-23 roared through the darkening sky toward the thunderstorms ahead, he thought back to how these aircraft projects had begun.

Sore Need

It was May 1942, nearly midway in the dark first year after Pearl Harbor. F.H. Hoge, Jr. of the War Production Board's planning committee pondered the latest report of losses to German submarines. During the week ending May 10, 1942, the United Nations lost approximately 300,000 deadweight tons of shipping that carried approximately 200,000 tons of cargo.[5]

Hoge knew that such losses were twice the rate of projected new ship launchings and dealt a triple-edged blow to the nation's war effort. The sinkings reduced the flow of troops and material to combat areas, impeded the return flow of essential raw materials to factories at home, and necessitated replacement ship construction that competed for scarce raw materials—a vicious circle.

Making imaginative use of America's industrial and technological strengths to solve such problems was the mission of the Planning Board. On May 22 Hoge submitted a thirteen-page secret memorandum to the chairman of the planning committee of the War Production Board. In it he proposed a "new method of transportation": not simply conventional cargo airplanes, but flying boats larger than any ever built.

His arguments were logical. Airplanes could leapfrog the submarine menace and make multiple crossings during the time it took a surface ship to make one trip. Aircraft efficiency for load-carrying over long ranges goes up with size: he pointed out that existing aircraft devoted thirty-eight percent of takeoff weight for a transoceanic flight to fuel and oil, but that a 300,000 pound plane would use only nineteen to twenty percent of the takeoff weight for that purpose. As to landing gear and runway requirements for such large airplanes, Hoge stressed that flying boats would need neither—this would also save the weight of landing gear, which accounted for fifteen percent of the net weight of conventional airplanes. Finally, suitable harbors existed around the world, even in combat areas where land-based facilities did not exist.[6]

But it was Henry J. Kaiser, miracle man of the nation's industrial west and the Paul Bunyan of shipbuilding, who pushed the idea into public view. Kaiser's past successes were based on seeing needs and filling them, and here was a real need. His approach to problem solving was to dream big and then to scheme like hell to make the dreams come true. Amazingly, no matter how grandiose and impossible his schemes sounded, his aggressive energy, disciplined use of time, and genius for organization, inventiveness, and improvisation had always seen him through to success. And among those successes were the nation's largest dams, including Hoover Dam and those at Bonneville, Grand Coulee, and Shasta.

Kaiser had seen the need for new ship construction when war began in Europe. In 1941, with accustomed vigor, he plunged into what for him was a completely new field: shipbuilding. His ideas revolutionized the industry. Through prefabrication and assembly line methods his yards set new records. By 1942 he had miraculously cut building time for a ten-thousand-ton freighter from 355 to forty-eight days, and by the end of the war his yard in Richmond, California would complete a 10,500-ton "Liberty Ship" in four days and fifteen hours from keel laying to launching.

Dismayed by the rapidity with which the ships he built were being sunk, Kaiser came up with two schemes. One was to convert some of his shipyard facilities to the mass production of giant seaplanes to overfly the submarine menace. The other was to mass produce antisubmarine aircraft carriers on Liberty Ship hulls. The former would lead to the construction of the world's largest airplane, the controversial "Spruce Goose." The second idea, initially opposed by some key officers in the Navy, would result in the production of some seventy escort carriers. By 1944, son Edgar J. Kaiser's Vancouver, Washington yard would launch an escort carrier a week. Such ships, working with destroyers and land-based aircraft, would play such havoc with enemy submarines that within two years giant cargo planes to avoid submarines would be unnecessary.

But in the summer of 1942 his idea for flying boats captured the nation's imagination. Kaiser chose Sunday, July 19 as the day to unveil his proposal. At the launching of the liberty ship *Harvey W. Scott* in Portland, Oregon he said, "There is no secret concerning the fact that the toll of merchant ships in the western Atlantic since our entry into the war will soon reach the appalling figure of 400." Actually, in the first seven months of 1942 German submarines sank an even more appalling total of 681 Allied ships. "I tell you frankly that this is a matter which has given me many a sleepless night."

Then Kaiser outlined his solution. "Our studies indicate that the answer lies in the aerial freighter. . . . Our engineers have plans on their drafting boards for gigantic flying ships beyond anything Jules Verne could ever have imagined. There are plans for flying ships of 200 tons, and after that plans for ships of 500 tons."

As an immediate first step he proposed that selected shipyards on the Pacific, the Gulf, and the Atlantic coasts mass produce seventy-ton Martin Mars flying boats capable of carrying a fourteen-ton payload. "That ship would carry a hundred men fully equipped. Five thousand of them could land 500,000 equipped men in England in a single day. And the next day they could fly over again with 70,000 tons of fresh milk, beefsteaks, sugar, and bombs. No submarine could shoot them down."

He proposed that hulls of giant flying boats be built on shipways, launched into the water, and towed to outfitting docks for addition of wings, motors, and finishing parts.

The first unofficial Navy reaction was noncommittal. When asked by reporters to comment on Kaiser's proposal, Adm. Howard L. Vickery, vice chairman of the United States Maritime Commission and head of the wartime merchant ship program, who was on hand to present Kaiser's Oregon Shipbuilding Corporation with a gold star for outstanding production achievement, commented, "I am a shipbuilder, not an airplane builder."

In Seattle, Phil G. Johnson, president of Boeing Aircraft Company, expressed skepticism. "I don't think it is possible to convert a shipyard into an aircraft plant—that is, readily."[7]

Kaiser followed up his initial proposal with a series of dramatic and highly publicized press statements. Because of his proven track record as a miracle worker the general public and many members of Congress were prepared to believe his most extravagant claims. When he pledged that "with the aid of the aviation industry and with the equipment already in place in the shipyards we can have the assembly line in production at six months or less," people listened. Kaiser also found sympathetic ears in the Roosevelt administration as one of the few industrialists who had supported the president.

But on July 29 Capt. Eddie Rickenbacker, World War I ace and president of Eastern Airlines, whose aviation judgment commanded enormous respect, testified before the Senate committee considering Kaiser's proposal. Rickenbacker did not see how Kaiser could make good on his claims. "There's a hell of a lot of difference between building ships and making airplanes."[8]

This stung Kaiser. The following day he testified before two Senate committees, one investigating cargo plane prospects and the other considering legislation to promote such planes. Kaiser said that until 1940 he had never even seen a ship launched and that "Army engineers told me it would be impossible to build Bonneville Dam." Kaiser's faith in the power of energy, initiative, and imagination came through loud and clear.

"It doesn't matter what can't be done," he said. "So long as we have to do it, we can do it."[9]

Not until Kaiser's intensive publicity and lobbying campaign was well under way did he go to the Army and Navy with his proposal. Responsible military officials thought the proposal impracticable, but they knew that the public and certain members of Congress believed otherwise. Not wanting to give the temperamental industrialist an unqualified no, they asked the Aircraft Division of the War Production Board to review his proposal and give him a complete insider's picture of production problems, shortages, schedules, and objectives.

Merrill C. Meigs, deputy director of the Aircraft Division, did the briefing. He pointed out to Kaiser that historical records showed that it took an average of over four years to develop a new airplane. Kaiser was unimpressed. When Meigs mentioned shortages Kaiser said, "Well, I will build a steel factory and I will build a magnesium plant . . . I will not rob the industry." When Meigs mentioned the shortage of engineers and draftsmen, Kaiser said he would educate and develop his own technicians and engineers. Nothing Meigs said dissuaded him.

Next Donald Nelson, head of the War Production Board, asked Meigs to set up a committee of manufacturers to hear Kaiser's plans. So in early August 1942, Meigs enlisted the services of Donald Douglas, Jack Northrop, Glenn L. Martin, and Grover Loening.

The aircraft manufacturers were not enthusiastic about Kaiser's entry into aircraft production. On August 12 Robert E. Gross, president of Lockheed Aircraft

Corporation, sent a letter to Donald Nelson and other key civil and military officials. Gross stated that Kaiser's program to build Martin Mars flying boats in Pacific Coast shipyards posed two threats to the Army aircraft procurement program and thereby to the entire war effort: "The first is the disposition, already demonstrated to us, by the Kaiser organization to secure key technical personnel from our organization. The second is the problem of the comparative wages paid to shop employees in the Pacific Coast Aircraft Industry and those paid in the Kaiser Shipyards." Gross then raised a key question. "In view of the fact that Lockheed Aircraft Corporation is already under commitment to produce cargo planes for the Army, is it your intention that the Kaiser program be carried forward in preference to the present accelerated programs which we have with you?"[10]

Eight days later, just before Kaiser was to meet with the committee of manufacturers, Donald Douglas telegraphed Nelson questioning the wording of his letter confirming Meigs's arrangements for the committee to "review" Mr. Kaiser's proposals. Nelson's letter had said that Kaiser had been advised that this committee was being set up "to act with him" in preparing a design for his giant flying boat.

Douglas objected strongly to this wording. To prepare a preliminary design for a 200-ton airplane, he said, "would require at least 100,000 engineering hours, or the use of forty competent and unavailable engineers for one year, while to prepare design and production drawings for only five airplanes of this size would require the use of 400 engineers of this type for one full year."[11]

As Nelson read the telegram, he took his pipe out of his mouth and studied the wording with great concern. A former chief executive of Sears Roebuck and Company, he had not realized the implications of what he had set in motion.

Very shortly, Douglas got an answer releasing the committee from such an obligation.

Hughes Hears of Kaiser's Proposal

Glenn Odekirk, longtime friend and close associate of Howard Hughes, listening to the radio news on Sunday, August 9, had heard of Kaiser's meetings with members of Congress to promote his idea for giant flying boats. Sensing an opportunity, Odekirk immediately dialed Hughes's unlisted number in Bel Air, California.

"Howard, did you hear what Henry Kaiser said about building flying boats?"

"No, I wasn't listening," Hughes drawled in his flat Texas twang. "What do you mean?"

"Well, when Kaiser proposed in Washington that he build giant flying boats to leapfrog the submarine menace they practically eased him out the door as though he didn't know what he was talking about," said Odekirk. "I've been thinking about it. This guy must be a hell of a production man—he builds these goddam boats so fast. Look, Howard, our engineers are just about finished with the D-2. Why don't we design a big boat and let Kaiser build it?"

Hughes had heretofore not considered building flying boats, but this was an opportunity worth looking into. "Well, call him," he said.

On Sunday, August 16, Odekirk put a call through to Kaiser on the East Coast. Kaiser, of course, fell for the idea. His voice was excited. "That would be great!" he said. "Now look, I'm leaving for Oakland tonight by train so I won't be there 'til Wednesday afternoon."

During the long train trip Kaiser called Odekirk from stops along the way. By the time the train reached Oakland they were on a first-name basis. When he called Odekirk in Culver City from Oakland on Wednesday, August 19, he said, "Now Odie, look, tomorrow night, Thursday, we're going to launch our first ten-day boat. I want you and Howard to come up. We'll be on national news and we'll announce we're going to join forces to build the biggest flying boats ever seen."

Odekirk was taken aback by the abrupt proposal. He had never met the man and neither had Hughes. "I'll have to talk with Howard," he said. "I'll call you back."

Hughes had been in San Francisco all week for a pre-showing of his latest motion picture *The Outlaw*. A bad cold had grown worse and now "he damn near had the flu," according to Odekirk. He was holed up in San Francisco's Fairmont Hotel under an assumed name.[12]

"Howard, we've got to shit or get off the pot," Odekirk said when Hughes answered his bedside phone, and he relayed Kaiser's proposal.

"Well, you'd better tell him where I am and that I haven't talked with him because I've been sick," said Hughes. "And you jump in your plane and come on up."

"Oh, goddamn," said Kaiser impetuously when he heard the news. "He's sick. I'll get him a doctor and go right over." With that he hung up before Odekirk could say another word.[13]

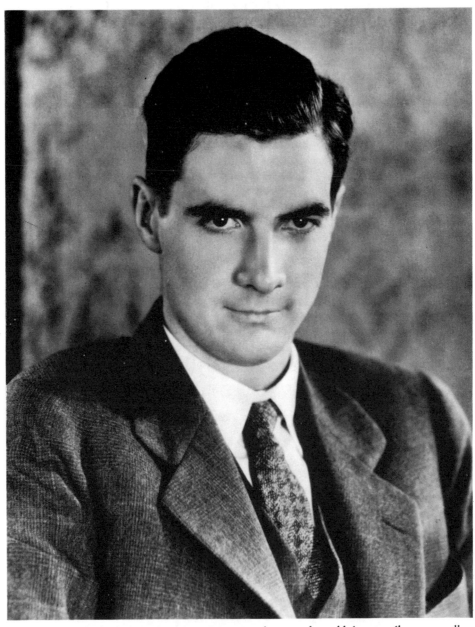

Howard Robard Hughes, Jr.—Motion picture producer and world famous flyer, as well as Chairman of the Board of Hughes Tool Company of Houston, Tex.

18

2

The Builder of the Spruce Goose

HOWARD ROBARD HUGHES, JR. was no typical industrialist, aviator, or anything else. He was one of a kind. Instead of the slight stoop the very tall sometimes develop when they want to appear less conspicuous, he carried his head bent slightly forward. His unpressed, casual dress, poor posture, and soft-spoken manner would seem to indicate humility, but at times he was imperious, sometimes displaying almost despotic arrogance.

He had a distinctive voice—curiously flat, high-pitched, nasal, and with a slight Texas twang. It was usually soft, but could become very abrasive.

He had sympathy for all living creatures; his friends mention many kindnesses and unpublicized good works. Yet he often appeared to be unfeeling and vindictive.

He had a passion for privacy, but not for anonymity. He wanted to be left alone, but at the same time he wanted to be widely known, respected, and recognized—on his terms.

He had a peculiar attitude of proprietorship over words and ideas and operated in secret and hidden ways. He formed the Rosemont Corporation to keep his name out of print, giving that organization the sole right to any biographical material. Would-be biographers were either bought off or sued. His attorneys drew up "no talk" contracts for his key employees. His Romaine Street command post in Hollywood was protected by twenty-four–hour guards and electronic gadgetry and warning devices.

He paid large sums for medical specialists, yet didn't appear to take their advice; went to great lengths to evade germs, yet failed to follow common-sense rules of diet, rest and exercise.

He was inventive, brilliant, fantastic in technical precocity and accomplishment, but suspicious, complex, contradictory and sometimes antediluvian in social outlook. He was involved in almost continuous litigation.

He had little interest in the liberal arts of history, philosophy, or religion. He read little other than technical manuals, balance sheets, film scripts, and comics.

19

Charles J. Kelly, Jr., commented on some of Hughes's peculiarities in his book, *The Sky's the Limit:* "Over the years, almost everyone has tried to explain Hughes' behavior in complex psychiatric terms. My opinion is quite simple. I think Howard Hughes has grown old without changing his little boy's fascination for airplanes, movies and girls. To the tired, middle-aged ethos of our business world, Hughes' intrigues and eccentricities are an enigma—but any small boy would instantly understand and appreciate the secret night negotiations and delight in his complicated dealings. Unpressed, unshaven, tieless and in dirty sneakers, Howard Hughes is the Huck Finn of American Industry."[1]

Hughes from the Beginning

To understand his relations with Kaiser and the government during his construction of the world's largest airplane, we must begin with a brief look at the shaping forces of family and fate.

Hughes's father, known to intimates as "Big Howard" after young Howard's birth, was born in 1869. The son of a Lancaster, Missouri lawyer who later moved his family to Keokuk, Iowa, Big Howard graduated from Harvard, earned his law degree at the University of Iowa, and hung his shingle alongside his father's in Keokuk.

But the private practice of law in his father's shadow was not the life for one of Big Howard's temperament. He was a plunger—an expansive, extroverted man of whim and fancy—and the stories of big mineral strikes in neighboring states captured his imagination. Leaving the security of a home town law practice, he sought to strike it rich in lead or zinc in nearby Missouri. Then the news of the great Spindletop oil strike lured him farther south to Texas.

With his legal background, Big Howard made a good "lease hound" as he sought out oil rights wherever the black gold might lurk below the surface. Eventually he found a partner, Walter B. Sharp. Together they started a drilling operation that probed for oil, both for themselves and under contract for others.

Being a lease hound and a wildcatter were not the surest ways to make a secure living. A few struck it rich, but many more barely managed to hang on or struck out altogether. Big Howard's fortunes fluctuated wildly. When he was up, he spent it. And when he was down, he was usually in debt. During one of his up periods he married the beautiful Allene Gano of a well-known Dallas family, and the couple left for an extended European honeymoon. When they returned he was nearly penniless and she was pregnant.

Howard Hughes, Jr. was born on Christmas Eve in 1905 in a modest rented house on an unpaved street in Houston while Big Howard's fortunes were still at low ebb. This would soon change.

When "Little Howard" or "Sonny" was just over a year old, the standard "fishtail" bits on one of his father's drilling rigs began blunting as they hit hard rock at a promising site near Pierce Junction, Texas. The same frustrating experience was repeated at Goose Creek. The problem was that the fishtail shape of the then-standard bit had only two cutting edges whose scraping action was nearly useless against rock. The partners agreed that there had to be a better way.

Big Howard was an inventive and innovative tinkerer, and he lucked into an inspired idea. In a bar he met a young millwright who showed him a model of a crudely fashioned drill made of wooden spools. Big Howard bought it on the spot for $150.[2]

Highly motivated—and backed financially by Sharp—he spent two weeks in Keokuk refining the idea for submission to the patent office. "The more cutting edges that could be brought into play, the better," he thought. "Their chipping action could replace the old scraping action of the fishtail."

It was truly an inspired idea. His final design called for mounting three hardened steel cones faced with many cutting teeth at the business end of a bit so that the cones were free to rotate as the bit turned in the hole. The rotation of the interlocking cones would cause each tooth to chip away at any resisting surface. In theory it looked good, but would it work in practice?

Sharp and the elder Hughes hired an engineer to perfect the design and had their first working model made in New England for reasons both of craftsmanship and secrecy. When they finally got their hands on the finished bit they quickly tested it in the same Goose Creek hole that had frustrated their earlier drilling attempt. In eleven hours the drill cut through fourteen feet of hard rock and brought in the first gusher in an area that became one of the great Gulf Coast oil fields. Next the bit struck oil in the Pierce Junction field.

Elated, the partners in 1908 formed the Sharp-Hughes Tool Company to manufacture the new bits. The U.S. patent had taken effect, and Hughes shrewdly patented the idea in every major patent office in the world, thus achieving a monopoly. And as a final strategy that would assure Howard Jr. of a virtually unlimited money supply, they established the policy of leasing the bit at a fixed price whether oil was struck or not.

Bits were not sold outright. When they became worn they had to be returned to the Sharp-Hughes Tool Company for overhaul. Years later a reporter asked Howard Hughes, Jr. whether it was true that the Hughes Tool Company was a monopoly, "Of course not," he replied. "People who want to drill for oil and not use the Hughes bit can always use a pick and shovel."

When drillers found that the new bit readily cut through rock, the demand was enormous. But Walter Sharp died in 1912 before the company became truly wealthy, and his widow soon discovered that Big Howard often spent more than the company earned. Fearing his extravagantly freewheeling "business expenses" would bankrupt the company and her with it, she sold her half interest in the company to oilman Ed Prather, a friend of both families. But Big Howard's spending continued uncontrolled, and after three years of worry Prather sold out to Hughes. Thus the one-shareholder Hughes Tool Company was created, the golden wellspring of his son's future wealth.

During his growing years young Howard led an affluent but lonely life. Big Howard worked hard and played hard. He and Allene were an extroverted, popular couple and young Howard was frequently alone. He became shy and introverted; his only pal was Dudley Sharp, son of his father's partner.

Howard envied those who, like his father, mingled easily and well. Writer Dwight Whitney ascribes this statement to Hughes:

"My father was plenty tough. He never suggested that I do something; he just told me. He shoved things down my throat, and I had to like it. But he had a hail-fellow-well-met quality that I never had.

"He was a terrifically loved man. I am not. I don't have the ability to win people the way he did.

"I suppose I'm not like other men. Most of them like to study people. I'm not nearly as interested in people as I should be, I guess. What I am tremendously interested in is science, nature in its various manifestations, the earth and the minerals that come out of it."

Howard's mother worried excessively about his health and went to great lengths to protect him from exposure to illness, and he acquired his fear of germs from her.

Howard showed an early aptitude for mechanical and technical things. He motorized his bicycle by installing a storage battery and an automobile self-starter motor which he bought at a junkyard. Later he and Dudley built a radio transmitter and receiver, and Howard obtained one of the early ham radio licenses, call sign 5CY. Big Howard encouraged his son's technical interests and provided a worktable at the plant where he could learn about machines and work with tools.

The Hughes family dentist, Dr. Walter Scherer, an outstanding dental surgeon in Houston, remembered the teenage Howard as a "real pistol." Dr. Scherer once saw young Howard push food right off a lunchroom counter when it failed to suit him.

When Howard sat in the dentist chair he was by no means a passive patient. He gave Dr. Scherer no trouble; he was just fascinated by the technology of it all. "He wanted to know *exactly* what I was doing," recalls Dr. Scherer, "why I was doing it, what the amalgam was made of—everything."[3]

In addition to mechanical ability and curiosity, young Howard early demonstrated his famous persistence by spending long hours teaching himself to play the ukelele and the saxophone. A beginner's sounds on the latter are hard for listeners to take and Howard's endless day and night practicing was torture. John Keats in his book *Howard Hughes* writes of one listener who spoke of Hughes as "this thing, a sort of nocturnal varmint type, six feet tall and a hundred and four pounds, sitting up in bed in a hotel room, playing the saxophone. No tune, just blowing."[4]

Hughes's First Flight

In the fall of 1920 when he was fourteen years old, Howard was sent to the

Fessenden School at West Newton, Massachusetts. There he flunked spelling (it was to remain atrocious), got one hundred percent on the algebra winter term final exam, did well in other subjects, and finished the year in the top third of his class.

He was also active in school activities. He played sax with the school jazz band, was a bench-warmer on the senior football team and runner-up in the golf tournament finals, and wrote for the school magazine. He is remembered by teachers and fellow students as intelligent, quiet, shy and retiring, but witty when he did join in conversation.

A key event in 1920 was Howard's first flight. He and his father had attended the Harvard-Yale boat races, and in the flush of his alma mater's victory Big Howard took his son for a ride in a Curtis flying boat that was hopping passengers at five dollars a head from the Thames River near New London, Connecticut. Howard's lifelong fascination with airplanes began that day as the flying boat spanked across the sparkling waters and then lifted, dripping, into the air. He would never forget that first sight of the green countryside dropping below, the miniature houses, the antlike figures of people, and the horizon beckoning in the distance.

While young Howard was at Fessenden some of Big Howard's oil business shifted to Southern California, where his younger brother Rupert worked for Samuel Goldwyn writing scripts for the fledgling movie industry. In a fateful move, young Howard was transferred to the Thatcher School in Ojai, California, fifty miles from Hollywood. Subsequent visits to movie sets with his uncle Rupert sparked his interest in moviemaking and beautiful girls—an interest that would prove enduring.

Then tragedy struck. During the spring term following his arrival at Thatcher, when Howard was sixteen, his mother died on the operating table in a Houston hospital. After the funeral his father persuaded Annette Gano, his wife's younger sister, to look after him for a year or so.

Midway through the school year Howard dropped out of Thatcher and he and Annette lived in Pasadena. His father managed to have him admitted to classes at Cal Tech, even though he had not yet finished high school, by contributing to the scholarship fund. Cal Tech kept no record of his scholastic performance. Meanwhile he had applied for admission to the prestigious Rice Institute in Houston and was accepted. He did well at Rice, especially in math. But at the end of his first term, just as he turned eighteen, his father died of a sudden heart attack.

Big Howard had prepared a new will after Allene died, but he had never signed it. The will still in effect, over ten years old, left half of the estate to Allene, twenty-five percent to young Howard, and the rest to his grandparents and his uncle Rupert. By Texas law Howard received his dead mother's share of the company. But he wanted full control of Hughes Tool and tried to buy out his relatives. There were two problems: they were reluctant to sell and he, at eighteen, was not legally competent to take over. Instead he went to Europe with the widow Sharp and Dudley. By the time he came back he had decided on a course of action.

23

The Texas Civil Code provides that if a minor can convince the court that he has the ability to handle his own affairs he can be declared competent to enter into binding contracts. The young Hughes went to court and convinced the judge—with whom he had played golf—that he was perfectly capable of doing just that. Armed with his new legal status, he simply wore his relatives down until they agreed to sell. At nineteen, Howard Hughes became sole owner of the Hughes Tool Company, moved into his father's office and took over, learning the business as he went along.

He had no lasting interest in his father's business, except for the money that came from it. Like Big Howard, he wanted to get out from under his father's shadow. His visits to Samuel Goldwyn's movie sets with Uncle Rupert had exposed him to the glamour, excitement, and opportunities of Hollywood. The motion picture world combined technological challenge with the promise of big rewards just as the oilfields had for his father.

His relatives urged him to complete his education. Instead, in the summer of 1925, he married Ella Rice, daughter of the founding family of Rice Institute. Shortly thereafter the newlyweds moved to Hollywood; Hughes was never to make Houston home again. For a time Hughes and Ella stayed with Rupert. Then they moved into a suite at the Ambassador Hotel. In a fortunate decision that fall, he hired able, experienced Noah Dietrich to manage his business affairs, freeing himself to try to make movies.

His first picture was a flop and was never released. Doubling the stakes, he tried again. This time he hired an experienced director, kept hands off, and achieved a modest success. His third picture, *Two Arabian Knights*, won an Oscar in 1928 for director Lewis Milestone. He was now ready for what he really wanted to do: *Hell's Angels*, a World War I flying picture.

This time Hughes went all out. He was a perfectionist, and simulation would not do; he had to have the real thing. He used people and money lavishly, employed thousands of extras for battle scenes instead of using old newsreel footage. When the script called for the destruction of the Zeppelin, he bought the real thing and burned it. That sequence cost half a million dollars alone. He reworked whole flying sequences because they lacked cloud backdrops and the dogfights appeared static.

But he could not find a real German bomber for the air raid sequences, he had to settle for colorful Roscoe Turner's twin-engine Sikorsky, at that time the largest airplane in the United States.[5] Hughes's technicians made the plane over to look like a Gotha. Turner flew this "Gotha" during filming. Turner was a celebrity aviator and as famed for his natty uniforms and mustache as for his innovative and enterprising use of airplanes. During one sequence Turner became irked by Hughes's demands. "Hughes was kind of working with his director," Turner remembers. "He kept wanting me to get lower and lower, so I just put the wheels down and hit the cameras on one trip."[6]

Hughes permitted himself another trick: he had all the German planes painted black and the allied planes painted white so the audience could clearly tell who was who in the dog-fights.

Hell's Angels also marked the real start of Hughes's flying career. Shooting on the film started in 1927, and in the fall of that year Hughes began dual flight instruction in a serious way at Santa Monica's Clover Field under the watchful eye of Charlie LaJotte, a 22-year-old Army-trained aviator (the same age as Hughes) fresh out of the National Guard. Although Hughes had received some previous instruction from J.B. Alexander in 1925, according to Noah Dietrich, he apparently kept this secret from LaJotte in order to get as much dual as possible before he soloed.

"He wasn't interested in just soloing," LaJotte recalls today. "He was there to learn all he could from me. He was a terrific pilot, not just a dumb cluck."[7]

By December 1927 Hughes had passed his private pilot's written exam and successfully flown his check ride with a CAA inspector in his Waco biplane. By the end of August 1928 he had his commercial rating, to which later he would add multi-engine and instrument ratings.

During the filming of *Hell's Angels* it was said that Hughes would not ask his pilots to do anything he himself could not do. One day Frank Clarke, one of the film's stunt pilots, balked when Hughes asked him to make a steep left turn after takeoff in a Thomas Morse Scout and dive past the cameras.

"Howard, the gyro forces of a LeRhone rotary engine will force you into the ground in such a turn," Frank said. So Hughes climbed in, started the engines, adjusted his goggles, took off, turned left, and crashed. He recovered, but the crash left its mark: a crushed cheekbone would trouble him in later years.

Hughes's quest for perfection in filming *Hell's Angels* led to an enormous number of retakes. Normally a director might shoot 80,000 feet of film to produce a ninety-minute film of 8,000 feet. Hughes shot more than 2,250,000 feet of film—almost 300 times the amount required for the final picture.

Moreover, the film was silent; and by the March 1929 sneak preview movies had become "talkies." The picture bombed. Overnight the market for silent films had disappeared. Planes zoomed, cannon fired, people talked and shouted, blazing planes smote the earth—but never a sound was heard. So the story was rewritten for the ear as well as the eye and for this second version Howard replaced the Swedish leading lady with an English-speaking platinum blonde, Jean Harlow. As a result, *Hell's Angels* took over three years to make and cost nearly four million dollars at a time when a million dollars was a lot of money.

In the midst of his concentration on movie making Hughes neglected his wife. Ella left to rejoin family and friends in Houston and divorced her obsessed husband in 1929 after four years of marriage. Hughes locked her bedroom door in their 211 Muirfield home and left everything just as she had left it until the house was sold years later.

Because of its cost *Hell's Angels* did not make a profit, according to Noah Dietrich, but it did bring in a lot of money. Encouraged, Hughes made three flops in a row before making *Scarface* and *The Front Page*. Both of these films received rave reviews and were box office successes. Hughes then decided to rest on his movie laurels for a time and give full attention to flying.

Howard Hughes shown above in typical role as movie director and below as Hollywood celebrity.

As a very young world famous celebrity Howard Hughes enjoyed the friendship of such other celebrities as Roscoe Turner, shown here with Mrs. Turner (in flying togs) and actress Gretta Nissen.

To broaden his airline knowledge, Howard Hughes flew with American Airways as co-pilot (and baggage handler) for two months during the summer of 1932.

Hughes Turns to Aviation

Since completing *Hell's Angels* in 1930 Hughes had spent more and more time "hangar flying" with pilots and mechanics, experimenting with modifications to his aircraft and their engines, and polishing his piloting and aerobatic skills. He never kept regular office hours at 7000 Romain Street, the stucco Hollywood building he had purchased in 1930 as a catchall headquarters for both his motion picture company and Hughes Tool's West Coast office. And the more deeply involved he became with airplanes the less often he showed up. In the summer of 1932 he disappeared completely for two months to add to his aeronautical knowledge and skill by flying for American Airlines in trimotor Fokkers on the Fort Worth-Cleveland run as copilot Charles Howard. (Later, in 1935, he would fly as copilot in Douglas DC-2s on TWA's transcontinental runs.)

Hughes's first airplane had been the Waco with which he earned his private flying license. In 1932, through special arrangements with Boeing and the Army Air Corps, he purchased a Boeing Model 100A, a two-seat, open-cockpit biplane, the civilian counterpart of the Army's P12B and the Navy's F4B. Not satisfied with the airplane as it was, Hughes had Douglas modify the P12B for him in accordance with his extensive, detailed, and everchanging requirements. The resulting $75,000 bill for the changes greatly exceeded the $45,000 original cost of the plane.

By 1933 the rather gawky-looking biplane with its uncowled engine and unstreamlined landing gear had been transformed into a sleek, single-seat biplane racer with every conceivable aerodynamic improvement from a landing gear elaborately streamlined by fairings and spats to a long-chord NACA cowling over a highly souped-up Pratt and Whitney 450 h.p. engine. Additionally, a streamlined headrest faired into the taller vertical fin and rudder assembly necessitated by the additional forward area created by the cowling and landing gear fairing.

He also bought a twin-engine Sikorsky S-38 amphibian and ordered it extensively modified at the shops of Pacific Airmotive. The job was handled by a young pilot-mechanic the same age as Hughes, Glenn Odekirk.

Odekirk was a superlative and ingenious craftsman. In the early 1920s he had made headlines in his home town of Portland, Oregon after touring the United States in a self-built automobile that excelled factory models in appearance and construction. Morton Bach, the pioneer California flier whose Bach Aircraft Company was looking for employees to build trimotor transports for the airlines, hired Odekirk on the spot when he saw the quality of workmanship on a second car Odekirk had built.

Odekirk first met Hughes in 1929 during the conversion of *Hell's Angels* to sound. During the filming of the silent version Hughes had deliberately crashed a twin-engine bomber that was no longer around to speak for itself. So he hired Bach Aircraft to produce the right sounds.

"We put two big tubes on the exhausts of the outboard engines on the trimotor and flew over their camera sound recorders with the center engine idling so that it sounded like a twin-engine going over," recalled Odekirk. "That's when I first met

Howard, but it was just at the airport in connection with this one little job we were doing for him."

But it was in 1933 that Odekirk began his forty-year association with Hughes as his copilot, mechanic, builder of the H-1 racer and technical confidant, and sometime manager of the Hughes Aircraft Culver City plant. Odekirk was assigned to work on the Sikorsky modifications when Timm Aircraft, his employer, was bought by Pacific Airmotive, which made the modifications.

Every day that Odekirk worked on the S-38 Hughes came in and watched his every move. Odekirk's abilities impressed him, and the two men got along well together.

A Flying Adventure

Hughes had two plans in 1933. One was to take an extended tour in his new S-38. The other was to race his new Boeing biplane racer. As he and Odekirk talked during the long hours they spent together, Odekirk heard of these plans and learned that Hughes was trying to hire a former Navy man who knew flying boats to go with him as copilot-mechanic.

"Mr. Hughes, I'd like that job," said Odekirk

"But you're married," said Hughes. "I'm going to be gone for at least three months. I don't think your wife would like that."

"She wouldn't mind," said Odekirk. "We don't have any children."

Hughes did not answer and started to walk away. Then he turned and said, "If you want the job, you can have it."

On April 13, 1933, after Odekirk had supervised the installation of a new radio receiver and transmitter by Western Electric technicians, the two young men climbed into the newly modified S-38, trundled out, took off, and departed Los Angeles on a flying adventure other twenty-seven year-olds could only dream about. It was the first time Odekirk had ever flown with Hughes, but Hughes let him fly the whole way to Phoenix while he fiddled with his new transmitter and receiver. When they landed to spend the night in Phoenix Hughes asked Odekirk to do him a favor.

"Yes, sir, if I can."

"Don't call me Mr. Hughes. Call me Howard. The other bothers me."

"Okay, Howard," said Odekirk.

The next day they flew to Houston. During the four days they spent there in the Rice Hotel. Odekirk gave the engines a twenty-hour servicing and Hughes gave him a tour of the Hughes Tool Company. The next stop was New Orleans.

As they approached New Orleans, a thundershower precluded an immediate landing. While they circled in the clear waiting for the storm to move on, the left engine suddenly quit without warning and Hughes landed in the Mississippi River about 30 miles below New Orleans. They anchored and the Coast Guard responded to their radioed request for a tow.

The river was at flood stage, all kinds of trees, limbs, and other debris were being carried downstream. Odekirk found that he had to keep the flying boat lined up directly behind the Coast Guard vessel or it would swing out to one side with great risk of being hit by debris.

Hughes kept him company for a while, then said, "Well, I'll go back and sleep a couple of hours." He slept all the way to New Orleans. They were under tow for ten hours.

It was April 22 before engine repairs were completed and they were able to take off again.

The next stop was Richmond, Virginia. Odekirk stayed with the plane while Hughes took a train to participate in a golf tournament. Six days later they headed for Bridgeport, Connecticut, where they kept the plane at the Sikorsky plant.

They spent the summer in the New York area. Hughes had a suite at the Drake Hotel while Odekirk stayed in Bridgeport. Whenever Hughes wanted to fly, he telephoned Odekirk to get the plane ready while he made the one-hour train trip from New York.

That summer they flew all over and around Long Island, including a two-week visit to the exclusive Hampton area. Wherever they went, Hughes introduced Odekirk as his associate. "He'd make me go through the door first and into elevators when we went to hotels and everything, like I was a guest or something," said Odekirk. "He was always that way."[8]

In those days a special aura of glamour and adventure attached to fliers, and this, combined with Hughes's tall, dark, youthful good looks, his wealth, and his reputation as a moviemaker, made him much sought after as a guest on the estates of the wealthy. He was a frequent guest of Sherman Fairchild, son of the founder, first president, and first chairman of the board of IBM. Fairchild was handsome, single, wealthy, and like Hughes was fascinated by the technology of aviation. But Fairchild, nine years older than Hughes, already was a leading figure in the aviation industry. In 1920 he had successfully demonstrated his automatic aerial camera (with the first truly workable between-the-lens shutter) and formed a company to manufacture it. Worldwide acceptance of the camera gave rise to a wholly new field of aerial surveying and mapping, which in turn established the need for an airplane that could provide a suitable platform for aerial photography. After five years of attempting to modify existing aircraft to meet the specific requirements of a good photoplane, Fairchild characteristically decided to build his own.

By 1928 Fairchild's company was the nation's largest builder of cabin monoplanes. One of his aircraft, *The City of New York*, held the record for the fastest trip around the world. Another, *The Stars and Stripes*, made the first flight from the Antarctic continent while serving with the 1928 Byrd expedition. Still another of the series successfully explored the unmapped interior of New Guinea, a most unlikely environment for an aircraft in 1928. For its time the Fairchild cabin monoplane was a superb bush country aircraft, and many of these machines were still flying during World War II.

Hughes and Fairchild, who had first met at a party in New York a couple of years before, had much in common, and their long friendship was to span two decades. In the years that followed, Hughes often flew to visit Fairchild at his Long Island estate. On one such visit, in November 1936, he crashed his amphibian on Long Island's North Beach Airport, apparently landing downwind and running out of runway.[9]

As the summer of 1933 drew to a close, Hughes asked Odekirk to come down to the Drake. A party was going on with Sherman Fairchild and other friends of Hughes when Odekirk arrived. Midway through the party, Hughes said, "Odie, I want to talk to you." In a back bedroom Hughes told him he was leaving for Europe the next day, would be gone a couple of months, and wanted Odekirk to have some work done on the airplane while he was gone.

In Europe in the fall of 1933 Hughes bought the 286-foot British-built twin-screw steam yacht *Rover*, which he registered in Panama, renamed *Southern Cross*, and arranged to have delivered to him in Florida. He returned to a New York white with the first snow, and he and Odekirk loaded the S-38 and headed south for the All-American Air Meet in Miami.

In Miami, Hughes operated from his usual hotel suite while Odekirk, who had been joined by his wife while Hughes was in Europe, found an apartment. As they settled in prior to the opening of the air meet, the *Southern Cross* approached the coast. Hughes and Odekirk landed alongside in the S-38, picked up Captain Flynn, and flew him to Miami to select his own berth. A 286-foot ship could not park just anywhere.

When the *Southern Cross* finally tied up, Hughes tried living aboard. Apparently it didn't suit him, because in two or three days he had moved back to his hotel.

The money for these goings-on came from Hughes Tool Company. It was the middle of the depression, and Toolco was not immune to hard times. Once, when Odekirk and Hughes shared a suite in Palm Beach, Odekirk overheard Hughes talking with Noah Dietrich in Houston.

"Well, Noah, I know things are a little rough," Odekirk heard Hughes say. "I'm trying to be careful of what I'm spending." He had just bought the world's fifth largest private yacht, was paying a crew of thirty to man it, plus was maintaining two airplanes in Florida. "In fact," said Hughes, "I'm trying to save some money. I've just moved from a thirty-dollar-a-day room to a twenty."[10]

The World's Fastest Airplane

In preparation for the All-American Air Meet Hughes had Odekirk tune and tweak the Boeing biplane racer's 1344 cubic inch Wasp engine to a maximum horsepower well above the 450 horsepower listed for that engine. When Hughes took the plane up for a test flight he averaged 225 miles per hour, a remarkable improvement over the plane's original top speed of 185 miles per hour.

On January 14 Hughes won the sportsman pilot free-for-all, averaging 185.7 miles per hour over a twenty-mile course and nearly lapping his nearest competitor. For good measure Hughes treated the crowd to a remarkably exhaustive and polished display of aerobatics before landing.

But this victory only whetted Hughes's appetite, and he knew that his biplane racer—fast as it was—would not be fast enough for what he wanted to do. Already the Wedell-Williams and Gee Bee racers were heralding the arrival of the low wing monoplane, and Hughes had been casting appraising eyes at the deeply filleted, low-wing, all-metal monoplanes from the small Northrop company in California. Furthermore, there were all kinds of new technical innovations that improved the performance of aircraft. It only remained for some enterprising designer and builder to put them all together in one airplane.

Odekirk put it to Hughes succinctly. "The only way you'll ever get a ship to please you one hundred percent will be to design it yourself."

So in the spring of 1934, after they had flown back to New York and sold the S-38, Hughes sent Odekirk back to California to rent hangar space and prepare for the design and construction of the world's fastest airplane. Odekirk would have the production responsibilities and Hughes, in an astute choice, picked Dick Palmer to share design responsibilities. Palmer had a bachelor's degree from the California Institute of Technology, a masters from the University of Minnesota, and had worked with Douglas, Fokker, and Aircraft Development Corporation. At thirty-one he was dynamic, sharp, and ready to try for the top.[11]

Other employees were selected with equal care. By mid-1934 a team of eighteen was working long hours in a walled-off section of Charles Babb's warehouse adjacent to Grand Central Air Terminal (then the Los Angeles airport) in Glendale. It never entered Hughes's mind that some of these men would spend more than three decades working for him. Unwittingly he had formed the nucleus of the future Hughes Aircraft Company. One of the young engineers was Robert W. Rummel, fresh out of engineering school, who later became chief engineer for TWA and a close associate of Hughes on airline transport matters.

The team had to have a name. When Odekirk had letterheads and invoices printed with "Hughes Aircraft Company" no such company had actually been formed; legally they were part of Hughes Tool Company. And at first even the airplane had no name; it was just "the racer." To outsiders it was "the Hughes mystery ship."[12]

Their main design problem was how to obtain maximum thrust and minimum drag in a safely controllable airframe. Hughes knew how he wanted the airplane to look, and he had the money to build it exactly as he wished. With Palmer he selected the air-cooled Pratt and Whitney Twin Wasp Jr. of 1,535 cubic inch displacement, because its fourteen cylinders were disposed radially in two rows with a diameter of a mere forty-four inches, compared with the fifty-two inches of the Wasp used in almost all other U.S. racers of the 1930s.

Then they designed a long, close-fitting cowling and its associated ducting so that the compact engine could breathe and cool properly, expel its exhaust efficiently, and yet have minimum drag—a major achievement. The rest of the airplane was to be as small as possible, but Hughes was adamant that it should be graceful and quite unlike the stumpy and dangerous Gee Bee ("the flying engine") that only Jimmy Doolittle could fly well.

Hughes had little formal engineering training. But he had tremendous natural aptitude and motivation for engineering and design, a mind quick to grasp complex technical relationships, and a retentive memory for technical detail. Furthermore, Hughes exploited his contacts in industrial and academic circles to gain information on the latest theories and developments. In May 1934, while Odekirk was setting up shop for the future Hughes Aircraft Company, Hughes attended the Ninth Annual Aircraft Engineering Research Conference at the National Advisory Committee's Langley Field Research Center along with such aviation notables as Orville Wright, Charles Lindberg, Grover Loening, and many others. Interestingly, NACA records of the conference list Hughes as with the Fairchild Aviation Corporation of New York City.

Palmer was well trained and experienced, and under Hughes's probing and prodding was able to implement Hughes's ideas to create a design that combined beauty with speed and safety. In September 1934, when Palmer tested their design in the ten-foot cooperative wind tunnel at Cal Tech, the results indicated a probable top speed of around 365 miles per hour.

Record-Breaking with the H-1

On August 17, 1935, after sixteen months of secret effort, they rolled their creation out into the California sunshine. A closely cowled, superbly streamlined monoplane, the H-1 looked like a winner. Despite some opposition from the others, Hughes did the testing himself; thus it was to be with every plane Hughes ever built. (Later, in the case of the XF-11, this practice would nearly cost him his life.)

The H-1 flew beautifully and was far faster than any aircraft previously built. Hughes determined to try to recapture the world landplane speed record, which had been taken for France the year before by Raymond Delmotte in a Caudron C-460 built in French Air Ministry facilities at a cost of over a million dollars. They tuned the Twin Wasp Jr. for maximum output using newly developed 100 octane fuel especially shipped in five-gallon containers from the Shell refinery in New Orleans.[13] In this way they got nearly 1,000 horsepower from an engine nominally rated at 700.

On September 13, 1935, at Santa Ana, California, representatives of the National Aeronautics Association and the *Internationale Federation Aeronautique*, including Amelia Earhart and Hollywood stunt pilot Paul Mantz, clocked Hughes and his racer at 352.39 miles per hour, nearly forty miles per hour faster than the existing record set by Delmotte.[14]

The speed runs that day nearly ended in tragedy. As Hughes completed his final pass along the measured three-kilometer course, the engine quit and the little silver

Howard Hughes with his modified Boeing Model 100A, a civilian version of the Air Corps' P12B pursuit. The original rather gawky looking biplane with its uncowled engine and unstreamlined landing gear has been transformed into a sleek, single-seat, biplane racer with every conceivable aerodynamic improvement from a landing gear elaborately streamlined by fairings and spats to a long-chord NACA cowling over a highly souped-up Pratt and Whitney 450 hp Wasp engine. On January 14, 1934, Howard Hughes won the sportsman pilot free-for-all at the Miami All-American Air Meet, averaging 185.7 mph over a 20-mile course, nearly lapping his nearest competitor.

34

In January 1936, Howard Hughes flew Jackie Cochran's Northrop Gamma and established a new trans-continental speed record from Los Angeles to Newark of nine hours and twenty-seven minutes. Subsequently he established other intercity records while flying the Gamma.

35

monoplane dropped out of sight into an adjoining ploughed field. When Odekirk and other observers got there Hughes was climbing down from the cockpit. Fortunately, the plane was scarcely damaged; a crash would have voided a new record.

Later they found a wad of steel wool in a fuel line. But according to Odekirk that did not stop the flow of fuel—Hughes had run out of gas. Odekirk had warned him to watch the time because he was only carrying a minimum fuel load to keep his weight down. But Hughes had been so intent on breaking the record that the engine quit before he could switch to an auxiliary tank containing a small reserve supply.

The Coast-to-Coast Record Falls

Hughes's next goal was to better the ten-hour coast-to-coast record set by Roscoe Turner in the 1934 Bendix Trophy Race. But it would be months before the H-1 could be repaired and fitted with a longer wing for distance racing. So Hughes looked with renewed interest at the new Northrop airplanes.

Famed aviatrix Jacqueline Cochran had recently purchased a Northrop Gamma, a sleek advanced monoplane she was readying for the Bendix race.[15] Hughes calculated that if he replaced the 1535 engine Cochran had on the plane with the latest Wright Cyclone R-1820G 850 horsepower engine coupled with a Hamilton Standard variable pitch propeller, he could easily better Turner's record.

At about eleven thirty one night the telephone rang in Cochran's hotel room. She groped sleepily for the phone at the bedside table.

"Hello."

"Jackie, this is Howard."

"Howard who?"

"Howard Hughes."

She was tired and in no mood for practical jokes at what for a working girl was a late hour. "Aw, come off it. It's late and I'm tired."

"No, really. It's Howard. I want to buy your airplane."

"Well, it's not for sale," she said. "I'm going to fly it in the Bendix."

"I don't want to fly it in the Bendix, I want to fly it transcontinental."

"So do I," said Jackie.

Hughes wouldn't be put off. "Come on out to Mines Field tomorrow, look at the racer and we'll talk about it some more."

The offer to inspect Hughes's "fabulous" racer was irresistible. She hadn't been able to keep her eyes off it whenever she had seen Hughes exercising it. "Aerodynamically," Cochran says, "the plane was as far apart from the then-accepted airplanes as the jets are from the planes of World War II. I had been looking at this racer with my mouth watering."

She got to sit in the airplane—she didn't get to fly it. Hughes, with his usual persistence, kept trying for weeks to work out a deal for the Gamma that she could not refuse. At that time Jackie was unmarried and supported her aviation activities through her efforts in the beauty and cosmetic business. Hughes knew that she was terribly short of funds.

Finally he offered to rent the Gamma from her for nearly as much as she had paid for it. "I couldn't afford not to rent it to him," she says.

Meanwhile, Hughes made eleven flights as a Douglas DC-2 copilot on TWA's transcontinental runs during 1935, apparently to build his transcontinental experience in preparation for the record attempt.[16]

On January 13, 1936 Hughes flew the modified Gamma from Burbank to Newark in nine hours and twenty-seven minutes at an average speed of 259.1 miles per hour for a new record. Then he went on to set intercity records for New York—Miami and Chicago—Los Angeles.

"It just broke my heart," said Cochran, "but I couldn't afford to do otherwise. Then the deadline was up for him to either return the Gamma or to purchase it. So he sent me a purchase check because he was in Chicago and too busy to return the airplane, I guess. Then he turned around and sold it back to me for much less a few days later—and he did a lot of work on it for me for practically nothing, which was interesting. He has a very interesting streak."[17]

For his achievements Hughes was awarded the coveted Harmon trophy. On January 20, 1937 enroute to the presentation ceremony he flew a revamped H-1, now fitted with a longer wing and a new Pratt and Whitney R-1535 Wasp engine of 700 horsepower, from Burbank to Newark in seven hours, twenty-eight minutes and thirty-five seconds. (Hughes built two sets of wings for the H-1, one with a span of only twenty-five feet that he used to set the closed course record, and the other with a span of thirty-one feet nine inches that he used for his long-distance runs. The wings were of wood and the fuselage was aluminum.) The little racer averaged 327.15 miles per hour over the 2,490-mile course for a record that was to stand for ten years. And he did it using only forty-eight percent power because he wanted to be sure and make it nonstop.[18]

The H-1: A Major Milestone

The H-1 had a great impact on the design of high performance aircraft. Noteworthy features were the close-fitting, bell-shaped engine cowling, the gently curved wing fillets that molded the wings to the fuselage, the retractable landing gear, the extremely smooth surfaces with countersunk rivets and flush joints, ailerons that drooped fifteen degrees when the flaps were fully extended (this increasing the lift along the full span of the wing during takeoff and landing), and the smoothly faired and totally enclosed cockpit with a sliding canopy windscreen for easy entrance and exit. Typical of everything on the H-1, the landing gear was so perfectly fitted that the gear fairings and doors were difficult to see when the gear was retracted.

So important is the H-1 in the history of flight technology that it is now enshrined at the Smithsonian's Air and Space Museum in Washington, D.C., where a plaque reads: "The Hughes H-1 racer was a major milestone on the road to such radial-engine powered World War II fighters as the American Grumman F6F Hellcat and Republic P-47 Thunderbolt, the Japanese Mitsubishi Type 0 (Zero), and the German Focke-Wulf 190. The H-1 demonstrated that properly designed radial engine aircraft could compete with the lower-drag inline designs."

Hughes's development of the H-1 racer made another vital contribution to American aviation, according to Jacqueline Cochran. "He had a group of young engineers working on that racer who became the backbone in the development of our wartime aircraft. And at that time they probably couldn't have gotten a job as a busboy in a cafeteria. We were in the heart of the depression in our country, and great talent would have just gone by the wayside if he hadn't put up the money for the development of that and many other things in aviation. . . . I have a lot of respect for him, frankly, in spite of his eccentric attitudes."[19]

While Hughes was still on the East Coast after his record-breaking transcontinental flight in the H-1 he was telephoned by General O. P. Echols, Commander of the Army Air Corps' Wright Field in Dayton, Ohio, a center for Air Corps testing and procurement. Echols told Hughes that the Air Corps was keenly interested in the H-1 because it was faster than anything they had at the time. "Can you stop by and let us see it on your way back to California?" Hughes agreed and Echols arranged for a group of top brass to be on hand to meet him.

According to Noah Dietrich, there now occurred the first of several incidents that would poison the minds of key Army Air Corps officers against Hughes for years to come. He overflew Wright Field, gassed up in Chicago, and continued on to California. Echols, who later became Chief of Air Corps procurement, never forgot the snub. He vowed that Howard Hughes would never get a "dime's worth of business" from him. Hughes told Dietrich that he just forgot to stop in Dayton. Dietrich thought the snub was intentional, that Howard simply "didn't want those generals snooping around his airplane and stealing his ideas."

Such an incident did occur, according to the testimony given in the 1947 Senate hearings, but not in the way Dietrich recalls in his book. According to information in Hughes's logbooks Hughes did not fly the racer home. The plane sat in Newark until Allen Russel, corporate pilot for William Randolph Hearst, flew it back to Burbank.

Around the World

Hughes's next achievement on the way to his stated goal of becoming the "world's greatest aviator" was his 1938 flight around the world. He had been greatly impressed by the one-eyed Wiley Post's 1933 solo flight around the world in the single-engine *Winnie Mae*—"one of the most remarkable feats of all time," Hughes said in later speeches. "I don't really know how that man could have done it all alone."

This was to be no catch-as-catch-can, seat-of-the-pants attempt. Hughes planned to circle the globe in a manner emphasizing the coming of age and safety of flying.

At first he planned to use an S-43 Sikorsky amphibian that he bought in 1937. But because of the slow speed he shopped around for something more suitable and selected a twin-engine, low-wing Lockheed Model 14 Lodestar.

Preparations for the world circling flight took two years. Typically, he was extremely meticulous about every detail and tried to provide for every possible contingency. Because the Lodestar was a landplane he had eighty pounds of Ping-Pong balls stuffed into all the empty recesses of the wings and fuselage so the plane would float if it were forced down at sea. He had Odekirk and his hangar crew strip the plane of all nonessential weight and install extra fuel tanks. All tanks were lined with neoprene to make them self-sealing. Hughes also carried ethyl on the flight to mix with low-test gas if he were unable to obtain the proper octane fuel along the way.

Hughes spared no expense in equipping the plane with the latest blind flying, communication, and navigation equipment, including the newly-perfected "Sperry Gyro Pilot," which could automatically maintain level flight and help to hold accurate headings on the long over-water legs of the flight.

He also stowed an impressive collection of survival equipment aboard the aircraft including a solar still for making fresh water from sea water, a kite for carrying a radio antenna aloft, portable bailout radios, and a shotgun. Although Hughes was meticulous enough to have a study made to determine what kind of bread would stay fresh the longest, his choice of provisions was not very impressive—mostly ham and cheese sandwiches and milk.

The Hughes talent for finding outstanding men to work with him was demonstrated again in his choice of crew members. Radioman Richard Stoddard, 38, was a former shipboard radio operator, a licensed airplane pilot, and an NBC communications engineer. Navigator Thomas Thurlow, 33, was an Army pilot and aerial navigator noted for his development of special navigation instruments. The combination copilot—alternate navigator was Harry P. McLean Conner, an expert navigator with transocean experience on previous record-breaking flights.

The flight engineer was to have been Odekirk. But he had been working long hours with little sleep to get the airplane ready for the flight; he had lost thirty-five pounds and was worn out. Nevertheless, he told Hughes that if weather delayed the departure long enough for him to get some rest, he would go. But in New York Hughes decided he wanted all new cylinders on the engines, so Odekirk had to work day and night with Wright Aeronautical people to get the job done. Consequently he was replaced by Ed Lund, a Hughes employee who was an expert on aircraft engine maintenance. (Lund made another special contribution to Hughes's effort; he was tall and looked a bit like Hughes, so when Hughes wanted to avoid crowds he would send Lund out first. While the crowd was distracted, Hughes could pass freely.)[20]

Al Lodwick, a vice president of Curtiss Wright, which made the plane's engines, handled advance arrangements for flight clearances, landing rights, and en route fuel provisions. William C. Rockefeller, advised by famed Cal Tech meteorologist

Add New Chapter to Aviation History With Record Flight

Richard Stoddart   Harry P. Connor   Howard Hughes   Lieut. T. L. Thurlow   Edward Lund

With four crewmen, Howard Hughes on July 14, 1938 established a new record for around-the-world flight of three days, nineteen hours and seventeen minutes; thus shattering Wiley Post's solo record of seven days, eighteen hours and forty-nine minutes which was established in 1933.

The crowd following the Lockheed 14 as it taxis up in front of the Administration Building of Floyd Bennett Field in New York City.

Above: Ticker tape parade down Broadway with Grover Whalen and Albert Lodwick, (7-15-38).
Below: Being introduced over microphone by Mayor La Guardia.

Thirty-year old Howard Hughes with his H-1 racer, which was a major milestone on the road to the development of radial-engine powered fighters for World War II.

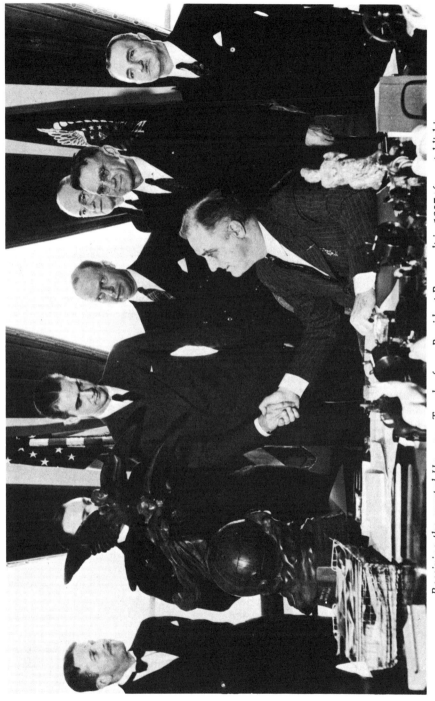

Receiving the coveted Harmann Trophy from President Roosevelt in 1937, for establishing the trans-continental record of nine hours and twenty-seven minutes in Jackie Cochran's Northrop Gamma. However, in his flight to Washington, D.C. to receive the trophy, he bettered that speed by hitting a new record time of seven hours, twenty-eight minutes and thirty-four seconds in his modified H-1 racer.

Dr. Irving Parkhurst Krick under whom Rockefeller had studied, helped choose routes and flight altitudes. According to longtime Hughes engineer Bruce Burk, Rockefeller worked for Hughes both as a meteorologist and an aerodynamicist and had been involved with tunnel testing the Hughes racer at Cal Tech.

Rockefeller established a 24-hour weather forecast center at the New York World's Fair grounds with the help of its manager, Grover Whalen. The latest teletypes funneled data from London, Paris, Berlin, Rome, Moscow, Manila, Honolulu, San Francisco, and Washington. Daily synoptic charts provided forecasts of wind direction and strength, temperatures, ceilings, visibilities, and storm warnings. A marvel of efficiency, this center was the forerunner of today's flight Advisory Weather Service.

On this flight Hughes used the Fairchild-Maxon Line-of-Position computer, manufactured by Fairchild Aviation, as one of his chief navigation instruments. The radio direction finder on his plane was also by Fairchild. Sherman Fairchild recalls going out to the hangar the night before Hughes took off and working with a crew on the adjustment of the magnetic compasses. "I was doing my best to get the compass on the airplane, he was insisting that all these engines be run all night to run them in, and with the darn thing jiggling it was hard to get the compass on. But he said, 'Look, to hell with the compass. It's more important that the engines run.'"[21]

Because the primary aim of the flight was to publicize the reliability and safety of flying, Hughes astutely arranged for it to represent the New York World's Fair, scheduled to open in 1939. He could thus avail himself of the services of Grover Whalen, president of the fair and New York's official greeter. Whalen cranked up a high-powered campaign that included radio, movie and press coverage of the official departure and arrival ceremonies, and flight progress releases. Millions of people around the world followed the flight avidly.

The Great Accomplishment

Hughes bettered the speed record previously held by Charles A. Lindbergh for the New York to Paris trip with a time of sixteen hours and thirty-five minutes at an average speed of 219.6 miles per hour. He set an around-the-world record of three days, nineteen hours, and nine minutes. For 15,000 miles he averaged 206 miles per hour. An outstanding feature was the excellence of navigation: the plane was never more than twenty miles off course during the entire flight.[22]

When Hughes landed in New York on July 13, 1938, ninety-one hours after his departure, a surging crowd made it difficult for Mayor Fiorello La Guardia and Grover Whalen to officially welcome him. La Guardia and Whalen accompanied him on the traditional ticker tape parade up Broadway—where, according to the New York sanitation department, the populace threw a greater weight of confetti and ticker tape in his honor than had been thrown during Lindbergh's reception after his solo transatlantic flight to Paris.

Throughout, Hughes was a smiling hero. "He had the face of a poet and the shyness of a schoolboy," said the *New York Times* of his city hall reception.

Of interest is that Jesse Jones, Secretary of Commerce, Chairman of the Reconstruction Finance Corporation, and an old family friend, was the second speaker after the mayor's city hall welcoming speech. The Defense Plant Corporation, an RFC subsidiary, would later let and supervise the contract on the flying boat.

Hughes was registered at the Drake Hotel, but he stayed at Fairchild's apartment during his New York visit. A formal reception and dinner was scheduled, and ambassadors and diplomats from all the countries Hughes had passed over were to attend. En route to the reception a Hughes public relations man handed Hughes a speech he had prepared for him to deliver at the dinner. The PR man stressed the importance of getting the names of the diplomats right and putting them in proper order—the order in which Hughes had passed over their respective countries—when he thanked them for their help. Hughes glanced at the speech and said, "Aw, I don't need this," and handed it back to the jittery public relations man. Once at the reception, Hughes disappeared for an hour or so. Everyone searched frantically for him until Fairchild finally located him in the men's room, locked in one of the stalls. Hughes was writing his own speech—on toilet paper. Fairchild says it was one of the best speeches he had ever heard. Furthermore, he observed, Hughes reeled off the diplomats' names as if he had been practicing them for days.[23]

Surprisingly, Hughes seemed to enjoy the limelight.

"Please remember," he said, "that I am but one of five persons who made that trip, and being taller than any of them I kept getting in the way and making a nuisance of myself. If you must praise anyone, save your shouts for Wiley Post, for by flying around the world, in the time he did, and with but one eye, he made the most amazing flight that has ever occurred."

Hughes also gave credit to the aviation industry and the thousands of people who had contributed to the success of his flight, which, he said, was in no way a stunt. He emphasized that the flight publicized the progress of American aircraft abroad. This last point was particularly well-received inasmuch as the country was just pulling out of the Depression.

In Houston, a quarter of a million Texans gave Hughes a tumultuous homecoming ovation after he set his silver monoplane down on the airport named in his honor. That night a homecoming banquet filled the big ballroom of the Rice Hotel to capacity. *The Houston Post* reported that he was as bashful as a schoolboy and just as captivating. After he was introduced Hughes dug down in his pocket and brought out a wad of notes from which he spoke. "If you don't believe I wrote this speech myself, just try to read the handwriting," he said.

Hughes paid tribute to the executives and employees of the two Houston companies that he headed: Hughes Tool and Gulf Brewing Company. "Anything I have done which you may consider worthwhile," he said, "has been made possible by the genius of my father and the faithfulness, diligence and enterprise of the men who comprise the various parts of the company he created."

So unassuming was his mention of his own part in the flight that toastmaster John T. Scott reminded the audience: "Don't forget, Howard Hughes was on that plane, too." But Hughes insisted on disclaiming any fame. "Why, I couldn't even get a job as first pilot on any airline in this country."[24]

For the moment, Hughes appeared to have achieved his ambition to be the greatest aviator in the world. The National Junior Chamber of Commerce selected him as one of the outstanding young men of 1938, and on the basis of his round-the-world flight the National Aeronautics Association named him Aviator of the Year. He also received the Octave Chanute Award, and President Franklin D. Roosevelt presented him with the Collier Trophy for aviation achievement.

On the Eve of the War

Hughes next planned to fly around the world on a goodwill tour of major world capitals in the first pressurized, high-altitude transport, the Boeing Model 307 Stratoliner. In the process, he bailed Boeing out of a difficult situation. Although ten Stratoliners had been ordered and were in various stages of construction—four for Pan American and six for TWA—Boeing had cash flow problems. It had spent a lot of money developing the Model 299 prototype of the famous B-17 Flying Fortress as its entry in an Air Corps bomber competition in the mid-1930s. Although the 299 performed beautifully during the competition, it crashed when control locks were not released prior to takeoff on one of the final routine test flights at Wright Field, and Douglas won the competition with its B-18, an outgrowth of the DC-3.

As part of its effort to recoup, Boeing went after airline money with its Stratoliner design, which incorporated the wings, powerplants, nacelles, and tail surfaces of the 299. But by the time Hughes and Odekirk went to Seattle to arrange payment for the TWA purchase, Boeing was hurting. The money was not coming in fast enough to make up for the loss of the bomber contract. Hughes now owned enough TWA stock to have controlling interest, and part of the deal was that Hughes was to get one of the six planes TWA had ordered.

Hughes arranged that the Hughes Tool Company would make weekly partial payments on TWA's six airplanes of about $100,000 a week. This helped Boeing through a lean period that ended when the Air Corps ordered thirty-nine B-17s in the fall of 1939.[25]

Germany's attack on Poland September 1, 1939 began World War II and ended Hughes's plans for another world flight. At first German air power ruled the skies as a key element of the blitzkrieg that carried the Nazi war machine to success after success. Shaken, the United States Army Air Corps launched a crash program to develop aircraft superior to that of Germany. It was then that Hughes decided to enter the competition for the development of a high-performance interceptor.

He conceived a radical design: a twin-engine, twin-boom fighter with the cockpit mounted in a pod midway on the wing between the booms. Again he clamped tight security around his Burbank hangar—so tight, in fact, that Hap Arnold, Commanding General of the United States Army Air Corps, was turned away by an armed guard when his party arrived to inspect the plane. Once again Hughes had affronted powerful people in the Air Corps.

Later, when a contract was awarded to Lockheed for what became the extremely successful twin-boom P-38, Hughes fumed that his ideas had been stolen and he became even more paranoid about secrecy. According to Noah Dietrich, Hughes never grasped the fact that an idea by itself is not patentable. As time went on and Hughes found that many of his ideas showed up in other people's work, his passion for secrecy increased.

Hughes, Fairchild, and "Success"

Hughes's friendship with Sherman Fairchild throws light on his personality and inclinations as an aviation pioneer searching for commercial success. The two men were good friends and in frequent contact with each other from about 1931 to the 1950s when Hughes began his publicized retreat from public view. Their personalities were similar, but they differed in critical ways which illuminate their respective careers. Both were wealthy, attractive, single, and shared an interest in beautiful women. And both were fascinated by, involved with, and had high aptitude for technology, particularly that associated with aviation. The two men would appear at the Stork Club or El Morocco with their dates and immediately become engrossed in some discussion of, say, the latest aircraft navigation equipment, while their dates sat staring into space.

But perhaps the most important trait they shared was a kind of waywardness in their powers of concentration. Both men were capable of intense concentration on a single interest: but neither could retain this interest for long. Through the 1930s Hughes turned from moviemaking to aviation to moviemaking again, while Fairchild shifted from aviation to photography to boats to the tennis courts and back to aviation. As a result, the aircraft industry did not take either too seriously. Professionals like Donald Douglas, or "Dutch" Kindelberger at North American Aviation, or Hap Arnold or Hugh Knerr in the Air Corps, whose whole lives were given over to aviation, could look on Fairchild and Hughes as amateurs—gifted to be sure, yet more interested in pursuing new ideas than in concentrating on the central business of the industry: building more and better airplanes than the next fellow.

It was typical of Fairchild that he should become much more interested in a new idea (such as Duramold, an idea he pursued to the detriment of the Fairchild company as a whole) than in developing a product more in line with the company's experience—and more likely to make money for it. Similarly, none of the major manufacturers would have spent nearly two years perfecting the Hughes Special, a plane that reached for a single goal—speed—and which could therefore never be sold in quantity. There was a feeling in the industry that Hughes and Fairchild—especially Hughes—were simply dilettantes who could afford to play around with aircraft ideas.

Yet, on the whole, the industry admired their contributions to the aviation art. Hughes broke the world's landplane speed record in the Hughes Special, and he added significantly to aeronautical know-how in the process. In connection with Duramold, Fairchild pioneered such techniques as electronic gluing, and as a structural material Duramold presaged modern sandwich and honeycomb structures.

Nevertheless, the developments of neither man—at least in the 1930s—led directly to a major *business* success; for neither had yet found the proper mix of technology and market readiness necessary at any given time for the economic success of an aircraft design.

For aviation success *was* an economic matter; an aircraft had to be marketable, which meant that it had to be useful to a significant number of aircraft buyers. By the end of the 1930s—certainly by 1939—it was apparent that such success in the 1940s would depend almost exclusively on building aircraft useful in war. Both Fairchild and Hughes wanted to succeed in the conventional business fashion. Hughes made persistent attempts to sell airplane designs to the skeptical professionals at Wright Field. But by concentrating to the point of obsession on the technology of speed, on breaking records, and on doing things his own way, Hughes blew his chances.

The two men's careers diverged where their personalities did. Fairchild was a reasonable man. If someone gave him a good reason why an idea would not work, he would agree and move on to another idea. He seemed to have been better able to learn from his mistakes than Hughes and was more willing to admit that he might be wrong.

But once Hughes had an idea in mind, nothing could change it. As the chaotic state of TWA in the 1950s would later prove, he—unlike Fairchild—didn't know his own limitations. He was like a cannon ball: once fired, he blasted all obstacles from his course.[26]

Hughes blamed much of his failure to sell airplanes to the Army on what he called "the Hate Howard Hughes Club." Over the years, he built up a litany of rationalizations as to why he could not get a contract. There was truth in certain of his allegations, and he appeared to believe that they explained his failures. But there is another side that should be reported.

During the 1947 Senate Hearings into his wartime contracts for the flying boat and the F-11 photoplane, Hughes again reviewed his dealings with the Army Air Corps' representatives at Wright Field. As a result of his testimony, concerned Senators and Congressmen sent letters of inquiry to the War Department asking the Air Corps to respond to his allegations. Here are its responses to his charges:

Charge: Hughes claimed that the Army turned down the H-1 racer because "at that time the Army did not think a cantilever monoplane was proper for a pursuit ship."[27]

Response: The YPB-2A delivered in January 1934 and the YP-29 delivered in August 1934 were both cantilever monoplanes. Furthermore, the January 22, 1936 Army specifications for a single-seat pursuit, which were cited in the Circular

Proposal issued March 12, 1936, stated that "an all-metal monocoque fuselage, cantilever wings and tail surfaces are desired." Hughes Aircraft, however, said that it was not interested in entering a bid.

Charge: Hughes submitted a two-engine design for an interceptor "with considerable fear" because at that time "nobody had considered seriously a two-engine interceptor or pursuit plane."[28]

Response: On March 30, 1936, Hughes Aircraft requested recent design studies of pursuit types, "particularly any multi-engined studies which might be available." On April 22 the Air Corps furnished Hughes with eight design studies including one of a twin-engine pursuit airplane.

Charge: When Hughes's two-engine design was finished, the Army told him "to sit on it for a period of months while they allowed Lockheed to make a similar design, and then the two would have to be evaluated in competition."[29]

Response: The Chief of the Materiel Division had on July 31, 1936 informed J.D. Alexander, Manager of Hughes Aircraft, that development funds had been impounded.[30] When funds became available, letters were sent on January 8, 1937 to Hughes Aircraft and four other aircraft companies announcing a design competition for an experimental two-engine pursuit aircraft.

Charge: "By some strange coincidence—and I might say, during the four-month period, I had to lay off some of my engineers, and they went to work for Lockheed—so by a strange coincidence, Lockheed also submitted a two-engine interceptor design."[31]

Response: "In view of the fact that Lockheed Aircraft Company was one of five airplane manufacturers which had been invited on January 8, 1937 to participate in the design competition for experimental two-engine pursuit airplanes, it does not appear 'a strange coincidence' that the design submitted by Lockheed was also a two-engine interceptor as called for in the specification."

Charge: The evaluation board liked the Hughes design better, but the Army thought that Lockheed, with its bigger plant, might be able to turn out more airplanes.[32]

Response: The Technical Subcommittee on the evaluation of the two-engine interceptor design competition awarded the Lockheed design a figure of merit of 65 percent while the Hughes design received only 47.3 percent. A review of the points awarded for the various factors indicated that this difference was primarily attributable to the greater high speed and shorter time of climb which could be expected from the Lockheed design. [33]

Hughes thought he had gotten rough treatment in this design competition. "So, I backed into my shell," he said, "and decided to design and build from the ground up with my own money an entirely new airplane which would be so sensational in its performance that the Army would have to accept it."[34] This became the D-2, a forerunner of the F-11 but not strictly its prototype.

Hughes also thought—and not without some justification—that one reason he had not been awarded the interceptor contract was that he lacked the necessary production capacity. Now with the D-2 under development they had to find space for a plant.

"Odie," Hughes said, "take your Waco out and see if you can spot any vacant real estate that'll meet our needs." So Odekirk made a flying search of the Los Angeles area. After he narrowed down the possibilities, he and Hughes flew over the likely properties together.

First they looked at an area in the San Fernando Valley that had multi-directional runways on a two-square-mile piece of land. "There isn't room enough for the length of the runway I want," said Hughes.

"Well, let's take a look at the area I found over by Culver City," said Odekirk.

As they approached the Pacific Ocean shoreline west of Los Angeles, Odekirk pointed at a long strip of land running perpendicular to the coast and paralleling the bluff on which stands Loyola University. Here was room for a 9,500-foot runway.

"Buy it," said Hughes.

Plant construction started early in 1941. But what with building the D-2, buying the land—Hughes wanted everything that was vacant to be bought to keep people from getting too near the airport—and building the first three buildings of the future Hughes Aircraft plant, they were spending, not making, lots of money. It was Hughes Tool Company that had to pay the bills. Noah Dietrich in Houston didn't think that was any way to run a business. Odekirk would ask Dietrich to send him a million or so to meet the payroll and pay the bills and Dietrich would stall.

One day Odekirk said, "Goddammit, Howard, I'm too busy to take Dietrich's stalling on sending me money."

"What? Is he doing that?"

"Yeah, and goddammit, I've gotta pay these bills and stuff."

"Well, I'll take care of *that*." Hughes telephoned Dietrich to leave Houston pronto and come out for a conference.

After the three men got together, Hughes said, "Now, Noah, Odie is doing what I want him to do. When he needs money, you *send* it to him."

According to Odekirk, that made Dietrich rougher and tougher than ever. "When Dietrich got back to Houston he called in former FBI man Tom Sisk, who had been on the Lindbergh kidnap case, and said, 'Now, look. They've opened the plant in Culver City and they're hiring a lot of people. Go out there and get a job.' So he came out and got a job in our personnel office."

Fifteen months later, Sisk went up to Odekirk's office and said, "Odie, I want to talk to you."

"Fine. Come on in."

"Do you know why I'm here?"

"What do you mean? Here, or working here, or what?"

"Yeah, workin' here."

"Sure. You've got a good job. You're doin' a good job."

"Well, I've gotta tell you something. I know I'll get fired, but I'm going to tell

50

you. Fifteen months ago Dietrich had me come out here and get a job to find where you were taking kickbacks or something in building these buildings so that he could go to Howard and give you a bad time. In fifteen months I haven't been able to find anything."

Odekirk said, "I'm running this joint. You're not going to get fired."

As Odekirk recalls it, "Old Dietrich was just trying to stop us from building. He thought it [Hughes Aircraft Co.] would never amount to anything."[35]

By Pearl Harbor Hughes had his new plant and was ready for bigger things. But his unorthodox business methods, secrecy, and desire to do things his own way contributed to his continuing failure to sell his D-2, or any other airplane, to the Air Corps.

Then along came Henry J. Kaiser in August 1942, and the story of the Spruce Goose began.

3

A Most Unusual Contract

AS SOON AS HENRY J. KAISER learned of Hughes's whereabouts from Odekirk that August day in 1942, he hung up the phone and buzzed his secretary. "Call my car." He spoke briefly with his assistant, then bustled out of his Oakland, California headquarters. The chauffeured limousine whisked him across the San Francisco Bay Bridge to the Fairmont Hotel, where his peppery enthusiasm was pitted against Hughes's low spirits.

"Sit up," he said, "we want to talk about winning the war." Kaiser, twenty-three years older than Hughes, went into an inspirational sales pitch for his flying boat idea. Even the skeptical Hughes, who knew something of the problems and time requirements in developing new aircraft, was intrigued by the possibility of designing the world's largest airplane.

By the weekend of August 22, 1942, after several days of talks in which Odekirk and Kaiser's son Edgar participated, they reached a handshake agreement. Hughes would design a flying boat; Kaiser would build it.

On Sunday evening Kaiser, elated, announced the agreement to the press in fulsome terms. On Monday morning Hughes viewed the headlines with distaste. The press release bound him publicly to goals and completion dates dreamed up by Kaiser and not yet fully studied by Hughes. Kaiser said that they had agreed to go forward in fulfilling "the most ambitious aviation program the world has ever known." Hughes would later testify before the 1947 Senate committee hearings that he did not recall any commitment "beyond possibly my word that I would study the matter or make a preliminary design."[1]

Hughes was not the only one who was worried. Officials in both the War and Navy Departments also worried that a go-ahead might be given to such a project during the most critical period of the war. This did not necessarily mean that Kaiser was wrong. The Navy had also opposed at first the Kaiser proposal to build a fleet of escort carriers on merchant ship hulls. And that program was a great success.

53

The position of the War Department had become known earlier that summer when reporters talked to Under Secretary of War Robert Patterson outside the hearing when Kaiser testified on July 30th. According to Patterson, the production of cargo planes would not be allowed to impede production of fighting planes, "as we must supply not only ourselves but our allies."[2]

Plane makers and high military and civilian officials communicated their concern to Senators Wallgren, Hatch, and Burton, who sat on the Subcommittee on Aviation and Light Metals of the Senate Special Committee to Investigate the National Defense Program (better known as the "Truman Committee," after its chairman). The senators made their points to the chairman and the committee in an August 5, 1942 memo:

1. There was already in effect a "well developed air cargo program" that included transport planes of the Army and Navy. The cargo ship program included the Lockheed Constellation and the Martin Mars.

2. There was a "tremendously important element of time involved in the production of the Kaiser Flying Cargo Ships . . . It is generally estimated that it would take two years to get into any appreciable production of the flying ships and that they still would be experimental models."

3. "Recognizing that the shipbuilding and present airplane progress cannot be permitted to cease it is obvious that the addition of a great program of Flying Cargo Ships would aggravate many of the existing transportation, labor and housing shortages."

4. "In view of the extraordinary genius and demonstrated production record of Henry J. Kaiser, any suggestion from him is entitled to respectful and careful consideration. On the other hand when the proposal involves entering into a new industry and possibly jeopardizing the entire war program of the country, it must also receive a thorough analysis and evaluation of its practicality before it is endorsed or undertaken."

5. "The Subcommittee discussed this matter confidentially with executives of the aviation industry. Each of them indicated a generous and patriotic willingness to cooperate in every way possible with this or any other development in the aviation industry. There was, however, a striking unanimity of opinion emphasizing the probable impracticality of the Kaiser proposal in the form in which it was presented through the newspapers."[3]

Admiral John Towers, who had been in aviation since 1911 and was Chief of the Navy's Bureau of Aeronautics, later testified before the Senate Committee during the 1947 hearings that: "Based on my experience over a long period of years in the procurement of aircraft and on my recent experience in connection with our contract for one Martin Mars, I was confident that it would be impossible for Mr. Kaiser to come anywhere near approaching his predictions . . . I felt that the development of plans and the construction of such planes in quantity could not be accomplished in time to be of any aid and assistance during the war."[4]

"The Heat of Hell"

How then, with seemingly everyone who mattered against the idea, did Kaiser and Hughes get a government go-ahead to build the airplane?

Kaiser had laid the groundwork during his first assault on Washington before he had met Hughes. During that first period, in July and August 1942, he made two proposals, although they were not always clearly differentiated. One was for the mass production of Martin Mars—type flying boats in association with shipbuilders and the aircraft industry. (Kaiser claimed that the Mars had been recommended to him by Donald Douglas.) The second proposal was for the design and development "in and for the future" of a 200-ton flying boat. Among the agency heads to whom he made these proposals was Donald Nelson of the War Production Board.

The War Production Board was a wartime super-agency of vast power and responsibility. Its head, taciturn, pipe-smoking, former Sears president Donald Marr Nelson, was a Roosevelt man and sensitive to the opinions of both his boss and the public. He avoided making hard decisions by finding ways to postpone them or to compromise.

Advising Nelson on aviation matters was the famed and very able Grover Loening, who at Columbia University in 1910 had received the first master's degree in aeronautics in the United States before becoming assistant to Orville Wright. During World War I Loening headed his own aircraft company and afterward pioneered in the development of a variety of military and civilian aircraft including the famous Loening Amphibian.

Loening had a soft spot in his heart for seaplanes. He was a wealthy man and had served on the board of directors of Pan American Airways in the late 1930s during arguments as to whether landplanes or flying boats should be used on the Atlantic runs. Loening's argument was that putting money into landplanes was foolishness, and that you shouldn't attempt to fly the Atlantic except in big boats. His opponent during those discussions was Charles Lindbergh, who recommended landplanes and at that time was a consultant for Pan American.[5]

On Friday afternoon, August 7, Kaiser and his executive assistant, Chad Calhoun, were ushered into Donald Nelson's office in the Social Security Building. According to Calhoun's later testimony, Nelson's first comment was, "Henry, I am going to take another chance on you."[6] (This referred to Nelson's previous authorization for building Kaiser's Fontana, California steel plant over strong opposition, a decision that turned out very well for the nation and the war effort.) Then, according to Calhoun, Nelson showed them a letter of intent prepared for the signature of Admiral Towers that would authorize Kaiser to proceed with the construction of 500 Mars-type flying boats. (The Navy balked at this and Towers never signed the letter.) Kaiser read the draft and then said, "How about the letter of intent to proceed with the design of the 200-ton plane?"

Nelson said that that would probably come through also, but probably not until after he returned, as he was leaving on a trip that weekend.

But on Monday, August 10, while Nelson was away, William Batt and Merrill Meigs of the WPB gave Kaiser two letters signed by Donald Nelson which Calhoun said "kissed off both ideas" by giving Kaiser "impossible conditions." (Kaiser thought that Meigs and Batt had waited until Nelson was out of town and then given him letters with rubber-stamped signatures.) On Thursday Kaiser departed Washington for New York and on Sunday boarded a train for Oakland and his meeting with Hughes.

After Nelson returned from his trip he sent Grover Loening to the San Francisco Bay area to inspect Kaiser's facilities. This inspection, made on August 22 and 23, overlapped Kaiser's meetings with Hughes, and Kaiser took advantage of the opportunity to ask Loening what he thought of the mystery man of aviation. According to Kaiser, Loening said that he thought Hughes was a brilliant engineer and that his aircraft work "was just about the best that we had in the factories of America."[7]

After his inspection Loening thought that the machinery and general tools of Kaiser's Bay Area yards were not suitable for aircraft construction. He was also concerned that no serious aircraft design work had been done by any Kaiser engineer, and that none of its engineers had been sent for aeronautical training, even though California universities giving such training had offered their facilities to the Kaiser organization.

In his report to Nelson, Loening also noted that during his meeting in Los Angeles on Monday, August 24 with the committee of aircraft builders, Kaiser had said that he greatly needed the assistance of the aircraft industry in designing a large, possibly 200-ton, aircraft for him. When it was pointed out to Kaiser that this was physically impossible due to other demands on the aircraft industry, Kaiser took this as a personal affront and said that he intended to enter into partnership with Howard Hughes in order to use the Hughes engineering group for design work.

Loening concluded from his West Coast visit that Kaiser had planned to make the aircraft industry design his airplane and the government build his factory so that "Mr. Kaiser's own contribution to adding aircraft facilities at the present crucial time would have been exactly nothing but newspaper buildup." But Loening was impressed with the efficient organization of Kaiser's enterprises, their orderly operations, the conceptual boldness of the assembly line methods, and the obvious competence of the men who worked for Kaiser. In his report to Nelson he recommended that "since Mr. Kaiser has become associated with Mr. Hughes and has in this way acquired some aeronautical staff, although not nearly large enough, that he be requested to design a new cargo carrying seaplane of at least one hundred tons gross weight size. An order should be given Hughes for the design only, in order to determine the fitness of himself and his organization to do work of this character."[8]

He also recommended to Nelson that "during the time that this design is being prepared, Mr. Kaiser be required to present to the government detailed plans of a factory that would use no strategic materials and of the assembly of a staff of engineers and factory workmen that would be trained from his own resources and not taken from the existing aircraft industry."[9]

With Hughes on his team, Kaiser gained powerful support from Jesse Jones, Hughes's old family friend and fellow Texan, who as Secretary of Commerce had built a financial empire in Texas. The towering, white-thatched "Emperor Jones" wielded wide influence because of his control of both Commerce and the Federal Loan Agency and through his ties with southerners on Capitol Hill.[10]

Some of Nelson's advisers, including Merrill Meigs, tried to dissuade Nelson from backing Kaiser. But others pushed him to decide in favor of building the giant flying boats. Col. Roy B. Lord, a strong advocate of transport aviation, wrote Nelson on August 31 expressing regret that Kaiser's proposal had run into so many snags and delays: "It is apparent that nothing constructive can be accomplished by continuing the committee of top men from the aircraft industry since they are naturally against permitting a new competitor to manufacture an air cargo plane which may put this competitor in the lead during the post-war period.

"With the strong tie-up between Kaiser Co., Inc. and Howard Hughes who has one of the best reputations as a designer in the industry, and with the general public as favorable to Kaiser as is indicated by the public polls and in the newspapers, I feel that it would be a grave mistake not to at least let Kaiser design and construct several of the large planes."[11]

Colonel Lord's letter was accompanied by a covering memorandum strongly endorsing Lord's recommendations and providing additional arguments designed to sway Nelson in Kaiser's favor. Its author, Nelson's assistant, Edwin A. Locke, Jr., made these points:

1. "If you take the advice of the aircraft industry, you will tell Kaiser to forget about producing airplanes and concentrate on providing raw materials. In that event, every newspaper in the country will 'go to town' in favor of Kaiser and against the WPB."

2. "I think the newspapers will be right. The general public and many of us in the war agencies have been deeply impressed by the Kaiser proposal and believe that under present critical conditions this country cannot afford to deny it, especially when presented by a man with a record such as Kaiser's for accomplishing the impossible."

3. "If you follow Colonel Lord's recommendation, what do you stand to lose: If the planes fail, the loss will be perhaps two or three million dollars and an infinitely small amount of materiel. If Kaiser succeeds, the benefits to the war effort will be great."

4. ". . . A contract to Kaiser will provide some very salutary competition for the Army, the Navy and the aircraft manufacturers."[12]

In fairness to the established aircraft manufacturers, it should be noted that they abandoned many ordinary peacetime competitive practices in order to produce Army and Navy aircraft in the shortest possible time. They cooperated with the automotive industry in its aircraft activities and worked together through Aircraft

War Production Councils. But it was natural they thought their own production more important to the war effort than the Kaiser scheme; such a conclusion was warranted by the facts as they saw them.

Nevertheless, Nelson was convinced he would be remiss if he did not give the flying boat project a go-ahead, and the press and public would have been quick to agree. Moreover, Kaiser was applying pressure through his influential and powerful friends in Washington, a process later described as "putting the heat of hell on Washington."

As a final step before issuing a letter of intent, Nelson had Harold Talbott check with the War and Navy Departments to make sure that the proposed project would not interfere with current programs. On September 12, 1942, R. Adm. John Towers, responding for the Navy, and Robert Lovett, Assistant Secretary of War for Air, responding for the Army, signed letters to Nelson agreeing to make standard engines and instruments available for three cargo planes as proposed. Both men stressed that the Kaiser-Hughes organization should be specifically prevented from hiring away key personnel from existing governmental aircraft contractors.[13]

On September 17 the Defense Plant Corporation, a subsidiary of Jesse Jones's Reconstruction Finance Corporation, authorized Kaiser and Hughes to proceed with the design engineering and construction of three flying boat type cargo planes. Two of these were to be flown and the third was to be for static tests. They were to be engineered and constructed "under the direction of Howard Hughes in his present plant at Culver City, California, with such additional facilities adjacent to a suitable water area as are necessary for final assembly." The design and engineering were to be approved by the National Advisory Committee for Aeronautics (NACA) and the Civil Aeronautics Authority (CAA).

Among the conditions imposed were that all construction would reduce to a minimum the use of any critical or strategic materials; that no fee or profit to Howard Hughes, Kaiser, or companies with which either was affiliated could be included in the cost; that no engineers, technicians, or other skilled personnel who were then working for manufacturers engaged in the war effort could be employed without the prior written consent of their respective employers; that the Kaiser-Hughes organization could spend no more than $18 million; and that the authorization was "limited to a period not to exceed 24 months from the date hereof."[14]

These conditions troubled Hughes and he complained to Merrill Meigs, the deputy director of the War Production Board's aircraft division. Meigs was in California on September 24 for a series of industry meetings, and it was midnight before he returned to his hotel room to see Hughes. For two hours Hughes told Meigs his problems and his worries.

"I can't make a boat that big in less than two years," said Hughes, who complained about the conditions at length. Meigs noted in his diary that "Hughes is a very tired, worried, sincere young man, and left my room at 2 o'clock with very good reason to be worried."[15]

Nonetheless, all of the conditions contained in the original letter of intent were included in the formal contract signed November 16, 1942. (Since this contract was let outside the normal Army-Navy procurement channels, endless difficulties later arose over materiel priorities and the procurement of equipment and supplies.)

Kaiser and Hughes were free at last to go to work. But they quickly discovered that there was very little work they could do in concert.

"Partners"

It is hard to imagine two more dissimilar men than the tall, slender, introverted Howard Hughes and the short, roly-poly, extroverted Henry Kaiser. Hughes shunned publicity; Kaiser sought it. Hughes was a perfectionist; Kaiser was a pragmatist. Kaiser was hard-driving, punctual, and lived according to a rigorous schedule. Hughes was dilatory, kept no regular office hours and seemed to run his business by telephone from wherever he might be at the moment.

When Kaiser would say, "Get Mr. Hughes on the phone," his staff would call Hughes's Romaine street office in Hollywood and call again, and then again. Each time the young minions on duty at Hughes would be vague about the whereabouts of their master and would ask the caller to leave a message. Hughes could never be reached on the spur of the moment. Even his uncle Rupert complained that "I can get through to the Almighty by dropping to my knees, but I don't know how to get in touch with Howard."

As soon as the letter of intent had been issued, Kaiser took a handpicked team of production men and engineers to the Hughes Aircraft plant in Culver City. Odekirk had only a small office in front of their new factory, as their office building had not yet been built. He was overwhelmed by the size of Kaiser's groups. "He had about ten or twelve men with him, and they were planning to build a waterway from the plant out into the ocean to launch the flying boats and so on," Odekirk recalls.

For two weeks Odekirk was Kaiser's main contact with Hughes Aircraft. Hughes was not feeling well and was at any rate busy with other matters. Kaiser did a lot of sitting around waiting for Hughes to show up, according to Odekirk— extremely exasperating for a man accustomed to getting things done in a hurry— and, in Odekirk's words, "Kaiser got real upset with Howard."[16]

After suffering weeks of frustration, the Kaiser engineers and production people returned to Kaiser headquarters in Oakland. But the two "partners" did manage to set up the Kaiser-Hughes Corporation with offices in Culver City.

Despite the joint name, Hughes continued to go it alone. He began making frequent flights to Lake Mead, Nevada to experiment with takeoffs and landings in the Sikorsky flying boat he had purchased in 1937. And he continued to monitor and supervise his many defense activities. These included the building of machine gun feed chutes that would eventually equip ninety percent of all U.S. bombers; work on an electrically operated booster drive to speed machine gun firing rates; subcontracts for landing gear struts, wings, fuselages, and aircraft seats for other aircraft manufacturers; the manufacture of artillery shells and cannon barrels; and work on his experimental D-2 aircraft (later to become the XF-11). And there was always TWA to monitor. At night he personally cut, scored, and edited his latest motion picture, *The Outlaw*, starring Jane Russell.

Hughes's reputation grew for immersing himself in detail, for tinkering with designs and specifications, for being difficult to locate when needed, and for failing to follow accepted business practices. Key people in government and the military began to feel that the war could not wait for a dilatory Howard Hughes who sought perfection in unorthodox ways. Hughes's aircraft projects were given a Group V priority, the lowest rating.

According to the letter of intent between Kaiser and Hughes, Kaiser was left almost powerless to interfere: *"It is understood that the engineering and construction will be done under the direction of Howard Hughes."* Moreover, according to Kaiser, Jesse Jones had told him explicitly to keep hands off the project: "I want it understood that Hughes has the responsibility and you do not interfere with him."[17]

The result was that Kaiser-Hughes was something less than a working entity. The flying boat was a Hughes Aircraft project from the beginning.

4

Design and Construction

HUGHES ALMOST NEVER ATTEMPTED a design that was not bigger, faster, or in some other way unique compared to anything and everything built by others. In later years, however, he sometimes accepted contracts because of the need to keep his engineering group busy between projects that really interested him.

His first contract for helicopters was an example of this. When Rae Hopper, his chief engineer at the time, proposed going after helicopter contracts, Hughes told him, "I know your arguments. If you don't have something for them to do, the good ones will quit and the poor ones will stay on forever." So Hughes allowed himself to drift into helicopter production, a type of craft in which he had little interest.[1]

But Hughes drew the line at gliders. During the war, when Hopper asked him if he wanted to compete for a contract to build gliders for the Army Air Corps, he exploded: "Gliders! chrissakes, you tell 'em we're big boys now. We can build airplanes."[2]

Design

Hughes's ideas permeated every aircraft design, and the flying boat, which was his life for about two years, was no exception.

He not only made all decisions relating to external appearance and size, but also was involved with power plants, flight controls, and instrument panel design. He spent much time on the hydraulic system, less on the electrical system.[3]

How did Hughes manage to function in the forefront of aviation in all these fields with practically no formal training in engineering? Carl Babberger, Hughes's chief aerodynamicist during the design of the F-11 and the flying boat, believes it was because he used the lawyer-like techniques of cross-examination and brain picking.

"He talked on the phone practically eighteen hours a day, all the time he wasn't sleeping," says Babberger, "and to anybody anywhere. I've been there when he got

61

long distance calls from Europe and India. In my case, he'd talk to the top aerodynamicists and then spring something on me."[4]

Hughes called on experts regularly—usually the number one engineer or scientist in some phase of aircraft or engine design. He had such contacts at Curtiss Wright, Boeing, Douglas, Pratt and Whitney, Lockheed, Hamilton Standard, Cal Tech, and other places.

Earl Martin, president of Hamilton Standard Propellers during the 1940s, said that Hughes used to telephone him all the time and at all hours of the day or night. "He was very smart, a very meticulous individual," said Martin, "but I thought he beat things to death."[5]

Prior to the end of World War II, Hughes had frequent contact with Lockheed's chief engineer, Clarence L. ("Kelly") Johnson. Johnson became less available to Hughes after the war, probably because much of the original contact between the two men related to the development of the Lockheed Constellation for TWA. Later, Hughes's lengthy calls not only interfered with Johnson's work for Lockheed, but often cut into Johnson's weekends. Hughes called so often that Johnson complained to Lockheed's president Robert Gross. Thereafter, Johnson refused to talk with Hughes on matters that did not concern Lockheed.

It appears, too, that Hughes and Johnson did not get along well together. In the famous telephone interview of January 7, 1971, when seven veteran newsmen gathered in Hollywood to talk with Hughes three thousand miles away in the Bahamas in order to determine if it was really he, Hughes recalled Kelly Johnson as "a man I used to lock horns with at Lockheed . . . the engineer who worked with me on the Constellation and who claimed credit, really, for the design . . . our jealousies ran all through that period."

When Kelly Johnson was asked about this, he said, "There was a hell of a lot of jealousy because he was coming out in the newspapers as a great designer. I got so damn mad at him that he and [TWA president] Jack Frye sent me a letter offering to put an ad in *Aviation* magazine saying that I had designed the Constellation. They said that they 'applied' it. And of course they did. They *bought* it. That's the most important thing they did for the Constellation."[6]

Since the mid-1930s, while they were designing the record-breaking H-1, Hughes's brilliant mind, flair for engineering, and quick grasp of the essence of technical problems had enabled him to learn a great deal from Dick Palmer. And during the design of the D-2, the F-11, and the HK-1, Hughes spent thousands of hours with Bell, Ridley, Hopper, Grant, Babberger and others on design problems. These ranged from the detailed design of fittings to meet anticipated stresses and strains to the design of control systems, power plant installations, hydraulic systems, and the overall configuration of the aircraft.

After a number of years of this on-the-job training Hughes became an expert in several fields. In fact, some of his engineers feel that much of the time Hughes spent with them was not because he personally wanted to do the design, but primarily in order to learn something.

Whether or not this was true, Hughes left no doubt as to who was in charge. Once he spent hours with a group of his engineers on the design of the eight nacelles for the engines of the flying boat. One argued question was whether a seam in the metal skin of the nacelle should have one row of 5/32 inch rivets or two rows of 1/8 inch rivets.

Kenneth Ridley, then chief engineer, finally said, "We really shouldn't spend too much time arguing over this kind of detail at this point. We're not even sure what engines we're going to use. The nacelles might not even look like this."

"I'll have you know one thing," Hughes said angrily. "It's going to have two rows of one-eighth inch rivets and it's going to look just like *that*!" And he slammed his folders shut and stalked from the room.[7] Babberger, however, observes with a laugh, "I never saw that side of him. I tried to do everything he told me. He never raised his voice—didn't have to. He was a quiet, soft-spoken fella."[8]

But Hughes could be very difficult, Babberger concedes. "We'd give him everything that looked fine to us and if he had any reason in the world for not making a decision at that time, he would not make it. And so we'd . . . either try some other design or twiddle our thumbs until we heard from him again and he accepted something. And practically everything required his approval, down to pretty fine nuts and bolts. He used to hold us up a lot by not making decisions. All of us had to contend with that damn foolishness."[9]

Design of the Flying Boat

After the go-ahead to build the flying boat was signed in September 1942, Hughes got together with his engineers to decide its size, shape, and general configuration. The first big question was whether it should be twin-hulled or single-hulled.

James V. Martin (not Glenn L. Martin of Martin Aircraft), an eccentric aviation pioneer and creative genius, had earlier proposed a giant swooping gull-winged catamaran "Twin Hull Martin Oceanplane" that had interested Winston Churchill and the British Admiralty.[10] Churchill, in turn, had piqued the interest of President Roosevelt; and members of the Air Cargo Board (which Nelson had established under the auspices of the War Production Board that past May) strongly favored such a design. Twin hulls would eliminate the extra drag and weight of wing tip floats and make it easier to beach the flying boat to discharge cargo in amphibious operations.

Loening dreamed that the big boat would be used for Pacific Island amphibious operations to land in the sheltered water of lagoons and discharge troops and cargo from a bow ramp before backing off the beach with reversible-pitch propellers.[11]

Hughes himself had been impressed by the successful Savoia-Marchetti twin-hulled flying boats, twelve of which had completed a mass flight from Italy to Brazil in 1931 under the command of Gen. Italo Balbo. Balbo also led a 1933 mass flight of the planes from Italy to Chicago.

For weeks, every evening between 5:30 and 6 p.m., Hughes would arrive to argue the twin-hull-or-single-hull question. Kenneth Ridley would argue that twin hulls would weigh more for the same capacity: "Why have little hulls when you can have a bigger one?" But Hughes would disagree.

Hughes was persistent and stubborn in arguments and usually got his way. He did change his mind at times; but if he himself had made the original proposal, there was no way he would change his mind—until he could think that the change was his own idea. Just as Ridley finally conceded that the twin hull design was right for the flying boat, Hughes opted for the single hull. This pleased the structural engineers, who had concluded that the twisting loads on the center section between the two hulls would be excessive.[12]

The single hull design would have its own problems, because the mammoth size Hughes was to choose for his design would require an overhang wingspan fifty percent greater than the Martin Mars, which would invite new torsional, wing flutter, vibration, deflection, and control problems never before tested.

The next big question was size. When the contract was let in 1942 the government had envisioned a plane somewhat larger than the Martin Mars whose design gross weight was 145,000 pounds. Hughes finally settled on a design gross weight of 400,000 pounds. His choice resulted initially from a requirement to transport an eighty-ton Sherman tank. But at a May 4, 1943 meeting in the NACA conference room in Washington, Ridley was asked to give a brief review of how they had arrived at an aircraft size of 400,000 pounds. He stated in effect that their objective had been to design the largest aircraft possible using eight of the largest engines currently in sight. Eight was considered the maximum number of engines that at the time seemed practicable to mount on one aircraft.[13]

The size question arose again at an October 21, 1943 meeting attended by Hughes in Donald Nelson's office at the War Production Board. Grover Loening, the WPB consultant on aircraft, agreed that the objective was to build the largest possible load-carrying plane, but observed that the design was Hughes's own interpretation of the "largest possible." In Loening's opinion, "the largest possible" at that time meant eight Pratt and Whitney 2800 engines in a plane of about 250,000 pounds gross weight. "The engine Mr. Hughes has chosen," he said, "is not in production even yet and certainly was not at that time." Hughes accepted complete responsibility for the choice of engines and size without further qualifications.[14]

Loening was also concerned about the plane's weight, because aircraft efficiency does not indefinitely increase with increasing size. Only the previous month he had written: "It so happens that while larger airplanes get more efficient and faster as they increase in size due to the smaller relative drag of the body and relative weights of necessary items, like a pilot to fly them, there is also, due to the law of the cube, an increase in the relative weight of the wing structure with size. After the line of favorable decreases crosses the line of unfavorable increases, like wing weight, there is no further advantage to larger size aircraft." In Loening's opinion the Hughes design had reached the latter category, particularly since the construction was of wood rather than new alloy metals that would have permitted the design of a lighter wing.[15]

Hughes became concerned about another size-related problem. He felt that many new design features would need testing in flight, but that the team should not have to depend on flying the giant eight-engine boat every time some little gadget had to be checked. So in August 1943 Hughes's engineers proposed to Loening that they be allowed to build a .45 scale flying model of the HK-1 with eight air-cooled "putt-putt" engines. Loening recommended instead "that the Navy be required to loan to Kaiser-Hughes at once a PB2Y3 flying boat stripped of all military equipment and to be used by Mr. Hughes as his flying laboratory in connection with this contract."[16]

After the size, number of engines, and the single hull design had been decided upon, the Hughes team was ready to determine the specifics of shape and design. Hughes, a dedicated disciple of technology, was impressed with the work of the National Advisory Committee for Aeronautics' Research Center at Langley Field, Virginia (now a NASA research center). He had read an old NACA report by John B. Parkinson, then Assistant Chief of NACA's Hydrodynamics Division under Starr Truscott, that showed seaplane hulls drawn around streamlined bodies to minimize drag. "Make it like that," he told chief designer Rae E. Hopper.

Design Work at Langley

Hopper and Kenneth Ridley, who ran the engineering division, called in preliminary design group engineers Roy Wendahl and Gene Blandford and told them to go to Langley to obtain NACA's latest design criteria for flying boats, inasmuch as the company had had no previous experience with such aircraft. This was very unusual, says Wendahl. "Prior to our arriving at Langley and asking for their design criteria, the only people who ever came to Langley were those who had already designed their boats, got in trouble, and then brought their models to the towing basin to ask for help. We went down there with nothing in hand and asked them to help us design one."[17]

Hopper and aerodynamicist Carl Babberger also went to Langley, but Hopper spent only a short time there. He was needed at Culver City to direct the overall design effort in coordination with Hughes.

For some months the Hughesmen operated out of Parkinson's office and worked with the various NACA experts. Soon they were doing three-views of what was to become the biggest airplane in the world.

As Parkinson remembers it, "I guess they did a hundred overlays. They'd do a three-view and then bring in people like me to comment and suggest changes. We put in all the latest things we knew and were finding out all that time in our research work."[18]

Roy Wendahl drew up the hull three-views and sent them to Culver City as the basis for the preliminary design. There Hopper's design crew prepared sixteen profile views of the proposed airplane which were then taken to Hughes at his house for approval.

In some cases the variations between drawings were minute, but Hughes had an outstanding visual memory for the smallest detail. One time an engineer, taking the latest proposals to Hughes for review, sneaked in an old drawing that Hughes had already seen. Hughes spotted it immediately "We've had that one before," he said, and tossed it aside.[19]

After Hughes had made the final decisions on hull shape, his craftsmen at Culver City reproduced the beautiful and properly proportioned dynamic test model for tests at the NACA towing basin. Langley experts told Loening in February 1943 that this model was the finest job they had ever received from a contractor.[20] It would be nearly a year before the hydrodynamic and aerodynamic tests were completed.[21]

"The hull design was only part of the work done at Langley. The wing section was recommended by NACA's Eastman N. Jacobs and use was made of Langley's low-turbulence wind tunnel. Carl Babberger believes that the result was "one of the finest low-drag, high-lift sections that ever was put together." Parkinson says that even unpublished ideas were applied to the nacelles so that they and their associated internal cooling systems represented the latest and the best in low-drag design. "All in all, aerodynamically and hydrodynamically, the Hughes flying boat was very superior," said Parkinson. "We had high hopes of using it after the war as a research airplane simply because it did have such outstanding aerodynamic and hydrodynamic features. It had probably the largest Reynolds number I've ever heard of. We could have gotten a lot of aerodynamic data off of it. It had a finish just like a piano—probably the smoothest airplane that was ever built. That was one dividend from the Duramold plywood." Duramold, as will be seen later, was a special wood lamination process developed by Fairchild and used by Hughes for this project.

The model eventually used in the NACA towing tank and wind tunnel tests was a powered dynamic test model with electric motors to drive the scale-size propellers. The wings and hull could be tested separately or together. Some wind tunnel tests were also conducted in Cal Tech's ten-foot tunnel by Dick Murrow using a 1/80th scale model with a four-foot wing span.

During this design period Hughes carried on an intermittent, indirect dialogue with the NACA experts. He communicated in a kind of three-way conversation through Babberger, Roy Wendell, or other Hughesmen at Langley. Often it was Hopper who relayed Hughes's thoughts.

Babberger says that Hughes did not come to Langley while they were there. "He never went to a wind tunnel test or anything like that." But he did phone frequently. Howard would tell you what he wanted. Then he would review it. Then he would summarize it. And then maybe you'd have to tell it back to him. One time he gave me a half-hour set of instructions to call Wright Field after seven p.m. when rates went down."

Takeoffs and Landings . . .

Occasionally Hughes disagreed with NACA. Like all pilots, he had strong ideas about everything concerning airplanes, Parkinson recalls. "He challenged his own people and he challenged us in many cases." A case in point was the design and location of the step in the bottom of the hull of the flying boat.

"We'd done a lot of work on Navy seaplanes trying to determine how deep that step had to be," said Parkinson. "The step was an aerodynamic drag item and designers liked to make it as small as possible. Usually they made it too small, which gave rise to troubles during takeoffs and landings. So we had the chance to say what it ought to be on the Hughes boat, and according to our formulas (it was such a big thing—sixteen foot beam) it came out [to be] two feet, which is an enormous thing to have to drag through the air. We had quite a discussion with Hughes over that."[22]

But even with a two-foot step the Hughes hull had the lowest profile drag over the equivalent streamlined body of any airplane fuselage or body NACA had ever tested, and was probably the lowest drag seaplane hull that had ever been designed—simply because it had the area distribution of a streamlined body.

"We made it that way," says Parkinson. "It was built around circular sections. It was just like it ought to be. That two-foot step was insignificant compared with the overall size."[23]

But it was the *location* of the step that Hughes argued about. "He had it firmly in his mind that the step ought to be relatively far aft, and he had the idea that when the plane [with such a step] touched on landing it would tend to put the nose down and kill the lift so that it would stay on the water," says Parkinson. Hughes was convinced that the reason many flying boats skipped and bounced on landing—sometimes dangerously—was that the center of gravity was not far enough ahead of the step. There was merit to Hughes's argument, but, characteristically, he was dogged about pursuing it.

To prove his point, he ran tests with his S-43 Sikorsky amphibian, ballasting it to move the center of gravity farther and farther ahead. As Earl Martyn remembers it, "We'd go up to Lake Mead and shoot landings all day long and at every attitude and every angle he could think of. The plane was unstable on the water after it got below flying speed, so we added two rudders and vertical stabilizers, one in back of each engine, and that helped a lot."[24]

Aerodynamicist Dick Murrow said, "We collected a lot of data up at Lake Mead with the amphibian. It had such lousy water handling characteristics that Howard wanted to make sure we avoided that on the big boat. [The Sikorsky] porpoised so badly on landing that the Navy would not let their pilots land it on water. It was a terrifying thing to be in it when it was porpoising. You could land it as gently as though you were putting it down on an egg in a nice three-point position and it would porpoise due to the fact that the step on the hull was not deep enough to vent properly. We had a speedboat that we used to film the thing on landing, and you could see a curl of water come up from under the step and hit the bottom of the hull 'way aft of the step. This created a suction on the aft end of the airplane and tilted it to increase the angle of attack enough that, at the speed it was going, it would come out of the water again. Only a foot or so the first hop, but then it would repeat and the second hop would be much more violent so that the airplane would be out of the water five feet or so, losing speed all the time. By about the third hop, it sounded like a ton of garbage cans when it hit. It really was rough."[25]

Odekirk estimated that Hughes made six thousand takeoffs and landings in a four-month period, But Hughes's flight test engineer, Charles E. "Gene" Blandford, says that the question of center of gravity location was mainly Hughes's excuse to go out and fly the airplane. The whole operation was so disorganized that the data was never used.[26] But Hughes gained firsthand experience as to how the plane handled with various centers of gravity.

. . . And Disaster

Earlier, in 1942, a chain of events had been set in motion that would lead to a tragic accident. Hughes had landed the Sikorsky on Lake Tahoe one day and then could not take off. No matter how he had rocked, pushed, and pulled, the old boat would not break loose from the water. The engines simply had not had sufficient power to take off at Tahoe's elevation of 6,229 feet. Hughes had to wait for the wind to pick up and a chop to develop before the plane could take to the air. (Envious stay-at-homes later accused the crew of fixing the Sikorsky so it could not take off so that they could vacation in the high Sierra.)[27]

Disgusted, Hughes flew back to Culver City and ordered the original engines replaced with Wright G-205A engines. This increased the total power to 2,000 horsepower but also added weight and moved the center of gravity forward. The change in the engines and the modification of the tail necessitated a CAA flight test as a prerequisite to an updated airworthiness certificate before Hughes could complete a planned sale of the plane to the Army Corps of Engineers the following year.

C. W. ("Ted") Von Rosenberg, an engineering test pilot in the old Civil Aeronautics Authority sixth region headquarters at Santa Monica, was assigned to work with Hughes on the project. Flight tests of the Sikorsky with the new engines were completed by mid-May 1943. Only water tests remained, which were to be conducted on Lake Mead.

On the afternoon of May 16, 1943, the day before the water test, Von Rosenberg with copilot Ceco Cline, Chief of the Manufacturing Inspection Branch at the Santa Monica headquarters, flew the aircraft to Boulder City on the south end of Lake Mead. Also in the plane were Hughes, flight test engineer Gene Blandford, flight engineer Dick Felt, and American Airlines pilot Howard West and his copilot. West and the copilot were to fly the airplane in and out of Greenland, Iceland, and other such places for the Army under an American Airlines contract.[28]

Tests began the morning of May 17. The aircraft was configured in accordance with purchaser requirements. Radio equipment and a radio operator's position had been installed in the rear, so the rear ballast had been removed. Earl Martyn had gone into Las Vegas to pick up West, who had overslept. This chance occurrence saved Martyn and West from possible death or serious injury.[29]

At one point Von Rosenberg asked, "Howard, you don't really have time to devote yourself to being a test pilot. Why don't you hire somebody to do that work?"

"Hell," Hughes answered, "why should I pay somebody else to have all the fun?"[30]

As the test began, Hughes took off from Boulder City Airport and flew to the north end of the lake for a landing on the water. Hughes was in the left seat, Von Rosenberg was in the right seat, and Felt, acting as flight engineer, was leaning through the cockpit door. Blandford sat in a jump seat on the pilot's side and Cline was in the upholstered chair at the navigator's table facing forward on the right side.

As Hughes turned to line up for the final approach, Blandford leaned over to Cline and said, "Change seats with me, Ceco, so I can get the equipment ready." Blandford's temperature measuring equipment for the upcoming taxi cooling tests was on the nav table. Cline unbuckled and moved to the jump seat while Blandford took the nav seat about thirty seconds before touchdown. Blandford is alive today because of that move.

Hughes normally landed the Sikorsky fast and flat. The plane had very poor water handling characteristics, and the higher speed gave more rudder control while the flat touchdown seemed to initiate a better runout. But this time, unknown to the crew, the center of gravity was ahead of the forward limit for safe operation. Not only had rear ballast been removed, but Dick Felt's tool chest weighing about a hundred pounds, normally stowed in the far aft end of the plane, had been brought forward. Moreover, there was very little fuel in the hull tanks, which were aft of the center of gravity, and all the people on board were forward.

Blandford fastened his seat belt and looked out the little porthole at the nav station. They were right on the water and about to touch. As usual with Hughes at the controls, the touchdown was very smooth. But as the plane settled in the water and picked up water drag, the nose was sucked down suddenly and the resulting water resistance became centered ahead of the plane's center of gravity—an extremely unstable condition.

Suddenly the nose pulled to the left and the plane started to skid sideways. Hughes kicked full right rudder. For a moment it looked as if he had regained control. Blandford, feeling the swerve, grabbed the nav table. "We're probably going to tear off a tip float this time," he thought.

Then all hell broke loose. The aircraft was completely crossways. The right wing tip and float dug into the water, wracking the wing. Struts collapsed or were torn out. The whirling blades of the left propeller slashed through the hull right at Cline's jump seat.

Finally the plane came to a stop. It was right side up but steeply nose down and listing about forty-five degrees to the right. Water gushed through the hole in the side of the hull slashed by the prop. The plane was sinking.

Blandford disentangled himself from the nav table and looked for Cline. Where the jump seat had been was a gaping hole, and Cline was nowhere to be seen. Blandford felt around in the rising water looking for him and found Dick Felt instead. Felt was horribly wounded; the prop had hit him in the back of the head.

In the cockpit, Von Rosenberg jerked his seat belt loose and looked across at Hughes, who sat strapped in his seat, dazed and glassy-eyed from a blow on the head.

"Come on, Howard, let's get out of here! It's going to sink!" Hughes didn't move. Von Rosenberg moved over, unbuckled his seat belt, and shook him several times. "We've got to get out of here, Howard!" Hughes began to stir.

The water was rising fast as Von Rosenberg began pushing Hughes out of the plane through the pilot's side window. The window was small, and Von Rosenberg feared that Hughes might get stuck and block his own escape. As he pushed Hughes halfway out he remembered the overhead escape hatch. When Hughes was nearly through the window Von Rosenberg opened the hatch and floated out.

Meanwhile, Blandford worked Felt over to the hole in the side of the airplane where Rosenberg, who was outside now, helped him float Felt out through the hole.

"Where's Ceco?" said Rosenberg.

"Well, he's not in there," said Blandford. "Maybe he went aft before the crash."

By this time Hughes, stunned, was in the water hanging on to the radio mast.

"Here, hold Dick," Blandford told Hughes. ("The only time I ever gave Howard an order," he recalled later.) Then he and Von Rosenberg climbed up on the sloping back of the plane and down into the back hatch to look for Cline.

By this time the compartment Blandford had been in was flooded. But the rear compartments, elevated because of the plane's nose-down attitude, could still be entered. While looking for Cline, Blandford found all the ship's life preservers stowed in boxes behind the tied-open hatch to the radio compartment—another indication of Hughes's informal flight operations. He went into the compartment as far as he could without letting go of the flange on the bulkhead. There was no sign of Ceco. Von Rosenberg had no better luck, so the two men climbed back out.

They remembered that a life raft was stowed in a compartment on top of the wing. The two of them got it out, plopped it in the water near where Hughes was holding Felt, and Blandford pulled the string. Compressed air hissed, the raft began to take shape, but remained limp. Someone had left the air valves open. Quickly they rigged the hand pump.

Hughes had regained full consciousness. "Get Dick in the boat," he said.

A couple of people in a small outboard arrived on the scene to offer assistance. "Get Dick in the outboard and take him to the hospital," said Hughes.

Blandford, the least injured, went with Felt. When they were about two hundred yards away he looked back. Hughes was sitting in the rubber boat working the hand pump. The Sikorsky was beginning to go down.

Von Rosenberg suffered severe back injuries in the crash and spent the night in the hospital in Boulder City. The following day he was flown to Los Angeles in a TWA aircraft. With him on the plane was a Los Angeles specialist brought in the previous afternoon by Hughes to insure that he had the best of care.

The only identifiable injuries Blandford had were bruises and strains that aggravated a bad vertebra which had never bothered him before. "It was a great shock to my faith in airplanes," Blandford recalled.[31]

The crash gave Hughes a head injury and dealt him a severe psychological blow. He had killed two men. Dick Felt had flown with him in the Sikorsky for many years, and Hughes was closer to his personally selected flight engineer mechanics than to other people. As for Ceco Cline, Odekirk rented a small plane and he and a mechanic Van Storm searched in and out of all the small inlets day after day in the hope that his body would surface. It never did.[32]

The Sikorsky, too, was an old friend. He had personally supervised its birth at the Sikorsky plant in Connecticut some six years before and was responsible for a number of its special features such as flush riveting. All in all, the crash gravely affected Hughes's pride and confidence as a pilot.

The plane was salvaged from Lake Mead—no simple chore. Van Storm, who took part in the search, recovery, and rebuilding of the Sikorsky, says that they looked for days before Navy divers under Commander Garland (Jack) Suggs found the plane in 180 feet of water. Former Hughes power plant mechanic John H. Glenn says, "And by God, he put it back together. He must have put hundreds of thousands of dollars into that thing in labor and material." And this, it must be noted, was during the war when everything was in short supply.

The Project Drags On

As 1943 began, Hughes was still involved with preliminary design problems with the flying boat. WPB chairman Donald Nelson, who had taken the chance in approving the Kaiser-Hughes contract, grew worried by the lack of progress and instructed Grover Loening to make a surprise visit to the Hughes Aircraft Company on January 10. Loening was not impressed. Among other things, "it was difficult to get hold of Mr. Hughes, as he was busy on other matters."[33]

Following Loening's suggestion that Hughes be forced to give full attention to the flying boat, Nelson sent a rather sharp letter to Hughes on February 8, 1943:

"The skill with which you complete this craft in a satisfactory enough state to be of distinct service is more important than any skill which might result in an ultimate perfection at the expense of time."[34] (This belies a later Hughes assertion that "I was specifically instructed that it was a research project and I was told to take my time.")[35]

In his reply to Nelson—*six* weeks later—Hughes wrote that "after all, the question of whether Grover Loening's criticism of me is fair or unfair is not very important. The main thing is to get the airplane built."[36]

Hughes was rarely seen by most of the men who worked for him. His nightowl work habits, penchant for secrecy, and involvement in myriad simultaneous projects—plus a reluctance to delegate authority in matters of design—made working for Hughes a unique and often frustrating experience. Important decisions could be delayed for days because Hughes's executives could not contact their elusive boss.

Edward Bern, general manager of Hughes Aircraft Company for several months in the summer of 1943, later testified that he saw Hughes at the plant only once. However, as Bern was quick to add, "it is my understanding that many times at two or three o'clock in the morning Howard would come in there with a ham sandwich and a glass of milk and work all night, but I did not see him."[37]

Hughes took little interest in administrative matters. It never entered his mind that anyone would retire. Pay raises and vacations were not details he would think of on his own. He understood things, not people. As one of his chief engineers said, "If he couldn't see it or touch it, he wasn't much interested."

Project Management

For administration and tight operational control he needed competent help. Some of his appointments were shrewd and longlasting. But others were of short duration—primarily because his eccentric ways of doing business handicapped and frustrated his managers. In addition, he was always interfering—he simply couldn't keep hands off.

At the start of the flying boat project Hughes Aircraft Division of Hughes Tool Company was a small experimental group that had designed and constructed the H-1 racer and was involved with the design and construction of the D-2. It was essentially a small engineering group.

During the first seven months of the project Hughes acted as general manager with the heads of the production and engineering departments reporting directly to him. Henry Kaiser, after his unsuccessful first attempt at combining forces with Hughes, had nothing more to do with the project except to help out with a few personnel at the start and to drop in every few months for a hurried visit.

Shortly before the project got underway, Hughes brought in an outsider from the automotive industry, John LeDuc, who had no aircraft or woodworking experience. As works manager, LeDuc would head up the manufacturing organization. Kenneth Ridley, a young aeronautical engineer who had come to Hughes from Douglas about four years earlier, was placed in charge of the engineering group.

LeDuc and Ridley held parallel positions. This seemed an impossible arrangement to the supervising engineer of the Defense Plant Corporation's Culver City office. He made an effort to get Neil S. McCarthy, the executive vice president of the relatively ineffective and inactive Kaiser-Hughes organization who had also been Hughes's personal attorney since about 1925, to bring in a general manager to properly coordinate all efforts.[38]

For a time LeDuc and Ridley seemed to work well together and LeDuc, a man with great drive and force, began to get the group organized. However, LeDuc had difficulty finding good personnel—Hughes was not supposed to raid the industry—

and, thrown into a new and unfamiliar field of work, made many mistakes. As a result, the engineering and manufacturing departments began to split into two factions composed of the "hometown boys" and the "outsiders."[39]

By May, 1943, Hughes brought in Edward H. Bern as general manager. Bern had long experience in American Airlines and had a background in sales and promotions. He moved aggressively to organize the group and to push the work, but he soon had a falling out with Ridley. And Hughes, because of his long association with Ridley, began discussing management problems with Ridley without the participation of Bern.

On August 27, 1943, Bern telephoned WPB Chairman Donald Nelson. "We have got a terribly chaotic situation out here. It is going to blow right up in your face. . . . I have been in the business for twenty-six years and I am trying to clean things up and they will not let me."

"Who will not let you?" Nelson asked.

"Howard interferes. Howard owns the company. The only time we see him is at home late at night—at ten, eleven, twelve or one or two in the morning. He calls you up and tries to get the picture . . . . The last man that talks to him of his old bunch is the one who can sell him the idea of doing something."[40]

Bern resigned that same day, saying that Hughes insisted on organizational changes which he, Bern, felt rightfully belonged within his purview as general manager.

There was a flurry of changes in the executive lineup at Hughes Aircraft in the summer of 1943. Mathewson, head of production engineering, resigned in June. Morgan, night superintendent of manufacturing, was discharged on June 18. Armstrong, general superintendent of manufacturing, resigned in June. Blydenburgh was promoted to head production engineering in June. Rivers, general superintendent of manufacturing, was hired in July. Bern, general manager, resigned August 27. LeDuc, works manager, resigned August 27. Ridley, chief engineer, was promoted to general manager of the cargo division, August 28.[41]

Dick Murrow briefly replaced Babberger as chief of aerodynamics, and Babberger went over to 7000 Romaine to work on the F-11 photoplane.[42] (Murrow had joined Hughes in 1941 during work on the D-2 at the Burbank hangar, and after the move to Culver City he was principally involved in the flying boat. He also participated in tests to determine why the D-2 was having aileron control problems.) Regarding this period of delay and disorganization in the flying boat project, Murrow said:

"I got worried because the project was getting so far behind schedule, and actually it was because Hughes wouldn't relinquish control of things to his people out there. He would spend all night worrying about the most minute details that any young engineer was quite capable of handling. He insisted on digging into details way beyond what he should. We'd spend sessions up there in the middle of the night and then have to be at work at 7 o'clock *wartime* in the morning, and it was driving us crazy. Then he would disappear for weeks at a time and nothing could

The immensity of the Flying Boat is evidenced in the pictures on these two pages. With a wing span of almost 320 feet and a maximum hull depth of almost 30 feet, even the workmen look small.

All finished surfaces required meticulous hand sanding as noted in the insert above.

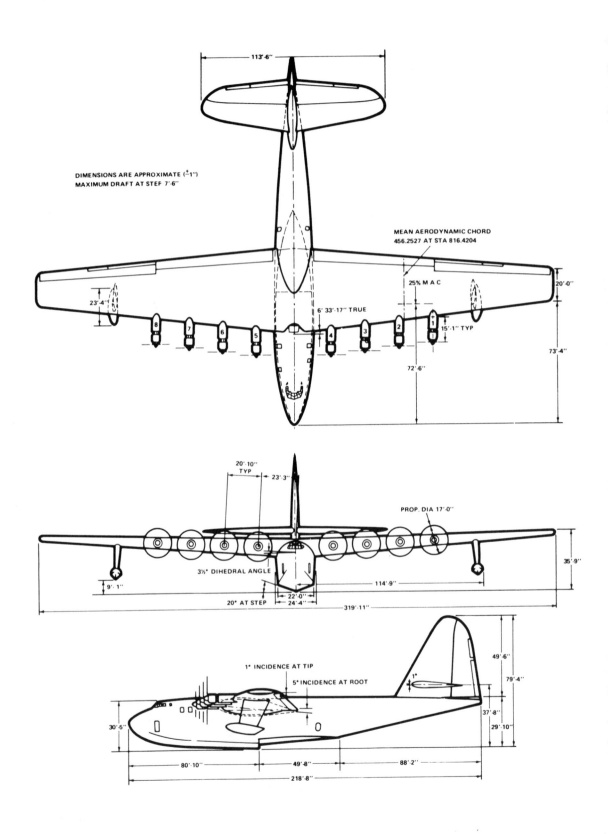

DIMENSIONS ARE APPROXIMATE (±1")
MAXIMUM DRAFT AT STEP 7'-6"

MEAN AERODYNAMIC CHORD
456.2527 AT STA 816.4204

25% M A C

23'-4"

6' 33'-17" TRUE

20'-0"

15'-1" TYP

73'-4"

72'-6"

20'-10"
TYP

23'-3"

PROP. DIA 17'-0"

3½° DIHEDRAL ANGLE

35'-9"

9'-1"

114'-9"

20° AT STEP

22'-0"

24'-4"

319'-11"

1° INCIDENCE AT TIP

5° INCIDENCE AT ROOT

1°

49'-6"

79'-4"

37'-8"

29'-10"

30'-5"

80'-10"

49'-8"

88'-2"

218'-8"

Howard Hughes Flying Boat Description

GENERAL — The Hughes Flying Boat is a cargo type airplane having eight Pratt and Whitney R4360-4A engines, single vertical tail, fixed wing tip floats, and full cantilever wing and tail surfaces. Its structure and surface are entirely of laminated wood; all primary control surfaces except the flaps, are fabric covered. Contained in the hull are a flight deck for the operating crew and a large cargo deck with a circular stairway providing access from one deck to the other. Below the cargo deck are located the fuel bays separated by watertight bulkheads. Beaching of the airplane is accomplished by the use of dry dock facilities.

The 3-View and the following data courtesy of
The Aero Club of Southern California & Wrather Port Properties, Ltd.

DIMENSIONS — WING AND EMPENNAGE

	Wing	Horizontal Tail	Vertical Tail
Area	11,430.0	2610.1	1703.443
Span (ft)	319.92	113.5	49.5

CONTROL SURFACES

	Flaps	Elevators (both)	Rudder	Ailerons (both)
Total area (sq ft)	1404.0	1110.2	650.56	1250
Span (ft)		104.318	47.661	143.5

FLYING TABS

	Elevator Flying Tabs	Rudder Flying Tabs	Aileron Flying Tabs
Area aft of hinge line (sq ft)	90.28	57.834	97.0
Span (ft)	46.800	23.069	62.08

TRIM TABS

	Elevator Trim Tabs	Rudder Trim Tabs	Aileron Trim Tabs
Area aft of hinge line (sq ft)	48.38	22.503	33.6
Span (ft)	15.526	11.875	25.0

PERFORMANCE

	Gross Weight 350,000 lb	Gross Weight 400,000 lb
High speed at sea level with T.O. power (mph)	235.5	234
High speed at sea level with normal rated power (mph)	222	218
High speed at 5000 ft with normal rated power (mph)	231	227
Operating speed at sea level with max. cruising power, 1675 BHP/2230 rpm (mph)	190	185
Initial cruising speed for max. range at 5000 ft altitude (mph)	141	150
Landing speed at sea level — 10% above stall, 45° flap (mph)	81	87
Range in miles at best cruising speed with no fuel reserve (8 engines) 12,500 gal. fuel	—	2,975
6,000 gal. fuel	1,575	1,430
Service ceiling (ft)	20,900	17,400

get done. I began keeping a set of hand written notes on the meetings—what was decided, when they took place, and so forth—because he got mad at his chief engineers and wouldn't talk to them, first Stan Bell and then Ridley. Us hirelings, like the heads of structures, aerodynamics, powerplants, and whatnot, would have these meetings with Hughes and then we'd have to go in the next day and tell the chief engineer what the hell the next step was. It was kind of ridiculous.

"Hughes was constantly hiring new plant managers, invariably telling them they were in complete charge of things down there. They'd come in with a bunch of their cronies and set up shop. We used to call them 'torpedoes.' They sat around at their desk with their hat on their head with a secretary and shuffled papers, and it wasn't long before they found out that they weren't running the place at all, that Hughes was. And so he'd get rid of those and bring in another bunch. Odekirk was the real plant manager for Hughes."[43]

In fairness, it must be said that the complex, often contradictory, aspects of Hughes's personality, character, and behavior (which caused such trouble for his managers) included strengths as well. One of Hughes's senior engineers said, "I can't give him enough credit. He had the ability to bring out the best in anyone."

According to this engineer, Hughes worked very closely with his people in matters he was particularly concerned with, yet he gave considerable freedom to his division chiefs. He allowed people he liked and trusted to do what they thought was right. If he thought that they were onto something, he saw that they had the means to do it.

When working with his engineers on the flying boat, Hughes did not worry about the bottom line. Function and performance were what counted in design, not money. Carl Babberger recalls that the Kaiser-Hughes project had the finest machine shop you could ask for. "Anything we needed we got. That's the truth. We were the first people in Southern California, I dare say, who got the Swiss-made SIP jig borers that could bore holes to a ten-thousandths of an inch center line spacing."[44]

Although Hughes did not skimp on equipment and materials for the design and construction of aircraft, he was chiseling and penny-pinching in business dealings with others, and in the payment—or rather nonpayment—of taxes. Typical of this, says Noah Dietrich, was when Howard balked at a $75,000 bill owed Douglas Aircraft for modifications to his Boeing biplane. Donald Douglas became exasperated and told Dietrich to have Hughes write a check for any amount he wanted, "And you tell him this for me—I never want to do business with him again." Hughes was delighted and made out a check for $15,000.[45]

For years people wondered about the rather bilious chartreuse color of the Hughes Aircraft plant. Color was not a consideration; price was. Hughes was able to purchase great amounts as war surplus because of the low demand for such a color.

Hughes often raised hell with his financial people if in purchasing, accounting, and contracting they did not extract the maximum possible financial advantages for

Hughes Aircraft. In February 1944, the Defense Plant Corporation's supervising engineer for the Kaiser-Hughes project reported a spirit of "soaking" the Defense Plant Corporation.[46]

Hughes the Employer

On the other hand, according to longtime Hughes employees, he paid good wages. People he liked—people who had done a good job for him—stayed on the payroll even if there was nothing for them to do.

For example, power plant mechanic John Glenn tells of the captain of the *Southern Cross*. "The skipper would come in once a week and look around and talk to us fellas—a very nice gentleman—used to tell us the most fabulous stories about Hughes's yachting days. Hughes had quite a few on his payroll like that. Didn't hit a lick. All they did was show up and pick up their paycheck—for years."[47] Actually, Capt. Carl B. Flynn had done more for Hughes than skipper the *Southern Cross*. During the 1940s he was in charge of all the work boats at the Terminal Island flying boat site. In April 1948 Comdr. Garland (Jack) Suggs replaced Flynn as commander of the Hughes fleet, but Flynn was kept on the payroll until his death in 1961. For years the *Southern Cross* was docked across from the old Ford plant in Los Angeles Harbor until it was sold in the early 1950s. Captain Flynn and Suggs kept two to six men on it until it was sold.[48]

In general, Hughes treated his working-level employees well, although he was often inconsiderate in his demands on those closest to him. Comments by longtime employees are revealing.

John H. Glenn, power plant mechanic: "Hughes certainly was good to work for. I think that we were the highest paid overall in the aviation industry when I worked for him. He knew a lot of old timers by name. You'd think that as little as he saw us he wouldn't remember, but he did. I'll never forget the time the union got into the plant after the war when there had been an influx of new workers and called a sit-down strike. The strikers all went over to the side of an aisle in the big hangar. After a while Hughes came in and told them, 'Either you go back to work or I'll shut this plant down.' Another fella and myself were working on a B-23—Douglas built—a good fast airplane. We used to put big engines on them and make plush jobs of 'em. . . . I just kept on working and he came up and said, 'How's it going, Johnny?' And I said, 'Oh, fine, Howard.' And he just looked at me and said, 'You'll never have to worry about a job in this plant.' That's all he said and he walked off with Rae Hopper."[49]

Jim Dallas, electrical engineer: "I came over from Lockheed. Worked for Hughes twenty-nine years. I started in the design staff on top of the Burbank TWA hangar. Stan Bell was chief engineer at that time. At Lookheed I had worked on what was called the Excalibur, an airplane designed in accordance with what customer research indicated the world's air transport companies wanted in a transport. The survey indicated that high speed was not an important consideration. Hughes didn't believe they understood the dynamics of the air transport industry.

He thought that a fast plane was what they had to have. So he started a competitive design that became the Constellation. Hughes was right. Over and over again I saw that. He was a great, great man. The finest mind of any person I've ever worked with.[50]

"I always found he was a real fine gentleman and very understanding. Most of the stuff you hear about him is pure newspaper bunk. One time I was working at the navigator's station on the flight load indicators Howard wanted to monitor control forces on the flying boat. Hughes came by and said, 'What the goddamn hell is all this stuff?' Then he smiled. I started to explain and then I could see that he knew. He was a friendly guy. . . . In actual design work, he was guiding. He was the authority. He was right in there all the time. He'd come down and stay all night, you know. Go over every drawing on the drawing board. He never went into a meeting or a conference that he didn't spend a lot of time so he knew everything up and down more than all the rest of the people there put together. That was actually the secret of his control."[51]

Harry Kaiser, power plant mechanic: "I was with him thirty years. He was a wonderful guy to work for! I had no complaint about that. He was very nice when he was getting ready to fly. When we had the DC-6, he'd just stick his head out and say, 'I got plenty of time now, boys, don't rush.' He appreciated us."[52] Chuck Jucker, service manager: "He was demanding, of course, but he paid well. If he said stand by, you stood by even if it was all night. If you did nothing but sit on the bench or in the office your pay went on."[53] Dave Grant, hydraulic staff engineer: "He really was a perfectionist and he really was in charge, but he was easy to work for. On the other hand, there was the primary difficulty of his weird hours and the fact that if you didn't agree with what he had to say it took quite a few hours of discussion to get to the final conclusion. But he didn't keep us up eighteen hours at a stretch. We were usually through by two in the morning."[54]

Al Geverink, power plant mechanic: "He was smart enough to get all the answers before he asked the questions. He always knew what he was talking about. He especially enjoyed experimental work and liked to get personally involved."[55] Chris Reising, electrical engineer: "People would make suggestions and he would review those and throw in his own ideas. If he liked an idea that came up he would so indicate it. He wasn't hard-nosed about it. He wanted to talk about it. He wanted to come up with the best design regardless of who suggested it and he didn't care how long it took. At my level, which was about three steps below reporting directly to the project manager, he was very kind, very thoughtful, very considerate. But if he thought anybody was trying to put anything over on him he indicated his displeasure."[56] Bill Noggle, hydraulics mechanic: "He was very soft spoken. He wasn't bossy at all. He knew his business, was very much interested in the details, and was very persistent."[57]

Homer ("Dave") Roe, powerplant engineer on Hughes Models D-2, F-11, and the HK-1 flying boat: "I had personal contact with Mr. Hughes on numerous occasions. I found him to be highly motivated and very involved with his projects and felt he was an outstanding leader, He would direct numerous unusual assignments and was technically very competent. He did not engage in small talk, but at times broke through with subtle humor."[58]

One of his senior engineers observed that Hughes wanted a day's work for a day's pay. Punctuality meant little to him as long as you delivered a day's work. Although he wanted personal loyalty—he wouldn't stand for even minor insubordination—he did not like yes-men. He respected those who stood up to him. You could argue with him until doomsday. But he was stubborn and persistent and usually got his way in the end. "He'd give you hell for failing to do what he told you to do, but not for making honest mistakes."[59]

Hughes it seems had very little contact with any but a handful of people in his organization. Yet in those contacts he was always pleasant to the people who worked for him on the lower levels. Working higher up in Hughes's organization was worse; he would call in the middle of the night and talk for hours. "Look, the bankers and others I have to call during the day," he told one of his executives, "but you work for me. I can call you any time."

"Actually, their lives weren't their own," says John Glenn, "and we always admired anybody who was higher up in the company. Sometimes he'd give them hell, and right in front of us. I've heard him chew out engineers like you wouldn't believe. He'd ask them a question and if they hemmed and hawed he'd tell them, 'If you don't know what you're talking about keep your goddamned mouth shut!' All they had to say was 'I don't know,' but you didn't fool him. This guy had a sharp mind on him and he knew that [flying] boat backside and frontside."

A trait that caused consternation at Hughes Aircraft was that Hughes never went through channels. He often worked with lower echelon people and then had them pass his instructions to their superiors. He would avoid taking time for first-hand contact if he could use an intermediary. Earl Martyn was often used for this purpose because Hughes would ponder his projects during their flights together.

As Earl remembers it, "We'd get in from a flight and Howard would give me a list of things he wanted me to tell Rae Hopper to do. This perturbed Hopper. He'd rather get it direct. But I couldn't help it. Hughes told me to do it, so I did it."[60] Flight engineer Van Storm gives a later example of this trait. "I can remember on returning from a flight in the Convair 240 Howard gave me a list of things to do, But first I was to call Lockheed president Robert Gross and tell him such and such. It was three a.m., but Howard told me to go ahead. Well, I did. And my ears rang for days. I never did deliver Howard's message to Gross, but I did deliver an unprintable message to Howard from Robert Gross. I now believe that was about the time Jack Real was made the Lockheed contact man for Hughes."[61] Carl Babberger was often an intermediary, too: "Hughes wasn't a typical executive by any manner of means. He didn't go for protocol. He just had whoever he was talking to carry messages. There were times when I had to go up to the general manager's office to tell him Hughes's latest instructions. Lots of time I had to pass messages to the chief engineer."[62]

Both despite and because of the quirks of Hughes's personality and his unorthodox ways of doing business, step-by-step progress was made on the flying boat during 1943. The close collaboration between Hughes and NACA resulted in an outstanding design aerodynamically and hydrodynamically. But the structure was another story.

Construction: The Duramold Process

Major problems resulted from combining wood construction with giant size. The Hughes Aircraft Company had had previous successful experiences in wood construction; but this experience was not always directly applicable to building the flying boat. Elaborate and costly jigs had to be devised and new glues and gluing procedures developed.

Intensive basic research in glues by two subcontractors resulted in the earliest practical solutions to the use of epoxy resins, which are chemical, thermosetting glues rather than organic glues. Further research and development resulted in special machinery and equipment for bonding, curing, and forming of high quality plywoods.

Three different types of epoxy resin glues were used: phenol formaldehyde resin cured by heating to 300°F, a urea formaldehyde resin which cured at 70°F or above, and a medium-temperature resorcinal formaldehyde type glue that became available after the project was well under way.

Glue pressure for attaching the hull skin was provided by thousands of small nails driven by specially developed nailing guns. After the glue was cured the nails were removed by specially developed nail pullers. Approximately eight tons of nails were used.[63]

It had been claimed that some of this research resulted in subsequent commercial applications. Wayne Thomis, for example, in a 1971 *Chicago Tribune* article quotes a Hughes Tool Company executive as saying that "the big wooden bird became a hen that laid golden eggs. Everyone in the country, and quite a few firms outside, that make plywood have been paying licenses and royalties to Howard ever since."

This is disputed, however, by Benjamin F. Schemmer in a hard hitting November 1972 article in *Armed Forces Journal*. He quotes John Ritchie, vice president and secretary of the American Plywood Association, as saying, "I'm sure that's not true . . . We would know it if it were." Furthermore, wrote Schemmer, "An extensive search of government patent files failed to unearth one single patent ever assigned to Hughes, Hughes Tool or Aircraft Companies, or to his key executives as a result of any HK-1 related work. Moreover, the government is entitled to royalty-free use of the HK-1 technology and any patents resulting from the plane." But GSA's sales division director Peter Glading says, "To the best of our knowledge, there are none."

Hughes himself testified at the 1947 hearings that "we have no patents which were intended to be used, we collected no royalty and I assure you we will not collect any and never had any intentions of collecting any."[64]

However, despite the lack of evidence of any resulting patents, challenging problems in constructing the large boat were licked by innovative solutions. Assistance in solving tooling problems was provided by consultants obtained from Los Angeles area woodworking firms doing subcontract work on subassemblies.

The subcontractors who assisted in the construction of the flying boat were: Weber Showcase & Fixture Company, Los Angeles, contracted to manufacture bulkheads for the hull; Edward J. Classen Manufacturing Company, Los Angeles, contracted to manufacture stringers for the wing; Modern Pattern & Foundry Company, Los Angeles, contracted to manufacture aluminum castings; Van Tuyle Engineering, Inc., Los Angeles, contracted to manufacture templates for parts manufacture; Jasper Wood Products, Jasper, Indiana, contracted to manufacture plywood flat panels.[65]

Hughes had purchased the partial rights to use the Duramold process for making molded plywood from Sherman Fairchild in 1939. This process was ideally suited for making smoothly molded fighter-size aircraft but had not been devised for anything as big as Hughes had in mind. The background is in and of itself an interesting story. Colonel Virginius E. ("Ginny") Clark, one of the early college-trained aeronautical engineers, was at one time, according to Fairchild, perhaps the top airplane designer in the world—a fine aerodynamicist. He was commanding officer of the old McCook Field in Dayton, Ohio, before it disappeared in 1923 to become Wright Field. "Ginny" Clark, among other pursuits, developed the Clark Y airfoil which became the standard airfoil section in most U.S. aircraft for many years.

Clark approached Sherman Fairchild in the 1930s and said that the answer to getting airplanes to go faster was to get them smoother. This meant using no rivets, he said. His efforts with Fairchild to discover how to build structurally strong airplanes with a material other than aluminum and with a glass-like smoothness resulted in the Duramold process.

In the beginning Clark did not have the information on glues and resins that was needed. So he and Fairchild went to George Meyercord of the Haskelite Company. There they developed the glues and resins and a pressure-cooking and molding technique. At Fairchild's Hagerstown plant they built on this development and added an ultra-high-frequency electronic gluing technique.

One effective but less sophisticated method of getting uniform glue lines in laminated wing spars was to put the spar in a box frame, drop in a second-hand piece of fire hose, put on the lid and turn on the water to get an absolutely even 60 pounds pressure. "The fire hose just happened to be the right thickness," said Fairchild.[66]

As Fairchild remembers the Duramold development, "We started in with pressure kilns and molds, bags, and methods of molding a fuselage in two halves." The result was the 12-cylinder Ranger engine–powered Fairchild 46. "This airplane was just amazing in speed and everything . . . . People just couldn't believe it went so fast."[67] But the public distrust of wood precluded any wide sale of the F-46.

83

Fairchild later used some of the Duramold processes to mold tail surfaces for the successful Fairchild trainer, the PT-19.

In the meantime, Clark became difficult. He had a tendency to look down on ordinary airplane manufacturers who did not have the money or vision to fully back him.

Clark was tremendously interested in the aerodynamic effects of the smooth skin produced by Duramold. He felt that he had demonstrated those in the F-46. And he had a single-engine fighter design that on paper outflew everything. But Fairchild had money problems at that time, so Clark contacted his friend, Glenn Martin. Martin agreed to back the fighter design, but only if he could have complete control. Meanwhile, Fairchild was struggling to find any deal where he could get the needed cash to keep control of Duramold and Clark.

The year before, Hughes had bailed out Fairchild when money had been a problem. Hughes did so again and obtained the license to Duramold in the deal. Hughes was sold on Duramold anyway because of the external smoothness that it produced. So Fairchild and his attorney, Roswell Gilpatric, flew out to Culver City.

Hughes was one of Fairchild's closest friends, but the friendship was not necessarily based on the amount of time they spent together. They were both extremely busy with their own projects. When Fairchild and Gilpatric arrived in California to see Hughes and arrange the deal, they waited in Hughes's office for three days. Hughes never appeared. Nonetheless, Hughes came through for Fairchild and agreed to buy the Duramold rights for aircraft above 20,000 pounds leaving the rights below that figure to Fairchild and George Meyercord of Haskelite.[68]

Along with the Duramold process, Hughes acquired the services of Ginny Clark and a Maine wood expert, George Allward, who had been trained in England. Clark, of course, hoped that Hughes would build his single-engine fighter, but he never did. Instead, the Duramold process was applied to the Hughes D-2 and later to the flying boat.

The Hughes engineer assigned to work with Clark and Allward in the development of Duramold processes for Hughes Aircraft was mechanical engineer Louis Tribbett, who had started work for Hughes on September 1, 1939, in the old Western Air Express hangar at Burbank.

"I was the 17th person hired in the Hughes Aircraft Company," says Tribbett. "That included shop men and all. About half of those were engineers. Then he hired steadily from the first week in September. There was a new engineer every week practically. I think we were at the Western Air Express hangar there in Burbank for about half a year. When we moved to the new factory at Culver City we probably had thirty or forty engineers. I would estimate . . . that on the day of Pearl Harbor Hughes had a hundred people working in the engineering department. I would say that half of those were engineers and they were some of the finest engineers that money could get."[69]

Ken Ridley, Rae Hopper, Warren Reed, and Tribbett all came to Hughes from Douglas Aircraft Company at about the same time. The chief engineer then was

Stan Bell. Aerodynamicist Carl Babberger was already at Hughes.

Colonel Clark came to work at Hughes in October 1939, shortly after Tribbett began. Clark was not put in charge of anything, but had an office as a consultant advisor. George Allward became Tribbett's boss. "Allward really was good," says Tribbett. "He really knew his business."

But during the war, Allward was hired away from Hughes by the Higgins Company of New Orleans while Tribbett was in the Pacific on military duty. Hughes was furious and filed a lawsuit against Higgins.

Tribbett's work was primarily in support of the D-2, but this laid the groundwork for the building of the flying boat. Under Allward's supervision he tested all kinds of U.S. woods and selected birch as the primary structural material. Spruce, otherwise a good structural wood, could not take bolts well. But by laminating birch in both directions they could get the necessary grip of wood to bolt. They found, too, that for high stress applications birch in terms of weight was better. Additionally, birch made better molded plywood when glued and steam heated than spruce. (Carl Babberger says that they developed seventeen types of Duramold. All had thin laminations and varied from all birch to mostly poplar.)

"I personally wrote the design book, *Duramold and Aircraft*," says Tribbett. "I forget how many thousands of tests I ran on different kinds of woods and combinations. I worked out the formulas for the curved sections and where and how to use the wood, the matter of bolts, the whole thing. When I left the company in 1942 I had seven or eight engineers under me working full time on it."

Duramold, as Fairchild said, was really better for smaller aircraft and for small radius curvatures. It really was not appropriate for large aircraft such as Hughes was building. Tribbett recalls that on the very front page of the design data book he and his engineers prepared he wrote that from his studies he recommended that wood never be used in aircraft with gross weights of more than 16,000 pounds. "And later, when the boat turned out so dismally, I was glad I'd put that in there," said Tribbett.[70] (During the initial static load tests of the stabilizer some Duramold skin began to separate from the underlying stringers.)

Hughes was lavish with equipment for Duramold, says Tribbett. "We could have most anything we wanted. We went out and bought a steam tank, about ten feet in diameter, I think, and about forty feet long with a massive door on one end so we could move a whole [D-2] wing section in. We'd put this glue and plywood in there in enormous molds and covered with rubber bags and then press it with steam pressure in order to 'cook' it.

"We had to start from scratch with everything because the Fairchild data wasn't suitable for what we were doing, and when we tried to use some of the data from the government's Forest Products Laboratory they weren't worth a damn. It ended up that a lot of the research we did ended up in the new forest products book they copied from us.

"We didn't have any wood construction subcontractors until 1942. The Hughes company just went out and hired a bunch of Swedes and good woodworking men—

some real fine people. The man we sent to Wisconsin to buy the selected woods was Gus Seidel, a personal friend of Hughes."

After the contract for the flying boat was let, they had to expand the Duramold technology still further, according to Carl Babberger. "We built some fantastic types of Duramold plywood designed for the job it had to do—whether it was bearing or shear or tension—and developed special corner angles to replace glue blocks. We demonstrated that glue blocks were a serious problem in wood construction because of differential expansion with and across the grain. I would say that the corner angle substitute for the glue block was the greatest development in plywood history. We went to real thin plies, maybe a hundredths of an inch thick, and then built up angles that had maybe ten or more plies with little fillets glued in at the angle."

"The men wore white gloves," said Babberger, "in order not to put fingerprints on the laminations when they were building them up. A fingerprint was assumed to create a bum glue joint. We used the best woods and the best glues that were known.

"We also pioneered a special lofting technique. All templates were faired mathematically, machined out, and hand filed to a 1:16 scale. Then an enormous camera was used to project the templates to full scale. This produced continuous curves—beautiful things. After all, a spline is only as good as the eye of the man that uses it. But we could define everything, and did, to the thousandths of an inch. We were the first ones to try that stunt."[71]

Birch was selected as the main structural material, not only because of the structural properties previously mentioned, and its good strength-weight ratio, but also because spruce of the quality desired was difficult to obtain. However, spruce, poplar, maple, and some balsa for fairings were also used.

The main structural material for the flying boat was built up by bonding several plies of birch veneer with a urea-formaldehyde glue. The bonds were formed under both heat and pressure, but some cold setting was used in certain cases.

Sharply curved surfaces, like the nose covering of the wings, were made using the usual Duramold process. But here the pieces were so large and the strategic material required for steel dies so hard to obtain and so expensive that Hughes experimented with "Gunite," a hard plaster.

This development of new tools, materials and methods was often by trial-and-error. Mistakes consumed time, material, and money. Progress was slow through spring 1943.

5

Hughes Versus the Experts

IN LATER YEARS Hughes partially blamed delays in building the giant flying boat on the requirement that he build it of nonstrategic materials—that is, of wood. "You might as well have built a ship that big out of putty," he said in a 1947 *Washington Daily News* interview. But government records show that very early in the life of the contract, Hughes was given the option of switching to metal and made no effort to do so. It seems that the effort he had expended, the progress the Hughes team had made in pioneering innovative methods of wood construction, and Hughes's attraction to the smooth external finish of the Duramold plywood made him reluctant to change materials after the start of the project.

NACA engineer John Parkinson says that "the story I got from my friends was that by the time aluminum became plentiful, his [Hughes's] people had gotten so sold on this pioneering plywood design that they didn't want to change. They thought they were building a better, lower-weight airplane using the plywood techniques that they developed. But it didn't turn out that way because the stuff started coming apart."[1]

The Wood Problem

The opening gun in the wood-versus-metal controversy was fired by Grover Loening on April 3, 1943, in commenting on the preliminary general specifications for the airplane. "The use of wood, because of strategic shortages, is not now needed," he wrote. He recommended that the wing be designed for metal.[2]

On May 4, William Burden, who as Special Aviation Assistant to the Secretary of Commerce represented the Defense Plant Corporation, chaired a meeting in the NACA conference room to review the progress on the HK-1. Henry Kaiser was present; Hughes was not. Representing Hughes were Kenneth Ridley, his chief engineer, and Edward Bern, then general manager of the Hughes Aircraft Cargo Division.

Midway in the meeting Burden turned to Ridley and asked, "Are you satisfied with the wooden construction that has been specified for this work?"

Ridley, undoubtedly speaking for Hughes, replied that he would not ask for any change in material whatever. "I do not feel that there would be any advantage whatever in going to metal construction. On the contrary, I think it would take longer to build, cost more, and might even be heavier."

Capt. L. S. Stevens, representing the U.S. Navy, said, "The Bureau of Aeronautics is definitely on record against wood construction for a project of this character. The Navy feels the design is very good, but we're skeptical of wood and the time of construction."[3]

Up until about August 1943, Hughes refused to consider switching to metal. Carl Babberger says that Hughes might have thought wood was better, "but that wasn't the opinion of the engineering department. Hughes may have feared that if he switched to metal they'd say, 'Well, you're going to be delayed some more, the war will be over, we'll just cancel the project.' "[4]

For several days, beginning on August 2, Loening, Burden, and Dr. George W. Lewis of the National Advisory Committee for Aeronautics, under whose direction NACA had helped with the design of hull and wings and conducted aerodynamic and hydrodynamic testing, visited with Hughes and his staff in Culver City.

"The general progress of the Kaiser-Hughes project can be reported on as satisfactory," wrote Loening in his report of the visit. "It is, of course, difficult to appraise work of this character, but the progress on the engineering seems particularly noteworthy. The design of the KH-1 aircraft, aerodynamically and hydrodynamically, appears excellent. It is in no sense a freak, but is, on the other hand, a very fine and graceful layout in a fairly conservative but thoroughly modern type of aircraft in which giant size alone is the principal new contribution." (Reference here is to the HK-1).

Then Loening again launched into the wood problem. "Several times in the past, your consultant has called attention to the serious question involved in building the huge 320-foot span wing of this design out of wood. Originally this was mandatory upon Hughes, because it was and still is distinctly understood that this project must not 'raid' strategic materials from military aircraft production. However, since that time the situation has reversed itself in that wood, particularly birch veneer, is becoming very scarce, and metal is becoming a great deal easier. For this reason, the question of developing a metal wing for this design was again taken up in detail with Mr. Hughes. In the discussions on this subject, Mr. Hughes finally expressed agreement and said that he would be entirely willing to proceed at once with the metal wing."

Loening concluded his report on an optimistic, upbeat note (though this would become more muted in future reporting): "Since there is growing very quickly now an appreciation of what is coming in Air Power development in the way of invasion task forces that move entirely by air, the Kaiser-Hughes development is daily assuming more sense and importance, despite the skepticism in its early days. . . . In general, the Kaiser-Hughes organization is showing imagination, initiative and lots of push in connection with this work. They are meeting with all kinds of troubles, but they are facing them properly, and it is again urged that this development be pushed to the utmost."[5]

Three weeks later Loening admitted that he had been conned. LeDuc, Bern, and half a dozen others resigned after Hughes had represented to Loening "that his management and organization were in running order." At the same time, Loening reported to Nelson his great concern that the finishing of the stabilizer indicated a very great overweight—"far beyond what would be permissible and of a nature requiring immediate review of the project."[6]

Nelson's response was to send Loening for an intensive three-day investigation of the situation at Culver City. In his report of this September 20–22 visit, Loening said that although he saw difficulties in the manufacturing organization he thought these did not warrant any kind of indictment of Hughes's management. "As a matter of fact," he said, "conditions in the fabricating end of the plant were generally reported as greatly improved since the recent resignations of Messrs. LeDuc, Bern and others. There is not, therefore, any particular necessity for appraising the progress of this contract and the future plans for it in the light of management difficulties, but only in the light of technical considerations of the design itself. The most serious thing that is taking extra time . . . is that the method of construction has not yet been wholly devised and *actually, the government is financing an experimental development of a new wooden construction method*—at a time when it thought it was financing the development of a giant aircraft built on known structural fabricating methods."[8]

Due to the outsized members in the huge wing that were to take the stresses, a great deal of work went into making up the "billets" from which these members were shaped. These billets might be composed of as many as fifty laminations all pressed together with a very fine glue-line tolerance. If the glue was too heavy or thick, the strength was impaired—and the weight increased—and if the glue was too thin a good bond was not obtained. There were frequent rejections of parts due to glue lines indicating insufficient bond, and in Loening's opinion there was no way to inspect the actual internal quality of the bond. This proved to be a major point against wooden construction of this type, and Loening jumped on it.

"Unlike the ability we have in metal with magnaflux and x-ray devices to determine the character of metal joints, these wooden joints must be taken on faith and on their external inspection only. Yet structural loads including vibrations, flutters, etc., and finally, weathering effects, will definitely strain these joints with forces other than shears (in which they are manifestly strong) and thus give to the entire structure an element of unreliability that is definitely 'scary' for aircraft."[9]

One of Hughes's aircraft inspectors, Clarence Selberg, comments on this: "In quality standards and workmanship, [the flying boat] is perhaps the best wood structured aircraft ever built. Hughes was very meticulous regarding stress of materials, quality of workmanship, and appearance. Wood parts to be assembled were mated to each other at the glue bond area to a maximum of .003 inches gap. Blue chalking on one of the glue bond area faces was checked for transfer to the other. Where possible, feeler gauges were also used to insure precision fit. And a method of testing soundness of glue joints was developed using sonic as well as x-ray methods.[10]

Loening concluded the report of his late September visit by saying, "It is the details of construction material used and likelihood of serious overweight, the miscalculating of time needed and cost, the choice of engines, and consequently the practical availability of the aircraft for this war that warrant a very serious review of the desirability of this project from here on."[11]

Similar doubts were expressed by a CAA inspection team. They stated that in view of the unconventional size of the project, the materials used in its construction, and the difficulties encountered, "it is our considered opinion that further work on this project would have very doubtful value if the construction of the aircraft is to be considered a war project."[12]

The "very serious review" of the flying boat project recommended by Loening began on October 4, 1943 with a meeting of the Aircraft Production Board, a subordinate activity of the WPB. This meeting was chaired by Charles E. Wilson, the WPB's Executive Vice Chairman. Minutes were taken by Loening.

After detailed review and discussion of Loening's recent reports, "It was the decision of the Board that the contract should be cancelled, inasmuch as the project offers no useful contribution to the War effort, and the facility is required for production of important military types." Brig. Gen. B. E. ("Benny") Meyers, who represented the Army Air Force on the Board, advised that they were "ready to place a contract for the Hughes photographic type airplane immediately upon availability of the facility for the purpose."[13]

Following this Board meeting, and on that same day, Wilson chaired a second meeting—this one attended by William Burden, Assistant Secretary of Commerce for Air; Grover Loening, Aircraft Consultant, WPB; C. L. Stanton, Civil Aeronautics Authority; Dr. George W. Lewis, Director of Aeronautical Research, NACA; and A. A. Vollmecke, Civil Aeronautics Authority. After the situation and the relevant factors were reviewed, it was understood that unless the Services objected the project would be cancelled.[14]

To give Kaiser and Hughes ample opportunity to answer all the points that had been raised at these meetings, they were invited to Washington for three days of conferences. The first meeting, in Nelson's office at the War Production Board on Thursday, October 21, was chaired by Grover Loening. Loening opened the meeting with a brief review of the history of the project and the altered circumstances that led to the decision on October 4 to abandon the project. Then Burden and Vollmecke expressed their opposition to wood construction and Loening quoted Dr. Lewis's opposition.

Hughes listened with growing impatience, then said, "Only one wood plane, that in which Knute Rockne was killed, has cracked up as a result of structural defects. My own planes have all met the most strenuous tests. It was in a plane with wood wings, for example, that I made the record flight from Los Angeles to New York eight years ago at an average speed of 325 miles per hour."

Burden said that in contrast to British practice, the trend in this country has been away from wood.

Hughes said he did not believe that wood had been dropped for metal entirely on the grounds that wood is an inferior material. "Other factors played a part in the switch from wood to metal. One, the public was easily led to believe that metal is safer than wood. Two, the suppliers of light metal are more aggressive, and perhaps more willing to cooperate with the plane manufacturers, than are the suppliers of wood. And three, it is likely that financial tie-ups between the producers of planes and light metals have had something to do with the switch. If the Army and Navy have given up wood, as Mr. Burden says, I think the decision might have been influenced by the fact that the builders for the Army and Navy have not always been skilled in wood construction. And the recent development of phenolic glues places wood construction in an entirely different light."

Loening looked at Hughes and asked, "Do you consider wood satisfactory in the construction of seaplanes as well as land planes?"

Hughes replied, "With phenolic glues wood might even be considered superior to metal for seaplanes."

Loening raised the question of water soakage, and in the ensuing discussion he and Hughes seemed to be far apart in their estimates of the amount of water the HK-1 would absorb.

Burden, the Assistant Secretary of Commerce for Air and speaking for the Defense Plant Corporation, said, "I very much doubt that this plane can be completed before the end of 1944."

Hughes disagreed. "I'm certain that we can deliver the first plane within one year, and as a guarantee, my company will forfeit a half million dollars if that schedule cannot be met."

When Loening commented again on the excellence of the design and stressed that he strongly favored redoing it in metal, Hughes said, "I see no reason why wood is not as good today as it was a year ago. But if the War Production Board now takes the view that wood is unsatisfactory, it follows that the War Production Board was ill-advised to authorize the project in the first instance."

This nettled Loening. "The circumstances under which the original decision was made have been radically altered," he said, "and in any case the question under consideration is not whether the original decision was a wise one but whether the project should now be continued."

Kaiser suggested that one plane be constructed of wood and one of metal so that they could be tested and compared. But Loening objected. "I favor proceeding in metal only, but it's not certain that Hughes's design staff is qualified to work in metal."

Hughes bridled. "I can assure you that my staff is perfectly capable of switching to metal," he said.

The meeting adjourned with no formal action taken. But the group appeared generally agreed on the desirability of salvaging the design.[15]

After the meeting, Kaiser and Hughes hurried to Wilson's office. Both men believed in a frontal attack at the top, not in skirmishing with the troops. They found Wilson cordial and soothing in manner. Wilson did not argue, but strove to understand their side of the story. He knew full well the potential power of the Kaiser-Hughes financial, political, and public relations clout, and he knew that he could not afford to be wrong.

Kaiser and Hughes were persuasive, impassioned, and persistent. Hughes was adept at fashioning arguments of great plausibility. He had answers for everything. Kaiser spoke of how Douglas, Martin, and the established aircraft manufacturers had been against him from the start. With just a hint of paranoia in his voice he implied that a monopolistic conspiracy had fought their project every step of the way. Between the two of them they managed to extract a very significant concession from Wilson. According to a memo by a Miss McCray of the WPB executive office, "Mr. Wilson made a verbal agreement with Mr. Hughes when he was here and is not going to put it in writing. He has a modified 30-day extension and says he will have some part of the plane completed at the end of that time [by December 1]. He plans to talk to Mr. Loening about the letter and agreement. The Army and Navy are in agreement on the procedure and have promised to loan experts to go out and examine the operation there." (This typed memo, dated November 3, 1943, was stapled to the minutes of the October 21 meeting as filed in the National Archives.)

Wilson advised the Air Production Board at their October 25 meeting that "the cancellation of the Defense Plant Corporation contract for the Kaiser-Hughes cargo airplanes has been deferred for thirty days, after which a reappraisal of the project will be made from an engineering point of view."[16]

The situation was clarified at the Aircraft Production Board meeting on November 1. "The final decision is that the Kaiser-Hughes Company will be allowed approximately 30 days [until December 1, 1943] to static test a number of subassemblies, at which time an examining board of engineering experts will be sent to the Kaiser-Hughes factory to determine the engineering feasibility of the project. The Examining Board will make its report to the Aircraft Production Board, where the final decision will be made relative to the disposition of the project."[17]

Grover Loening was very unhappy with this temporizing. Before the Engineering Examining Board had even begun its work, CAA inspectors and engineers reported that static tests of the flying boat's stabilizer conducted prior to the December 1 deadline had been unsuccessful:

"The test stabilizer was completed on October 23. The first test [maneuvering up load] was started and discontinued on November 13 due to failure at 55 percent of the required design loading. The principal failures involved were glue joints (skin-stringers). Several of these glue joints were reinforced prior to the next test.

"On November 19 and 20 the stabilizer was successfully tested to limit loading (67% design loading) for the maneuvering up load. Prior to the next test, however, additional reinforcements to the structure were added.

"On November 26 tests for the second condition (balancing-down load) were discontinued because of glue failure at 50% of the required ultimate loading. Following this test, all stringer to skin attachments that had not already been reinforced were reinforced."[18]

On November 29, Loening sent a memo to Wilson saying that with the expiration of the 30-day period agreed upon, the unsuccessful tests should be brought to the attention of the Aircraft Production Board at once. In his last paragraph he said: "The recommendations made to you by Dr. Lewis of the National Advisory Committee for Aeronautics, Mr. Burden of the Department of Commerce, Mr. Vollmecke of the Civil Aeronautics Administration, and myself, for the immediate cancellation of this wooden construction, appear to be further reinforced by the lack of successful results in the last few weeks. In view of the expert knowledge of the National Advisory Committee representatives and the inspectors and engineers of the Civil Aeronautics Administration, additional engineering investigations would appear to involve an undesirable delay in stopping the expenditures of public moneys."[19]

Loening also thought that the static testing of the tail was not nearly as important as testing for flutter, because the possibility of flutter is very serious in wooden aircraft. "Due to the peculiar action of wood in various humidity conditions, one day it will be perfectly okay, and the next day its rigidity will be quite different, and that has always been one of the reasons why aircraft engineers would like to leave wood and go to metal, because they can count on it more surely. The stress can be figured more accurately."[20]

The November 29 meeting of the Aircraft Production Board considered Loening's recommendation that the wooden construction be immediately discontinued and that the Engineering Examining Board investigation be cancelled. But the Board concluded that "in view of the War Production Board's agreement with the Kaiser-Hughes Company to appoint an 'Engineering Examining Board' to determine the engineering feasibility of the particular type airplane, the investigation shall proceed as originally planned."[21]

Wilson explained the rationale to Loening in a memo on December 8: "It would appear to me that if we follow the procedure on which we obtained a substantial agreement, our case will be stronger in combatting the almost certain pressure from various outside groups if and when cancellation is finally effected. . . . Failure to do so will give Messrs. Hughes and Kaiser material on which to pin a story of violation of agreement, persecution, etc. Furthermore, as nearly 20 million dollars of the taxpayers' money has been spent on a single model, it seems to me that, even if the final decision is to cancel, the development experts should make such a decision on the ground, in view of the magnitude of the proposition."[22]

Because of the gluing difficulties revealed by the structural tests, the CAA on

December 14, 1943 arranged for a glue expert from the Forest Products Laboratory to consult with the Hughes Company on these problems. Since October the Forest Products Laboratory had been conducting intensive tests of a new and very promising resorcinal glue that could be applied cold.[23]

By now, however, Loening had become convinced that the project had little chance of making a wartime contribution. On January 27, 1944 he asked Dr. George Lewis of NACA whether or not the general progress and prestige of American aviation from a postwar technical standpoint would be adversely affected by cancellation of the construction in wood of the HK-1.[24]

Dr. Lewis replied: "This project of constructing the HK-1 flying boat of wood serves no useful purpose in the interest of advancing the American aviation art."[25]

Meanwhile, the Engineering Examining Board under Dr. E. P. Warner of the CAA had completed its work. Someone, probably Loening, extracted some lessons from the memo report on February 3, 1944, which said in part:

" The HK-1 design is of such a conservative and normal pattern that its performance can be very accurately predicted. This has been done by Dr. Warner's committee and the indicated performances are definitely of an inferior nature due to this excessive over-weight. It is unnecessary to complete the plane in order to verify these performances . . . . A most valuable lesson learned from the HK-1 development is a clear indication that efficiency of cargo carrying aircraft does not increase indefinitely with size in any such degree as had been generally considered likely before this work was undertaken. The over-weight difficulties on the Hughes design emphasize that the size has gotten too big and into a white elephant class where efficiency in load carrying becomes sacrificed to an excessive structural weight empty of the aircraft itself. The indications are that the most efficient size would be about half way between the Martin Mars and the Hughes design, even if the latter were to be built in metal."[26]

During this period, Loening and Nelson had visited the Martin plant and inspected the Mars program. They liked what they saw. Loening added a new argument to his recommendation to cancel the Kaiser-Hughes contract: "The successful development and demonstration of the Mars flying boat makes further prosecution of the Kaiser-Hughes boat of no vital interest to WPB."[27]

Hughes and Kaiser Apply Pressure

It looked as though contract cancellation was inevitable, but Hughes was not defeated yet. Shortly after the Warner report was issued, Kaiser and Hughes began telephoning Donald Nelson. Nelson had not even had time to read the 65-page report, which he had planned to read that weekend, when he received the first phone call from Kaiser on Saturday morning, January 29.

Kaiser's pitch was strangely emotional for a pragmatic businessman whom one would expect to be more factual and rational. "Grover Loening double-crossed me so much on the coast, as you know, and he has been doing it ever since in connection with this plane, and I am not afraid to come out and say publicly what I think about him and what he has done to me. I will get the whole goddam thing out in the open, including Donald Douglas and Martin and how they treated me and how they took evidence and then destroyed the evidence."[28]

"Will that help win the war, Henry?" asked Nelson.

"Well . . ."

"Now, I know, but keep your eye on the ball."

"I *will* keep my eye on the ball, but I don't propose to take a licking from guys like that, and I don't propose to let monopoly control the works. *It* has something to do with the ball, too."

"Henry, why don't you read the report and talk facts?"

After give and take Nelson again cautioned Kaiser, advising him not to go off half-cocked until he got the facts. "The Truman Committee has got hold of this now," said Nelson, "and they are at work on it. And we have got to do the right thing regardless of passion or prejudice or anything else. I am not going to let any of that influence me, and it must not influence you."[29]

A few hours later, Hughes telephoned and asked if he could call Nelson at home during the weekend. Nelson gave him a suggested time.

On Monday, January 31 Nelson received a five-page telegram from Kaiser, less emotional in tone but notable for its shading of the facts. Nelson had said he would read the engineering report of January 15 over the weekend. So Kaiser said, "You probably have now reached the same conclusion as our engineers have that there is nothing in the report on which to base the stoppage of this important development program. . . . You will note the committee made no recommendations as to whether the project should be cancelled and that all their recommendations are based upon continuance of the project."

Despite the fact that the government had always envisioned the fastest possible development of aircraft to carry wartime cargoes, Kaiser in his telegram assumed that the flying boat project had been solely experimental from the beginning. "The Kaiser-Hughes flying boat is purely a development project," the telegram said. "It was conceived as such and recognized as purely development prototype project and is now in an advanced state of completion. . . . In furtherance of air cargo with courage and vision in 1942 you courageously authorized the contract with Kaiser-Hughes this prototype for a large flying boat as an experimental project. We accepted it as a no-fee contract on that basis and I was forced to forego my plan of producing in quantity the Mars type plane on the insistent promise that development was an important essential. . . . I can hardly conceive now when the plane is near completion and over ten or twelve millions have been spent that we must hesitate and fall."

Kaiser concluded his telegram by saying that Howard Hughes wanted the Aircraft Production Board to hear him analyze and present his answers to the January 15th report. "Certainly he should be accorded this hearing."[30]

On February 16 Jesse Jones as Secretary of Commerce acknowledged receiving Nelson's letter of the 11th requesting immediate cancellation of the existing contract between Defense Plant Corporation and Kaiser-Hughes. Further, as Nelson had requested, DPC had invited a prompt and reasonably detailed proposal from Kaiser-Hughes for the development of the HK-1 design in metal.[31]

The next morning Nelson had second thoughts and telephoned Jones or his Assistant Secretary, W. L. Clayton, to request that Hughes be allowed to continue work for a few days on the wooden airplanes until receipt of his new proposal.[32]

It did not take Hughes long to get the word. That same day he telephoned Nelson: "I talked to Will Clayton. He said that they would continue the project for a few days pending your consideration of our proposal."

"That is right."

Hughes said that in his bid he had inserted a paragraph stating that the job will be done at cost and that if the cost exceeded the fixed price bid, "we will bear the burden, and there will be no cost to the government."

Nelson complimented Hughes's patriotism, but Hughes said, "It is not necessarily patriotic. It is my interest in the development of aviation."

Nelson again emphasized what to him was the key consideration: "I think the whole thing is dependent entirely on whether or not a plane of this type made of metal, started now, will be of value in winning a war. . . . Then the other question to be decided is, is it of value to the building of a metal plane to finish this prototype in wood? There is a great difference of opinion on that between you and all of the other people here."

Hughes bridled. "Well, I just can't help but feel that anyone who expresses that opinion has either a very incomplete knowledge of how the process is gone through in building the first article of any airplane and the testing of it, or else it must be someone who has some reason to see this thing stopped."

Nelson said, "The question is if in the flying of this wood ship will we gain experience that will enable us to make it better in metal?"

"Well, Jesus, there's no question in the world," Hughes snapped.

"But in the minds of all these men that I have talked to there is a question, Mr. Hughes, and I want to thrash it out and get the facts on it . . . if I am subject to any criticism at all, it's for going ahead long after everybody in the picture told me it ought to have been stopped . . . . But at any rate it doesn't pay for us to argue this over the phone. Let's see what comes of it and then I will be glad to talk to you about it."[33]

Late Friday morning, February 18, Donald Nelson called to order the meeting that was supposed to have given him the information he needed to decide on the desirability of doing the flying boat in metal and of completing the wood construction as a prototype. The roster of attendees was impressive but did not include Howard Hughes. The oversight would mean yet another meeting on the same subject. By the end of the meeting Ridley himself was convinced by the weight of expert opinion and agreed that there was little value to the wooden construction other than to have finished up what had been started. But he still felt that there would be some kind of a saving in time in completing the wooden job.[34] (In a phone conversation with Nelson that afternoon, Hughes seemed surprised and annoyed that Ridley conceded so much.)

At the conclusion of the meeting Nelson had to rush to a cabinet meeting. Shortly after he got back to his office Hughes telephoned. Hughes said that Ridley told him what happened at the meeting, adding "but I didn't know what you decided."

"Well, I haven't made a decision on it yet," said Nelson. "I am going over to talk to Mr. Jones tomorrow."

"Well, you call me in the morning any time. I will be here all morning."

"And will you hold your mind open on it until then?"

"I will hold my mind open on it until then."[35]

In the meantime Hughes had been talking with his old friend Jesse Jones. Jones did not know much about the expert opinion on the flying boat, but he was well informed on Hughes's side of the story. After the Friday cabinet meeting, Jones had a visit with the President, as was his custom on matters he did not want to bring up during the meeting. Roosevelt had been interested in the giant flying boat from the beginning. Jones knew of this interest and had occasionally discussed it with him casually. (Jones later testified in the 1947 hearings on Hughes's wartime contracts that he "merely brought it to his attention, not with any idea of getting the contract reinstated, because I had tried my best to get Hughes to quit in his own interest and do something else rather than this."[36]

Jones's memorandum of this conversation with the President, dictated after he returned to his office from the White House, read:

"I spoke to the President after Cabinet today about the big Kaiser-Hughes plane, and told him that we had been instructed by Mr. Donald Nelson to cancel the contract.

"I explained that the estimate that Mr. Kaiser furnished us at the time the construction of these big planes was being considered was that three of the planes including the prototype would cost $18,000,000, and that approximately $13,000,000 had already been expended on the building, equipment, and prototype; that it was now estimated that to complete the prototype alone would cost probably $5,000,000 or $6,000,000; that Mr. Nelson had ordered the contract cancelled due to the extra time it would require to complete it, and upon the advice of experts in the aviation field.

"The President stated that he thought the experience to be obtained by completing one plane would be of too much value to throw away the money already expended, and that the contract should not be cancelled."[37]

The next day Jones planned to lunch with Nelson. But first Hughes hit Nelson with another telephone call. Nelson had already spent the morning discussing the Kaiser-Hughes flying boat situation with his executive vice chairman, Charlie Wilson. The call from Hughes came shortly before he was to go to lunch with Jones.

Hughes said, "I tell you, I feel very definitely that certain of the so-called experts are prejudiced in this matter, and particularly Mr. Loening, because I would like to call your attention to Loening's report of last August . . . . Mr. Loening's report at that time was most favorable and he said this project should go ahead. Now then, in the short period of two months he changed completely, and with no foundation whatsoever that I know of, except the fact that he made a trip up to Martin's and they let him fly the Mars around and rubbed him in the right direction."

Nelson was angry. "I can assure you, Mr. Hughes, that is not true. There is no truth to that, honestly. We are not going on Grover Loening's advice alone in this thing. We are going on a whole group, and you are just so dead wrong, Mr. Hughes, really. Honestly, dead wrong, and I can give you my word on that."

The conversation went on for four pages of single-spaced transcript before Nelson's annoyance began to get vocal.

Hughes said, "May I ask you this, Mr. Nelson, so that I can have a clear understanding of this to convey to Mr. Kaiser, because—"

"Let me talk directly to Mr. Kaiser," interrupted Nelson. "I have got to go over now and have a luncheon date with Mr. Jesse Jones. I will talk directly to Henry [Nelson called Kaiser "Henry," but Hughes was always "Mr. Hughes"], and I will send you a complete transcript of our conversation of last Saturday . . . ."

Hughes was forever interpreting conversations to fit his situation—and this was another of those instances.

"My understanding of that conversation was that the going ahead with the metal airplane depended solely upon our submitting a reasonable proposal," Hughes said.

"I told you very definitely that the criteria would be whether a metal airplane of the large size could be used in the winning of this war," said Nelson.

The conversation showed no sign of ending. "Now, Mr. Hughes," said Nelson, I know your reluctance, but I honestly believe if you would fly on here and talk about this thing, we would be months ahead. This business of trying at long distance telephone conversation hour by the hour on the thing is not satisfactory to you and it certainly is not satisfactory to me . . . . I have never had the opportunity of talking to you, it's always these long talks over the phone . . . if we could sit down and look each other in the eye and talk this thing through, I am sure we would get somewhere, but I don't believe in these interminable conversations over the telephone."

Hughes talked on as if Nelson had said nothing.

An exasperated Nelson finally said, "Now Mr. Hughes, honestly, I can't talk any more over the phone about this thing at the moment. I just can't do it . . . . But I honestly think you and I ought to get together instead of constantly talking over the telephone. I don't talk well over the telephone. I like to look at you, like to see you, like to tell you the thing face to face instead of talking interminably over the telephone about it."

After two more pages of conversation, Hughes at long last said, "I will call you then later on."

"All right," said Nelson with a sigh of relief.[38]

There is no record of the luncheon conversation between Jesse Jones and Donald Nelson that Saturday, but Jones undoubtedly gave Nelson considerable food for thought. In addition, Howard Hughes finally appeared in Washington to spend five weeks crusading for his flying boat.

To accommodate Hughes, Nelson called a meeting on February 29. This gave Hughes an opportunity to more fully present his objections to any cancellation of the HK-1 contract. Present at the meeting were Nelson, Wilson, Burden, Vollmecke, Lewis, Locke, Hughes, Ridley, Loening, Captain Smith of NATS and Colonel Brown of AAF.

Figures do not lie, but statisticians do; and engineers can be equally adept at misleading themselves and others with their figures. Loening, in his notes on the meeting, gave a number of examples of what he called "the Hughes twist." "The general feeling of those present who heard Mr. Hughes," wrote Loening, "was that he was adroit in twisting arguments in his favor, which did not stand up when analyzed, and unreasonable in his insistence that his estimates were correct, fully to be relied upon and infallible—to such a degree that anyone who questioned them was prejudiced. Also he always had some involved excuse as to why he was late in delivery or had used up so much money."

In closing the meeting Nelson stated that he would arrange a meeting the following day with Mr. Hughes, at which Dr. Warner could be present to discuss the features of his report.[39]

On March 2 Nelson wrote to Loening listing a number of points that still troubled him about the matter and requested that Harold E. Talbott, who had been Chairman of the 1942 Cargo Plane Committee within the WPB, reconvene the committee to consider promptly the points he had raised.

On March 4 Talbott replied that the Committee had met and then reported: "It is the consensus of opinion of the Committee that the construction of the present HK-1 design in metal would not contribute to the War effort. With reference to size of aircraft and general type that would be within feasible range of materially assisting in the War it was the judgment of the members of the Committee that the present work being done for the Army and Navy by the Aircraft Industry, in producing current types and developing new types of cargo aircraft and power plants, is now effective and sufficient for the War needs. It is further noted that since July 1942, a change in the character of the War has, for the present, greatly abated any War need for giant cargo aircraft of spanning transoceanic distance carrying round trip fuel loads. The Committee naturally views with satisfaction the splendid progress now being made on cargo carrying by air. [This referred to the work of the Air Transport Command, the Naval Air Transport Service, and the airlines.]"[40]

The Kaiser-Hughes flying boat project had been so thoroughly studied, dissected, analyzed, and rehashed that Nelson could not delay decision any longer by asking for another study or another meeting. And no matter what group, agency, or committee had done the work, published the reports, or held the meetings, the results all favored cancellation of the project.

The Breakthrough

What transpired during the first weeks of March 1944 to swing the decision in Hughes's favor? All the facts will never be known. But what is known is that Hughes worked out of his suite at the Carlton Hotel telephoning anyone and everyone who might help him while keeping the pressure on Donald Nelson with that unique Hughes persistence akin to Chinese water torture. And at cabinet meetings Nelson saw the President and Jesse Jones, both of whom were in favor of the flying boat project. Nelson had no desire to cross either the President, Jones, or Hughes; it was easier to go along than to resist.

Hughes returned to Culver City about mid-March and fired one last salvo in a letter to Nelson on March 17.

"I am writing this letter to advise strongly against stopping construction of the HK-1 flying boat now being built by Hughes Tool Company for Kaiser-Hughes. . . .

"Either it was a mistake to start building this airplane or it is a mistake to stop its construction in its present unfinished state. . . .

"If we are going to keep abreast of development in aviation, then we must reconcile ourselves to the necessity of building bigger and bigger airplanes. This being true, why throw away the $14,000,000 already expended on the HK-1 and later start from scratch on another?

"I feel I have made certain contributions to aviation in this country and that you are aware of this fact. I believe I know a good deal about designing and constructing airplanes, probably as much as others who advise scrapping the HK-1. . . .

"I do not believe anyone can say definitely when the war in the Pacific will end. Irrespective of this, our military and naval services are both going ahead with big airplanes which are behind the HK-1 in state of progress. . . .

"I sincerely hope you will rescind your order to discontinue construction of the HK-1 and will allow it to be completed on the basis outlined in this letter.

"Because of my company's desire to be of every possible assistance in winning the war, it is willing to complete the prototype at the total cost to the government of $18,000,000, provided my company may have the privilege of using the plane at customary rental rates (same to be satisfactory to the government), for a sufficient length of time so that the rental will reimburse the excess cost to my company in completing the plane, such reimbursement not to exceed $2,000,000. Our engineers estimate that to complete the plane will cost more than $2,000,000, in addition to the government's expenditure."[41]

Despite all the expert testimony leading to the decision to terminate the contract, the scales finally tipped in Hughes's favor. Some thought this an illuminating instance of how, in the Roosevelt administration, administrative procedures, duly established by law and public policy, meant less than the passing remarks of the President to a cabinet member.

Later, Republican Senator Owen Brewster would try to prove some kind of wrongdoing on the part of the President, but that partisan attack was countered by Democratic Senator Claude Pepper of Florida when he posed the following question to Hughes during the Senate Hearings in 1947:

"If, in 1944, Mr. Donald Nelson was disposed to cancel the government contract for the construction of the big cargo ship, and if Mr. Jesse Jones, who was at that time the responsible head of the Defense Plant Corporation, which was the government corporation which actually had the contract with you and Mr. Kaiser to build this ship, took the matter up with President Franklin D. Roosevelt to consult him as to whether the contract should be canceled and the plane junked, as it were; or whether the government should put up an additional five million and attempt to carry the construction of the plane on to completion, and if President Roosevelt at that time told Mr. Jones that he felt that, in view of the fact that the government already had $13,000,000 in the plane which would be wasted if it were not completed, he thought it would be in the public interest to put up the additional $5,000,000 and carry the plane on to completion, would you say that President Roosevelt acted at that time with fair regard to the public interest?"[42]

On March 27, 1944 the contract was reinstated, but with Hughes alone. Kaiser was out.

In the meantime, Hughes had been active in pushing the development of the Lockheed Constellation and in the spring of 1944 he and Jack Fry flew one of the new Connies coast-to-coast in six hours fifty-eight minutes to inaugurate a new advance in air transportation.

Work now continued on the massive components of the flying boat without further serious threats of cancellation. A competition was held among Hughes employees to rename the plane. The winning suggestion was *Hughes H-4 Hercules*, but to Howard it would always be simply the Hughes Flying Boat.

By the fall of 1945, Germany and Japan had surrendered, but the giant seaplane that was to have transported wartime cargoes over submarine infested seas was still in pieces in the Culver City plant. It would require one of the most spectacular moving jobs in history before the massive sub-assemblies could be brought together near a body of water large enough for takeoff.

Howard Hughes inspecting a photo plane during July 1943 with Stanley Bell, Kenneth Ridley to his right and Glenn Odekirk facing him.

6

Accidents and Eccentricities

A HOST OF PRESSURES AND PROBLEMS brought Hughes to the breaking point in 1944. His fight to save the flying boat in February and March had drained him physically and emotionally. The contract for the F-11 photo plane had run into difficulties and was delayed. Hughes's detractors in the Air Corps adamantly opposed his haggling to recoup his development costs for the D-2, which he had built on his own and in their view bore little resemblance to the F-11 as a prototype (the D-2 was of wood; the F-11 was of metal). Moreover, troubles with Neil S. McCarthy, his attorney, led to McCarthy's quitting in August. And in the meantime Hughes had been active in pushing the development of the Lockheed Constellation. These pressures would force Hughes to make his first lengthy retreat from public view in the fall of 1944. For six months not even Noah Dietrich would know where he was.

The Problems Pile Up

Hughes testified during the 1947 Senate hearings that when the photo-reconnaissance group under Colonel Elliott Roosevelt saw the D-2 at Harpers Lake, "they thought it was a terrific airplane and just what they wanted." But instead of a contract to build the D-2, he finally got a contract under the jurisdiction of Wright Field—which forced so many changes, Hughes said, "I had to build a whole new prototype from the ground up, which I couldn't possibly put into production during the war."[1]

Discussions at Wright Field in the spring of 1944 led to a review by the Under Secretary of War. After all the reports and documentation were in, the chief of the Contracts and Facilities Division concluded that "the contracts should be approved, despite the unsatisfactory nature of the terms, but that prior assurance should be obtained from the CG, AAF, positively stating the necessity for the procurement of the F-11, and his recommendation that the Hughes contract be signed."[2]

103

On July 17, 1944 Hap Arnold, Commanding General of the Army Air Forces, informed the Under Secretary of War that "a long-range, high speed, high altitude, land-based, photographic reconnaissance airplane, stressed for active evasive action, is an urgent military necessity. I believe the best available method of obtaining such airplanes is by placing with Hughes Tool Company a contract for the F-11 aircraft engineered by that concern. Accordingly, I approve the recommendation set forth in the attached papers that the formal contract for one hundred such airplanes now before you for approval be placed with that concern at once."[3]

But in the meantime, the Hughes Aircraft division of the Hughes Tool Company (Toolco) had proceeded with the development of the F-11, based on a letter of intent of the year before. But progress was slow. The Aircraft Division had been without a general manager since Bern had quit, and Hughes needed a strong, competent production man to take charge.

Maj. Gen. Bennett E. ("Benny") Meyers of the Materiel Command advised Hughes to try and get crack production man Charles W. Perelle. (Perelle, who started work as a painter's helper at Boeing and during the 1930s rose to be a major division manager there, became general manager of Vultee in the early 1940s, where he introduced innovative assembly-line techniques for aircraft manufacture. When Vultee merged with Consolidated in 1943, Perelle became senior vice president for manufacturing.)

Perelle did not succumb easily to Hughes's blandishments. This only made Hughes more insistent. In September 1944, Hughes finally got his man with an offer of $75,000 a year. Perelle was to be vice president and general manager of the Hughes Tool Company, manager of the Hughes Aircraft Company, and a director of Transcontinental and Western Air (TWA).

Indicative of Hughes's desperation to get the supposed production expert to join him was that Hughes gave Perelle an option to buy 10,000 shares of TWA stock at the current market value. If the stock went up in the future, the option could be exercised and Perelle would make a tidy profit. The high salary, the key positions, and the stock option, plus Hughes's promise to give him a free hand, proved irresistible.

In the meantime there had been labor trouble at Toolco in Houston. When the United Steel Workers had organized the plant, management refused to bargain with them. A strike resulted, and for a time the army took over operations, as production was essential to the war effort.

In addition, Hughes was worried about how his longtime associate and attorney, Neil S. McCarthy, had handled rejection of Gen. Benny Meyers's requests for employment and a long-term, low-interest loan so that the general could buy stock on margin. It was actually Hughes's fault that the general blew up, because Hughes hadn't telephoned him as promised. Still Hughes blamed McCarthy for somehow not being able to placate Meyers. He was concerned that Meyers might somehow hold up the F-11 contract, and he badgered McCarthy with late-night phone calls to rehash what had happened.

McCarthy quit in August. During the Senate hearings in 1947, he testified that "the basic reason why I left Howard was that I probably would have been dead today if I had stayed with him. Howard works until away [sic] early in the morning, two and three o'clock in the morning, and he never hesitates to call you at any time he wants to, and he himself went into a nervous breakdown about that time, and I would have done the same thing. I decided that I would rather not practice law that way and wrote him and told him so."[4]

However, in 1972 shortly before his death, McCarthy told Nadine Henley that he had quit because of Noah Dietrich and that he and Hughes had remained friends and often talked together. Confirming this are Hughes's "call lists" from the late 1950s in his own handwriting, found when Hughes's temporary Las Vegas residence, the "Green House," was opened after his death.[5]

McCarthy's resignation came at a bad time for Hughes. Hughes argued and cajoled but McCarthy was adamant. Hughes later testified that he had a profound respect for McCarthy but that their relationship had broken up under rather bitter terms "after he had been representing my company, I believe, for fifteen years.'

The Constellation: Flying Lockheed's Way

In addition to these pressures, during this time Hughes also had to push development of the Lockheed Constellation for TWA. After returning from Washington and the threat of cancellation of the flying boat project in March, Hughes went to the Lockheed flight line in Burbank for his first checkout flight in the Constellation. TWA president Jack Frye accompanied him.

They were met by Lockheed chief engineer Kelly Johnson and Lockheed test pilot Milo Burcham. The four-engined, triple-tailed craft with its arched shark's body and tapered nose was gassed, preflighted and standing by on the bustling Lockheed line when they arrived. Burcham took the left seat for this initial checkout, Hughes the right. Hughes made the takeoff, climbed to 10,000 feet, and headed away from the smog and urban buildup of the Los Angeles area toward Palmdale Airport in the uncrowded desert beyond the mountains to the northeast.

After they had leveled off, Hughes turned to Burcham and said, "How does this thing stall?"

"It gives plenty of warning," Burcham answered. "Recovers nicely. Here, I'll show you." Whereupon he pulled the power off and pulled up the nose. As the wing began to stall with the yoke all the way back, the plane began to buffet and shake from the disturbed airflow. Burcham eased the nose down and added power. The plane made a smooth recovery to cruise airspeed.

"Goddammit! That isn't the way to stall this thing," said Hughes, who took the controls, extended full flap and, as he pulled the nose up, added full power to all four engines.

Johnson, who was standing behind the pilots, was appalled. "It was the only time I've every seen zero indicated airspeed on a big airplane," he recalls. "It had so damn much thrust that the airplane was just hanging on the props. Hell, I knew that in the recovery we wouldn't have much control over what the damn airspeed was going to be so I hollered, 'Up flaps! Up flaps!' so we wouldn't exceed the flap speed."

Burcham started the flaps up, took over the airplane, and recovered. By this time they were approaching Palmdale, so Burcham instructed Hughes in the procedures for let-down, traffic pattern entry, and landing. The procedures were somewhat different than those in Hughes's previous experience because of the need for close coordination between the pilot and the flight engineer, who had his own instrument panel and engine and propeller controls. Moreover, the hydraulically boosted flight controls felt different than the controls Hughes had handled heretofore.

The procedures called for practice landings with both boost on and boost off. Hughes did six takeoffs and landings and apparently did not follow the precise procedures that Burcham had demonstrated. "His takeoffs were weird," says Johnson. "He pulled the thing off at too slow an airspeed so that he didn't have one-engine-out control speed, and he drifted to the left. Hell, on the sixth takeoff he damn near drifted right into the control tower."

Johnson went back to see Jack Frye. "Jack, this is getting worse and worse. What should I do? I'm responsible for this airplane."

"Kelly, you do what you think is right," said Frye. So Johnson went back to the cockpit and said, "Milo, we're taking this thing home."

Hughes turned around and looked at Johnson as though Johnson had just shot him. He gave Burcham the controls and just sat there the rest of the way back to Burbank.

The Lockheed sales people were wild at Johnson for taking the airplane away from their best customer. But in the ensuing discussions, Hughes agreed that he would follow the Lockheed procedures absolutely during the subsequent check-out and would learn to fly the airplane their way. This he did. But Johnson said, "We paid our flight crew a bonus to fly with him."

"Howard got real mad at me for giving him the ultimate insult of taking the airplane away from him," said Johnson. Did this influence Hughes's foot-dragging later when Lockheed had immediate need for hangar space at Burbank to work on the U-2 spy plane that Johnson's "Skunk Works" had developed? Johnson asked Hughes if they could use a hangar where Hughes kept a Lockheed Electra—a hangar that Hughes kept sealed up with tape and under twenty-four—hour guard. It took thirty days for Hughes to get his plane and gear out.[7]

After Hughes completed his transition training in the Constellation in the spring of 1944, he and Jack Frye flew a load of press people in one of the new "Connies" coast-to-coast in six hours fifty-eight minutes to inaugurate a new advance in air transportation. The flight was marred when Hughes flew into a thunderstorm out of Denver while some of his passengers were wandering around the cabin. Three of them were hurt.[8]

In Washington, Hughes invited Jacqueline Cochran to fly with him as co-pilot on a demonstration flight for a number of Congressmen. One of their passengers was Sen. Owen Brewster of Maine—who later was to sparkplug the Senate investigation into Hughes's wartime contracts.

Hughes's Disappearance

All of these anxieties—as well as overwork, his peculiar lifestyle, a high-strung temperament, and the physical and mental after-effects of three violent accidents—aggravated Hughes's already eccentric behavior and brought him to the edge of a nervous breakdown.

Dietrich always felt that these accidents had played a part in Hughes's deterioration. The crash in the Thomas Morse Scout during the filming of *Hell's Angels* had crushed his cheek bone, rendering him unconscious, and affected his mind to the point that he had not recognized Dietrich when he first came to. An auto accident during the war had left him incoherent and semiconscious for several days. And the May 1943 crash in the Sikorsky on Lake Mead had caused yet another severe concussion.

During that summer of 1944 Dietrich grew concerned by Hughes's odd mental lapses and his repetitiveness. One day during a telephone conversation Hughes repeated the same sentence thirty-three times. Appalled, Dietrich urged him to see a doctor, who ordered him to get away from the pressure of business completely for an extended period before he broke down.[9] (Interestingly, Nadine Henley, who worked closely with Hughes on his will during middle and late 1944, noticed no such lapses.)[10]

The secrecy surrounding Hughes's strange nearly yearlong odyssey in 1944-45 was first lifted by Joe Petrali, former Chief of Services and Flight at Hughes Aircraft, during taping sessions with western newsman Maury Green before Petrali died in 1973. Presented here are additional details, which have never before been published, of that mysterious disappearance.

The crashed Sikorsky had been rebuilt and refitted with the old single fin and rudder that had been in storage during the Lake Mead testing. Every week Hughes called Petrali and asked, "When will the boat be ready?"

"It's ready to fly now," Petrali would say.

"I'll be out to test it."

So Petrali would roll out the amphibian, preflight it, run up the engines and wait. Week after week for three months Hughes called and asked the same question. Finally, Petrali showed his impatience.

"Well, Howard, it's been ready for three months. Like I keep telling you, I've been waiting for you to give it its first check out."

This time Hughes was ready to go. Perelle had been hired, Odekirk and Dietrich were still in place, and Hughes was ready to follow his doctor's orders. It was October 1944.

"How long will it take you to gas this thing for a trip?"

"Give me an hour," said Petrali.

Petrali called his wife for some clothes and serviced the airplane.[11]

Flight mechanic Dick Beatie—whom Hughes probably considered especially trustworthy because he was a Mormon, and because he had previously flown under Dick Felt in the Sikorsky—was tagged to go with them. Beatie barely had time to collect a change of clothes, shaving kit, and toothbrush and to tell his wife he would be gone for a couple of days. He had no idea he would be away for nearly five months.

It was late fall when Hughes took off from the long airstrip at Culver City, banked in a climbing turn over the Pacific, and headed for Las Vegas. To avoid publicity, he did not land at McCarren Field but turned off and landed at a small dirt airport north of town.

Unfortunately, a twenty to twenty-five mile per hour diagonal crosswind led him to select the shorter of the two crossed runways. He touched down on one wheel with the right wing dipped into the wind; but the narrow tread of the ungainly amphibian's landing gear, the large fin and rudder area, and a center of gravity behind the main wheels made the Sikorsky terrible to handle in a cross wind. In addition, the plane was too heavy for its small brakes and Hughes saw that he was going to run out of runway.

About midfield, the plane either weathercocked to the right or Hughes tried to turn off onto the longer runway. He did not make it. For whatever reason, the plane suddenly ran off the edge of the runway, slammed over the berm, and tore off through the mesquite, banging across desert sand knolls with jolting, destructive force. Loose gear flew about the cabin. Beatie, who had unfastened his seat belt after touchdown, grabbed frantically for solid support. Finally, the plane slowed its headlong, slam-bang charge. Hughes added nearly full throttle to keep the airplane moving through the soft sand and blasted it back onto the runway.

He guided the limping airplane to a parking spot at the small flight service hangar and they soberly inspected the damage. The tail wheel had been smashed and torn loose. There was some buckling of fuselage skin near the wing attachments.[12]

The next morning, Hughes came out to the field, inspected the airplane more closely, and carefully wrote down what he wanted fixed. Then he gave the men characteristically detailed instructions to keep their location and the whole affair secret and yet to get the airplane repaired.

Petrali and Beatie went back to Culver City, loaded a truck with repair materials and equipment, and returned with several sheet metal and airframe experts, including mechanic Bill Grant, all pledged to secrecy. The repair took little more than a week, but Grant was kept on for another month before he was allowed to return home to be with his very pregnant wife.

Most of that first period was spent in Las Vegas, says Grant. Hughes planned to leave every day at 3:30, but never did while Grant was there. Every day they would check out of the hotel, go down to the airplane, get the plane ready, and then return to the hotel again.[13] Grant thought Hughes was spending his time with a number of different women in the Las Vegas area, but Beatie thinks that that was just the conventional wisdom and that Hughes really was avoiding people, just getting away from it all. Hughes spent most of his time at the little individual cabin he had rented at the El Rancho.

After Grant left, Hughes, Petrali, and Beatie shuttled between Las Vegas, Palm Springs, and Reno, but spent most of their time in Las Vegas. Since it was wartime, hotel rooms and rental cars were scarce, but Hughes and his crew managed to tie up cars and rooms in all three cities.

In Las Vegas, because of a shortage of suitable cars, the manager of the agency rented Hughes his personal Chrysler station wagon. Naturally, he became very upset when Hughes "lost" it at Christmas time.

This Christmas caper started when Beatie told Petrali, "I'm going home for Christmas." Petrali, of course, wanted to go too. But when he had asked Hughes's permission to go home for Thanksgiving, Hughes had ignored his request. This time they decided not to ask, but to leave a note wishing him a happy birthday and saying that since no flight was planned they were going home to their families for Christmas and would return Christmas night. As soon as Hughes read the note Petrali shoved under his door at the El Rancho, he tried to intercept them at the Sal Sagev, their hotel, thinking that they would have to pack before leaving.

"I'm sorry," said the clerk, "they've already left for Los Angeles."

"Don't give me any of that crap!" Hughes shouted. "They have to pack a bag or something. I'll wait."

He waited two hours before he gave up. Whether he intended to leave Las Vegas at that particular moment just because they were not available, or whether he had planned the trip all along, he drove off to Reno in the rented Chrysler without leaving word with anybody as to where he had gone or when he would return. When Petrali and Beatie got back to Las Vegas their boss was nowhere to be found.

"O.K, so he got mad at us just for going home for Christmas," said Petrali. "The hell with it! If he wants to get mad about that he's just going to have to get mad."

Beatie agreed with Petrali that Hughes could not get far before he ran out of gas ration stamps, that he could take care of himself, and that he would return eventually. So the two men stayed on at the Sal Sagev and continued their morning trips to the airport to run-up the airplane.

Some time later, Petrali received an irate phone call from the rental car manager. "Your boss abandoned my car with an empty gas tank in Beverly Hills!" he shouted.

Petrali soothed him as best he could and telephoned Odekirk at Culver City for help in getting the car back—no easy matter with wartime gas rationing.

As February approached, Beatie had had enough of nothing to do. He had even overhauled the airport manager's car just to be doing something useful while he waited for Hughes to show up and fly somewhere. Bob Martin came over from Los Angeles by train to replace him.

Several days later, after three to four weeks' absence, Hughes rolled up to the Sal Sagev in a taxi and went up to Petrali's room as if nothing had happened.

"Down in that cab there's a box," he said. "I want you to have it brought up here."

"Okay, Howard."[14]

Petrali and Martin lugged the heavy, coffin-sized box up to the room where Hughes instructed them at length and in great detail what to do with it.

"Wrap this in heavy butcher paper," he said. "And don't use sticky tape. No stickum."

"Okay, Howard, no stickum."

"And when it's wrapped securely, take it out to the airplane and carefully slant it through the rear hatch and stow it in the aft section." All of these instructions were repeated with variations and in great detail.

"And, Joe, don't look in the box. Don't open it."

"Okay, Howard."

This last was too much for Petrali. After they were alone, he said to Martin, "By gosh, I think we'll open this box and take a look." But then he thought better of it and said, "No, just as soon as we open this up that son of a gun will be knocking on the door."

"Aw, the heck with it. Let's open it up."

Just as he and Martin got over to the mystery box lying on the floor, there was a "knock, knock, knock." Petrali opened the door. It was Hughes. He stood in the doorway, repeated some instructions, and left again.

Petrali looked at Martin and said, "I'll bet you he won't be back again soon. Let's grab a quick look now.

Once again they went back to the box. And once again, just in time, there was another knock on the door. It was as if Hughes had some way of seeing into the room. Again Hughes looked in, said something inconsequential, went out and closed the door.

"The hell with it," said Petrali. "That's it." They wrapped the box and stowed it as directed.[15]

After Martin's arrival in Las Vegas there was no more shuttling to Palm Springs and Reno. But Hughes did take the airplane out for touch-and-go landing practice.

"He shot twenty-two landings in an hour and a half," said Martin. "I had to go to the bathroom so bad I could taste it, but he wouldn't stop. Up-and-down. Up-and-down. He was just checking to see that the plane was alright and to refresh himself."

Hughes's obsession with secrecy surfaced weirdly. One afternoon in Las Vegas he hopped in his rented car and drove the forty miles to the small TWA office at Boulder.

"I'd like to borrow your office to write a letter," he told the manager. Of course, the manager willingly moved out so that the lanky owner of TWA could take over. Hughes locked himself in. All through the night he typed and retyped secret instructions for those who would accompany him on the next legs of his strange journey. Satisfied at last, he sealed the product of his labor in a manila envelope and returned to the El Rancho.

Later he went to Petrali's room at the Sal Sagev and spent several hours and many sheets of hotel stationery preparing a handwritten note telling Petrali how to handle the typed instructions. The next day Hughes gave the sealed instructions to Petrali and harangued him in a loud voice—very uncharacteristic of Hughes—telling him to study the instructions for eight hours a day for a couple of days and that the instructions in the envelope "shall remain in force so long as you shall live!" After Hughes left Petrali read the handwritten note. It told him to wash his hands with soap and water before opening the manila envelope. He did so and opened the envelope. Inside was a single typewritten sheet, which read: "Do not convey, communicate, telephone or telegraph any message from me to anyone in California unless I repeat it to you word for word ten consecutive times." That was it—there was nothing else!

Hughes also gave Martin a copy of the note. "This is a secret," Hughes said. "I don't want anybody to know anything about it. Twenty years from now if the Senate calls up and tells you that they want to know all about this, you just take the note, put it in the toilet, and flush it."

About two days later—presumably after Petrali had studied the instructions eight hours a day—they took off for Orlando, Florida with an overnight stop at Shreveport, Louisiana. The Sikorsky needed gas and they needed sleep.

For eight hours during the flight Hughes said not one word to Petrali, who sat next to him in the copilot's seat. After landing, Hughes explained his silence by saying that he had been praying to God that Petrali would follow his instructions to the letter.

That night Petrali and Martin went to a movie. When they got back to the New Jefferson Hotel the room clerk called Petrali aside.

"The police called for you," he said. "They've picked up some guy who claims he's Howard Hughes and that you can vouch for him."

The two men ran the half block to the police station, but they were too late to help. By this time Mr. Long, the local Hughes Tool Company representative, had already identified Hughes and the police had released him.

"Hughes called me a goddamn country cop," Chief of Detectives Davis told them. "I was trained by the FBI and he called me a country cop." Then Davis laughed and said, "I told him that if he was Howard Hughes I was Shirley Temple."

Apparently, Hughes had bought a bag of cupcakes and a quart of milk for his dinner and stood in the gas pump lane of a darkened service station to eat his meal and wait for the rain to slacken. When he finished his meal, he rinsed his mouth and filled it with mouthwash. Hughes had a bone in his face that had never healed properly, and he often filled his mouth with antiseptic from a little bottle that he carried with him.

It was wartime. A tall, gaunt stranger in scruffy clothes wearing a hat whose brim drooped low over his forehead, carrying a paper bag clutched in one hand, and standing in a darkened service station when gasoline was in short supply, was naturally suspect. A passing policeman who saw the suspicious figure lurking in the shadows stopped to investigate.

"What are you doing here?"

Hughes said nothing, his mouth full of mouthwash.

"Who are you?"

Still there was no response from Hughes; he just turned his back and ignored the man.

"All right," said the policeman. "Come with me."

The arresting officer told Bob Martin that on the way to the police station near the New Jefferson "Hughes spit out that stuff and gave me hell."

At the station Hughes could not prove who he was because he carried no identification.

Long, the manager of Toolco's Shreveport facility, notified the home office of this incident and thus provided Dietrich with the first information he had had of Hughes's whereabouts since Hughes had left Culver City four months earlier.

Hughes did not eat for several days following this incident. Day and night, Petrali in the next room could hear him pacing back and forth. Worried, Petrali telephoned Nadine Henley for advice. "There's nothing you can do," she said.[16]

Finally, Hughes told Petrali, "Get the plane ready. We're leaving." After landing in Orlando, Hughes got on a bus, leaving Petrali and Martin to care for the airplane. He did not return for nearly three months.[17]

As Petrali's fifth month away from home came and went, he telephoned Culver City and asked to go home. He was replaced by flight engineer Ray Kirkpatrick, who had started at Hughes Aircraft in 1939 and knew the old Sikorsky as well or better than anyone else in the Hughes organization.

The first day Kirkpatrick went out to the airport with Martin to check the amphibian he spotted the strange box wrapped in butcher paper.

"Bob, what the hell's in the box?"

"I don't have any idea," said Martin. "It's Howard's secret."

"Does he get into it?"

"No, he's never opened it since we put it in there. He's never looked in there."

"Okay," said Kirkpatrick. "We'll leave it alone."

Before long Kirkpatrick's wife came out from California to join him. Toward the end of their stay the phone rang about nine o'clock one evening. Kirkpatrick answered it.

"Who is this?" Hughes asked in his flat Texas twang.

"Ray Kirkpatrick."

"Kirk, I'll be coming back to pick up the airplane in a few days, but I need some money. I want you to get forty-five hundred dollars to the Roney Plaza in Miami by tomorrow at one o'clock."

Kirkpatrick told Hughes he was sure he could not get the money to him on time.

First he would have to have the money sent to him; then he would have to go to Miami, more than 250 miles from Orlando. "I could get it the day after."

"Boy, this phone connection sure is bad," said Hughes.

Kirkpatrick tried again. "What I'm trying to tell you is that I don't have any way that I could get forty-five hundred dollars to you by tomorrow at one o'clock."

"This is a terrible connection," said Hughes. "A very bad connection."

Kirkpatrick put his hand over the phone and in an aside to his wife said, "He says we have a terrible connection. Watch it clear up." He removed his hand and spoke to Hughes again.

"Howard, don't bother. I'll try to get forty-five hundred dollars by tomorrow."

"Oh, great!" Hughes replied. "That's just great."

Kirkpatrick immediately called Odekirk in California and told him the trouble. Odekirk, who held things together at Culver City during those years and was the flight crews' point of contact, wired Kirkpatrick the cash. As soon as he got the money Kirkpatrick jumped in his rented car and headed south. The car was not supposed to leave Orlando, he barely had enough gas stamps for a round trip to Miami, and Hughes had not yet arrived at the hotel. Nevertheless, Kirkpatrick left him the money and the car as arranged and flew back to Orlando.

A few days later, Hughes called; he was on his way back. Kirkpatrick and Martin waited for him at the airplane. When he finally drove up they saw that the Chevy was jammed with boxes—just ordinary cardboard cartons stacked everywhere, on the seats and in the trunk. Hughes never carried conventional luggage; instead he had all his belongings in boxes. ("Kind of practical," recalls Kirkpatrick. "They stack nicely. Just tie a little string around them, you know. That's how he moved around. In those damn cartons.")

After they transferred the boxes to the amphibian, Hughes said, "How many have we got, Kirk?"

"Well, it looks like you've got twelve of them here."

"That's all of 'em," said Hughes.

Leaving Orlando at last, they headed north to Newark.

Newark Airport was crowded with military aircraft, and only aircraft on official business were allowed to land. Hughes, however, was always conveniently hard of hearing whenever anyone mentioned anything limiting his freedom of action. He just barged in and landed without prior permission and sent Kirkpatrick to flight operations to explain.

Kirkpatrick pointed out that although the airplane was being flown by a civilian, it was marked with an Army star, and Hughes was going to be there on military business, making trips to Washington, and the like.

"All right, you can park it here," the duty officer said.

When Kirkpatrick told Hughes that the Army had bought his line of crap, Hughes, pleased, prepared to head for New York and asked, "Where are you going to stay?"

"Well, I'm going to stay at the Lexington," said Kirkpatrick. "I've always stayed there before."

"No," said Hughes. "Listen, I'd rather have you closer to the airplane. I'd like to have you live in Newark."

"Newark!"

"Listen, Newark is beautiful. You'll like Newark. They've got a great hotel there."

"Well, Newark is the pits," Kirkpatrick recalls. "It always was. He just didn't want me in New York at all. He was going to race around and he just didn't want me sharing the town with him."

The day after their arrival, Kirkpatrick and Martin went back to Newark Airport to check the Sikorsky. A ruptured autopilot line had soaked the butcher paper around Pandora's box with hydraulic fluid.

"My God, this will look bad for us if that oil gets inside and screws up anything," Kirkpatrick told Martin. They were dying for an excuse to open the box. "We'd better take care of it."

First they peeked out the windows to make sure no one was near. Carefully, they undid the twine and removed the oil-soaked paper. Nervously they lifted the lid and peered inside. The box was filled with funny papers—stacks of them—mostly from the *Los Angeles Times*. Kirkpatrick could not believe that it was just a weird idiosyncracy. "Maybe his housekeeper saved them for him. She babied him a lot—and he just took them along to please her." Bob Martin thought the top layer was a series of Red Ryder comics that Hughes was reviewing for a possible movie script and that there were shirts, boots, and other items under the papers. "He even had a couple of douche bags in there," says Martin.

Later, when Kirkpatrick finally got back to Culver City and turned the Sikorsky over to Service and Flight with a list of discrepancies that would "choke a horse," one of Petrali's mechanics peeked into the box and found a dentist drill buried in the funny papers.

Every morning while they were in the New York area, Kirkpatrick read Earl Wilson's *New York Post* column, "It Happened Last Night," looking for clues to his boss's activities and future plans. Hughes's name began to appear in the paper in early June, 1945. One column said, "Howard Hughes wears tennis shoes around New York proving something fascinating about men's fashions: If you're Howard Hughes, it doesn't matter."

At the Stork Club, Hughes explained to Wilson that he had worn out his shoes in Florida and not having shoe coupons had to buy nonrationed canvas shoes. But he continued to wear sneakers to posh night spots after he had obtained coupons and bought new shoes and a prominent "footician" later told Wilson that a projecting bone in one foot was the reason.

One morning, Kirkpatrick picked up the paper and read: "Howard Hughes chases Yvonne DeCarlo into Canada." "Oh, oh. We're in trouble," he thought. Sure enough, the phone rang. It was Colonel Clary, officer in charge at Newark Airport. "Your boss just wore out his welcome. Get that airplane off this airport." Boat pilot Al Zotack, whom Odekirk knew, was hired to move the airplane to a Long Island airfield near Sperry Gyroscope.

Some time around August 1945, Hughes returned to Culver City after an absence of about nine months, leaving Kirkpatrick and Martin behind with the airplane. When Kirkpatrick went over to the Plaza to close up Hughes's suite and put a lock on the telephone, he saw plenty of shoes in the closet plus a supply of douche bags. This last item may indicate the nature of Hughes's activities in New York.

By now, Kirkpatrick and Martin had been on the East Coast for approximately nine months; and although Kirkpatrick's wife was with him, there came a time when enough was enough. It was October and getting cold, and Kirkpatrick was having trouble getting the Sikorsky's engines started for their daily run-up. He called Odekirk. "We've either got to take this thing to Florida or we've got to take it home." Of course, recalls Kirkpatrick, they could have pickled it and left it out in the snow. But Hughes liked to keep his airplanes hangared in those days.

Odekirk sent Frank Williams out to fly the airplane back to Culver City. But on takeoff, with a full load of gas, the airplane drifted off the runway to the left, ground-looped, and tore off the tail.

Back at the hotel, Kirkpatrick asked Martin for an explanation. "There's something funny about this airplane. It drifts to the left when the tailwheel is down and locked. Now, you'd better sit down and tell me what happened to that thing."

So Kirkpatrick heard for the first time of the Las Vegas incident. Apparently, the men had so honored Hughes's desire for secrecy that they neither logged the accident and its repair nor told Kirkpatrick about it. As a further result of this accident, the aircraft developed a gas leak from a wing tank down through the cabane strut into the cabin. They limped back to Culver City nearly sick from fuel fumes.[18]

Hughes and company had left for Las Vegas in late fall 1944. Hughes had turned up in New York in June 1945. And he had finally returned to Culver City in September 1945. This story of his strange year-long odyssey tells us something about the man, as do stories of other longtime Hughesmen. But he was so complex, contradictory, and various that there seems to be no one "true" view of the man. As flight engineer Earl Martyn's wife says (she is also Odekirk's sister), "He was a many-faceted man and I always felt that there were many, many people who knew different sides of him. He could show a different side of himself to different people, and he would act differently at different times, very compassionate or quite cool, depending on the problems he was facing at the time."[19]

See Appendix for further revealing stories of Howard Hughes by other longtime Hughes employees and associates.

Three photographs of the XF-11 photo-reconnaissance plane. Above: Hughes flies over Southern California. Below: The dual, contra-rotating props are clearly visible as the plane sits at the Culver City plant of Hughes Aircraft Company. Right: July 7, 1946 shot of Hughes as he prepares for the ill-fated test of his XF-11.

7

The Move to Terminal Island
and the XF-11 Crash

DURING HUGHES'S LONG ABSENCE from Culver City, the war ended and so did his dream of becoming a major wartime builder of military airplanes. Three weeks after Germany surrendered on May 8, 1945, his one big airplane contract, the production order for one hundred F-11s, was cut to two planes. By the time Japan surrendered on September 2, 1945, the giant flying boat that was to have carried wartime cargoes over submarine-infested seas was still in pieces at Culver City. Hughes seemed subdued, dejected. He had gone from lean and lanky to gaunt and shaggy.

With his return to the West Coast, relations with Perelle rapidly soured. Not everyone at Hughes Aircraft had been convinced Perelle was the production wizard he claimed to be. "He wasn't so damn smart himself," said one high-level Hughesman. "He just used others who were." A key Hughes engineer thought Perelle was "pretty much of a fake—a little Mussolini" who liked to flash fifty-dollar bills.

Nevertheless, real progress had been made by Perelle. On October 29 Perelle wrote Hughes a personal and confidential letter, addressed to 7000 Romaine Street, detailing Hughes's management problems. The text of the letter is significant enough as a "status report" of the Hughes operation at that time—if only in Perelle's view—to be quoted entirely.

"Dear Howard:

"I have from time to time verbally called to your attention some of the many problems confronting the operations of the Hughes Tool Company and the Hughes Aircraft Company.

"There is some doubt in my mind as to whether or not my comments have impressed you sufficiently enough for you to recognize their importance. I am, therefore, as a matter of record, reviewing the situation for you in order to clarify some of the misinformation and misquotes, of which you undoubtedly are aware.

"You will recall that prior to my actually assuming duties for you a banquet was held at the Ambassador Hotel, at which time you publicly announced that I was to have complete and unrestricted control of your operations. This is a matter of record. That this policy has not been carried out is also a matter of record, as I will subsequently point out to you.

"I would like to call your attention to the fact that your original invitation to me to join your organization as executive in charge of the Culver City operations only was rejected as not being a position of sufficient magnitude to be attractive to me. Unable to accomplish this objective, you later included under the terms of my contract other more attractive fields of endeavor. That I have been precluded from functioning to your benefit or the benefit of the company in any of these organizations is evident.

"Prior to my coming with you, you made the statement that you had absolutely no organization upon which you could depend. I am now in a position to concur with you in that statement. In spite of all the opposition and restrictions encountered, I now feel that we have been able to put together something in the way of an organization which has possibilities of functioning. That nothing short of a miracle has been achieved at the Culver City plant during the past year is a matter of factual record, some of which is set forth in subsequent paragraphs of this letter.

"Contractual relationships with the Government were at absolutely the lowest level that I have ever encountered. The attempted short-circuiting of Wright Field has had serious repercussions. I know from personal experience that it was impossible to discuss this program with any one individual without the presence of other Government officials. The F-11 contract apparently had a very bad 'tinge,' which added to the difficulty we were encountering. . . . The many restrictions placed upon our operations by the War Manpower Commission and the Salary Stabilization Unit are well known to you.

"We were frozen with a salary scale far below that which we should have had because of bad past practices. The lack of a priority of any kind for the Cargo Ship made progress tedious, and as I have stated before, the lack of an overall comprehensive program enthusiastically supported by all members of management of Hughes Tool Company further complicated our problem.

"The three departments—Aircraft, Radio, and Armament—were combined into a single operating unit, thereby effecting great economies. The three purchasing departments were merged into one, the two plant engineering departments were combined, the two tooling departments were integrated, and the two industrial relations departments were merged. In payroll reductions alone these administrative changes effected a saving to the company of more than $25,000 monthly. Charges for rents have been reduced through the consolidation of operations, excess personnel have been eliminated, and some of the payroll parasites without assigned duties have been dispensed with. Reductions in executive personnel have likewise been accomplished.

"Apparently this company had made no effort to maintain good relations or to cooperate with the Treasury Department. There was no Treasury-approved salary plan. Numerous inexcusable Treasury Department violations were on file. These were subsequently corrected; a salary plan in accordance with accepted Government practices was installed and Government approval obtained.

"That we have been completely in the dark from an operating point of view with respect to accounting information is a fact well known to everyone connected with this operation. This has been discussed on many occasions and at great length with all concerned. The present practice of absorbing large amounts of expense which in no way contributes to the operation is, of course, very detrimental. The practice of carrying on our payroll persons who in no way contribute to the operation serves only to add to our overhead.

"The apparent hidden expense accounts from the Hollywood operation still further aggravate the condition. A continuation of these practices, which serve only to cause abnormally high overheads, will preclude us from any competitive field of operation from a standpoint of pricing. This practice must be stopped and true operating figures available or we will price ourselves out of business.

ARMAMENT DIVISION

"Armament sales, as you know, to the Government were practically nil. Government approval had not been obtained for any of the division's products. Immediate steps were taken to have tests conducted at both Wright Field and Patuxent, with the result that both Army and Navy approval were obtained. Thus new and heretofore unobtainable business was opened up to us, and contracts in the amount of $7,622,937 were entered into as a result of this program. These contracts, of course, were subsequently terminated with the cessation of hostilities.

F-11 PROJECT

"As you know, there has been considerable delay in the F-11 project. This can be accounted for, not excused, by some of the following facts: At the time we discussed a March delivery date which you had set, you advised me that engineering was 90% complete. And, certainly if engineering had been 90% complete it was reasonable to expect that an airplane could be produced during the ensuing six months. However, subsequent investigation revealed that the engineering was less than 40 percent complete and that all of the engineering done at the La Brea Division prior to its transfer to Culver City had to be thrown out. As of today the engineering still is not complete. No doubt the figures were given to you optimistically in order that contracts with the Government could be retained. As I recall, you advised me that serious consideration was being given by the Army Air Forces to cancellation of the F-11 project, and that a change in management was imperative if the contract was to be retained.

"The poor quality of engineering as accomplished by the engineering department is no doubt well known to you. The complete lack of experience in the design and construction of airplanes in general, as well as the fact that they were lacking in experience in the design of metal aircraft, was in itself a tremendous handicap. The ability of a group of engineers to function as a unit in the design of aircraft can only be achieved by long experience working collectively on basic types of airplanes and airplane construction. This fact is well-known in all industry. Even the experience of the engineering department at Houston is publicized as such in the oil tool field. Further, the lack of desire to profit from the experience of other qualified people has led to constructional difficulties of serious proportions.

"These faults have not been solved, partially because of the various fixes which have precluded action in the matter. The internal bickering in the Engineering Department caused by various conditions existent prior to my coming here, including the fact that too many people previously had an opportunity to approach you directly, has not been completely eliminated as yet. Time is the only cure for some of these ills.

"The type of contract which we have covering the F-11 has also contributed materially to the conditions which are very unsatisfactory from a performance point of view. The tying in of an experimental plane with a production order has long been recognized as a fallacy in the aircraft industry. That considerable improvement in the performance from a manufacturing point of view has been achieved is evidenced by the fact that the costs are now far below that anticipated by you and the Government at the time the contract was negotiated.

"The various attempts by the Government to cancel this project as a whole have contributed materially to retarding progress. Wright Field had been short-circuited and antagonized to the extent that it was necessary for me to devote considerable time to overcome a rather volatile situation.

"Pressurization of the F-11, as such, was a complete failure because of irresponsible engineering and inspection. Less than one-half pound of air could be pumped into the fuselage. This has not been entirely corrected yet, due to a lack of proper engineering from the beginning. The continued failure of the induction system on actual test is a further contributing factor. The failure of the hydraulic system—faulty valves bursting due to poor design and inferior quality of vendor's workmanship accepted by our inspection—results in our having to redesign and remanufacture with considerable delay. Many, many other reasons for delay could be cited; these are but a few of the most obvious examples.

"The termination of the 98 airplanes, the cessation of hostilities in the Jap War, the mandatory reduction to a 40-hour work-week on Government contracts . . . all contributed to a further delay in the program. These are statements of fact for your information. Whether or not a more expeditious program could have been achieved is a matter of conjecture, I know of no one in this organization, other than myself, who, from either an experience point of view or knowledge of the problem, is qualified to comment one way or the other.

CARGO SHIP

"Progress on the Cargo Ship [the flying boat] is somewhat analogous to that on the F-11. There have been some delays, partly occasioned by the Government's classification of the project as nonessential and the red tape resulting from the cumbersome Kaiser-Hughes set-up at the inception. The confused contractual arrangement and the divided responsibility now set up, which you had promised to clear up, leaves this program completely suspended, and no completion dates can ever be ascertained under the present conditions. This has been called to your attention numerous times and despite your comments to the effect that you didn't mean exactly what you said when you advised me I was to have complete responsibility for this program and make my own decisions, I do not now and never will concur in any program which has a divided responsibility.

"Shortly after I came here and when all of the surfaces were practically complete, a 4,000-pound tail-heavy condition developed which necessitated redesigning and rebuilding the tail surfaces. This can be attributed only to inferior engineering.

"Nevertheless, the project as a whole, in my opinion, considering the various problems, has moved satisfactorily. The numerous day-to-day errors which are attributable to inadequate engineering, poor inspection, etc., have gradually been overcome. You cannot build quality into the individuals overnight; it must be achieved slowly. The poor administration of the Engineering Department, and on occasions our inability to obtain qualified personnel, is a situation with which I am sure you are familiar. The many restrictions placed upon us by the low wage scale with which Hughes Aircraft Company found itself saddled did not attract adequately trained personnel. The lack of a comprehensive program was a further contributing factor.

"As you know, I originated the program for the launching of the Cargo Ship at Government expense, and this program resulted in the successful negotiation of a contract now awaiting your approval, which awards us an additional $1,500,000.

RADIO DIVISION

"In the short period that the Radio Division had been in existence prior to my taking it over it had incurred a deficit of several hundred thousands of dollars. Certain changes were made by me in personnel who were unwilling to acknowledge my authority or cooperate with us in the basic program. Through subsequent negotiation with the Government we acquired some very lucrative contracts, totaling $719,841.30, which bid well to improve activity in the department and should result in further increment to the company providing we can have a continued workable policy. . . .

ACCOUNTING DEPARTMENT

"While it is a long recognized and accepted business practice to have a controller to perform the necessary checking of the accounting program of a company—and again I wish to call your attention to the fact that this was discussed with you prior to my coming into the organization and accepted by me—at no time did I ever accept or ever consent to the accounting department reporting to anyone other than the general manager.

"Far more drastic action would have been taken by me months ago had it not been for the fact that this point was not clarified by you with the other parties involved, and also had it not been for the fact that Mr. McDonnall continued to tell me he was resigning. Because of his pending resignation I saw no point in attempting to change his point of view. There can be no compromise in a situation of this kind. I refer you again to your public pronouncement at the Ambassador Hotel, which is a matter of public record.

"That the various top officials of the Hughes Tool Company in Houston from time to time have openly discussed, and with Army officials, the thought of closing or relegating the aircraft division to a plaything for your personal use is also a matter of record. This results in the lowering of employee morale within the plant and in the discouragement of qualified people outside the plant from becoming associated with us.

"The various commitments, promises, and public comments made by your Mr. Meyer, as your spokesman, to the effect that he was closing down the Culver City Division, that he was making personnel changes, and that you were so dissatisfied with my performance that you had given me an ultimatum of 90 days in which to perform or be thrown out, have all greatly added to the confusion, not to mention my personal embarrassment. These conditions have all been called to your attention before. I merely wish to make them a matter of record at this time. The public apologies of Mr. Meyer only serve to authenticate his original misstatements.

"At the time I came to Culver City Mr. Meyer was on the payroll, but was not on the job, although he maintained an office and secretary. He refused to acknowledge the authority of management and contributed absolutely nothing to the regular operations of the plant, despite the fact that he secured Selective Service deferment from the armed forces as a member of the working organization.

"My duties and responsibilities as vice-president in charge of manufacturing of the Hughes Tool Company have been completely ignored by the Houston organization. They have refused to cooperate even to the extent of sending me comprehensive reports of operations. No attempt was made to provide me with office space, temporary or otherwise. Plants were shut down completely, personnel changed in others, etc. and public announcements appeared in the newspapers, without even the courtesy of advice to me. I have not at any time been properly posted on activities of the Hughes Tool Company.

"You advised me that you anticipated certain difficulties in setting me up in the Houston organization, not because of me as an individual, but because of an inherent resistance to anyone coming into the company whose abilities along certain lines had national recognition. That you have not been prepared to face the difficulties encountered is very evident to me. And, again, I must call your attention to the responsibilities which you incurred when inviting me into the organization under these conditions. As I have previously explained to you, I would be quite capable of taking care of myself within the Houston organization, without your support, although my efforts might for some time be ineffectual and at considerable expense to you due to the great resistance inherent in that organization.

"The activities of my directorship on the Board of Transcontinental and Western Air, Inc., have been discussed with you. As I recall your comments on a particular night in the Town House, you stated that I would have complete voice in representing you on the Board of TWA. I subsequently found that this is not the case at all.

"Likewise, you advised that the president of TWA was to report to me for whatever actions and/or decisions would be required on behalf of TWA and/or Hughes Tool Company. This, too, as you know, has not been accomplished in any sense of the word. Various restrictive measures imposed by Hughes Tool Company have precluded my functioning to any extent whatsoever. As I previously told you, I am not interested in wasting my time with ineffective or dummy directorship or management titles. The recent financing program wherein you, Mr. Dietrich, and Mr. Frye completely short-circuited me in its development is evidence of bad faith on your part in the execution of the spirit and intent of my contractual arrangements with you.

"From the foregoing you can readily see that I must necessarily doubt in my mind as to whether or not you were acting in good faith at the time you gave me your word in the foregoing matter.

"This record is prepared for your perusal, and I am herewith asking you what action you propose to take regarding these all-inclusive problems, pertaining particularly to the over-all benefits which should accrue to the Hughes Tool Company by a more comprehensive program as we discussed prior to my joining the organization.

Sincerely,

C. W. Perelle"[1]

Evidently this colossus of a letter had no effect whatever on Howard Hughes's methods of doing business. In December he called up two men he knew in the engineering department of Hughes Aircraft and told them to report to 7000 Romaine Street for a special assignment. After four years of withholding release of his bosomy western starring Jane Russell while he battled censors—thus incited public interest—finally Hughes was going to premier The Outlaw. The Hughesmen were to assist with a promotional flight in a huge blimp over Los Angeles the night before the showing.

Perelle exploded.

"Dear Howard: I am advised that you have recently contacted some personnel in the Engineering Department below the immediate lines of supervision and have taken them away from their work without the knowledge of their supervisor to function in art work in connection with your moving-picture enterprise. As I have previously advised you, this interruption to organization will not be tolerated. We will be most happy to assist you in any of your problems, providing you extend reciprocal cooperation in my efforts to maintain sound organization by making your requests known through proper lines of authority.

"The practice of allowing subordinates to advise their superiors as to what their activities are to consist of is the most demoralizing thing that we can possibly do to organization. I am sure you recognize this fact, inasmuch as you have admitted to me previously that you knew it existed. Continuance of such break-down of organization will undoubtedly be very embarrassing to you and others involved. I trust that you will not make this necessary.

Kindest personal regards,

C. W. Perelle"[2]

That did it for Hughes. No one had ever spoken to him like that. Through Dietrich he fired Perelle for insubordination and never spoke with him again.

The Flying Boat Moves to Terminal Island

Still awaiting Hughes's approval was the contract Perelle had negotiated with the Reconstruction Finance Corporation providing for an additional $1,500,000 to move the flying boat. Hughes was dragging his feet; the contract stipulated that the RFC would choose the pilots for test flights, and Hughes intended to fly the plane himself. Perelle had tried for three months to get Hughes to change his mind, but without success.[3]

The RFC was anxious to get the plane away from Culver City in order to sell the big wooden plant that housed the hull and other component parts—RFC at that time had title to both the plant and the flying boat. But as usual, Hughes got his way.

After careful investigation, Hughes had chosen Long Beach Harbor's Terminal Island as the final assembly site. It was protected by two major breakwaters, fronted a water area ample for maneuvering the flying boat, and was conveniently accessible from both land and sea. The site was procured from the Long Beach Harbor Department by a two-year lease with option to renew for an additional three years. Little did the City of Long Beach realize that their eccentric tenant would occupy the site for more than thirty-three years.

How to move the massive components from Culver City to Terminal Island was the next question. Barging by sea was rejected in favor of an overland move, so Hughes's men studied combinations of highways between the two points using hull size as the governing factor. The route finally chosen had several blocks of trees on Rosecrans Avenue that would have to be trimmed and 2300 wires (owned by twenty-one separate utility companies) that would have to be moved. But this was less costly than what would be required using any other combination of highways.

By June 1946, the assembly and dry dock site on Terminal Island adjacent to the eastern boundary of the Long Beach Naval Base was ready to receive its winged tenant. On June 11, Star House Movers, low bidders for the move at $16,970, placed the giant 160-foot wing sections on moving dollies at a height just sufficient to clear parked cars along the twenty-eight mile route. Then the strange caravan inched out of the plant and on to the highways. Ahead of them, the police of ten cities and towns, together with California State Highway Patrol officers and sheriff's personnel, blocked off cross streets and re-directed traffic. Overhead the blimp Hughes had bought from the Navy to promote *The Outlaw* cruised majestically while crewmen photographed the move.[4]

On June 16, Star House Movers, aided by the maintenance crew at Hughes Aircraft, loaded the 220-foot hull, and it too began the long journey. Reporters estimated that 100,000 lined the streets to watch the huge hull move slowly by.

Battalions of telephone and power company linesmen preceded the load, cut power and telephone lines that could not be moved in advance, then hurriedly spliced them again as the load passed. Toward the end of the route a right angle turn brought the towering fuselage to a standstill. After an hour of jockeying, of inching this way and that, they negotiated the difficult turn. Plant engineer John Stearns, responsible for the move, felt relief and elation. At no point had it been necessary to remove a tree, pole, or other structure, so carefully had the problem been studied.[5]

Reaching the assembly site at last, they eased the hull down an inclined ramp into its dry dock between the wings laid out in a position for attachment. The long-awaited final assembly was at hand.

The Demise of the D-2

Meanwhile, Hughes was busy with his F-11 photo plane. Although he appeared to be involved in a whirlwind of simultaneous activities and projects, he really became deeply involved in only one airplane at a time; and it was not until the basic design work on the flying boat had been completed that he switched his attention to the XF-11. ("X" indicated that the aircraft was experimental.) Before going away on his strange get-away-from-it-all odyssey in 1944, he had spent much time on the engineering of the F-11 and in negotiating with the Materiel Command for a production contract that would reimburse him for his work on the D-2. Although the D-2 outwardly resembled the F-11, it was really a different airplane, and Hughes's persistent efforts to include reimbursement for it in the F-11 contract not only delayed the signing of that contract but further alienated some of the air officers involved.

The D-2 was not a successful airplane. After Hughes had flown it for the first

Above is a wing flap section—not a wing—on its way to Terminal Island. Below: Looking down on the empennage on Roosevelt Highway.

Wing sections, above and below, being hauled along a Redondo Beach, California highway en route to graving dock at Terminal Island.

Above: Flying Boat hull being moved out of the hangar at Hughes Aircraft Company in Culver City, California. Below: Hull turning corner on Roosevelt Highway in San Pedro, California.

Above: Police escort lined up in front of Flying Boat on Roosevelt Highway in San Pedro, California. Below: Rear angle shot of hull also on Roosevelt Highway in San Pedro.

Above: Here the wing and float attachments were complete; and the right wing float is shown in its individual dry dock. Below: The hull has finally arrived at Terminal Island, Long Beach, California, and is ready to be lowered into its nest.

Above: The massive hull moving through the small communities from Culver City to Long Beach drew interested crowds everywhere. Below: The great Flying Boat had been given great publicity and schools along the route were temporarily closed to permit children to witness this unprecedented move.

Overall view of Terminal Island assembly site before any shelter had been erected to protect the plant from the weather or to shield it from the eyes of the curious.

time, then chief engineer Stan Bell rubbed his hands and said, "Howard, how did it go? How did it go?"

"Stan, I don't know. Stan, this thing, uh, it nibbles."

Bell just looked at Hughes, walked out of the room and said, "I just heard some kind of new engineering term. Howard says the airplane nibbles. Do you guys know what that means?" Apparently, it was a pitch problem for which Hughes invented a word. Perhaps the elevator was a little too low behind the wing. Additionally, according to Hughes aerodynamicist Carl Babberger, the 16-series airfoil they chose for the wing turned out to have too great a trailing edge angle and caused elevator and aileron control problems.

"We tried everything trying to clean up that problem and couldn't," said Ray Kirkpatrick. "We extended the trailing edge of the wing about another ten inches to try to get a smoother airflow. Didn't work. Howard didn't like that airplane at all."

During taxi tests one night at Harper's Dry Lake Hughes was warned to stay away from the north end of the lake because a natural spring there created a sort of marsh. "You'll sink out of sight there—really wreck the airplane."

"Okay, okay," said Hughes.

After a couple of taxi tests he let the D-2 roll at sixty or seventy miles an hour right into the soft ground. Kirkpatrick thinks that Hughes was hoping it would rip the gear off and damage the airplane beyond repair. However, the aircraft withstood the rough treatment; it only got well bogged down in the muck.

There was a crew of about ten men on hand at the time with a variety of vehicles. One was Hughes's old Deusenberg that had been converted to a fire truck. They lined up all the vehicles, hooked them together with ropes, and attempted to pull the airplane backward out of the swamp from the main gear. The Deusenberg strained mightily, and then something broke.

"Jeeze, we broke the axle," somebody said.

"Broke the axle!" Howard nearly cried. "On the Deusenberg! Impossible!" It really shattered his faith in cars when the mighty Deusenberg broke an axle.

With Hughes acting as foreman, it was quite a night. "He had a lot of fun trying to get us all to pull together," said Kirkpatrick. "I wouldn't say he was any better than any other foreman, but we knew he was kind of enjoying it. So outside of being late and cold we didn't mind so much what he wanted to do."

The D-2 was a wooden plane kept in a wooden hangar. One day a mysterious fire totally destroyed hangar and contents. According to Kirkpatrick's buddy, Hughes employee Wayne Gaston, "That thing was struck by lightning."

"In clear weather, right?" said Kirkpatrick.

"Yeah, mister, you wouldn't believe it."

Kirkpatrick was asked if he thought the fire was an act of God or was purposely set. "Well, I don't think it was planned, but I don't think God had a hell of a lot to do with it either. I have yet to see lightning strike in clear air. That's not to say that some crazy thing like that couldn't happen. But we had an old diesel generator, and I have a hunch that maybe the electrical system burned it down. I don't believe that anybody really, truly planned it. But we sure had our doubts. Kirkpatrick thinks that Hughes was happy about the way the D-2 ended; it gave him a chance to start over."[6]

The XF-11: Unheeded Warnings

The first XF-11 was ready for its maiden test flight in late spring 1946. Hughes was to make this and subsequent test flights himself. What follows is the first complete account of the events leading up to the plane's flaming crash in Beverly Hills on July 7 that nearly killed Hughes and affected the course of his life.

On the day of the first test flight on April 15, Hughes sat in the cockpit of the photoplane familiarizing himself with the instruments and controls. Then he signaled for the chocks to be pulled and moved away from the ramp and onto the grass runway at Culver City. Frank J. Prinz, service engineer for Hamilton Standard Propellers, rode with him to check propeller operation. "Frank, I can't get the proper manifold pressure the way the props are set," Hughes had said. "Ride with me on this taxi run and take a look."

As Prinz settled behind Hughes and the canopy was closed, Hughes immediately advanced the throttles to full power and the airplane charged down the runway. Both men were absorbed in the instrument readings and did not realize how fast the two-mile strip was being eaten up by the high taxi speed. When they looked up they were fast approaching the line of eucalyptus trees at the end of the field! Hughes slammed the throttles closed and clamped down on the brakes. Smoke came from the wheels. The right outboard tire blew. Even Culver City's 9,000-foot strip, the longest privately owned runway in the world, was not long enough this time.

Prinz reached over Hughes's shoulder, flipped up the red guard covers over the prop reversing switches, and flipped the toggles. Electric solenoid valves ported high pressure hydraulic fluid to the propeller hub mechanisms. The propeller blades moved into reverse pitch and stopped the plane before it crashed into the trees. Hughes took one look at Prinz, said nothing, and turned back to the hangars.[7]

Neither Odekirk nor Hughes's flight test engineer Charles E. ("Gene") Blandford were informed of this reversal.

"Howard didn't communicate very well," says Blandford. "He never told anybody anything. He'd come out and get in the airplane and do what he was going to do and then he'd get in his car and drive away. If he had any knowledge of what happened, he didn't tell anybody."[8] The Air Materiel Command Safety Inspection Team, having just completed a three-day safety inspection of the aircraft, included in their report that the propellers had reversed for no apparent reason.[9]

It should be noted that the prop blades could be mechanically prevented from going into reverse pitch by setting stops in the propeller hub mechanisms. This, of course, was a ground maintenance operation. But Frank Prinz had suggested to Hughes that the stops be set to allow for reversing during the taxi test phase to save wear and tear on the brakes, which were in short supply. Later, William George Dickman, a former senior test engineer with Hamilton Standard and at the time of the XF-11 test flight an employee of Hughes Aircraft's Radio Division, testified on this point: "To my knowledge, Mr. Hughes would have preferred not to have had [the reversing mechanism] connected, but it was strongly suggested to him for use during high-speed taxi runs, and I understand it is only for this reason he agreed to have the modifications made."[10]

During some of the first high-speed taxi runs Odekirk lay in the camera compartment of the F-11 and watched operation of the nose gear shock struts and wheels through the camera windows.[11]

On June 16, following extensive rework to the hydraulic system, the airplane was jacked up and the landing gear operation checked. By July 2 the airplane was ready for the first flight tests, having been accepted by both Army and Hughes inspectors, and was awaiting satisfactory weather for the first flight. That afternoon it was decided that additional rudder rework was required. Still dissatisfied with the high rudder forces required during the taxi tests, Hughes postponed the flight until Sunday, July 7.[12]

Prior to July 7, Hughes already had accumulated several hours of taxi time in the XF-11, including fifty minutes on June 30th after inspection and reinstallation of the propellers, thirty-five minutes on July 1, and thirty-five minutes on July 5. Frank Prinz rode with him during these runs.

Leaving the propeller stops set to allow for propeller reversing for the test flight was probably against Hughes's judgment. He undoubtedly knew that the Army Air Forces had accepted the Hamilton Standard Super Hydromatic Propeller as an experimental model only. It had not yet passed its type test.[13] Previous malfunctions of the reversing system had occurred. The operation of the propeller was such that if actuating oil pressure was lost, centrifugal twisting moments would cause the blades to reverse pitch.

On the preflight inspections the day following each taxi test, oil had to be added to the propellers, particularly to the right-hand pair. This was a warning signal to which not enough attention was paid.[14] Flight test engineer Gene Blandford says that the Northrop flying wing, which used the same propeller, had previously experienced a loss of propeller oil back into the engine through the thrust ring resulting in propeller reversal. This oil loss, being internal, was not outwardly evident. Subsequent testing and experience indicated that the prop could be run for at least an hour and a half before prop oil dropped to the danger point. The full test flight for the XF-11 was only supposed to last for forty-five minutes.

Sunday, July 7, dawned with sky conditions clear—just the usual Los Angeles area haze limited visibility a bit. Hughes met with a few of his engineers at breakfast in the company cafeteria. Hydraulics engineer Dave Grant remembers that he seemed tensely excited but well controlled. But it was Hughes's breakfast menu that stood out in Grant's mind: a cafeteria banana cream pie a la mode.[15]

Out on the flight line, the twin-tailed plane looked sleek and powerful as it sat high on its tricycle landing gear while Hughes flight service people readied it for flight. Viewed head-on, the closely cowled radial engines looked bigger around than the slim, needle-nosed, pod-like fuselage mounted midway on the wing between them.

Tapered extensions of the engine nacelles, like twin booms, extended aft where twin fins and rudders bracketed a straight stabilizer and elevator assembly. The clear plastic cockpit canopy was smoothly molded in one continuous piece with no structural obstructions to vision. Huge contra-rotating double props on each engine were fitted with streamlined bullet-shaped spinners that concealed the hub mechanisms. Large oil cooler scoops were smoothly faired into the underside of each nacelle, and gill-like cowl flaps ringed the aft end of the engine cowlings, looking somewhat like metal shingles hinged at one end. It was a beautiful plane.

When Hughes arrived at the flight line, he first discussed the preliminary high-speed ground runs with Gene Blandford. If any thoughts existed that only four years earlier Blandford had been flight test engineer on his ill-fated Sikorsky, he did not show it.

He spent the morning on taxi runs, a total of one hour and fifty-five minutes worth, including several brief hops into the air. Satisfied, he taxied in for a final servicing before taking his beautiful creation into the air for its first real flight.

For some reason no one had notified Frank Prinz, the Hamilton Standard service representative, of the rescheduling of the test flight to Sunday. Prinz had cancelled a weekend trip so as to be available, but no one called. In his absence no check was made of the propellers to ascertain if they were full of oil. (Some Hughes men muttered later that Joe Petrali should have been strung up for this oversight.)

Hughes instructed the service crew to gas the plane to twelve hundred gallons without consulting Blandford. This was six hundred gallons more than Blandford thought desirable for the test.[16] At about six pounds per gallon, this added nearly thirty-six hundred pounds to the takeoff weight. However, Blandford believes that this extra weight represented no real danger. "The airplane had plenty of power. The extra gas just let him goof around longer than the forty-five minutes called for by the day's test plan."[17]

About midday Jean Peters, a budding new actress Hughes had met just two days before and invited to witness the test, arrived at the Culver City airstrip with war-hero-turned-actor Audie Murphy and Bill Cagney, James Cagney's brother. Hughes spoke with them briefly and then took Odekirk aside. "Odie, you take those two bums with you in the back of the A-20 while we're flying. I want Johnny Meyer to look after her and set things up for me."[18]

Hughes then rejoined Blandford, who reviewed the test plan item by item. Blandford did not discuss retracting the landing gear because the initial test plan did not include landing gear retraction, which was scheduled for the second flight.[19] Nonetheless, Hughes did intend to operate the landing gear immediately after the first takeoff so that he would be aware of its status from the beginning, a reasonable idea, still another instance of Hughes doing things his way.[20]

Flying—especially test flying—is like managing a cage full of lions. If you let one of them get out of control, others act up and problems multiply. That is why flight test programs avoid simultaneous or unnecessary operations. Each system, each item that could possibly cause trouble, is checked step by step. Not until those particular "lions" are under control do you bring another one into the cage.

In accordance with Hughes's instructions, the gas crew pumped high octane avgas into the wing tanks until 1,200 gallons registered on the dipsticks, then reeled up their hose and drove off. Meanwhile, another Hughes employee loaded film into the two electrically driven photorecorders. They would automatically take pictures of flight instruments, engine power instruments, control surface position indicators, and miscellaneous temperature and pressure indicators at the rate of ten frames per minute for a duration of forty-five minutes, the scheduled duration of the flight. [21]

Finally, the last technician and mechanic finished their checks and servicing. Hughes had a final word with Odekirk and walked under the plane to where a retractable ladder extended down about eight feet from the access hatch in the belly of the slender fuselage. So high did the plane sit on its landing gear—in order to provide ground clearance for the 17-foot diameter props—that even the six-foot-four Hughes could walk under the fuselage without stooping.

Getting up and in was awkward. Hughes did not like the ladder and had asked his engineering department to devise a better one. Mechanical engineer Louis Tribbett had yet been unable to come up with an improvement, so often Hughes just used a folding stepladder. [22]

Soon Hughes was in the cockpit, the engines were running, and he was ready to taxi out. Then he signaled the ground crew to pull the chocks. Given the all clear, he released the brakes, eased up the throttles, and moved out of his parking spot. At the east or Culver City end of the field he turned into the wind, set the brakes and began a final checkout and warmup. At one point he throttled back to allow Blandford to climb up and join him in the cockpit. Hughes was checking his instruments, controls, and equipment and reviewing the emergency hydraulic procedures. He asked Blandford a few questions, but they did little talking.

Then Blandford asked, "Howard, do you want me to go with you or are you going to go alone?" He had brought his parachute and other flight gear in the jeep just in case.

"Well," Hughes said and hesitated. "I'll go alone."

Blandford just tapped him on the shoulder in acknowledgment, started the photorecorders, and climbed down. [23] It was another ten minutes before Hughes was finally ready.

He made final adjustments to trim tabs, set the prop controls for takeoff rpm, and visually checked all other controls for proper setting and the engine instruments for proper reading. Then he lined the plane up on the runway and smoothly advanced the throttles to takeoff power. The engines and propellers responded with a deep-throated crescendo and the plane trembled. He released the brakes and the plane surged ahead. Observers on the ground noted the time: 5:20 p.m.

As the takeoff roll started, Hughes checked the manifold pressure and adjusted the throttles with his left hand so that both engine instruments indicated the desired power setting. He was careful that neither propeller exceeded the 2,300 rpm maximum limit set for the first flight.

The acceleration pushed him back in the seat. The ground streamed past faster and faster. He checked the instruments once more; everything appeared normal. Hughes felt the plane coming alive, ready for flight; still he held it down. The nose wheel was still on the ground as he passed the speed at which he had hopped into the air on the taxi runs. This time he wanted plenty of margin above stall speed before he committed the plane to flight.

After some thirty seconds of ground roll the airspeed read one hundred fifty miles per hour. He eased back on the control wheel with the fingers of his right hand. The nose wheel lifted from the runway, and almost immediately the plane was airborne. He caught a glimpse of the group on the ramp watching him flash by. As the runway dropped away he moved the landing gear control to "up" and throttled back to climb power. The landing gear came free of the down locks and the red gear warning light came on as it was supposed to do. Everything felt good.

As he climbed straight ahead away from the field the landing gear warning light still gleamed red. "The gear should be retracted by now," he thought. He continued his climb and started a wide left circle of the field. Sky conditions were clear in his vicinity, and within the limits of ten miles visibility in the usual Los Angeles area haze he could see no other aircraft. The plane handled well. All instrument readings were normal.

It was just that damn red light. At a comfortable altitude he recycled the landing gear. The light stayed on. He put the gear down and then up again. Still the light indicated incomplete retraction. On the next cycle he pushed sharply forward on the control wheel as the gear retracted. This lifted him against the seat belt. The gear thunked into the uplocks. The light went out. Nagged by dissatisfaction with the operation of the landing gear, he recycled it two more times, completing each retraction by exerting sharp forward pressure on the control wheel. The light went out each time.

For about forty minutes he continued circling his Culver City field at about 5,000 feet altitude. The first thirty-five minutes of the flight were recorded by the flight test photo recorders before they ran out of film. His maximum altitude was 5,130 feet, and he appeared to approach stalled flight on several occasions as called for by the test plan. Then Hughes decided to fly low across the field with gear extended so that the ground crew could visually check that all three of his landing gear did in fact appear fully extended.[24] Oddly, he did not call Hughes Ground Control and tell them the problem.

Headquarters Air Materiel Command had assigned a "C" channel frequency of 150 megacycles to the Hughes Company for use in the flight test program of the XF-11. Hughes Ground Control operated on this frequency, and a radio check had been made during preflight several hours before takeoff. There is no record, however, that Hughes himself made a radio check immediately prior to takeoff.[25]

When questioned later by the accident board convened by the Air Force if he had attempted to call anyone on "C" channel, Hughes replied that he had not and had had no reason to since "B" channel had been available. "B" channel was the standard frequency used by most control towers.

To get a visual check before landing Hughes descended in a left-hand pattern around Hughes Field. At 2,000 feet he saw that the A-20 was also airborne.

Odekirk recalls that he watched Hughes take off then followed in the A-20 with Blandford, Murphy, and Cagney who were riding in the four-seat passenger compartment, originally the bomb bay of what had been a World War II attack bomber. They kept Hughes in sight the entire time except for the last few minutes of the flight. According to Odekirk, most of the flight was at 10,000 feet, not 5,000 as stated in the report of the accident investigation.[26]

Hughes wanted Odekirk to observe his landing gear and tried to fly close to them while climbing back to altitude. Unfortunately, there was no radio contact between the two planes. (The A-20 flight communications had not been coordinated with Hughes.) Odekirk stayed inside the left turn and above and to the rear of Hughes's plane so that they saw only the top of the XF-11; they could not see the landing gear at all.

Hughes, exasperated, picked up his mike and made a call on "B" channel to "any tower."

Dick M. Fischer, controller on duty at Los Angeles Municipal Airport Control Tower, made quick reply: "Army 47155, this is Los Angeles Tower."

"Los Angeles Tower from 47155, how do you read me?"

"I read you R-5."

"47155 to Los Angeles Tower, this is a test ship out of Hughes Aircraft. Will you see if you can contact the A-20 that is on this flight with me and tell him I am having gear trouble? If you are unable to contact him, call Hughes Aircraft at Ashley 4-3361 and find out what frequency he is using."[27]

Desperate Maneuvers

Hughes did not know it, but he had just lost critical time. He could have had instant contact with his home field from the beginning merely by switching to "C" channel. Now it was too late; as he finished talking with Los Angeles Tower the airplane suddenly felt as if someone had tied a barn door broadside onto the right wing.[28]

Hughes was two or three miles east of home field heading north at approximately 5,000 feet. He allowed the aircraft to turn right until it headed almost due east. Then he stopped the turn and forced the plane to make a 180-degree turn to the left. The aircraft lost altitude rapidly all the while.[29]

Odekirk and Blandford misinterpreted these maneuvers. They thought he was maneuvering to enter a left-hand pattern preparatory to landing at Culver City. They broke off and made a short approach in order to land well ahead of the XF-11.[30]

Dick Fischer in the Los Angeles Control Tower saw the A-20's landing approach and noted the time: 1840 hours, or 6:40 p.m.[31]

Hughes loosened his seat belt and controlled the aircraft with his left hand on the control wheel while he moved about the cockpit straining to see as much of the aircraft as he could through the canopy. Nothing he saw explained the problem, yet it felt "as if some giant had the right of the airplane in his hand and was pushing it back and down."

He had to hurry now; no time to refasten his seat belt. He took the control wheel with his right hand and with his left increased the manifold pressure to fifty or more inches of mercury and ran the props up to 2,800 rpm. No help. He reduced power to about the original setting and then tried full throttle and about 2200 rpm on the right engine. No help. He reduced power on the right engine. Still no help. By now he was down to about 2,500 feet. He thought of bailing out, but it was probably too low for that now. Perhaps there was still time to locate the trouble.

He had to hold full left rudder and full left aileron to keep the aircraft approximately level. This raised the spoilers on the left wing to their full "up" position and caused further loss of lift. He could control the direction of flight but not the altitude.

Now he was below 1,000 feet, tail low, power on, but still going down, heading northwesterly above the rooftops and swimming pools of Beverly Hills. "Maybe a landing gear door or some other underside surface has torn loose and turned broadside to the wind," he thought. He dropped the gear thinking it might knock the offending structure loose, but as soon as the gear was down he knew that wasn't the problem.

He was going to crash. He planted his feet high on the instrument panel and attempted to flare into the roof of the house directly ahead, Hollywood stunt pilot style. He hit in a climbing attitude, tail down, right wing low. The right landing gear and engine crashed through the second story wall and roof, the left landing gear struck the peak of the roof, then the right wing tip struck the neighboring house. This sequence slewed the aircraft violently to the right, and it hurtled sideways through the air striking a power pole with its left side and breaking the pilot's canopy.

The remainder of the right wing crashed through the roof of the garage next door. What was left of the airplane struck the ground across the alley, then bounced and skidded sideways so that the left wing penetrated the rear of a house at 808 Whittier Drive.[32]

This breaking of wings, landing gear, and other peripheral parts of the airplane as they crashed through yielding structures on the ground dissipated much of the stricken craft's kinetic energy. The center section finally skidded to a stop between two houses without directly suffering catastrophic impact with any substantial structure. Flames burst out in an explosive flare as spilled gasoline ignited.

Hughes in a Burning Inferno

A few doors down the street, Marine sergeant William Lloyd Durkin was dozing in the living room of friends when he heard the stricken craft approaching. It sounded like a big diesel, then like a four-engine R5D (C-54) passing within fifteen feet of him on takeoff.

"Oh, Christ!" he thought. "He's way too low." As the plane hit Durkin was up and running. He reached the street and saw a ball of fire and black smoke roiling upward. He turned left and ran up the alley across the street which divided the triangular block in two. His friend was right behind him. Now he saw the tail section and a piece of wing; that tail section looked wrong for an R5D, he thought.

It was hotter than hell. The plane had broken a small gas main, from which flames shot up about six feet. The house and the plane itself were burning. It was difficult to see clearly because of the smoke. The owner of the burning house, Lieutenant Colonel Charles A. Meyer, was in Germany as a bilingual attorney at the War Crimes Trials. Durkin could see Mrs. Meyer walking around inside and throwing pillows out the window.

"What a thing to save," he thought. "Is there anybody else in the house?" he asked her through the window.

"No," she said.

Durkin pointed to his friend. "This man will take you out the front. Now get the hell out of that house now!"

Durkin turned to his friend. "Jack, get that gal out the front and stay there. I'm going around to the right and see what I can do."

As Durkin circled the house broken shrubbery slowed his progress. It was like going through a briar patch. He jumped on the leading edge of the right wing to see better. Just then he heard a rumbling and thought the gas tanks were going to blow. He jumped headlong through the hedge and nearly plunged into a swimming pool. Powered by adrenalin, he cleared the corner of the pool with a tremendous leap and ran on around the house. Out front he saw a big radial engine with double props smoking on the front lawn and thought, "That's funny. Two props." He still thought it was an R5D.

The engine torn loose from the left wing had clipped a row of poplar trees about three feet above the ground and laid them out toward the street. These impeded Durkin's approach to the plane's nose and the left wing's leading edge because he was going against the slant of the branches.

He crouched and tried to see if anyone was moving. The heat was intense; when he moved, his hot shirt burned wherever it touched his skin. He started to get up, but the heat was worse. "I'm being stupid. Nobody could live through that." He slipped slightly and started to feel panic rising. He dropped to his belly to collect himself, annoyed to be shaken by something like that.

"Christ, there isn't much left of the plane, but some poor sonofabitch might be in there." He decided to call out. "Over here!" he yelled. Then yelled again. The third time he heard a banging that he thought came from the cockpit. It was the sound of Hughes falling on the wing and then to the ground.

The plane had hit some eucalyptus trees as it crashed, and the blow from one had trapped Hughes's left foot. Another tree had split the canopy right down the seam.

After Hughes had freed his foot he stood up on the seat, threw his shoulder into the plexiglass—which was so hot by this time that even though it was over an inch thick it bent out without shattering—stepped out on the wing, and collapsed. As he fell, he hit the leading edge and dropped to the ground. This Durkin heard, but did not see.

"Somebody's stumbling around in there," he thought. He took a deep breath, put his hand over his nose and mouth, closed his eyes and jumped toward the sound. He lucked out and landed right on Hughes. With one hand Durkin yanked him around as though he weighed nothing. Flames were burning an eight to ten inch strip of Hughes's clothing from above the armpit down to his waist. Durkin took Hughes's wrist, lifted the arm clear, and with his own forearm brushed the fire out. Hughes's hand looked as though he had stuck it in a deep fat fryer.

Durkin yanked his burden a few more feet before being stopped by the fallen trees. "Hell, the accumulators, tanks, and whatnot are still going to go up on this thing, but with this goddam brush how am I ever going to get out of here?"

By this time a crowd had collected and Durkin spotted a fireman through the smoke. "Hey, give me a hand in there!" he yelled.

"Wait a minute till I get a hose," the fireman said.

"How can a guy be so stupid," thought Durkin. "I've got a poor man about to burn to death!" he yelled. Thinking that no one would help him, he bent down and spoke to the man he was trying to save. "I'm going to prop you against this stump and leave for a minute. You stay there if you can hold yourself."

But Hughes never spoke. His eyes were open, but Durkin didn't know if he was conscious or not.

"You just stay that way and we've got it made. If you can't, and you fall over, I'm not going to be able to reach you, and all they'll find in here is a couple of little balls of ashes. One's going to be you and the other will be me." Durkin got back on his belly, crawled over to the poplar logs, then reached down and grabbed Hughes by the clothes at his neck and by his belt. He could not lift him.

Durkin looked toward the wing and saw that the self-sealing rubber lining in the fuel tanks had started to burn. The wind, which had been nearly stagnant, stirred and shifted. He thought he saw a big ball of fire coming right at him. Suddenly he had enormous strength; he picked up Hughes as if he weighed two pounds. As he did so he felt a hand on his shoulder. It was the fire chief. He had come in after all!

"You take him by the wrists," Durkin said. "Don't touch his hands. I'll take him by the ankles. Keep him stretched out. He's got a broken back." Durkin didn't know that for certain, but he was taking no chances.

Going with the grain of the fallen limbs, they did not slip once. When well clear, they stretched him out on the ground. Durkin bent down.

"How many more people are in there?" he asked.

"I was by myself," Hughes said.

Two policemen came up. "There's nobody else on the plane," said Durkin. "If you want me I'll be across the street. I'm going home."[33]

Van Storm and two other Hughesmen, racing toward the crash site in their commandeered company car, saw the ambulance carrying Hughes leaving the scene and were the first to reach the crash site who knew who the pilot was.

The ambulance first took Hughes to the Beverly Hills Emergency Hospital. "I'm Howard Hughes," he said on arrival, then passed out again.[34] Hospital personnel ministered to Hughes as best they could, put him in an oxygen tent, and moved him to Good Samaritan Hospital for surgery. Glenn Odekirk and a Dr. Hall, whom Odekirk had brought with him, followed the ambulance to Good Samaritan, a fortunate arrangement. Since it was Sunday there were no doctors at Good Samaritan. Hughes's personal physician, Dr. Vern Mason, was on Balboa Island and did not arrive until a few hours later.[35]

The Long Vigil

Hughes nearly died. The crash occurred at 6:42 p.m. on Sunday, July 7. In the early morning hours of July 8 he suffered severe internal bleeding into the pleural space around his left lung followed by a seeping of the bloody fluid into his chest. His left lung had suffered contusions from severe crushing of the chest and was not functioning.[36]

As Dr. Mason, Dr. Lawrence Chaffin, and a team of nurses and technicians struggled to save his life, Hughes's blood pressure fell rapidly and he slipped into profound shock. Swiftly, efficiently, they gave him two transfusions while administering a constant flow of pure oxygen. They drained 3,400 cc's of bloody fluid from the pleural space in three separate tappings.[37] Gradually, as the hours passed, Hughes's blood pressure rose and he began to come out of shock. Now the excruciating pain began, and for this they gave him injections of morphine.

This was the start of a thirty-year drug habit that eventually killed him, claims Forest S. Tennant, Jr. of the University of California's School of Public Health in Los Angeles. Tennant compiled the Hughes medical history for the Federal Drug Enforcement Administration when authorities investigated a possible murder conspiracy by Hughes's aides after Hughes's death in 1976.[38]

Odekirk is skeptical of this conclusion. He says that at times Hughes would read the doctor's instructions posted at the foot of the bed. He did not want to take as much pain killer as prescribed, and told Odekirk that he wanted only enough to get by, and no more. According to Odekirk, he would take only a third, or a half at most, of the amount prescribed.[39]

Van Storm also questions this conclusion. "I flew with him in 1952 through 1956 and was with him for long periods, even in the bathroom. At that time there was no indication of a dope habit. I was never led to believe by his actions that he was influenced by drugs. There was no gossip among his aircraft crews and flight engineers about his being on dope."[40]

140

The Recovery

Hughes spent thirty-five days in Good Samaritan Hospital. During that time, Odekirk was the only person other than doctors and nurses allowed to see him. Newspaper accounts said that Odekirk was the first visitor; actually, at Hughes's request he stayed in a room next to Hughes with the door open between them during the entire period.

Guards were posted near the elevators to prevent unauthorized persons from entering sections of the hall leading to Hughes's room, and Odekirk arranged for Marian Miller, later Nadine Henley's secretary, to receive visitors in a small reception room. At times Hughes sent Odekirk out to tell special visitors that the only reason they could not visit him was that since he was covered with burns and cuts he did not want them to see him in such bad condition.[41] As he recovered he began to fear that his bedside phone was tapped. So he asked Odekirk to make calls for him on an outside phone.

Lying in bed was extremely painful. To move was torture. So Hughes asked Odekirk to have the plant build a new kind of hospital bed with motor-driven segments that would allow him to adjust his body position with no effort on his part other than to finger a control panel. Odekirk relayed his instructions, Jack Jerman drew up the plans, and Service and Flight Department mechanics built it. The men worked around the clock. Some never went home until the job was done. Some only left for about four hours sleep before rushing back to the job. The bed was delivered to the hospital in record time, but it was never used; it is still in storage in Culver City.[42]

According to Odekirk, Hughes improved rapidly, but he had an eye on the public impact and drama of his situation. Hughes himself briefed Dr. Mason on what to tell the press and refused to see visitors. Even his mother's sister, Annette Gano Lummis, who had lived with Hughes for a year in California after his mother's death, was turned away. Visitors would diminish the impact of his dramatic fight for life.

"He *loved* publicity," said Odekirk, "but he tried to act like he didn't want any."[43]

The Investigation

Odekirk had given orders that nothing at the crash site was to be touched until he said so. He went there a day or so after the crash and marked the collars of the propellers at the hubs to show the blade settings before the wreckage was moved to the plant. The right rear propeller was in fourteen degrees reverse pitch.

On July 11 Hughes prepared a statement that he was convinced that the rear set of blades on the right propeller had reversed.

"The front four blades of the propeller were trying to pull the airplane ahead while the rear four blades were trying equally hard to push it backward," he said. "To make matters worse, these eight large propeller blades, whirling around fighting one another, created a dead drag on the right-hand side. Seventeen feet in diameter turned broadside to the wind at several hundred miles per hour. This also destroyed the flow of air over the right wing and created a tremendous loss of lift."[44]

During the investigation that followed, the propeller laboratory at Wright Field concluded that all available evidence indicated that the pitch-change mechanism of the right rear propeller component failed due to fluid loss. The propeller had separate hydraulic systems for the front and rear components, which were independent of the engines. Loss of more than forty ounces of fluid from either component would permit the blades in that component to go into reverse pitch and the propeller controls to become ineffective. Stops in the propeller hubs were originally set to prevent reversing, but had been reset during taxi tests.

Seals on the rear propeller components were known to permit loss of fluid, probably to the engine gear box, which was at a slightly reduced pressure for scavenging. Fluid leakage of approximately four ounces per hour had occurred on test stands and on other airplanes.

The propeller lab also noted for the record that Hughes took off on an Air Materiel Command approved 45-minute flight and flew for approximately one hour and twenty minutes. "He did not follow the approved flight test program in that attention was concentrated on operation of the landing gear, which prolonged flight duration and was not scheduled until the second hour."

During the last few minutes of the flight, a "powerful drag" developed on the right side of the airplane and it began to lose altitude at approximately 1500 feet per minute. A propeller pitch indicator in the flight test instrumentation indicated a positive pitch on all propellers, even though one set of blades was in reverse, because the indicator was connected to the governor control mechanism, which functioned normally, and not to the actual propeller blades. This "normal" indication apparently helped deflect Hughes's attention from the true cause of his difficulties. He became preoccupied with the possibility that the drag was related to the landing gear difficulties he had previously experienced.

The XF-11's estimated single engine ceiling with the dead propeller feathered (the propeller stationary in minimum drag position) was in excess of 30,000 feet. So Air Force technicians said that he should have been able to continue flight with the right propeller windmilling in any pitch if he had pulled the right throttle back and advanced the left.[45]

Gene Blandford, flight test engineer for the XF-11, says, "Sure, if he'd pulled his power off on the right side his drag would have been reduced. But show me a pilot who figures he's got a broken panel sticking out on the right wing who's going to pull power off on that side. All engine and prop instruments indicated normal operation. As he applied power on the right engine with the rear prop on that side going into reverse, the front prop automatically tried to hold the rpm constant by going into a higher pitch. So he didn't get any clue from his instruments at all. His rpm, manifold pressure, and torquemeter all read normally."[46]

The final report of the Accident Investigating Board assigned primary blame to the propeller malfunction, but faulted Hughes for the way he operated the airplane and conducted the flight. He was criticized in particular for not using the special radio frequency and facilities provided, for not being sufficiently acquainted with emergency operating procedures for the propeller, for retracting the landing gear, for not giving proper attention to the possibility of an emergency landing when sufficient altitude and directional control were available, and for failing to analyze and evaluate the problem by reducing power on both engines simultaneously in order to distinguish between structural and power failure. The Board thought that this accident was avoidable after the earlier propeller trouble was experienced.[47]

Hughes's aerodynamicist, Carl Babberger, says, "The airplane was designed with plenty of capacity to take it. If he'd either cut that engine or cut power he could have come down nicely. He got spooked on that one."[48]

Hydraulics engineer Dave Grant, who was present at the test and later discussed it with Blandford, Bill Dickman, and others, says that Hughes "was kind of funny in being very thorough about many things, but relative to the flight test he didn't check everything out the way he should have, including communications. Subsequently, he did sue Ham Standard and my understanding was that the main reason for suing was that accident report and wanting to vindicate his own ability."[49]

The suit against Hamilton Standard was settled out of court. During the settlement, Earl Martin, then president of Hamilton Standard, together with an insurance representative of Liberty Mutual, spent two days with Hughes in California. Hughes said that if they would accept responsibility and make a settlement he would be glad to forget the whole thing, and not only that, TWA would never use anything but Hamilton propellers.[50]

After a tentative agreement between Hughes and Martin, the Liberty Mutual man met with Hughes for a few minutes and everything was settled amicably. The settlement of $175,000 was for "personal injury" and thus tax free. Martin said that Hughes was very easy to deal with face-to-face "except that he went over everything over and over and over again."

During the two days Martin was in California, Hughes took him to Terminal Island and walked him through the flying boat.

The final blow to Hughes's pride as a pilot was that as a result of the accident his old antagonist Wright Field requested Hughes Aircraft to "furnish the name of a test pilot, other than Mr. H. R. Hughes, for approval for XF-11 second article flights."[51] Galled, Hughes fought back. Early in 1947 he flew to Washington and appealed his case personally to Gens. Ira C. Eaker and Carl Spaatz, the Deputy Commander and Commanding General of the Air Force. He cited his familiarity with the airplane and offered to "pay the government" $5,000,000 if the plane crashed with him at the controls.[52] Spaatz had no objections and said he would issue the necessary orders to Wright Field.

Hughes's Rescuer: A Sequel

Noah Dietrich in his book with Bob Thomas, *Howard, the Amazing Mr. Hughes*, states that he was present when Hughes urged Durkin to remain in the service. "You must serve out your full enlistment with the Marines. It's your duty to your country. Then, when you come out of the service, I'll establish you in any line of business that you select." Years later, according to Dietrich, Durkin completed his thirty years of service and telephoned Dietrich for help because he was not able to contact Hughes to collect on this offer.[53]

When asked about this story recently, Durkin said, "Let me say something about Noah Dietrich, and you can quote me. I have never in my life talked to him, written to him, heard from him, or communicated with him in any way, shape, or form. The first one to contact me was Charlie McVarish from Carl Byoir Associates [Hughes's public relations firm]. Odekirk was second."[54]

Durkin's story is that after the rescue he went to north China with the Marines, and while there he received a letter from Hughes saying that Hughes was giving him $200 a month as a reward for saving his life. ("It's strange nobody's ever asked me to look at that signature," laughs Durkin.)

In 1949, back in the States on leave, Durkin called McVarish, who was a reserve Marine captain, and through him met Glenn Odekirk. Odekirk telephoned Durkin one day and said, "I want to meet you. Charlie McVarish is going to come along. Let's meet at the Beverly Hills Hotel."

After they met Odekirk asked, "Would you like to look at the new XF-11?"

"Hell, yeah," said Durkin.

"Well, let me know where you are and I'll give you a call and you can come out and take a look at it."

Three or four days later Odekirk called. "Come on out to the hangar. I'll meet you at the airport cafe and we'll have a steak and then look at the airplane."

After a tour of the shop, Odekirk said, "By the way, I want to show you my old office." After they had looked around a bit, Odekirk said, "The Old Man never had an office. We built one here for him, but he never used it. Would you like to see it?"

"Sure," said Durkin.

Odekirk opened the door to an adjoining office and there sat Howard Hughes. It was the first time the two men had met since the crash.

They shook hands and Durkin said, "Well, you look a little better."

"Well," said Hughes, "I'm glad you didn't get hurt."[55]

Apparently this meeting had been set up according to instructions from Hughes. Odekirk says that Dietrich was wrong in saying that Durkin stayed in the Marine Corps at Hughes's urging. "He didn't want to leave the Marines because in four years he would be retired and draw retired pay from then on. So it ended up just giving him a check."[56] Durkin retired a Marine Corps captain and now lives in Palm Springs.

8

Final Assembly

BY SUMMER 1946 the flying boat had sprouted wings. Although the bottom half of the hull rested below ground level in its dry dock at the tip of Terminal Island and a high board fence marked the landward perimeter of the assembly site, no shelter of any kind yet blocked the view from the water. The awesome bulk of the largest plane ever built was clearly visible from passing ships.

The 320-foot wing was twenty feet longer than a football field, a hundred feet longer than the wing of the giant Lockheed C-5A Galaxy, today's largest Air Force transport.[1] The vertical fin towered eight stories (eighty-five feet) above the keel. The horizontal tail surface was over five feet longer than the 108-foot wingspan of a 163-passenger tri-jet Boeing 727. Eight engines, each tipped by a four-blade propeller, were mounted on the leading edge of the wing.

At the site, Hughes technicians had begun work on the myriad details that would give life to the winged marvel. Step by step they were installing the electrical, hydraulic, and control systems and were tying together the associated wiring, plumbing, and control cables.

Working conditions were spartan. The men's room was a five-holer. For the first few months, no shelter protected the aircraft. Then a canvas shelter was rigged up on a metal pipe and angle iron frame over the fuselage and each wing. As electrical mechanic Ben Jiminez remembers, "It was just out in the open at first, and boy, that skin really got hot. I'd be behind the damn panel with my head right up against the skin, burning—you could hear those heat waves coming in." After the canvas was installed, Jiminez recalls, "every time the wind blew we had to go up there and roll the canvas up."[2]

Electrical System

The electrical system devised for the Hughes flying boat was unique: a 120-volt DC three-wire system. "The only other aircraft that ever had a 120-volt DC system was the Northrop F-89, I believe," says former Hughes electrical engineer Chris Reising.[3] This system was developed at Culver City by Jim Dallas and L. B. Hillman.[4] They chose a high-voltage system in order to reduce wire size, an important consideration in an aircraft that required very long runs for the wiring. Doubling the voltage reduced the system weight by seventy-five percent.

Jim Dallas, the engineer in charge of the 120-volt design, emphasizes this point. "If we'd used 24 volts, the main power feeds for the 195 kilowatts required would have had to be solid aluminum rods two inches in diameter and several hundred feet long! So 24 volts was impossible. As to whether to use DC or three phase AC, a cargo airplane requires ten times more high torque motor applications than AC applications. So we used 120-volt DC to suit the purpose for which the airplane was designed."[5]

Harold Hoekstra, a Civil Aeronautics Authority engineer associated with the flying boat, remembers walking into the wing, which was supported by a laminated wooden spar thirteen feet high and three feet wide. "It was like walking into a huge closet, a plywood hallway with catwalks leading to the engines."[11]

Some called the engines "corn cob" engines because they were huge radials with four rows of seven cylinders each. "This added up to 224 cylinders," Hoekstra calculated, "448 spark plugs and 28,000 horsepower, which in those days was an enormous amount of power." Each engine drove a four-bladed, hydromatic, full-feathering Hamilton Standard propeller seventeen feet two inches in diameter. The four inboard propellers could provide reverse thrust. Initially, the four inboard propellers could provide reverse thrust, but this capability was deleted after the F-11 crash." Carburetor air inlet scoops were underslung on each nacelle. The scoop fairing also enclosed the oil coolers. Individual oil tanks in each nacelle were replenished from a 280 gallon central oil reservoir by a semiautomatic control system. Two transfer pumps supplied fuel to a service tank in each wing from fourteen huge tanks of over 1,000 gallons each located within the watertight hull compartments. Each wing's service tank provided fuel to four engines. A separate emergency fuel system could provide pressurized fuel directly from the hull tanks to the engines. To allow for wing deflection—which at the wing tip could be as much as thirteen feet—"slip" joints and "floating" fairleads were incorporated in the fuel lines.

All engine throttles at first were operated by "pneudynes," devices which used compressed air instead of hydraulic fluid to transmit very small motions a long distance. The receiving pneudyne was supposed to maintain the correct position called for by the transmitting pneudyne despite changes in atmospheric temperature and pressure. The pneudyne system's electrically driven air compressors automatically maintained pressure in the bottled air supply. Moisture absorbing devices protected them against freezing. Since only a small amount of make-up air was required during flight, the bottled air supply would outlast a normal flight even if the compressors failed.[12]

However, pneudynes did not work out as expected. An argument developed between project manager Bill Berry and the lab people who had to endorse or approve the system to be used. The key issue was the throttles; the pneudynes just would not come up in the same spot.

Ben Jiminez remembers Rae Hopper going up on the flight deck and playing with them like a pinball machine: "They had indicating lights, and wherever the son of a gun sought and set up at, that's when the light came on. But once you got your electrical throttles in there, no problem. They'd lock in and they'd stay there."

Engine mechanic Al Geverink says that once they got the power plants installed and were operating the engines and their associated systems and controls, Howard Hughes came down to the Terminal Island site routinely. "He was up on the flight deck and we were back of the engines. We had all air controls at that time before we changed over to electricity. They were a pain in the A. It was pretty hard to control them. No valve will operate the same with the same amount of given pressure. The pilot only having four throttles—one throttle operating two engines—why, we had to get back there and adjust them. The flight engineer had eight throttles, but a lot of times we could even them up out in the wing better than he could at the instrument panel."[13]

Hughes wanted a fail-safe design, so they developed a zoned electrical system with complete redundancy throughout. All electrical subsystems had fallback arrangements. Bill Berry, the program manager, made a trip to New York City to see how Consolidated Edison handled short circuits while still feeding power to unaffected areas. The resultant design was a three-wire system with current limiters for each wire. If one line shorted, two remained to carry the load.[6] They also were very careful to ensure that all electrical relays would work at high altitudes. Such electrical equipment had to be built especially for this 120-volt DC system, and most of it was provided under contract to Hughes by Bendix. Backup or standby electrical power was provided by two 30-kilowatt auxiliary power units by Jack and Heintz. In addition, emergency battery power was provided by ten 12-volt batteries in two banks.[7]

The aircraft taking shape was indeed something special. Its cargo space was equal to that of two railroad box cars. The cargo deck could carry 125 pounds per square foot. If the load was distributed by heavy planks, a sixty-ton Army tank could roll in under its own power without dismantling. Originally, the design called for clamshell nose doors and a nose loading ramp. These were not installed on the test airplane. The hull's inch-thick bottom skin could take a much higher bottom pressure than that of smaller flying boats. Below the cargo deck the hull was divided into eighteen watertight compartments. If twelve of these were flooded the ship would still float.

As additional protection in case of flooding, Hughes at first had beach balls placed in the hull. Like the Ping-Pong balls used in his round-the-world Lockheed Lodestar, they were to provide buoyancy in case of an accident on the water. Interior photographs of the hull taken during this period clearly show the balls, but the captions sometimes erred as to their purpose: they were not to protect people who fell from the catwalk, as one caption explained. A net placed over the balls ensured that buoyancy would be applied to the lowest points at which the net was fastened to the hull.[8] After the test flight, however, the beach balls were replaced by styrofoam meticulously contoured to the ship and placed alongside the catwalk. ("We never used the beach balls," says Ben Jiminez. "We gave those to the kids. Everybody got a few.")

The exterior finish developed by Hughes consisted of one coat of wood filler, one coat of sealer that acted as a cement for a coat of thin tissue paper placed over it, two coats of spar varnish, and one coat of aluminized spar varnish.[9]

Engine Systems and Controls

As Merle Coffee, Jack Jacobsen, Ben Jiminez, and other electricians hooked up the electrical circuits and made functional checks of the electrical equipment, engine man Harry Kaiser and his crew of power plant mechanics (including Al Geverink, Mel Glaser, Don Shirey, and John Glenn) put the power plants together, hung the engines, and mounted the props.

Harry Kaiser, like other longtime Hughes employees, grew up with aviation. He helped fly the mail back in 1926 and had been crew chief on Amelia Earhart's plane at one time. "A fine, fine engine man," according to other Hughes power plant mechanics, he designed and built the engine test stand used to test and break in the engines used on the flying boat.

The first set of engines was obtained from the Navy on the West Coast. "We got hold of nine 4360s, the model A, from the Navy in San Francisco and brought them up to the B class," says Kaiser. In addition to other modifications, recalls Kaiser, they added different manifolds.[10]

The eight air-cooled, radial R-4360 Pratt and Whitney Wasp Major engines rated at more than 3,000 horsepower each, were accessible for in-flight inspection and minor repairs through a passage in front of the main spar, and then through the nacelles and firewall doors. The wing was thirteen feet thick at the hull. All fuel, oil, hydraulic and pneumatic plumbing was routed along the spar, which provided for quick inspection. All cowling and other structures forward of the firewalls were of metal.

The pneudyne-operated throttles were used for the one and only flight of the flying boat but were subsequently replaced by electrically operated throttles.

As final assembly, outfittings, and instrumentation neared completion, Hughes and his engineers found that they would have to redesign the flight control system. From the beginning, they knew that they had designed an airplane that was too big for a man to operate the ailerons, rudder, and elevators unaided. What was needed was a powered system that would transmit exactly the smallest movement of the controls by the pilot in the cockpit to the control surfaces, but with a force multiplied two hundred times. Unfortunately, their first design was completely unstable and oscillated violently at the slightest attempt to move the controls.

In April 1946, just two months before the flying boat was moved from Culver City to Terminal Island, David Grant, a Wright Field specialist in hydraulics and controls whom Hughes engineers had previously consulted on the XF-11, was persuaded to work for Hughes on the control problem as hydraulic staff engineer.

Grant soon discovered that major modifications were necessary. Minor changes to eliminate instability did not improve the responsiveness of the existing system.

"One problem," said Grant, "was that Howard didnt like that feeling of pumping oil."

As Grant tells it, "Lockheed's Constellation preceded us. Some of the Lockheed people were a big help to me in terms of telling me all that they had been through. So I used their technology. But we had to go much further because the job was just that much tougher. Size made the job tougher. Plus the fact that Howard Hughes was a control perfectionist. He wanted more response than he really needed.

In the system as Grant found it, the pilot's flight controls were directly connected to hydraulic servo valves in the cockpit that ported pressurized oil all the way to the actuating units at the controls themselves. Although conventional 3/16-inch diameter control cable also directly connected cockpit controls to the control surfaces, they did not by themselves move the surfaces. They provided a follow-up that ensured the proper relationship between the pilot's control positions and the actual deflections of the surfaces.[14]

Grant's most fundamental change to the system was to move the servo valves from the cockpit to mountings directly on the actuating units at the control surfaces. With this arrangement, the control cables actually transmitted the pilot's control movements out to the actuators rather than providing only a "follow-up" function.

For safety, each control surface was operated by two independent hydraulic servo-actuators powered by separate hydraulic systems and separate pairs of engine-driven hydraulic pumps. The two independent hydraulic systems were both on for normal operation so that if one system failed there was no lag in maintaining control. Furthermore, if one system failed or was turned off, the other could maintain full load. This contrasts with even present day aircraft where if one or more of the redundant systems fails, there is a partial loss of load capability. In addition, after the test flight, two electric motor driven hydraulic pumps were added as a backup source of hydraulic power to provide even greater redundancy.

Because Hughes was concerned about problems resulting when engines became separated from aircraft structure, as had happened to several propeller-driven aircraft, he had Grant design self-sealing automatic disconnects to prevent the loss of hydraulic fluid. These disconnects, which were designed and built in-house, were also provided for the fuel and oil systems and were unique to this airplane.

"Howard indicated that I was to be his copilot throughout the flight test program," said Grant. "One of the reasons for this was that he didn't want any regular copilot getting in his way. But the other reason was my involvement with what he considered the most critical part of the airplane at that point (the control system) because when I came with the company that was really what was holding it up."[15]

Hughes was also fussy about instrumentation. He spent a great deal of time getting the kinds of indicators he wanted and on their precise placement. "My contacts with Howard were not involved with the electrical system as much as they were with instrumentation and the arrangements for the instrument panel," says electrical engineer Chris Reising. "He was very meticulous in how he wanted the panel arranged. It took long, arduous pains to get the instrumentation just to his liking. He wanted it almost foolproof so that you could follow the flow of the systems. The CO_2 fire extinguishing system was very elaborate. The hydraulic system instrumentation showed the flow and the switches involved. The air pressure system that supercharged the hydraulic reservoirs was also very meticulous in design. He wanted those just precise. He went over them in several meetings and marked up drawings and then he'd come back again. We had two or three such meetings before he finally approved each system's control and instrumentation layout.

"There were usually four or five people at these meetings. The drawings would be laid on the table and he would go into the systems in great detail. He had very good basic technical knowledge. He knew what he wanted and belabored each point until he got exactly what he wanted—and he usually had a good sound engineering principle behind the way he wanted it. He would work on us, discuss it and talk about it for hours. He wasn't hard-nosed about it. He wanted to come up with the best design regardless of who suggested it."[16]

Reising recalls an episode that illustrates Hughes's relationship with his engineers: "There were two auxiliary hydraulic pressure systems with separate reservoirs pressurized by the air pressure system. Originally we planned on two air pressure gauges side by side. But in going over the drawings with him on a Sunday morning he asked me if we could get a single dual air pressure gauge. I said yes. Because there were so many dual pressure gauges, no problem. So he looks at me and he says, 'Are you sure we can get a dual air pressure gauge?' And I told him yes. I wasn't about to say no.

"During the whole session while we were reviewing that panel he asked me no less than five times point blank, 'Can you get a dual air pressure gauge?' And I said yes every time. He didn't remember ever seeing one.

"I couldn't wait to get into work the next day—and there was no such animal! There was just no dual air pressure gauge available anywhere. No one had ever heard of one. So what we got was a dual oil pressure gauge and converted it to the proper pressure and that's what we used. I think that he knew that there was no such thing and was testing me."

By 1947 the world's largest airplane neared completion. But by that time, too, the Senate Special Committee to Investigate the National Defense Program was casting an appraising eye on the controversy that had accompanied its design and construction.

9

Maneuvers Before Battle

AS HUGHES READIED HIS GIANT AIRCRAFT for test in 1947, the special Senate committee to investigate the National Defense Program zeroed in on his wartime contracts. It was not unexpected. Three years before, Hugh Fulton, then Chief Counsel for the Committee, sent a letter to E. A. Locke, Jr., the assistant to the chairman of the War Production Board, asking for "whatever information is available concerning the status of the Kaiser-Hughes Transport Airplane Project."[1]

Senators Ralph Owen Brewster of Maine and Homer Ferguson of Michigan, who had been committee members under Harry S Truman, were aware of the cancellation of the contract and its reinstatement in the face of unanimous expert opinion that "the contract should be cancelled inasmuch as the project offers no useful contribution to the War effort."

On January 31, 1947, Francis D. Flanagan, the assistant chief counsel for the Committee, submitted a memorandum to George Meader, the chief counsel, in which he concluded: "Based upon my investigation to date, it is my opinion that this entire flying boat project, which never had the wholehearted approval, and in some cases actually had the disapproval of responsible government agencies, must have received strong backing from some persons with considerable influence in high government places."[2]

To Brewster, Ferguson, and their fellow Republicans, the Hughes contracts seemed low risk, high yield targets. Not only might they be examples of the kind of wartime profiteering and wrongdoing the committee had been set up to expose, but also that very exposure might tarnish the image of Roosevelt's Democratic administration, always a high-priority Republican goal.

Elliott Roosevelt, the President's son, had recommended Hughes's experimental XF-11 as a photoplane for the Air Corps despite the objections of General Echols and other Air Corps officers responsible for the development and procurement of aircraft for the war effort. Indeed, the President himself had interceded in favor of reinstating the flying boat contract after the Government's own experts had agreed unanimously that the contract should be cancelled. Furthermore, although Hughes had received $60 million to produce the two planes, neither was finished by war's end.

Moreover, in 1946, Hughes's Trans World Airways had begun flights to Europe in competition with Pan American Airways. Brewster sincerely believed that the United States needed a single American flag-carrier to compete successfully with foreign government-sponsored airlines on international routes. In line with this belief, and in response to special advocacy by Pan American's Juan Trippe, Brewster had sponsored the so-called Chosen Instrument Bill which, if enacted, would have resulted in Pan Am becoming the U.S. flag-carrier in international air transportation.

Vigorous lobbying by Hughes's TWA and other airlines blocked enactment of that bill, but Brewster persisted. Now he was salesman for a somewhat similar bill (the "same baby in a different set of diapers," in Hughes's opinion), Senator McCarran's Community Airline Bill, which if enacted would probably achieve the same end result as the previous bill.

This was an anathema to Hughes. As the major stockholder in TWA, he had no intention of seeing his airline either relegated to domestic service or merged with Pan American. But TWA was in financial difficulties, as Brewster well knew. In January 1947 Brewster, as head of the aviation subcommittee of the Senate Interstate and Foreign Commerce Committee, had taken testimony from Civil Aeronautics Board Chairman Landis in executive session on TWA's financial condition.[3] All things considered, Brewster may have felt that the threat of an investigation might persuade Hughes of the merits of the single flag-carrier idea. It did not.

In 1945, according to Hughes, right after the Civil Aeronautics Board first awarded TWA the right to fly the Atlantic, TWA's president Jack Frye had warned him of Pan American's political clout: "Howard, you are going to learn that Pan American Airways has the biggest, most complex and strongest political machine that has ever hit Washington. Juan Trippe feels you have moved in on his territory, which he considers to be the entire world outside the U.S., and he is going to make your life miserable. You have no idea the lengths to which these people will go."[4]

Merger Smokescreen

Hughes could go to great lengths too. "In some matters Howard could teach a few lessons to the master of manipulation, Machiavelli himself," wrote Noah Dietrich in recalling these events.[5] His opening gambit in early 1947 was to begin negotiating with Pan Am president Trippe for a merger of the two airlines. Trippe thought he meant it; but Hughes, in devious fashion, was only buying time while laying the groundwork for an offensive of his own.

In December 1946 Senator Brewster had been elected chairman of the Special Committee to Investigate the National Defense Program, as part of the spoils due the Republicans with their new congressional majority. On the morning of

February 1—even before the formal selection of its Democratic membership—Brewster launched into a preliminary hearing to open his promised grand-scale inquiry into the war spending of the Roosevelt and Truman Administrations. An hour or so later, after the Senate had convened, announcement was made of the Democratic list of four members, a deliberately "strong" panel to keep watch on the Republicans in an inquiry regarded in both parties as certain to produce many political implications.[6] On February 3, the *New York Times* editorialized that "The Democrats may be pardoned if they fear that this investigation has some connection with next year's Presidential campaign."[7]

Rumors, leaks, and press speculation convinced Hughes that an inquiry into his multimillion dollar contract to build the wooden flying boat was high on the committee's list of key investigations. So near the end of that first week in February, Hughes hopped into his B-23 and flew to the east coast, first to New York and then to Washington. This key objective was to forestall a full-scale public inquiry.

Hughes arrived in Washington the weekend of February 8. He first telephoned Brewster's apartment but found that Brewster was in Kansas City. Hughes telephoned Brewster there on Sunday morning to say that he was in Washington and ready to talk to him. Hughes later testified that he desired to make whatever statements were wanted by the committee so that he would not have to return to Washington again.[7]

Hughes and Brewster disagree as to what followed this initial contact, the first time they had talked since Brewster and other Congressmen had been given a demonstration ride in Hughes's new Constellation several years before. Brewster had speaking engagements in Kansas City, Morgantown, West Virginia, and Columbus, Ohio and told Hughes he would not be back in Washington until Wednesday. According to Brewster, Hughes told him, "I cannot wait until Wednesday. If you will get back here on Monday, I will see that you are flown up there."[8]

But according to Hughes, Brewster already held a ticket on TWA to return to Washington on Sunday and accepted free transportation from Hughes by choice, not to accommodate his schedule to that of Hughes.

On Monday, February 10, Hughes, accompanied by a local attorney named Hefron, called on Brewster at his office. According to Hughes, he had been advised that Senator Brewster "was very tricky" and that he should have someone with him to be sure that Brewster could not later claim he had made statements which he did not make.[9]

"When I met him in his office," said Hughes, "he immediately launched into the community airline bill. He didn't have much to say about this investigation, so he talked about British supremacy, jet propulsion, and labor differential and how it was impossible for the present competitive American systems to succeed because foreign lines could supply services at the lower foreign labor rate, in direct competition with us, and I told him I did not agree.

"Furthermore, I did not agree about England's technical supremacy over us. I said that the United States in my opinion always led in commercial aviation and probably always would. I said that some foreign countries exceeded us in flash performance of various military types but that when it came to sound, safe commercial aviation this country had always led, and I felt it always would, and I felt that people might even be willing to pay a little premium to ride on the United States line because I thought it would be safer and the public would appreciate that.

"So, anyway, we had some argument on that matter and then I told him I was in Washington and while here I would like to testify before his committee if he so desired and dispose of the matter because I did not want to come back to Washington again. . . . Some time previously I had heard that this investigation was brewing, I also heard that Pan American was behind it, and I thought rather than wait until I was subpoenaed that I would offer voluntarily to testify."[10]

Brewster testified later that he did not recall the Monday morning conversation quite as Hughes did. Brewster said that Hughes was primarily interested in the investigation. "I did not know how he had learned about it," Brewster said. "But he inquired what it was all about, what we wanted to know, and said that he had come on to discuss this matter with us, and that he wanted a hearing in the matter 'right now.' "[11]

After some discussion Brewster finally told Hughes, "I am sure that the committee will be glad to hear your story in executive session. That will not involve any unfortunate publicity for anyone concerned, and I will call the committee together." Accordingly, it was decided to have an executive session the next day, Tuesday morning.

Hughes arranged for Jack Frye's executive plane to fly Brewster to Morgantown that Monday evening for his speaking engagement. The next day the executive session of the committee convened at eleven a.m. to give Hughes his opportunity to answer questions. Hughes hoped that this appearance would suffice. Moreover, he was encouraging Brewster to believe that merger negotiations with Juan Trippe were underway.

The hearing was held in room 457 in the east or First Street side of the old Senate Office Building. The committee members sat in red leather chairs at a U-shaped desk of dark mahogany elevated by a dais so that the members looked down on Hughes as if he were a specimen in an operating amphitheater.

Hughes, again accompanied by Hefron, sat at a long table at the mouth of the U facing an eagle carved into the dark wood of the desk below where Brewster, as the presiding chairman, sat looking down at him. The setting appeared designed to impress petitioners and witnesses with the majesty of Senatorial power and with their own vulnerability and aloneness in facing that power.

From all accounts, the hearing proceeded amicably and was concluded that afternoon. At one point Senator Hatch asked: "Mr. Hughes, you are willing for someone from the committee to come out and go over all of your books and give them all of the information that you have out there?"

Hughes did not hear the question clearly. "What is that?" he asked.

Mr. Meader, counsel for the committee, rephrased the question: "Senator Hatch would like to know if you are willing for a representative of the committee to come and inspect your books concerning this matter."

Hughes replied, "Oh, certainly; of course."[12]

Brewster interpreted this as an invitation to visit Culver City and freely inspect any and all records of Hughes's aviation business. Hughes, on the other hand, thought that this invitation was limited to those records pertinent to the specific matter then under discussion. This misunderstanding later became a point of controversy.

Tuesday evening, after the hearing, Hughes personally flew Brewster and Senator Bricker of Ohio to Columbus in his B-23 for another Lincoln Club dinner. During the flight Hughes invited Brewster to sit in the copilot's seat. Their conversation was limited by engine noise and Hughes's hearing problem, but according to Brewster there was some mention of the "community company."[13]

When the senators returned to the airport immediately following their speeches, Hughes had already flown back to Washington and Frye's TWA plane was waiting for them. Meanwhile, Hughes had decided to stay over Wednesday in Washington and Brewster had invited him to lunch.

Hughes was met at the Mayflower Hotel the next day by both Senator and Mrs. Brewster. After a few pleasantries were exchanged, Mrs. Brewster excused herself and left the men to lunch together in the Senator's suite. Since no witnesses were present, the subject of their conversation was known only to themselves—and later one of them was to lie about it under oath. Hughes recalled that he told Brewster he had previously discussed the possibility of TWA merging with Pan American with Juan Trippe during dinner in Trippe's apartment at the Mayflower and that he had promised to give Trippe an answer in thirty days.[14]

Following Hughes's visit in Washington there were stories in the press that either the two companies would merge or Hughes would withdraw his opposition to the community company. This press speculation followed an *Aviation News*, February 24, 1947 report: "The leading proponent of the community airline on Capitol Hill is conducting a one-man missionary campaign on Howard Hughes. Senator Brewster and the west coast aviation executive have spent many hours together recently, some of it traveling. Hughes is said to be leaning toward a community-company idea and high TWA executives wondered whether it is because of the threat of a full-fledged quiz into the Hughes-Kaiser cargo-plane deal by Brewster's war investigating committee."

Both men were later questioned by reporters concerning the *Aviation News* story. During the week of March 3 Hughes telephoned Brewster, ostensibly because "I thought I ought to speak with you before talking with the press." Brewster replied that "they asked me the two questions, 'Did you say that you were going to merge Overseas?' and 'Did you say you believed in the community company?' And I said 'The answer to both questions is no.' "

Hughes said, "Well, I had to deny the merger because that put the whole TWA organization into a spin, as you can well imagine."[15] Although Hughes acted as though the stories had been published without his knowledge, they did serve to bolster the case he was building against Brewster.

In the meantime, Hughes continued his charade of merger negotiations and sent Noah Dietrich to New York to continue talks with Trippe. Balance sheets were even exchanged. But Trippe's offer of merger was refused as inequitable to TWA stockholders.[16]

Flanagan: Pressure from Brewster?

On Friday, March 14, Francis D. Flanagan, former administrative assistant to FBI Chief J. Edgar Hoover and an FBI agent for six years before going to work on the committee in 1944, arrived in Culver City and requested to look at Hughes's records.[17] There was nothing sinister in the timing of this event; Hughes *had* invited the committee to look at his books. But Hughes later testified that because of its timing in relation to Dietrich's refusal of Trippe's merger offer, he felt the two were "definitely connected."[18]

However, Flanagan recalls that he and Hughes discussed the visit at some length while Hughes was still in Washington and at that time Hughes was affable and cooperative:

"I'll be there Monday night," Flanagan recalls telling him.

"Well someone from my office will get in touch with you eleven o'clock Tuesday morning," said Hughes.

On Tuesday morning, March 11, at eleven o'clock on the dot ("You could set your clock by it," said Flanagan), the phone rang. Flanagan recognized the voice. It was Hughes.

"Mr. Hughes?" Flanagan asked.

"No, I'm calling for Mr. Hughes. Are you Mr. Flanagan?"

"Yes."

"Your coming out here is to get an appointment with Mr. Hughes?"

"Yes."

"Go outside, not on the park side [Flanagan was staying at the big hotel on Pershing Park in Los Angeles—he could not recall the name] but to the side street. There you'll find a station wagon with California number . . ." Flanagan did as instructed and found Hughes waiting for him.

After they had talked for three or four hours that day Hughes said, "Well, how about tomorrow?"

"All right," said Flanagan.

"Eleven o'clock," said Hughes.

"Okay," said Flanagan.

Every day there was the same procedure. Hughes would say, "A man will call you at eleven." Right at eleven the phone would ring. It would be Hughes with the same instructions as before. One day as Hughes dropped Flanagan off at his hotel and made the same arrangements, Flanagan said, "What kind of bullshit is this anyway?" Hughes looked at him a moment and then they both laughed.

Hughes spent five or six hours one day giving Flanagan a tour of the flying boat. His pride was obvious as he tried to impress Flanagan with its virtues. At another point during the two-week visit Flanagan met with Noah Dietrich and a Texas lawyer who had been or was then the mayor of Houston. Dietrich said, "Now listen. I know why you're out here, I know what Brewster's after, and that what you're after is Roosevelt."

This was news to Flanagan. He and the committee staff knew that Brewster was very close to Pan American people and suspected that Brewster and Hughes might have been talking about Pan American and TWA. But that had nothing to do with the investigation as far as Flanagan was concerned. What he was looking for was how, in the middle of a war, could all that manpower and money be spent on two planes—neither of which was ever put into production or completed. What kind of mismanagement allowed that to happen? Flanagan even doubted that the original impetus for the investigation came from Brewster.

Dietrich and Hughes, however, professed to believe that Brewster was using the investigation to pressure Hughes and blacken the Roosevelt administration. Probably Hughes was paranoid enough to believe the worst and really did interpret everything accordingly.

Flanagan believes that Hughes's prime motive in inviting him to Culver City was to head off a public hearing, to con him around into recommending that the investigation be dropped. Hughes and Dietrich thought that the investigation could be stopped or fixed in some way, and Dietrich was ready to throw Roosevelt to the wolves.

"You lay off us and we'll give you all the stuff on Elliott Roosevelt. We've got the records," Dietrich said.

That got Flanagan interested in the records. Hughes "never trusted Johnny Meyer or anyone else," said Flanagan. "That's why he made them keep these detailed expense accounts. He insisted on precise records."[19]

As of 1947, Johnny Meyer, pudgy, fast-talking, fun-loving exponent of wine, women, and song, had known Hughes for about eleven years. Meyer's background was in the back-slapping, gift-giving, party-going high-powered public relations world of southern California, first with the Caliente, Mexico Race Track, then as operator of Hollywood's La Congo night club, and then as a public relations expert for two years for Warner Brothers. This last job led to his joining Hughes Productions, the motion picture arm of Hughes's empire, on December 1, 1941. However, after Pearl Harbor Meyer's name was transferred to the Hughes Aircraft payroll, an assignment that enabled him to obtain six draft deferments during the course of the war. His title was "Assistant to the President and Public Relations Director."[20]

During the period of their association Hughes and Meyer were often seen together at night spots in Hollywood and Las Vegas. It was natural that when Hughes decided to compete on the entertainment front with the other aircraft manufacturers, Johnny Meyer would handle the job. One of Meyer's jobs had been to look after Col. Elliott Roosevelt and his group of experts from North Africa who had come to look for a photo reconnaissance airplane. During the course of Roosevelt's visit to the United States Meyer introduced him to actress Faye Emerson, whom Roosevelt married four months later.

When Flanagan asked Hughes for Meyer's expense account records, Hughes at first refused to turn them over. But under threat of subpoena he finally made all the records available to Flanagan by the end of March.[21]

Hughes thought he was being pressured by Trippe and Brewster, so his next ploy was to telephone Juan Trippe in New York. "Look, there is no chance of us getting together unless we discuss this matter in person." Trippe agreed and arranged to meet with Hughes in California.[22]

According to Dietrich, the meeting was held in Palm Springs in a house in the desert rented by Hughes for the occasion. Trippe arrived from New York in his personal airplane, Dietrich from Houston in his, and Hughes in his B-23. "Howard was extremely cordial to Trippe," said Dietrich, "even though he hated Trippe's guts for his efforts to monopolize overseas air travel for Pan American. The talks continued into the evening of the first day and were resumed on the morning of the next day."[23] The dates of these Palm Springs meetings were April 12 and 13.[24]

During the meeting, Hughes brought up the question of Brewster's investigation as though this were a matter that Trippe could control. By Hughes's account, Trippe was not bothered by this and talked "as though Brewster worked for him."[25]

Not long after the Palm Springs meetings Trippe finally realized that Hughes had no intention of merging TWA with Pan American. Meanwhile, the investigation was moving ahead at an accelerated pace, and Hughes realized that revelations of Meyer's expense account would figure prominently.

Hughes knew that not much could be said in defense of Johnny Meyer's activities except that everyone was doing it. Furthermore, he knew that he was vulnerable to critical inquiry into the poor management and delays in fulfilling his two contracts. Obviously the most effective way of defending himself and his works would be to mount a slashing counterattack.

The Second F-11

In the meantime, Hughes pushed the flying boat toward completion and readied his second F-11 for testing. The contrarotating dual props of the original plane had been replaced by single sixteen-foot, four-bladed Curtis electric propellers.

Hughes made the final test flight himself on April 5, 1947. Hydraulics engineer Dave Grant ran into Hughes shortly afterward. Hughes was upbeat. Uncharacteristically, he invited Grant to lunch in the company cafeteria, and the conversation centered on the F-11. "Howard thought that was the world's greatest airplane. He just couldn't stop raving about how everything was working well on it. The controls were all mechanical, and Howard had spent a great deal of time until he got them just the way he wanted them. He was just as ecstatic about the way the F-11 responded."[26]

The F-11 contract called for Hughes Aircraft to complete successfully a series of flight tests before delivery of the first plane to the Air Force. Most of these tests were flown by Hughes accompanied by Gene Blandford, his flight test engineer.

Hughes was good at providing pilot's reactions to how a plane felt and handled. Qualitative testing suited his style of doing things. But he was too much an individualist, too undisciplined, to provide the kind of hard data needed for quantitative testing.

Hughes would come to the plant before a flight for steak and a bowl of peas in a little private room of the cafeteria. He would say to Blandford, "Well, what are we going to do today?"

Blandford would go over the Air Force procedures that he had outlined in a little book. He would say, for example, "Now, here we'll hold the power and vary the wing flap position." (The usual practice was to vary one thing at a time so that the results could be plotted on a curve.) Hughes would say, "Okay, okay." But when they got in the air, Hughes would do it all wrong: "Well, I don't like that. Let's hold this flap position and vary the power." He would always find some reason to do the test slightly differently.

This meant that Blandford was unable to plot nice smooth curves based on one variable. Instead, he got mountains of data he could not put together. "We very seldom got any decent data with him in the plane," said Blandford. "So one time I didn't turn on the recorders."

When Hughes landed, he said, "do you have a lot of data?" Blandford told him what he had done. "When you sit there I have a room full of data that I can't touch."

Hughes was madder than hell. "Well for Christ's sake, what's all that stuff in there for?"

One day they climbed to altitude to determine stall characteristics, that is, the airspeed at which the airplane would quit flying in different configurations—gear up, gear down, flaps at various settings, power on, power off—and how the airplane behaved at the various stall points. Suddenly, acrid smoke filled the cockpit.

"It smells like an electrical fire," said Blandford. Hughes returned to Culver City and had the ground crew investigate. The mechanics found nothing wrong.

"Well, let's take off again," said Hughes. Halfway to Catalina Island, while they were approaching a stall with partial flaps, the blue haze of acrid smoke filled the cockpit again.

Blandford called the field. "We're full of smoke. Clear the runway. We're coming in."

A small vent forward gave Hughes some fresh air, but Blandford wasn't helped much by that. As they started the approach, Hughes said, "You really think we should land?"

"You're goddamn right I do," said Blandford. "I'm suffocatin'. Besides, if I were flying this airplane under the conditions you're flying it, I'd get it on the ground."

Hughes said nothing; he just landed. Finally, the mechanics decided that at certain airspeeds and flap settings smoke was sucked from the left engine through the flap well and into the fuselage behind the pressure bulkhead just aft of the cockpit. The plastic bubble that normally sealed a port in the pressure bulkhead was missing.

"Well, that's nothing," Hughes said. "We don't have to worry about that."

"There's carbon monoxide," said Blandford.

"That's not going to hurt anything. Let's go."

"Hell no," said Blandford. "I'm not going to get in the goddamn thing until it's fixed."

Hughes called Joe Petrali over. "How long will it take to put the pressure bulkhead in, Joe?"

"It'll take twenty or thirty minutes," said Petrali. Hughes grumbled around while mechanics installed the bubble, then off they went again. Finally, all stall tests were completed except the most difficult one: a stall at METO power (maximum except take off), flaps full down forty-five degrees, and gear down.

Hughes loved to stall airplanes. Instead of stalling partially, he went the whole way. But this time, with the F-11's power, the airplane refused to stall. It just kept climbing and climbing until Hughes had the yoke all the way back against the stops with the airplane practically standing on its tail while he held it with the rudder. They were at 14,350 feet.

Suddenly, as the airspeed dropped to the stall point, the airplane flipped over on its back as though a string had been cut on one side, and the nose dropped in a screaming dive. Hughes retracted the wing flaps—they would have blown off if he had left them down—reached over and grabbed a handful of knobs to reduce the power, and started gradually pulling the airplane out of the dive, maintaining little more than one g positive. But he left the gear down, and this helped limit its speed.

Unfortunately, when he pulled the throttles back he also pulled the mixture and electric propeller controls off. This locked the propellers in full low pitch so that they could not now automatically limit windmill rpm by going to a higher pitch. The engines oversped with a rising, terrifying banshee wail.

The airplane did not have dual controls or side-by-side seating—the navigator's seat was low behind the pilot—so Blandford had been sitting on a little milk stool to the right of Hughes. From there he could see what was going on and still reach his own panel. As the terrifying dive started, Blandford stowed his stool, crawled back over the hatch to the nav station, and grabbed his mike.

"Feather the prop! Hit the feather switches!" Blandford yelled. Hughes did not respond. As the monstrous 4360 engines revved up to 3700 rpm in a rising crescendo, Blandford thought, "If anything hits that cowl from the inside, I'm leaving."

Clarence Shoop, a former Air Force pilot with Hughes Flight Test, was flying chase plane in an A-26. When he saw the F-11 dive vertically through a layer of low cloud he thought, "They'll hit the deck for sure." But Hughes levelled out at 4,000 feet after completing a 10,000-foot split S and started coming up with props and throttles. There was no response; the mixture controls were in idle cut-off position.

His hand jumped to move the levers forward. By the time he recovered power they were at 3,000 feet.

Blandford radioed the A-26. "Shoopy, we're heading for the farm and everything seems to be all right. Come on and give us a check."

Shoop flew up alongside and looked them over. "You look all right," he said. "The landing gear doors are still aboard. The gear looks all right." Blandford called the tower for landing clearance.

By this time it was almost dark and low scuddy clouds have blown in from the sea. Hughes threaded his way in, landed, and taxied to the hangar. When they were safely in the hangar Hughes said, "Did you get that data?"

"Well, I think so," said Blandford. "But if we didn't get the data, you can find somebody else to go with you next time." Hughes just grunted a bit. As they were wrapping things up, Hughes said, "What the hell were you *yellin'* so much about while we were going through that?"

"I was yellin' for you to use the feather switches to control that overspeed rpm."

"Oh," said Hughes, and he didn't say another word about it. But when they were ready to leave Hughes insisted on driving Blandford home, and even dropped him off right at his door.

About two weeks later Hughes came into Blandford's office carrying the manual of operating instructions for the Curtis Electric Propeller. He had gone through the manual and underlined in red every reference to overspeed control. He placed the manual on Blandford's desk and without saying a word, showed him the underlined material page by page. Then he picked up the manual, closed it, turned around, and walked out.

"The manual said to use the feather switches in case of overspeed, so he wasn't trying to educate me," says Blandford. "Besides, I couldn't have reached the control switches anyway. They were on Hughes's side of the airplane. . . . Maybe he was just showing me that he took the incident seriously and now he knew all about it. He was strange, even in those days. He could be as gracious and polite as anybody, and then the next day he'd walk right past you and not even see you."

Hughes finally finished his part of the F-11 flight test program, and as they sat in the hangar finishing their reports he instructed Blandford and Bill Dickman (who flew some of the test flights in Blandford's place) with regard to getting the plane ready for delivery to the Air Force.

"If you get it delivered by November first," he said, "I'll give you a two-week vacation with pay."

"I'll hold you to that," said Blandford. He had selected a picture of Hughes in the F-11 from the photo lab. When they'd finished their paperwork, he handed it across the desk to Hughes.

"You know, Howard, we're all through with this foolishness. Would you autograph this picture for me?"

Hughes hated to sign his name to anything. He looked at the picture and then looked at Blandford for fully three good minutes. He was sure Blandford had something in there that was going to be embarrassing. Finally, satisfied that it was just a photo lab picture, he said, "How do you spell 'intrepid'?"

When he finished, the inscription read: "To Gene, my intrepid, fearless companion on the XF-11 test program."

Hughes also autographed a photo for Bill Dickman who had been on a flight when the nose gear, which rotated as it retracted, had stuck crosswise. On that occasion, Hughes had radioed for Blandford to go to the control tower with engineering drawings of the nose gear actuating system to answer questions. When they finally got the nose gear down straight, Blandford said, "I suggest you land this time without putting it back up."

Hughes really gave him a blast. "What do you think I am?" he rasped.[27]

Final Maneuvers

After the first successful F-11 test flight, Hughes spent more and more time with the flying boat. Meanwhile, Senator Brewster started leaking charges and salacious items to the press.

"We never intended to put ninety percent of these expense account items about actresses and whatnot in the record," said Flanagan. "But we had the originals and made one set of copies which we punched and put in a loose-leaf notebook. One day a member of Brewster's staff asked to see the expense account records, so we sent him the copies with the holes in them. The next day when photocopies of Meyer's expense accounts appeared in the newspapers, Brewster called an executive meeting to find out how the leak occurred. Flanagan told him the copies printed in the paper were the ones with the holes that his staff had borrowed. 'Well, call off the meeting,' said Brewster. He knew we knew. He was very brash that way. You'd catch him in something and it wouldn't faze him. He'd just laugh it off.

"He was a very bright guy, Brewster. He wasn't a real crook, he just had that streak of burglary in him. If he hadn't, he'd have been a hell of a senator. One of the brightest guys in the Senate. But everything he did was conspiratorial. If you could walk in the front door, he'd sneak in the back window. He was that kind of guy."[28]

For weeks Hughes remained silent while the scandalous revelations made headlines. But this apparent passivity in the face of attack by his enemies was misleading. Behind the scenes he was using his wealth, connections, and cunning to lay the groundwork for his coming offensive.

After striking out with Flanagan in March, Hughes had telephoned Hugh Fulton, the former chief counsel for the Investigating Committee who had been replaced by George Meader. Hughes told Fulton that when he had appeared in Washington he had not believed that he needed counsel, because he had thought that the committee was concerned only with the engineering aspects of his aircraft contract with the government, and that he had felt perfectly competent to handle any inquiries along that line himself. Hughes was confident that that kind of an investigation would disclose creditable performance on his part. But after Flanagan had contacted him in Los Angeles and requested Johnny Meyer's expense account, he became convinced that the Committee was out to smear him.[29]

Fulton thereafter reported to Brewster that: "It was Hughes's contention that the Committee's investigation of the aircraft contracts was being utilized in behalf of Pan American Airways and the proponents of the Chosen Instrument Bill; that Hughes was aware of a close association between Senator Brewster and Pan American Airways, including entertainment of Senator Brewster by Pan American Airways without charge to Senator Brewster; and that in the event of a public hearing which exposed the relationship between Howard Hughes, Brigadier General Elliott Roosevelt, and certain entertainment of General Roosevelt by Hughes and representatives of the Hughes Tool Company, it would be Hughes's intention to counterattack by exposing relationships between Senator Brewster and Pan American Airways.[30]

According to Fulton, Brewster was incensed at the suggestion and stated that the investigation was not one which he originated, that it had been developed by Meader and Flanagan and the staff before he was acquainted with it. In fact, Brewster claimed, the investigation had been under consideration by the Committee in one form or another for several years, even back to the time when Fulton was chief counsel. The suggestion that the investigation was related in any way to his advocacy of the Chosen Instrument Bill was incorrect and unwarranted, he claimed, and his attitude toward the progress of the investigation would not be in any way influenced by the fact that such a suggestion had been made.

Fulton reported the results of this conversation to Hughes by telegram.[31]

On Easter Sunday, Hughes called Fulton again and asked that he represent him in connection with the Committee's investigation. Hughes told Fulton that he was convinced that the Committee was out to smear him. Fulton (according to his statement to Meader) accepted employment only in the limited sense of ascertaining whether or not some means could be found to avoid the sensational aspects of public exploration of entertainment activities and leave in abeyance the question of whether or not he would represent Hughes in any critical investigation conducted by the Committee in case his primary effort was unsuccessful.

On April 8, Fulton sent Rudolf Halley, his law partner and the former associate counsel and chief counsel to the Investigating Committee, to Los Angeles. Halley apparently reported that Noah Dietrich still did not believe that the investigation amounted to very much and thought that Hughes was unnecessarily excited about it. However, Halley seemed to think the case was pretty bad for Hughes.

Fulton told Meader that if the Committee seemed determined to go into a full and complete public examination of Hughes's affairs—including transportation and entertainment furnished to public officials—he would be inclined to represent Hughes. He said further that he was inclined to concur in Hughes's strategy of defending himself by counterattacking on the grounds that this was a political investigation to smear the Democrats, Hughes, and Elliott Roosevelt to the detriment of Transcontinental and Western Airlines and to the advantage of Pan American Airways, and to attack Senator Brewster's association with Pan American Airways.

163

Meader wrote in his memorandum of the event that "Fulton stated that his only reason for discussing the matter with me was to apprise me fully of all the circumstances and to caution me that in the event of a hot public controversy, I should bear in mind that I might be in the thick of it with brickbats flying."[32]

Meader replied to Fulton's monologue by saying that Hughes had brought on what publicity had already attended the investigation by rushing to Washington and insisting on speaking to the senators themselves. This resulted in an executive hearing on which there was some publicity. Hughes's attempt to control the way the Committee conducted the investigation by stating the terms on which his files would be made available to Flanagan resulted in the Committee's decision to issue a subpoena. This subpoena was announced to the press by Senator Brewster.

Meader thought Hughes had been ill-advised in these actions, "since the staff had simply been conducting a preliminary investigation, as we have done on a great number of matters which have never been mentioned publicly and concerning which we have not been in the practice of releasing any information to the public until the preliminary investigation was substantially completed." Fulton told Meader that he agreed and that if he had been Hughes's counsel he would have advised him against such actions.[33]

Hughes Foxes the Committee

This was how Fulton and Halley, with their insiders' knowledge of Committee procedures and of the disposition of potential cases against Pan American which Brewster had quietly shelved, came into the employ of Howard Hughes.

Hughes also hired investigators to dig up evidence of Brewster's close connections with Pan American and of his acceptance of gifts and favors. In addition, he sent Johnny Meyer on an extended trip around South America and to Europe to uncover evidence of Pan American largess to the Brewsters during their trips abroad. Finally, he contacted journalists and publishers who might help him in his fight.

One important ally was Drew Pearson, Washington gadfly and muckraking columnist whose "Washington Merry-Go-Round" was widely read and much feared. Pearson had long inveighed against Pan American Airways for wielding such political influence that it was supported by taxpayers' subsidies and protected by exclusive government franchises. Pearson also bore a particular animus toward Brewster, whom he called "the kept Senator of Pan American Airways."[34]

Pearson and his assistant, Jack Anderson, provided Hughes with tactical advice on dealing with inquisitorial senators, as well as information from their sources that might be of help to Hughes. For his part, Hughes gave them information that he had gleaned from his own intelligence network. Pearson ingeniously wove the anti-Brewster material into his columns, ostensibly praising Brewster for his work but adding that it stopped short of investigating Pan American.[35]

William Randolph Hearst became another important ally. Right after the public hearings into Hughes's two contracts opened in Washington on July 28, Hearst's *Los Angeles Examiner* published a copyrighted open letter from Hughes to Brewster that was carried in Hearst papers throughout the country and reprinted by other major papers. After days of public silence while the press ran sensational stories about his lobbying activities and Brewster's version of his role in the unfolding melodrama, Hughes was at last striking back—and hard. All the bits and pieces of information that he had developed during the past six months now fell into place.

"You know, Senator," he wrote, "if you hadn't gone too far overboard, I might have been willing to take a certain shellacking in this publicity spree of yours.

"Yes, I might have been willing to sit back and take a certain amount of abuse simply because I am only a private citizen while you are a Senator with all sorts of rights and powers to subpoena me, make me drop my work, and travel 2,500 miles back there to Washington and otherwise cause me no end of inconvenience.

"So I sat back and let you do the talking for five days."

The open letter continued in this vein for some paragraphs, making the points that Hughes was not a politician but an ordinary citizen, and that he had been in the airplane business for thirteen years and lost $14,000,000 ("So I don't think I have been defrauding the Government"). Then he moved from defense to attack.

"Why not tell the whole truth?" he challenged. "Why not tell when this investigation was really born?

"Why not tell that this investigation was really born on the day that TWA (Trans World Airline) first flew the Atlantic? On the day when TWA first invaded Juan Trippe's territory—on the day when TWA first challenged the generally accepted theory that only Juan Trippe's great Pan American Airways had the sacred right to fly the Atlantic?

"And why not tell about my answer: That I would have to think it over for thirty days, and that I would let Trippe know at the end of that time?

"And why not tell about Mr. Trippe's flight to the Coast to see me, and how Mr. Trippe and Mr. Dietrich and I spent two days at Palm Springs, Calif. [April 12 and 13, 1947], and why not tell what we were talking about for those two days? (Noah Dietrich is executive vice president of the Hughes Tool Company.)

"And while you are at it, Senator, why not tell about the two airplane trips you bummed off of me?"[36]

On July 30, Hughes issued a statement to the press that directed four questions at Senator Brewster and demanded an answer: "1. At lunch in your suite at the Mayflower Hotel, Washington, D.C. did you or did you not offer to call off this entire investigation if I would agree to merge TWA with Pan American Airways and support your community airline bill? 2. Did I or did I not reply that I had already promised Juan Trippe that I would give him my answer in thirty days? 3. And did Juan Trippe subsequently make a flight across the country to see me, and spend two days closeted in secret conference with me at Palm Springs, Calif., or did he not? 4. And when you returned from Europe thereafter, did Juan Trippe tell you to hold up and not push this investigation for a while, as he and I were still trying to get together, or did he not?"[37]

Each day brought new press statements as Hughes delayed appearing in

Washington in defiance of requests to do so by Sen. Homer Ferguson (who had taken over as chairman of the subcommittee set up at the request of Sen. Taft to handle the investigation so that Brewster would be free to answer Hughes's charges as a private citizen). "It is a sad situation when a United States Senator has to drag a lot of innocent girls into a Congressional hearing in order to achieve personal publicity," Hughes stated on July 31. His reference to "a lot of innocent girls" apparently was prompted by the subpoenas issued for Judy Cook, a swimmer, and Martha Goldwaite, a model.[38]

Hughes also attacked committee demands that he rush to Washington. "So far I have not had more than two hours sleep for the last week which as you know was one of the hottest in history. In addition, I have not completely recovered from my accident of last year. So it was under these circumstances that Senator Ferguson called me on the phone yesterday afternoon at 5:30 p.m. and told me to appear in Washington before his committee this morning at 10 a.m. I simply replied that under the circumstances I refused to jump through a hoop like a trained seal and fly all night and appear the next morning without any sleep to testify all day on a most important matter. I am a little tired of being pushed around and intimidated by Senators Brewster and Ferguson just because they have some very strong powers which are granted to all Senators but which were not intended to be misused for the promotion of a three-ring publicity circus."[39]

Ferguson's response to Hughes's foot-dragging and newspaper salvos from the sidelines was to sign a subpoena for his appearance to be delivered to Hughes in California the following day, Friday, August 1. Hughes, however, held to the original date set for his appearance. In Los Angeles he stated that he would be in Washington the next Wednesday to answer questions, and that pressure of business would prevent his going there until then.[40]

Drew Pearson had advised Hughes that he could not win just through lawyers, columnists, and PR men; neither could he ride out the storm unscathed by lying low. Although the basic ingredients of public sympathy lay on his side, Pearson observed he would have to come out of seclusion and face the lions personally.[41]

Hughes agreed, and his own experience as a moviemaker prompted him to cultivate the mystique of the western hero who, armed with moral right, rides alone into a town controlled by his enemies for a confrontation at high noon—or of an average citizen who singlehandedly takes on powerful and corrupt elements of the establishment as in *Mr. Smith Goes to Washington*.

Hughes also slyly cultivated the underdog image: "Juan Trippe and Brewster made it very clear to me that they only needed TWA in order to put their community company airline bill through Congress and make it a law. They could shove it down the throats of the other overseas airlines if they could just get TWA on their team. Then Juan Trippe, who already has the biggest airline in the world, would wind up with a complete monopoly, automatically and quite legally, putting all the smaller airlines out of business and taking over their routes and airplanes."[42]

As U.S. Marshals sought to deliver Ferguson's subpoena into Hughes's hands,

Hughes disappeared from public view. Everyday Americans were tickled by Hughes's defiance and by the committee's inability to find him; public interest in his every word and action increased. Moreover, the committee, having to put on a show every day, would soon run through the lesser witnesses, thereby clearing the stage for the climactic event: Hughes's face-to-face confrontation with Senator Brewster.

Columnist Jack Anderson later noted another significant factor: the passing of time lessened the risk that Hughes would be trivialized by a joint appearance with clown prince Johnny Meyer because the effective period of Meyer's subpoena was fast running out.[43]

In the meantime, a confident Brewster in an August 3 radio interview taunted Hughes, saying that he hoped to expose "the whites of his lies."[44]

Enterprising newsmen kept watch on Hughes's B-23 at Burbank Airport hoping to spot Hughes when he left for Washington, so Hughes called Odekirk. "Odie, you fly the B-23 to Culver City. That way I can leave when I want without being bothered by anybody."

When watchers saw the B-23 take off, they checked with the tower.

"Who flew that plane out of here?"

"I don't know," said the controller.

"Well, did it sound like Howard Hughes?" The controller did not think that it did. As the plane climbed out of Burbank, Odekirk banked to the east as a diversionary maneuver. He later swung around to drop down unobtrusively and land on the Hughes Aircraft Company's long private runway.[45]

On Monday night, August 4, Hughes materialized briefly in Las Vegas and spent several hours in the public rooms of the Last Frontier. The next day at 2:32 p.m. Pacific Standard Time, he, flight engineer Earl Martyn, and his two bodyguards took off from Culver City for the long flight to Washington. U. S. Marshal Robert Clark ruefully admitted that the subpoena was still undelivered.

"He ducked," he said.[46]

Howard Hughes listening very attentively in the Senate Sub-committee hearings in Washington, D.C. on August 7, 1947.

10

The Hearings

IT WAS NOT A RESTFUL FLIGHT to Washington. Lightning flashed in a line of thunderstorms ahead. Hughes, who had rested in the pilot's seat while Earl Martyn maintained course and altitude, tightened his seat belt, took the controls, and peered intently into the blackness. Carefully he noted the location of each flash, flicker, and flare as indicators of the really heavy turbulence. As he watched he adjusted his heading so as to pass between what appeared to be the more violent areas. At one point Martyn helped him even up the engine power for best penetration speed—a judicious compromise between being too fast and risking structural failure when the plane slammed into the boiling violence of the storm, or of being too slow and stalling out of control in a sudden lull between gusts.

The first rain spattered the windshield. A flare of lightning revealed a tumbled mass of cloud towering above them and the plane shuddered as it hit the initial stirrings in the air. Then a jolting upward surge slammed them into their seats and lifted the plane with a force that flexed the wings. The plane grunted as though hit by a giant.

Almost immediately, a sickening roller coaster drop lifted them against their belts. Boiling currents of air rocked and buffetted the plane, boosting it at 2,000 feet per minute one moment and then dropping it at 2,000 feet per minute the next. Smoothly but firmly, Hughes moved his controls in response to the glowing needles and dials of his flight instruments, striving to approximate a level attitude so that the airspeed would stay within safe limits. Smooth handling was important. Roughness on the controls could combine with gust loads to cause structural failure. Lightning flashed around them. Little snakes of St. Elmo's fire danced along the edges of the windshield. The prop arcs were rimmed with blue fire. Rain impacted on the windshield and aluminum skin with a sustained tinny roar.

Martyn went back to check on their two passengers. It was cold in the cabin and the two guards huddled in their seats near the tail of the plane.

"Come on up in the cockpit where it's warm and sit," said Martyn.

The whites of the men's eyes shone in a flare of lightning. "No, we'll stay here," one said.[1]

Soon they passed into better weather, but before the night was over there would be more.

The First Day

By daylight the storms were behind them. The weather was clear as they descended across the Georgetown Homer, a holding fix for aircraft waiting their turn for instrument approaches to Washington National Airport during bad weather. Washington Tower cleared them for an immediate visual approach to runway 18.

Hughes lowered the landing gear as they crossed over the Memorial Bridge not yet crowded by rush-hour traffic, made a shallow right turn to the runway heading as they passed over the 14th Street Bridge, followed by his usual smooth touchdown. Turning off the runway, he taxied immediately to the TWA parking ramp.

After braking to a stop and shutting down the engines, he jackknifed his tall frame through the aft door of the B-23 and half-jumped to the ground, skipping the bottom step of the short metal entrance ladder that hung from the door sill. He was wearing his usual hat, brim snapped down in front, a white dress shirt open at the neck, and a grey double-breasted suit with coat unbuttoned. Grim faced, he strode purposefully past the cameras.[2]

"There was a whole crowd of people there yelling for him," recalls Earl Martyn. "I guess they knew he was coming."[3] Noah Dietrich, who had met the plane, maneuvered Hughes into a waiting car, and they headed for the Carlton Hotel.

Hughes had promised to appear before the committee at ten that morning, but he was exhausted. "Noah, I've got to get some rest. Ask them to postpone the hearing until afternoon."[4]

At 10 a.m. in the caucus room of the Senate Office Building, when Senator Homer Ferguson called the committee's morning session to order, Hughes's attorney, Thomas A. Slack of Houston, asked to be heard. "I wanted to tell this committee," he said, "that pursuant to its request, Mr. Hughes is here and ready and anxious to testify before the committee whenever it suits the convenience of the committee."

Ferguson observed that "here" must mean in Washington "rather than present in this room."

Slack replied smoothly. "Last night we read in the press that you had issued the statement that Mr. Hughes would not be used this morning, that he would have to await the finishing of testimony of other witnesses, and may I say that it was on my own suggestion that I make this announcement to you, and that Mr. Hughes is awaiting your pleasure and he will be available on your request at any time."[5]

This left Ferguson little option but to say that "rather than delay until he gets here we will proceed with this morning's proceedings . . . and then recess for an early afternoon session at which time Mr. Hughes will be called as the first witness."

This gave Hughes an initial advantage. Rather than having to wait for Johnny Meyer and Roy H. Sherwood, the assistant comptroller of the Hughes Aircraft Company, to finish their testimony, he could enter as the star attraction for whom everyone was waiting. He derived further psychological advantage by arriving forty-two minutes late for the afternoon session, which had been scheduled for two o'clock.[6]

At 2:15 p.m., Senator Ferguson, grandfatherly with his white hair, round cherubic face, and rimless glasses, banged the gavel and called the committee to order. "I want to announce that Mr. Hughes will be here at two-thirty when the session will start, and I will put on the record now a memorandum that has been handed me by the War Department. . . ."[7] With that business concluded, he again recessed the Committee to await the arrival of "Mr. Hughes."

While the members of the Committee idled at their places, the waiting spectators, who were jammed into the high-ceilinged, chandelier-lit caucus room, eyed the great oak entrance doors expectantly. As the time ticked on, senatorial majesty wilted; but for the spectators the approaching moment of Hughes's entrance became even more dramatic.

William P. Rogers, new Chief Counsel for the Committee, turned to Slack.

"Tom, what the hell is he doing?"

"Well, the last time I saw him he was sitting on the bed in his hotel room picking his toes," said Slack.[8]

As two-thirty came and passed, Ferguson was visibly restive. "Mr. Slack, what is the latest news from the front?"

"I reported to you the latest news, Senator, that they were leaving right away."[9]

The car carrying Hughes and Dietrich from the Carlton Hotel proceeded up Constitution Avenue toward Capitol Hill, swung left at Delaware Avenue, and stopped at the corner. Newsreel cameramen followed every move.

Hughes got out, tucked a small stack of folders and papers under his left arm, and started walking toward the building. A press photographer stepped into the line of advance as Hughes and his small entourage passed a group of women in light summer dresses who had been waiting on the sidewalk. A flashbulb flashed.

The group proceeded directly across the walk, up the marble steps, and through the main entrance at the southwest corner of the Senate Office Building into the domed rotunda. The route was lined with well-wishers and the curious.

As he approached the massive oak doors of the ornate second floor caucus room, he could see that he was playing to a standing-room-only crowd that trailed out into the corridor and snaked out of sight into the corridors beyond. Loudspeakers had been set up so that those standing in the corridors could follow the testimony given inside the room.

As Hughes entered, the crowd clapped and welcomed him noisily. It was, said *Newsweek*, the biggest circus that had pitched its tent in Washington in many years. Six movie cameras and one television camera whirred. It was the first congressional hearing to be televised and was being watched by five thousand pioneer viewers in Washington and New York.[10]

The Hearing Begins

Senator Ferguson pounded a glass ashtray on the desk. "Let it be known that we must have quiet in the room. Mr. Hughes, will you come to the witness chair, please." The spectators watched the lank, dark-mustached man in a loosely fitting grey suit, his neck sticking out of a too-large collar, as he made his way through the room. Twenty press photographers rushed to surround the witness table. Ferguson continued. "Will you just raise your right hand and be sworn?" Hughes deposited his stack of folders on the table before him and raised his right hand. "Do you solemnly swear that in the matter now pending before this committee, you will tell the truth, the whole truth, and nothing but the truth, so help you God?"

"I do," Hughes said firmly and sat down. He looked darkly at his interrogators. Batteries of microphones for seven radio stations faced him on the witness table as they did the committee at their long table covered with green felt. Since there was no dais, witness and committee faced each other at eye level.

As preliminary questions progressed from name and residence to details of Hughes's business, Hughes said, "Senator, with all this noise and these cameras, I have trouble hearing you. Can we take the pictures first and then go on with the testimony?"

After the pictures were taken, Senator Ferguson said, "It will be understood that there are to be no more camera shots. If there is anybody that has not finished, he had better take it now. All right, Mr. Hughes." Hughes requested more time to review the transcript of previous testimony before he testified on any of the matters covered by that testimony. "Do you have anything else that we could go into that was not covered in this particular memorandum so that . . . we would not lose any time?" Ferguson asked.

"Well, if you have any other material that you want to discuss with me, I would be glad to go ahead with it."

But Ferguson would not take the hint. He felt strongly that the purpose of the hearings was to look into the F-11 and the flying boat contracts, and he wished to avoid or postpone any digression into the "side issue" of Hughes's personal charges against Senator Brewster. "I do not know of any other matters that we could take up except what is covered in this memorandum," he replied. "It covered both the F-11 and the cargo boat."

The audience became restive. Brewster, too, was ready. "May I speak?" he asked from his end of the committee table. With that, the audience—jam-packed fifteen hundred strong into a room meant to hold about one third that number—noisily urged the committee to get on with it.

Ferguson banged his ashtray on the table with exasperation. "Just one moment. I must have quiet in the room. . . . We understand that this is a public business and that people are entitled to come here and to hear the evidence, but we must have quiet and we want no remarks. . . . The officers have been very courteous in allow-ing more than the room would normally accommodate, and that is perfectly all right—but it must be understood that we must have it quiet, and we want no in-terference with either the witness or the committee."[11]

"Now, Senator Brewster, you have asked to be recognized."

Brewster, in his mellow, resonant, senatorial voice, opened the subject everyone was waiting for.

"I think the audience is entitled to a certain amount of consideration," he said, "and I trust that no undue delicacy on the part of the committee will prevent our moving forward. There has been a considerable delay, and I thought that I under-stood Mr. Hughes to say that he might take up, I thought he said, the other matter. Is that correct?"

"I did not hear that, Senator," said Hughes. "Will you repeat it?"

"Senator Brewster said that he understood you to say that you might take up the other matter," said Ferguson.

"Gladly, yes."

Brewster continued, "I can appreciate the committee may not want to begin an inquiry as it presents some problems, but I think that we all here fully realize what the situation is and that if the committee felt it advisable to proceed with certain matters of a somewhat more personal character, it might avoid any further delay in disposing of them . . ."

Ferguson then stated emphatically what he considered to be the real purpose of the hearings and concluded by saying, "It is hoped by the subcommittee that this matter having come up that we would dispose of this issue now, and that we would not have it brought into the various other matters in the hearing; but we would separate it from the real reason for the committee hearing, and that was to look into the letting and the continuation and the cancellation of the two war contracts that we had in mind."[12]

"Now I want to say to you, Mr. Hughes, do you understand what we have in mind?"

"Yes, I think I do," Hughes said evenly. The audience laughed.

"So, it is your desire, is it, Mr. Hughes, at the present time, to go into the matter as to the committee at the present time, or one of its members?"

"Not my desire, but I am very willing to."

"Then you may proceed. What is it that you want to tell the committee in rela-tion to this side issue, as the committee now sees it?"

"I do not have any particular desire to tell the committee anything. I think the committee is thoroughly familiar with it. I have made certain statements to the press, and I stand by those.

"Senator Brewster has then said that he would like me to repeat those statements under oath. I have no objection to so doing; and I think, however, if I do so, Senator Brewster should take the stand and allow me to cross-examine him and allow me to bring in such other witnesses as I desire, to clarify the issue."

Senator Ferguson bristled. The adversary relationship between Ferguson and Hughes was palpable to everyone in the room. "The subcommittee will not give to Senator Brewster the right to cross-examine you nor will you have the right to cross-examine Senator Brewster. . . . If there are any questions you or your counsel have, if you will submit them to the committee, then we will ask those questions. . . ."[13]

"Well, I only want the same privileges; however, it should be thoroughly understood that any questioning of me which you people carry out is in the nature of cross-examination, if the questions are directed from an unfriendly standpoint. Now, I think that I should have the same privilege with respect to Senator Brewster."

"Do you have any unfriendly questions up to date here?"

"Not at all."

"All right."

"Then, as I understand it, you want me to tell in direct testimony approximately what happened and then the Senator is going to tell what he says happened, and then you are going to ask me certain questions, and I shall have the right to ask him; is that correct?"

"That is right, through the committee."

"Will I have the right to call on such other witnesses as I deem desirable?"

"We will rule on that as you request them. . . ."

"Well, Senator, I do not desire to launch into this matter and then have my hands tied."

"Now, Mr. Hughes, as far as the Chair can do, you will not have your hands tied. It is not desire of the committee to bring a citizen in here and tie his hands and he has not a fair hearing. . . . If at the close of this hearing, you will tell us what witnesses you desire, the committee will then make a decision. . . ."

"Well, I am willing to proceed on that basis. What is the first step?"

"Well, what do you have to say about this matter that we have been discussing?"

"I think my charges have been made pretty clear in the press. Do you want me to reiterate them?"

"They are not part of the record, and it is the desire of the committee, if any statements are made, that they be made here under oath and not through the medium of the press."

"Well," Hughes said, "I charge specifically that during a luncheon in the Mayflower Hotel with Senator Brewster, during the week commencing February 10, 1947, the Senator in so many words told me that if I would agree to merge TWA with Pan American Airways and go along on his community airline bill, there would be no further hearing in this matter."[14] He spoke in a rather flat, nasal tone, occasionally clearing his throat or saying "ah" between the phrases that he uttered in a matter-of-fact, unhurried way.[15] Then he stopped as though he had said all there was to say.

174

After a few questions to determine that the Mayflower luncheon had taken place after Hughes had testified at the executive session of February 11, Ferguson said, "All right. Now will you proceed?"

"Well, I have made my statement, Senator. Do you want me to amplify it?"

"Whatever took place, we would like to have it as full as possible, of your own knowledge."

"I think that I have told you what took place."

"Is there anything else that you want to discuss?"

"I thought Senator Brewster wanted to talk after that." There was a long pause. Hughes looked at Senator Brewster. The gaze of the audience swung from one to the other as if watching the challenge to a gun fight.

After some further questioning regarding Hughes's contacts with Senator Brewster, Juan Trippe, and Flanagan, Senator Ferguson asked Hughes, "Is that what you have to say on this side issue, or the outside issue that the subcommittee has before it?"

Hughes replied, "I think that is substantially it."[16]

Ferguson then turned to Brewster. "Senator Brewster, do you desire to take the stand?"

"Yes; I certainly do desire to take the stand."

Senator Ralph Owen Brewster (for some reason he preferred the name Owen to Ralph) was not a handsome man. The forepart of his head was billiard-bald. His meaty lower lip protruded slightly as though stuffed with chewing tobacco. But he carried himself as a confident man moving in familiar surroundings and among friends. After being sworn in, he took his seat at the witness table facing the committee. Hughes sat right behind him listening intently, occasionally shaking his head or snorting in disbelief.

Brewster projected the image of a reasonable man as he reviewed the history of the investigation. The committee had been interested in the Hughes contracts since Harry Truman had been chairman. The committee had given the contracts time to be vindicated. They had not been. What had happened to the eighteen million dollars poured into the cargo plane? As to Hughes's charges against him, it was Hughes, not he, who had suggested flying him to his speaking engagements so that he could meet with Hughes in Washington. It was Hughes, not he, who raised the subject of TWA merging with Pan American. Except for taking a demonstration ride with Hughes in the new Constellation several years before, Brewster had first met Hughes only two days before the alleged blackmail threat. "It is inconceivable to me," Brewster said, "that anyone would seriously contemplate that anyone who has been in public life as long as I have—in the state legislature, as governor, in the House and Senate—could, on such short acquaintance and in one short meeting, make so bald a proposition as he describes. It sounds more like Hollywood than Washington. No one of any competence or experience could make such a proposition. I can assure you I never did."[17]

It was a good point. It did seem unlikely that an old pro like Brewster would at first private meeting make such an offer to a dangerous stranger like Hughes.

Then Brewster told about the Fulton visit. "That reveals pretty clearly that they were seeking to lay a trap for me," Brewster said in a voice broken by deep emotion.

Brewster concluded his statement in a strong, resonant voice. "I promptly appointed a subcommittee headed by Senator Ferguson to handle this matter and let the chips fall where they may. I cannot and will not yield to a campaign of this character."

It should be noted at this point that the setting up of the subcommittee was not at Brewster's request. Rogers and Flanagan were concerned about how Brewster was handling himself. Fearing that damage to the committee's reputation might prejudice the case they were building against General Benny Meyers, they went to Ferguson and urged that he ask Senator Robert Taft, the majority leader, to remove Brewster from the committee.

"He's going to wreck the Senate's reputation, himself, and everyone connected with him," they said.

Ferguson discussed this matter with Taft who thereupon ordered Brewster to remove himself from the committee.[18]

After Brewster had made his statement, he was questioned briefly by Senator Ferguson in a manner tending to reinforce Brewster's side of the story. Then Ferguson said, "Mr. Hughes, I wanted to ask you now—rather, first I want to ask Senator Brewster whether he has any questions for Mr. Hughes, and Mr. Hughes, do you have any questions for Senator Brewster? If so, I would like to know."

Hughes replied, "You asked me if I have any questions. Yes, somewhere between two and five hundred. Can we get started on them?"

Senator Ferguson: "I beg your pardon?"

"I have between two and five hundred questions that I would like to ask him."

"Between two hundred and five hundred questions?"

"Just about."

"When can you submit those to the committee?"

"I will have to submit them as we go along; one would be predicated upon his answer of a previous."

Ferguson wasn't buying any of that. "I will ask both sides of this controversy to submit questions to the committee chairman at nine-fifteen tomorrow morning. . . . All questions will be in writing and submitted at that time."

Morning of the Second Day

Thursday morning, August 7, was hot and humid; this added to Senator Ferguson's discomfiture. A bad case of poison ivy on his feet made him irritable, and he was deeply annoyed with Howard Hughes and with the turn the conduct of the investigation had taken. It was not going at all like his one-man grand jury investigation he had conducted as a Michigan judge. That investigation had sent a Wayne County prosecutor, the immediate ex-mayor of Detroit, numerous police officials, and underworld figures to jail. But here, he and Brewster had tangled with a hawk with fierce eyes and sharp talons, eager to attack his captors.

Hughes's demeanor clearly indicated that he had come to make charges, not to answer them. If Ferguson didn't pull the reins taut this very morning his partial surrender of control over the hearings would become complete. Clearly, both he and the dignity of the Senate were being challenged.

As the last act of the previous day's session, he had made the procedure of submitting written questions a clear and explicit part of the record, specifying that such questions were to be submitted by 9:15 this morning. *Not one question was submitted.* With this in mind, Ferguson banged his gavel and called the committee to order.

"I will now ask, notwithstanding the fact that they have not been submitted, are there any questions upon your part, Mr. Hughes? . . . Do you have any written questions that you now desire to give to this subcommittee?"

In response, Hughes started to address Senator Brewster directly. "Senator Brewster, I would like to say—"

Ferguson quickly cut him off. "Just a moment."

Hughes turned to Ferguson. "Senator Ferguson, may I make a very brief statement of my feeling in this matter?"

Ferguson's exasperation and anger showed; he spoke very loudly. "I would like first to ask you this question: Do you have—and you will pardon me for speaking loud because I understand you have difficulty hearing—any questions in writing that you desire the subcommittee to ask Senator Brewster?"

"Senator Ferguson, I have, yes, one question that I will submit to start with. Now, last evening I tried to make my position very clear that it would be impossible for me to submit in advance all of the questions that I wished to ask Senator Brewster, because each question would be predicated upon his answer of the one before."

"We have given the forum to you and to Senator Brewster on this particular side . . . and we want to be courteous and we want to have both of you feel that you have had a fair hearing on the matter, but we cannot change the rules of the committee. . . . Do you have any questions to submit to the committee? This thing could go on for weeks if we are to have questions submitted in that manner, that you now ask us to do. Do you have any questions?"

"I believe that I answered that, Senator Ferguson."

"Will you just pass them to the chair?"

"Well, Senator, may I refer—"

"Now, we are going to get this thing settled. Do you or do you not have any questions? . . ."

"Yes; I have some questions."

"Then pass them to the chair."[19]

After more bickering Hughes's angry voice cracked like a whiplash as he emphasized each reference to Brewster with a short jabbing gesture toward him with the sheaf of papers clutched in his right hand. "I will submit these questions, but I want to make it very clear that these are not all of the questions that I desire to ask Senator Brewster, and furthermore, that when I entered into this controversy yesterday I was assured that I would be allowed to cross-question through the committee, that I could ask you questions, and you in turn could ask them of Senator Brewster. Now Senator Brewster's story as related here yesterday is a pack of lies, and I can tear it apart if allowed to cross-question him, and it is unfair to place me in the position of having my integrity questioned, and not being allowed to cross-examine Senator Brewster."[20]

Ferguson, somewhat taken aback by the vehemence of Hughes's attack, held firm. "You understood, and the record is clear, that you could submit questions through the committee. Now, have you any questions?"

"Yes; but these are the preliminary questions and not all of them by any means. . . . I cannot write the questions before I know Senator Brewster's answers. How can anyone cross-examine a witness if he is not allowed to ask questions predicated upon the answers given?"

Ferguson still held his ground saying that the committee was going to rule on the matter and "we are going to control the hearing."

At one point, Senator Ferguson turned to the press table and said, *sotto voce*: "He's a hard man to be nice to."

Hughes persisted. "May I ask you something, Senator Ferguson?"

"Not at the present time, until we go over these questions."

"May I make one very brief statement, please? Yesterday you told me that I would be accorded the same privilege as the Senator from Maine or anyone else here. Now, will you give me the questions in advance that you want to ask me while I am here, or will you give them to any third neutral party? Is it not true that you are going to propound the questions for me as I testify, and based upon what I testify as I go along? Are you willing to set aside the questions in advance which you will ask me?"

With that there were loud cheers and applause from the audience. A red-faced Ferguson tried to regain control. "The officers will clear the room except for the press. We are going to run this hearing properly."

Hughes spoke in an aside to the audience. "I want to say that I thank you, and at least I realize the people want to see fair play here."[21]

Above the tumult the voice of a young college student rang out: "I speak for the audience. We will be quiet. As American citizens we would like to hear this because—" Guards pounced on the student.[22]

Senator Ferguson, surveying the disorder with dismay, intervened. "He said he would be quiet. Do not remove him for saying he would be quiet."[23] When order was restored, the committee reviewed the questions submitted by Hughes and decided to ask them in the form in which they were presented except for the two last ones, the substance of which would be asked. Photographers closed in, cameras ready, as Senator Brewster again took the stand. Bulbs flashed and shutters clicked.

"Just as soon as the photographers are through," said Ferguson, "the committee will come to order."

As the cameramen drew back, Brewster made some preliminary comment. After a brief interchange between Ferguson and Brewster, Ferguson began asking Hughes's written questions one by one.

"Is it not true that you are a personal friend of Juan Trippe, president of Pan American Airways?"

"I have known Mr. Trippe for the past four or five years perhaps. . . . I think that I have had two dinners at which I was a guest of Mr. Trippe, once in his apartment in New York. Mrs. Brewster was present with me. And once in his country home in Connecticut where I stopped on the way home and had dinner with him . . ."

Ferguson looked at the paper in front of him and continued. "The next question submitted by Mr. Hughes: 'Is it not true that you are a close personal friend of Sam Pryor?' " Pryor was vice president of Pan American Airways.

"That certainly is true. I have been a close personal friend of his for a good many years."

Ferguson continued down Hughes's list without comment. "Is it not true that you are a close personal friend of Bill McEvoy, and what is his position?"

". . . I know Bill McEvoy, who is also a vice president of Pan American, and my associations with him have always been very pleasant, but very limited. . . ."

"Have you ever been a guest of Mr. Pryor, and partaken of his hospitality at his home in Florida?"

". . . Twice, I think in the last two years, Mrs. Brewster and I occupied for one week this small place which he has there of five rooms." Brewster went on chattily: "Mr. and Mrs. Pryor were not there. We had the exclusive occupancy and I hired a cook, whom I paid $5 a day, and I went over to the grocery store and bought the groceries, and the Thanksgiving turkey and I left the place pretty well stocked up, when I got through, with canned goods, as a sort of an expression of my appreciation for what had gone on."

"The next question submitted by Mr. Hughes is, 'Have you ever accepted free airplane trips from Pan American Airways in their special private airplane?' "

"I have."

"The next question is, 'Have you accepted such transportation to Raleigh, N.C.?' "

"I did."

"The next question submitted by Mr. Hughes is, 'What was the purpose of your visit there?' "

Senator Brewster's air of confidence, which had steadily evaporated as he realized the cumulative effects of his admissions, was replaced by a worried look. "I went down there to confer with Senator Bailey, who was ill, in connection with the community airline bill which was then pending before the committee, and it was necessary to determine what our procedure would be."

"The next question submitted by Mr. Hughes: 'Have you accepted free airplane trips in this same ship to Hobe Sound, Florida?' "

"Well, I may have . . ."

There were other questions. Step by step they led to Hughes's key questions: "Is it not true, Senator, that by virtue of this powerful position as chairman of this committee you held a whiphandle in one hand which you could easily use to the embarrassment of Howard Hughes, while with the other hand you wanted from him his support of the community airline bill, or the removal of his opposition to it?"

Brewster denied that he had the whip hand, that a chairman could control the actions of the committee.

"The next question submitted by Mr. Hughes is, 'Now, Senator, are you going to ask the public to believe that having this unique position you did not use the whip that was in your hand to try and extract from Howard Hughes the things that you wanted so badly?' " Ferguson apologized for the question and said, "The question is poorly framed, but we ask it exactly in the language that it is given in."

Brewster said the question challenged his good faith and the committee and the public would have to judge that from his record. But he made the point that the transcript of the March telephone conversation between Hughes and himself "does not sound to me in terms of anybody cracking a whip or making threats."

Ferguson went on to another question. " 'While occupying this unique position, did you or did you not lobby with Howard Hughes or attempt to sell him your community airline bill?' "

Brewster had to admit that he had discussed this matter with Hughes.[24]

All in all, the questioning did not go well for Senator Brewster. He minimized the amount and the frequency of favors he had received and attributed them to personal friendship divorced from politics. But the image that emerged was that he had close personal relationships with those who had the most to gain from Hughes's downfall: that while sponsoring a bill that would give Pan American a worldwide monopoly supported and enforced by the United States Government, he accepted free transportation from that company in order to promote the bill.

Despite these gains Hughes continued to attack vigorously. Ferguson had failed to follow up on the implications of Brewster's answers. "I have many other questions," he said, "but I do not see any point of submitting them in this manner. I think that Senator Brewster's statements were evasive, and in many cases it was not possible to get a direct answer, and I think that submitting the questions in advance this way and having them asked and never having his reply challenged by the chairman in any way, just accepting the answers on every occasion, is unsatisfactory, so I shan't submit any further in this way."

Ferguson said that the chair had not seen fit to change the questions or to challenge them in any way. "If there are no other questions, this phase of this particular hearing—the phase in relation to questions upon the part of Mr. Hughes . . .—that phase of the hearing is closed."[25]

At this point, Hughes's hostility, his refusal to accord the respect that senators ordinarily take for granted, his efforts to run the hearings his way, had so exasperated Ferguson that even the suggestion for a lunch break became a matter for argument. At about 12:25 p.m. Hughes said, "May we have a slight recess for me to get my material together here? It is lunchtime anyway."

Ferguson snapped back, "Well, again, you are trying to tell the committee what it should do." Nevertheless, the subcommittee recessed to reconvene at 1:30 p.m.[26]

Afternoon of the Second Day

Hughes began his afternoon testimony by saying that the public had witnessed "two men getting up here under oath and telling things which were quite contrary to one another. . . . Now, I believe that when you buy something you generally examine the reputation of the merchant, and I think that in deciding which one of us was telling the truth yesterday our reputations should be examined at least to some degree. . . . Now, I may be a little unkind in what I am going to say, but I shall also be unkind in the appraisal of my own reputation. I understand that Senator Brewster has the reputation of being clever, resourceful, a terrific public speaker, a man who can hold an audience in the palm of his hand, and that he has the reputation of being one of the greatest trick-shot artists in Washington, one of the most high-powered behind the scenes.

"Now, let us examine my reputation. I am supposed to be many things which are not complimentary. I am supposed to be capricious. I have been called a playboy, and I have been called eccentric, but I do not believe that I have the reputation of being a liar. For twenty-three years nobody has questioned my word. I think my reputation in that respect meets what most Texans consider important.

"Now, the statements I made on the stand here yesterday were true. I tried not to say anything which was a half-truth. I tried not to make any statements of which I was uncertain. . . . A man who carefully and diligently tries to tell only what he is certain of, that man should be believed before a man who makes certain obvious misstatements.

"Now, since the beginning of this affair, Senator Brewster has made a number of misstatements which are obviously untrue. One of these was his statement that he has no direct or indirect connection with Pan American Airways. Now most people in the aviation industry know that statement is untrue; and in Senator Brewster's testimony here this morning, he admitted a close relationship with Sam Pryor, the vice president of Pan American. . . . Now, I maintain that if Senator Brewster makes one statement which is known to be untrue, there certainly should be some considerable doubt attached to the other statements he has made."[27]

Hughes continued in a similar vein and was interrupted by Senator Brewster. "Mr. Chairman—I would simply like to make a point if I may, and I do not know whether you call it a point of order."

"You may."

"In what Mr. Hughes is now stating, he is reading from a prepared statement, and I think that it may be important at some point to determine whether or not these are the words of Mr. Carl Byoir, publicity manager formerly of German interests in this country and now acting as the publicity representative for Mr. Hughes. I would very much prefer to hear Mr. Hughes's testimony here rather than the voice of Mr. Byoir."

At this point, as he was to do increasingly during the rest of the hearing, Senator Claude Pepper, Democratic senator from Florida, objected strongly. "Mr. Chairman, I protest. Senator Brewster has no more right, since he has put himself in the position of a private individual, to interrupt Mr. Hughes's statement and to impute to him the influence of somebody else, than Mr. Hughes would have to interrupt him, which he did not do."[28]

Ferguson, however, ruled that the inquiry could and should be considered as a question. Hughes responded, "I will gladly state under oath that the document I have read thus far is in my own handwriting, scribbled mostly during the luncheon period." The reference to "German interests" was a rather under-handed way of attacking Hughes's testimony and further tarnished Brewster's image.

As Ferguson continued to question Hughes about his activities before and after the alleged blackmail threat, he frequently interrupted Hughes's responses. Finally, Hughes said, "Well, Senator, it is hard for me to swing from one thing to another. Now I am trying to make a point here, and Senator Brewster was not interrupted."

"Now, Mr. Hughes, I think we might as well make this thing clear right now . . . you are trying to discredit the committee so that it cannot properly carry out its functions. . . . It is obvious that you are trying to take control of the Senate hearings. If you believe that because you have great wealth and access to certain publicity channels, and therefore you can intimidate any member of the subcommittee, I want to advise you, Mr. Hughes, that you are mistaken, and that is final. . . . This extraneous matter, and your contempt for this committee, will not affect or cloud the real issue. This committee intends to carry out its functions. Now, is it clear?"[29]

Senator Pepper sided once again with Hughes. "Just allow me, as a member of the committee, to make an observation at this point," he said. "The chairman has evidently been reading from a prepared, typewritten statement which was supposed to be elicited by an incident that occurred just before the chairman made the statement, so it must have been that the typewritten statement . . . was prepared at some time prior to the time the incident occurred.

"Furthermore, I am authorized to say on behalf of the minority members of this committee, who are present, that . . . he does not speak for all of the members of the committee in making the charge against the witness, and it is not necessary, probably, to resort to recrimination and countercharge properly to conduct with appropriate decorum the hearings which we are now engaging in."[30]

But Ferguson was angry and would not be put off. "The chair has decided, and this is definitely final, that we are not going off in a side issue which was started, Mr. Hughes, by you, many weeks ago in the press. . . . We are not going to proceed along any such lines."

Slack, Hughes's attorney, tried to get the attention of the chair, "May I?"

"No, you may not," snapped Ferguson.

"Thank you, Senator for your courtesy."

"Mr. Hughes, you may proceed," said Ferguson.

"Senator, I only want to say this," said Hughes. "Number one, I did not suggest bringing this matter into the hearing. Senator Brewster made a statement to the press."

"Mr. Hughes, you started it in the public, so that it would discredit this committee. . . ."

"I deny that."

"What was your motive, Mr. Hughes?"

"I think my motive was very simple."

"What was it?"

"I felt that a great injustice had been done to me, and that I should be allowed to tell my story, and tell my side of it. . . . Before I issued those statements Senator Brewster here had made statements to the press which were absolutely false, one of which was that not even a cotter key had resulted from these contracts. . . . Now, I did not ask to bring this matter into this forum. Senator Brewster asked it. I requested, before going into it, an equal status with him. Now, that has been denied, because I was telling my side of this thing here and I was interrupted, and the Senator was not interrupted."[31]

Again, Ferguson hotly denied that Hughes was not getting equal treatment. Hughes then brought up Brewster's allegations of a "smear campaign."

"While we are talking about smear campaigns, I wonder if it was necessary to bring in a young airline hostess, who was not in any way involved in this matter? . . . The Senator stated to the press that this hostess absolutely refused to accompany us on our trip to Columbus, Ohio, because she did not dare to be alone with me in the airplane on the return flight."

Hughes then submitted affidavits from Harriet Appelwick, hostess, and M. E. Bell, the captain on the TWA plane that brought the senators back from Columbus. They clearly discredited Brewster's story and further substantiated Hughes's characterization of him as a trick-shot artist and a liar.

As the day drew to a close, Ferguson tried to establish a procedure that would wind up the "side issue."

"Senator Brewster has asked for ten minutes," Ferguson told Hughes. "Would you be satisfied to listen for the ten minutes: Then you would have, let us say twenty minutes . . ."

"No sir," said Hughes standing in front of Ferguson watching him intently, his face dark and angry, his left hand fidgeting in his pants pocket. "I am willing to let Senator Brewster have all day if I can cross-examine him."[32]

Press and spectators ringed the committee "like a mob watching a cock-fight."[33] Hughes leaned over supporting himself with arms straight and both hands on the table in front of Ferguson while Ferguson attempted to satisfy Hughes's objections though stopping short of cross-examination.

"I feel that Senator Brewster is not telling the truth," said Hughes angrily. "If I can cross-examine him I think I can prove it. If I do not have that right, I would like to drop the matter right at this point."[34]

Senator Pepper attempted to make peace. Both men, he said, had stated their positions for the record, and both men were "willing to let it stand as it is now."

Whereupon, Senator Ferguson ruled with some relief that "this issue is closed."

On Friday, Senator Brewster told newsmen that he regretted having brought up the story about the airline hostess. Then he quit the capitol and flew off—in an American Airlines plane—to vacation in Maine.[35]

Although little had been proved, Hughes's image had been enhanced and Brewster's diminished. Hughes had called Brewster a liar, and Brewster, by his own actions and testimony, had indicated this might be so. But as the *Washington Post* put it, conflicting testimony "created the impression of a series of distortion mirrors in a Coney Island house of fun."[36]

The Third Day

Friday was again hot. Again, the crowd overflowed the caucus room and lined the corridors. The women spectators "sighed over the 43-year-old Hughes as though he were Frank Sinatra, and the sound was like small winds murmuring in the spring."[37]

The Senate Caucus Room ordinarily holds only three hundred spectators. But all week around a thousand people crowded in (nine-tenths of them women), and there were another five hundred (nine-tenths of them women) standing in line in the corridor outside.[38]

Cameras flashed, klieg lights cast their hot glare, and the metallic blare from the loudspeakers reverberated in the room. Now that they had surmounted Hughes's diversionary delaying tactics, Ferguson was eager to begin the real investigation.

"You have been sworn, Mr. Hughes," Ferguson said. "Just be seated. I want to ask you some questions in relation to the flying boat contract."[39]

As questioning proceeded, it was clear the adversary relationship between Homer Ferguson and Howard Hughes had not been left behind with "the other issue." And Hughes was still an exasperating witness. He frequently could not recall matters with which it was reasonable to suppose he had been involved. He quibbled regarding the meanings of words and definitions of terms.

As the morning began, Hughes answered questions concerning his first meetings with Henry Kaiser and the attempts of Russell Birdwell (a Hollywood press agent who had ballyhooed *The Outlaw* for Hughes) to sell the D-2 to the government through White House contacts. Noah Dietrich took the stand for awhile and told how he had gone to see the Air Corps chief of procurement, General Echols, regarding the D-2. Dietrich said that Echols told him that he would not do business with Howard Hughes because he did not like him.[40]

Finally, questions to Dietrich concerning items on Birdwell's expense account led once again to Johnny Meyer.

"Do you know where Mr. Meyers is?" Ferguson asked Hughes.

"Meyers?"

"Yes; John Meyers."

"Oh, *Meyer*. No; no, I don't."

"Well, he was instructed to be here, and I am just advised by counsel that he is not here, and they are unable to locate him."

"Senator—"

"He works for you, does he not, Mr. Hughes?" Ferguson was very angry.

"He works for my company."

"It may be funny to you that he is not here."

"I didn't laugh, Senator. Somebody laughed back there." With that, there was an explosion of loud general laughter from the audience.

Ferguson persisted in his questioning as to the whereabouts of Meyer and Hughes's responsibility for previous difficulties in getting him to testify. Finally, Ferguson asked Hughes again, "I want to know now whether you know where he is?"

"I don't know where he is," said Hughes.

"He is in your employ, and why do you not know where he is?"

"There are, Senator—" Hughes turned in an aside to Dietrich and Slack, "about how many thousands of people?"

"Twenty-eight thousand," they said.

"There are a lot of people in my employ. Do I know where everyone is every day?"

As Ferguson continued bickering with Hughes, Senator Pepper tried unsuccessfully to get the floor. "We might have an understanding that you are not the only member of this committee," said Pepper.

"At least, when I am talking I am not going to be interrupted by you," retorted Ferguson.

"Well, now," Ferguson said to Hughes, "will you see that Mr. Meyer comes in at two o'clock?"

"What? Today?" said Hughes in an unbelieving voice.

"Yes."

"No. I don't think I will." It was a delicious moment for the audience and they laughed again.

"Do you think that Mr. Meyer [conducting] business at the present time is more important than this committee hearing?"

"Well, it is more important to my company, I can tell you *that*." Hughes's voice was flat and abrasive, and the last word cracked like a pistol shot.

"Who in your company will know the whereabouts of Mr. Meyer at the present time?"

"I don't know, but you have had him here for unlimited questioning, and I brought him back here twice from abroad. I don't see why I should do any more than that just to accommodate you; put him up here on the stand and make a publicity show out of it." Hughes's voice was rasping and angry.

"Is that the reason he is not here?"

"That is not the reason. I think that is the reason you want him back."[41]

Finally, Senator Pepper got the floor and objected to the way Senator Ferguson was handling the matter of Johnny Meyer's absence. "It seems to me that, if the chairman is going to be judicial in the matter," he said, "that things like that could be handled without a lot of insinuations against the witness."[42]

As the week of hearings neared their end, the committee was in disarray. Ferguson's adversary manner and inept questions continued to help Hughes improve his public image. The resulting public support was obvious and vocal, much to Ferguson's chagrin. But Ferguson asked for it. Late Friday morning during questions regarding the Kaiser-Hughes contract, Ferguson asked, "Is it not true, Mr. Hughes, that there would be no liability for breach of contract upon the part of the Kaiser-Hughes Corporation because you did use a nonprofit corporation such as you stated in the record was a country club?"

"I didn't say it was a country club. Now, Senator—"

"You referred to it as a country club charter."

"No, Senator, look: I feel that you have repeatedly changed my wording here and if you will read the testimony—" After further bickering, Hughes was given the transcript of the testimony where Meader had just asked him to describe what he meant by a nonprofit corporation. Hughes's reply was, "Well, it was organized in a manner similar to charitable corporations, or country clubs. Its charter specified that it was not organized for the purpose of profit." As he finished reading from the record, Hughes said, "Now, Mr. Chairman, I don't believe that means a country club corporation and I think your wording was intended to mislead."

Ferguson still maintained that Hughes had described his corporation as a country club. Hughes objected. "Wait a minute," Hughes said. "I said the technical, legal corporate charter was similar to the corporate charter used by a charitable organization or a country club."

"All right."

"Now, that is quite different."

"It is not," said Ferguson.[43]

Despite Ferguson's efforts, Hughes continued to dominate the hearings and deftly deflected testimony and allegations that would have seriously damaged a less confident, more defensive witness. Responding to charges by a Defense Plant Corporation inspector that he was rarely seen at the plant, he said that the man making the charges would hardly have access to the design departments of the factory. "I can tell you that I designed every nut and bolt that went into this airplane. I carried out the design to a greater degree than any other man that I know in the business; in fact, I am frequently accused of going too far and not delegating enough of the work to other people.

"I worked anywhere from eighteen to twenty hours a day on this project," continued Hughes, "for between six months and one year, and this, coupled with the F-11, the feed chute, and the other work I did during the war, resulted in me being so completely broken down physically that I was sent away for a total of seven months for a rest after the war. I do not know how anybody could have worked any harder than I did.

"If I made any mistake on this airplane it was not through neglect. It was through supervising each portion of it in too much detail; in other words, as I look back on it, if I could do the job over, I would have delegated more of the work to other people which might possibly have resulted in a faster job, but I am by nature a perfectionist, and I seem to have trouble allowing anything to go through in a half-perfect condition. So if I made any mistake it was in working too hard and in doing too much of it with my own two hands. And I can bring affidavits from everybody in my organization to back that up."[44]

The Fourth Day

On Saturday morning, he further amplified this theme: "Yesterday I said that I spent between eighteen and twenty hours a day for a period of between six months and a year. Now that was the concentrated, heavy design work on this plane; but from that point on I spent hours and hours every day for, oh, a period of years, on this project, and I am still spending a great deal of time on it. I put the sweat of my life into this thing. I have my reputation rolled up in it, and I have stated that if it was a failure I probably will leave this country and never come back, and I mean it."

Senator Pepper, a much more sympathetic questioner than Ferguson, asked, "Why, Mr. Hughes, have you put your company's money and your own personal effort and prestige into the construction of this cargo plane?"

"Well, because I so happen to believe in the future of aviation in this country," Hughes answered, "and I think this plane is a step forward."

"Do you consider that this plane has made and will make a contribution to aeronautical science and be of value to this country?" asked Pepper.

"I certainly do, Senator; I hope so, at least."

"Mr. Hughes, I don't recall that while I have been in the room that anybody has given a general description of the cargo plane. Would you give it to us at the present time?"

"Well, yes, sir; to the best of my ability. The wingspan is 320 feet. That is more than a football field, as you know; more than a city block. The length is over 200 feet. The circle on which the hull is built is twenty-four feet in diameter. It has eight engines, present rating of 3,000 horsepower each. . . . And when gasoline turbines or fuel-oil turbines become available, then the airplane should have a great deal of power. The wing area is 11,460 square feet, which I believe is almost three times any other plane that has ever been built at this time."[45]

Responding to charges that there was a spirit of "soaking" the Defense Plant Corporation, Hughes said, "May I also say that there was in the neighborhood of $150,000 or more of expense which went into the airplane and which I considered entirely legitimate and which the government auditors refused to pay and which my company bore as a loss. Now, I don't believe the government got the worst of this deal, and if there are any small instances where charges were put into this project which should not have gone into it, I think there were many more instances where my company had to pay for things that went into this airplane, which the government would not approve."

"Well, Mr. Hughes," said Ferguson, "this matter [the Defense Plant Corporation inspector's charges] that I read this morning here was a very serious charge against your company, was it not?"

"No; I don't consider it such in any way. I think that you will find that every contract that was ever performed for the government during the war was subject to criticism of some instance where the company apparently was charging something to it which the government did not consider correct."[46]

In responding to the charges of inefficiency and lengthy delay in fulfilling the contract, Hughes said, "I would like to say at this point that I have researched all of the airplanes that were designed and built during the last seven years, and I have discovered that this flying boat which is now being criticized so violently will cost the government less per pound and has taken less time per pound to complete than any other airplane, the first of a design. . . . The criticism that has been levelled at our supposedly inefficient operation does not really seem to be justified when you consider the result, because you can always find somebody around a factory who will bellyache and say the things are not going right, but just the same, if the result, the proof of the pudding is in the eating—if that measures up in relation to the other projects, I don't think the criticism is well founded."[47]

The flow of questions and answers smoothed out as Senator Pepper took his turn at questioning Hughes. Encouraged by Pepper's "sweetheart" questions, Hughes talked at length and without interruption regarding technical considerations and the potential value of his flying boat.

"We have discovered a great, great deal about the design and building of big airplanes," he said. "For example, it has long been considered that the bigger the airplane is, the more efficient it is. We have discovered, and I believe it to be quite important as a discovery—we have discovered that is not the fact.

"If I may be technical for just a minute. The body of the airplane becomes more efficient as it is larger. Now the reason for that is obvious. The skin area, which determines the drag, goes up as the square of the size; whereas the volume, which determines the cargo or passengers it can carry, the volume goes up as the cube.

"You can see that the cube will exceed the square, and therefore the carrying capacity will be greater in relation to drag as size goes up. But on the other hand, we have discovered that wing design is quite different, and that as the wing becomes larger, it weighs more per square foot than a smaller wing. In other words, a wing of 320-foot span, built according to the same design criteria, will weigh more in relation to its size than a smaller wing.

"Now, a point is reached, apparently, where the loss in wing efficiency, that is, in relation to its weight, exceeds the gain in body efficiency, and where those two lines cross, apparently, it is not desirable to build a bigger ship.

"Now, this one may have actually exceeded that point, but at least we will find out. And we have already found out a good deal in that direction. Now that, of course, is of some value. I think it is of considerable value in the design of further planes."[48] This last point may have been brought to Hughes's attention first by Grover Loening.

Senator Pepper elicited from Hughes that he had been working on the flying boat all together about five years and that the plane was in a drydock at Long Beach, California. "Are you prepared to give any general idea as to whether it is regarded as a relatively finished airplane, and relatively ready for flight?" asked Pepper.

Hughes said that it was structurally complete and had been for a number of months, but that the control system was delaying testing of the ship. He explained the control problem in a way that impressed all who heard him with his technical competence, the magnitude of the technical difficulties and the potential that successful completion of the flying boat project would make great contributions to aeronautical science.

"Now this airplane has crossed a barrier in size," said Hughes. "That barrier I consider to be the one where the control system can no longer be operated by a man, even in emergency. Now, up to this time, we have had airplanes which involved a booster system, like the boost on your brake on an automobile, just to make the controls easier to operate. But if that system ever failed, the pilot was still able to operate the controls manually, in an emergency, and I believe sincerely that this is the first time an airplane has ever been designed or built which was so large that no man could possibly work the controls under any circumstances.

"So, the flight of this airplane must depend completely on the power system of those controls. That has to be so accurate that every quarter-inch movement of the control up in the cabin will be accurately duplicated in the control surface of the tail of the airplane, or on the wing.

"Now, that is a tremendous problem, and we have been working on it since the start. We thought we had it licked, and we found that it was not satisfactory. The response was not quick enough, and it was not accurate enough. So we have been working overtime, and as hard as possible to lick that problem, and we think now, in our test system inside the hangar, that we have it licked, and we are now duplicating that system in the airplane, but it is a tremendous problem; and even if the airplane never flies, the research that we have done in that direction, and the knowledge we have gained, will be of considerable value to everyone in the building of bigger planes hereafter."[49]

During this portion of the hearings, what came across was the Howard Hughes of new ideas, experiment, risk, adventure, a genuine protagonist of aeronautical progress, a visionary challenging the established frontiers in aviation development. It was youth versus age. The daring of an innovative entrepreneur versus the hidebound conservatism of a bureaucratic establishment, challenging the undaring and the unimaginative. Hughes's appearance and demeanor projected all this but with an air of forthrightness and modesty.

He readily admitted the shortcomings of wood, even when glamorized with the name "Duramold." "If any more of these airplanes are ever built," he said, "they will undoubtedly be built out of metal, but I think that this airplane out of wood will serve its purpose experimentally if its other qualifications suffice.

"I am not pretending to say that this airplane will fly, or that it will be successful. I only hope it will, but I think that if it is successful, the fact that it is built of wood will not preclude its experimental value, or most of its experimental value.[50]

Now this . . . is not an airplane that can be used to haul excursion passengers from Coney Island to Staten Island. This is not an airplane which as one article can ever be used in a commercial sense. It can only be used for testing and research and to provide knowledge which will advance the art of aviation in this country.[51]

Hughes said that in 1944, when he had fought against cancellation of the flying boat contract, his thinking was that for a "comparatively small expense to the government we could finish and fly the biggest airplane in the world," and that the value of the information derived therefrom would exceed the additional expenditure, "when you weighed it in terms of what this government was paying for aeronautical research at the NACA laboratory and other places."[52]

Under Pepper's patient, friendly questioning, Hughes reviewed the history of his attempts to sell the Army Air Forces a pursuit ship based on his record-breaking racer—the plane that Jane's had called the "most efficient in the world." "But they turned it down," said Hughes, "because at that time the Army did not think a cantilever monoplane was proper for a pursuit ship."[53] He recounted his attempts to sell the Air Corps a high performance, two-engine interceptor with a revolutionary twin-boom tail design, and how the contract was given to Lockheed who then used the twin-boom idea.

"When they turned down my two-engine interceptor design and gave Lockheed the contract for it when I felt Lockheed got the two-engine idea from some of my engineers, I felt I had gotten rough treatment, so I backed into my shell and decided to design and build from the ground up with my own money an entirely new airplane which would be so sensational in its performance that the Army would have to accept it.

"Now, I designed and built that under closed doors, without any really important assistance from the Army. But they didn't like that because they like to have their fingers in everything, naturally. So the Alexander incident and the General Arnold incident, plus my closed-door policy on this new airplane, left me in a position where the Army did not want to touch me with a ten-foot pole and that is why I had so much trouble getting anything at the start of the war and that is why I wound up with two contracts, half-way through the war, and such little support on priorities and other assistance that I could not possibly finish the airplanes in time to be of use and nobody else could."[54]

The interrogation of Hughes had definitely run out of steam by midday. Hughes

Howard Hughes showing his flying boat to Senator Claude Pepper of Florida, a member of the Senate Committee investigating Hughes's wartime contracts. Pepper often sided with Hughes during the Senate Hearings.

managed to introduce into the record, over the niggardly objections of Ferguson, an August 2, 1947 news item quoting General Arnold as saying: "Hindsight and second guessing seem to be in order. That is what some people seem to have the most of. We wanted the best photo plane we could get. That seemed to be the British Mosquito (a plywood airplane). We tried to reproduce the Mosquito in this country. We could not get it. We tried to do it in Canada. We couldn't. The only plane that had the prospects of equaling the Mosquito was Howard Hughes's F-11. That is why we bought it."[55]

Then Hughes reviewed what he thought were the reasons why the officers at Wright Field opposed him. First, there were the incidents related to his go-it-alone, closed-doors policies. "Secondly," he said, "because they considered me to be stuck up. They considered that I thought I was too good for them, that I sat out in my bailiwick in Hollywood, I did not come to Wright Field to, let us say, kowtow to them there, and when they came to Hollywood, I ignored them. I did not meet them. I did not entertain them. I did not extend the type of reception they got from the other manufacturers."[56]

On this note, the hearings recessed at 12:45 p.m. until 10 a.m., Monday, August 11. "Another day like Saturday," editorialized the *Washington Post*, "and Mr. Hughes would have become a national hero."[57]

Hugh Fulton, denied a chance earlier to answer Brewster's charges of a plot in Hughes's interest, took his case to the press. In a 6,000-word statement he said that "Brewster was utterly unable to take issue with the fundamental charge of Hughes that while Brewster was chairman of a committee investigating Hughes and had occasion to meet Hughes only in connection with that investigation, Brewster had used that opportunity: (1) to obtain free transportation; and (2) to attempt to sell Hughes on a program to which he was known to be bitterly and publicly opposed.

"I respect the Senate Committee investigating the National Defense Program," said Fulton. "I gave four years of my life to working with the members of that committee and to developing it from an unknown committee to one of national stature with a world-wide reputation for thoroughness and fairness.

"I believe, therefore," Fulton continued, "that as one of the chief architects of the development of the committee, I have the right and the duty to point out to Owen Brewster that his conduct in this matter and the false statements which he has made in an effort to avoid the implications brought forward by Hughes have seriously impaired public confidence in the committee under his chairmanship."[58]

The Sixth Day—And a Surprise

On Monday morning Hughes entered the caucus room to the usual plaudits of his more vocal admirers. Determined and confident, he was prepared to broaden his charges that he had to "force" his way into war work over the "hatred" of some high Army officers. He had four hundred pages of notes at hand as he sat in the witness chair waiting for Homer Ferguson to call the committee to order.

Ferguson did call the committee to order—but only long enough to make a few remarks about the importance of John Meyer's testimony and that he had not yet been found. With that as an excuse, plus the fact that "all of the members of the committee have their work to do, some are going to leave the country for a six-week period, and other things are scheduled," he adjourned the hearings until the 17th day of November! "The announced decision," Senator Pepper later observed, with the faintest perceptible stress on the word "announced," was that "these hearings are to be resumed on November 17."[59]

An early end of public sessions—though not quite as early as happened—had been forecast by some subcommittee observers at the end of the session on Saturday. This was after Senator Arthur Vandenberg of Michigan, a key Republican party leader, and Senator Ferguson's own senior colleague, for the first time had quietly found a seat among the spectators and impassively followed proceedings.[60]

But the abrupt collapse of the hearing took Hughes completely by surprise. Grinning boyishly, he turned to reporters to predict the hearing would never be resumed. Obviously jubilant, Hughes fired a parting shot at Brewster for taking "a runout powder" and being "too cowardly to stay here and face the music."

At length, having been surrounded for twenty minutes or so by congratulating spectators, most of them women, Hughes took some paper and swiftly wrote out a statement for the newsreels, tossing it over to his attorney, Tom Slack.

"Here, is this libelous?"[61]

In this statement, which he read for the newsreels, he declared, "I have just been asked why I think the hearing was called off. I believe it was called off because the people of this country render the final decision in any controversy. The public is the final judge. It was very obvious from the time I first walked into this room that the public and the press were on my side. They believed that there was no justification for this investigation in the first place. As soon as Senator Brewster saw he was fighting a losing battle against public opinion he folded up and took a run-out powder. Yes, when Senator Brewster headed for the backwoods of Maine that was the tip-off. Washington was getting too hot for him! There was not reason for the other Senators on this committee to continue his battle for him if he was too cowardly to stay here and face the music. The other Senators saw no reason to carry Senator Brewster's banner against an overwhelming avalanche of public opinion.

"I thought this investigation would drag my reputation through the mud. But instead, due to the fact that the American public believes in fair play and because they supported me, I have more friends now than I ever had in my life. I want to thank the people of the country and the members of the press."[62]

Shortly after the bedlam in the hearing room had subsided and the room cleared, Senator Ferguson headed for the National Naval Medical Center in Bethesda, Maryland, for overdue treatment of his poison ivy infection.

Hughes's exit, however, was barred still by a cheering horde of autograph seekers whom he forbearingly indulged for the last time. When he reached the street to depart the Senate Office Building until November, the windows of the building were crowded with waving spectators.[63]

193

Howard Hughes eyes Shell Bowen's operation of the radio panel. Bowen flew a lot with Howard Hughes but wasn't on the one and only flight of the Flying Boat.

Above: Howard Hughes inspects the auxiliary electric power unit at aft end of flight deck. Hydraulic plumbing and wiring run along the forward face of the giant wing spar. The access to the catwalk inside the leading edge of the left wing is at the right. Note the loft socks on the men's shoes. Below: This is a view inside the fuselage looking to the rear, taken from mid-section on the day before she flew.

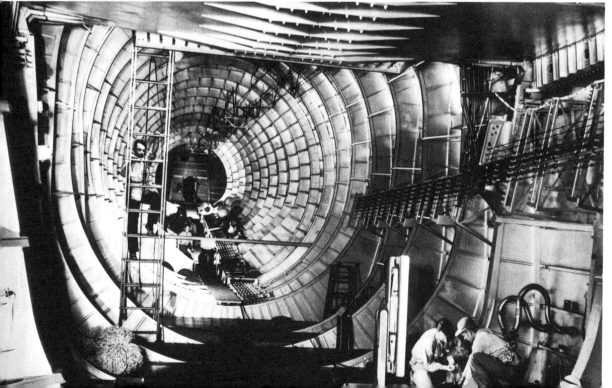

Howard Hughes in the cockpit of his Flying Boat (above) and conferring with his flight engineer (below) just prior to the historic taxi run and flight on November 2, 1947.

11

It Flies!

THE HEARINGS HAD ENHANCED Hughes's public image. But Brewster's derisive references to the flying boat as a "flying lumberyard" that would never fly stung Hughes's pride as an aircraft designer. "I don't build cluck airplanes," he told reporters the day of the adjournment.[1] Now he set out to prove it. Grim-faced, he flew back to California determined to test the plane before the hearings reconvened in November. As a first step, he sent Blandford off to Muroc Dry Lake with the XF-11 to wrap up the last flight tests and to deliver the plane to the Air Force.

"Deliver this thing by November first," he said, "or the next time you see me I'll be in jail."[2] This freed him to devote full time to the flying boat. Anger and hurt pride goaded him to super-human efforts. Money was no object. His crews worked around the clock.

Final Construction

"Howard came down every night during August, September, and October, 1947," recalls electrical supervisor Merle Coffee. "He would come in at the security gate and go over and talk with production head Jack Jerman and the plant security people there before we ever got started.

"We were running the engines, operating the hydraulic and electrical systems, and working on the controls at the time. I guess he was educating himself on how all the systems worked. A number of times while I was operating the electrical control panel he would stand there and ask me questions. He was trying to gain knowledge or just check me; I don't know which."[3]

Engine man John Glenn also remembered this period: "He came to the boat at night—he always worked at night. This man was unbelievable as far as mechanical engineering went. I remember one time we had some trouble with the rpm on one of the engines. Joe Petrali wasn't much help. Howard said, 'We'll pull that [propeller] off.' And sure enough, the stops were set wrong. He would sit there and run those

197

engines for hours on end. Feel them out and see how they were. He knew that airplane before he flew it backside and frontside. He was unbelievable."[4]

Chuck Jucker, crew chief on the flying boat, was called "the needle" by the other men. Uptight, he was always poking here and there. "Good boy," they said of him. During this period Jucker saw Hughes every night. There was never an idle word, claims Jucker. "It was always business with him. When he talked with me it was to ask how soon we could get the engines ready to run, or when we could check out the hydraulic system, that sort of thing.

"I'd say that ninety percent of the time he came down at night. Occasionally he brought Jean Peters down with him and sat her off in front of the flying boat in the car while he ran the engines. Jean Peters is the only one I ever saw with him, unless it was Rae Hopper, of course, or Joe Petrali."[5]

Flight engineer Don Smith recalls that one night Hughes drove up in his Chevy coupe and parked Miss Peters on the jetty right in front of number six engine. When they started running up the engines on that side someone asked, "Would you like me to take Miss Peters into the building away from the noise?"

"Oh, she'll be all right," replied Hughes. When the racket got too much for her, she got out of the car by herself and went inside.[6]

Electrical mechanic Ben Jiminez recalls that when Hughes ran up the engines, "he had a little old thing glued up there on the glass, and he'd sit and look through this 'horizon,' I guess it was, thinking about where he'd hold the nose at the takeoff point." Jiminez says that Hughes always had a lot of little work around he wanted done. "He'd say, 'Well, I want this switch right here'; and no matter what was behind the panel, that switch had to be *right there*." Placement was for operational convenience, not for appearance or for the electrician's convenience.[7]

Hydraulic engineer Dave Grant, who was to fly as Hughes's "copilot" on the test flight, confirms Jiminez's observation. "Howard probably spent more time positioning controls and instruments than he did anything. His cockpit arrangements were probably the best you could get."[8]

Engine man Harry Kaiser said that Hughes seemed to understand everything that was going on. "He had people quoting him on everything. He had us set up all the controls and everything just as he wanted them, and he knew the panel just like playin' a pie-ana before he ever flew the airplane."[9]

Hughes was very meticulous and observant. Power plant mechanic Al Geverink says, "You didn't dare walk on the wing and you didn't dare put your hand on the fuselage—he had various rules and his own ideas about what he wanted. If you followed through with those orders you had no problem."[10]

The men had to wear loft socks over their shoes whenever they entered the boat. He was quick to catch any variance with good aircraft practice. One day he noticed mechanic Vic Leonard hacksawing a piece of metal held in a metal vise. "That part is not going to be used in the airplane is it?" he asked. Both Vic and Hughes were relieved to know that it was not.[11]

The men who worked for Hughes all noticed his unorthodox eating habits. John

Glenn said that sometimes a meal was some crackers and a quart of milk. "In those days I guess the man had ulcers," says Glenn. "The usual, however, was a chicken sandwich with milk. Sometimes he'd bring it in a brown bag, but usually he'd send someone out about 12 or 1 o'clock in the morning. We'd always laugh about it. It seems he was always nipping on that bottle of milk. Howard was a funny man, as you know. The doctors would tell him to eat better, but he was so damn obstinate that he wouldn't pay any attention to them."[12] Merle Coffee said that when Hughes brought his lunch in a bag he would sometimes take off his hat, sit on one of the work benches and dangle his feet as he ate.

General mechanic Phil Thibodeau, who helped pick up the pieces of the crashed F-11 in Beverly Hills, thought that the after-effects of Hughes's injuries still bothered him. "Evidently he was taking a lot of physics, Ex-lax or something," says Thibodeau. "When we were running the engines in September or October, he'd have to leave the controls every hour or so and go to the toilet. Sometimes he'd go to his car, pick up a little brown bag, and then go to the five-holer. He'd sit there, going to the pot, eating a turkey sandwich, and reading a blueprint."[13]

One day, in addition to his usual long-sleeved open-neck white shirt and brown hat, Hughes wore a split in his grey slacks. A scaffolding had been built up to the flight deck door and Hughes had to bend over to exit right next to the APU mounting. His trousers ("they were kind of worn thin, you know,") ripped wide open.[14]

As Hughes had testified at the hearings, the development of a flight control system for such a giant airplane was a major problem. But by this time Dave Grant and his hydraulic mechanics had it nearly whipped. The system worked well in the mock-up at Culver City (it was actually more than a mock-up, because it simulated the static and dynamic loads on the control surfaces, duplicating the moment of inertia, the air loads, aerodynamic dampening, stiffness, and all such factors affecting flight control operation) and they were installing, hooking up, and adjusting this developed system in the airplane itself.

By the time the hearings adjourned in mid-August, the design was completed and the simulator was only used to work out design bugs. When Hughes first returned from Washington he spent a lot of time at the Culver City simulator looking for problems and asking for improvements. "We also used it to run an endurance test of the system and ran something like half a million cycles," said Grant.

There were two hydraulic systems for the flight controls, and Grant devised a "changeover valve" to switch from one to the other. This gadget created its own problems. "We didn't really get it all debugged until just before the flight," said Grant. "In fact, we were doing the final adjustment on that when Howard came aboard [for the taxi test and flight]."[15]

As the November 1 test day approached, Hughes turned Johnny Meyer loose to create a media event that would outshine the premieres of *Hell's Angels* and *The Outlaw*. He invited assorted dignitaries, journalists, and photographers to Long Beach for the big event. Some, like Owen Brewster, or journalists whose editors did

199

not think it ethical to accept Hughes's hospitality, refused. Those who did accept were wined, dined, and entertained with lavish hospitality. Hollywood stars and starlets mingled with the invited guests.

All the advance publicity carefully stipulated there would be only taxi tests on November 1. "Howard left himself all the opening he needed in case he didn't fly. In fact, he denied he was going to fly it," Dave Grant said.[16]

Did Hughes really intend to fly on the day set for the taxi test? No one knows. However, Merle Coffee recalls that on the night before the flight, Howard said to those gathered on the flight deck, "Everything looks good and we're going to take it out and fly it."

But crew chief Chuck Jucker, who rode between the pilots' seats during the taxi tests and lift-off, answers the question by saying, "Based on my instructions, I should say no. I was told to get the ship ready for taxi tests only."

Earlier in the year as the flying boat was nearing completion, the Government had made preparations for the flight test program. John Parkinson, the NACA hydrodynamicist who had worked so closely with the Hughes engineers at Langley, was a member of a committee formed to devise a test program to justify the government's investment. Hughes had said that if the plane was flown, he would fly it. NACA's chief pilot Mel Goff, who also was on the committee, objected to this. He thought that Hughes lacked flight experience in flying boats. As Parkinson remembers the incident, a representative of the Reconstruction Finance Corporation who was wiser in the ways of Howard Hughes laughed and said, "Gentlemen, you can talk all day about who's going to fly the airplane in your program. But let me tell you this, Hughes is bigger than the government. If Hughes says he's going to fly the airplane, he's going to do it. There isn't anything this committee or I or anybody else can do about it."

Hughes's money gave him special power in such matters. During a similar squabble in 1946 about who would test his XF-11, the question of insurance had been raised. Hughes had said, "Well, I'll be the insurance company."[17]

In reality, there was perhaps no pilot better qualified to fly the giant flying boat than Howard Hughes. He knew all the boat's systems intimately. He had run thousands of tests in his Sikorsky S-43 in studies of landing and takeoff performance with various load and balance conditions. And just a week prior to the November 2 tests Hughes had shot one hundred twenty-six landings in one afternoon with his Sikorsky on the Colorado River behind Parker Dam in furtherance of these studies.[18]

The First Stage

Saturday morning, November 1, dawned gloomily. Storm warnings were hoisted from Point Conception to Newport Harbor and brisk winds stirred up choppy seas in the outer harbor at Long Beach. Hughes anxiously checked the weather and then headed for Terminal Island.

By then the Terminal Island gang had cleared all scaffolding and movable obstructions away from the flying boat and opened inlet valves allowing harbor water to gush into the drydocks. Then they inflated sturdy rubber bags called "air jacks" to cushion the hull as it floated in the dock. They also fastened one air jack under the starboard wing tip float to prevent the hull from rocking from float to float during launching.

Hughes first checked these preparations when he arrived at the site. Then he walked out on the jetty that formed one side of the channel through which the hull would pass on its way to open water. Carefully he assessed the situation and decided that tests were off for that day, but that they would continue the launching so as to be ready when the weather improved.

By mid-morning workmen had hoisted the small cofferdams from the open ends of the individual wing tip float docks and swung the massive gate sealing the main dock outward and downward so that it lay flat on the channel bottom. A large crowd of onlookers, including Paramount and Movietone newsreel cameramen, gathered at the site. People were standing all around the boat, particularly on the two jetties that formed the short, sheltered channel for the hull.

All cameras were on Hughes as he arrived with his small entourage and walked past the spectators clustered on the paved surface forward of the right wing. He paused briefly, smiling dutifully. Then he walked with studied nonchalance to the gangplank leading to the personnel entrance hatch in the nose of the plane below the copilot's side window. At the gangplank he leaned forward, put one hand on each of the wooden posts flanking the entrance to the gangplank, supported himself with his arms stiff, and swung both feet up and on to the gangplank in one agile motion. It was all done with aplomb, much like Tom Sawyer showing off to Becky Thatcher while pretending he didn't know she was watching.

He walked casually between the nautical-looking manila lines that ran through holes in the wooden posts flanking the gangway. Then he stooped to enter the hatch, over which was printed "EXPERIMENTAL."[19] Inside the hull, he climbed the ladder leading to the top of the hull at the leading edge of the wing. Here a specially designed elevator platform had been hand cranked to its raised position to serve as a vantage point for directing launching and docking operations.[20] Jack Jerman and Joe Petrali joined him on the platform.

Hughes carefully checked everything visually, and with a walkie-talkie made contact with Harold Tegart, the launch engineer, who would direct the winch operation. Four tractors tended the lines that would keep the tail from swinging during launching. Everything looked good.

"Start easing her out," he said. Electric winches on shore growled, winding in the two lines that ran from the nose of the flying boat through pulleys anchored to the harbor bottom fifty feet apart some three hundred feet offshore and marked by two black and yellow striped rubber buoys. But as the big bird started to move out of its nest for the first time and into the channel between the finger jetties, a freshening wind pushed against the towering tail. The fore and aft restraining lines, tended by the D-6 and D-8 Caterpillar tractors, tightened.

"I think we ought to hold the plane here for the night," said Tegart.

"Why do you say this, Mr. Tegart?" Hughes asked.

"Well, these people have never towed this aircraft and the wind's quite high. It'd be safer for the airplane to just hold it here. I'm not sure they can handle it."

"Now's a hell of a good time to find out," said Hughes. "Take it out."[21]

Everything worked as planned except for one moment when the wind threatened to swing the tail against one of the jetties. Hughes thought during that moment that the tail was getting away from them.[22] "Watch it!" he yelled. But the restraining line tightened and held. The beautiful bird cleared the end of the jetties and was winched to a stop at the buoys, where the crew of a small Hughes craft made it fast to the mooring bridle for the following day's test.

Flight Day

Early Sunday morning, November 2, Glenn Odekirk picked Hughes up in Bel Air.

"How's the weather at Long Beach?" Hughes asked.

"It's not good, but it's better." Odekirk said.

As they drove to Terminal Island, Hughes said, "Odie, you don't mind if you're not aboard while I'm doing my taxi tests, do you?"

"Oh, come on," said Odekirk. "Don't give me that bullshit. I know if it feels right you're going to hop it." Hughes just smiled.

Odekirk also knew that Hughes didn't want another pilot aboard. That way no one could say, "Oh, he didn't fly it. The other guy did."[23]

At Terminal Island, chief engineer Rae Hopper talked briefly with Hughes before they boarded the flying boat. "We found a stress error in the aileron operating mechanism," he said. "Not too large and easy to fix, but it would be better not to fly until we do. If you want to go ahead and fly it, don't go over one hundred forty miles per hour."

"Don't worry, I won't," said Hughes.[24]

Hughes briefly visited the large, rectangular press tent before boarding and noted that his instructions to take good care of the press had been followed. Rows of tables set end to end and covered with heavy white paper filled half the tent. One such row supported batteries of telephones, some with hand-held receivers and megaphone mouth pieces, so that reporters could flash their stories to impatient editors. On other tables sat rows of bulky, black-framed Underwood typewriters, each with a folding chair in position ready for use. There was also food and drink, catered by Hughes's friend, Hollywood restaurant owner Dave Chasen. (Years later, when Chasen was recuperating from an illness, Howard was to have him and his wife flown to Las Vegas and put up in a luxurious suite—one of many kindnesses Howard did for his friends over the years.)[25]

About midday, Hughes invited the press to board his flying boat for the maiden taxi test—a three-mile run up the bay and back. Hughes's small craft ferried them the short distance to where the monster flying boat swung tethered to the buoys.

As his guests came aboard through the forward hatch, Howard cautioned them not to expect too much. "We'll reach speeds of only about forty miles per hour," he said. "The water is too choppy for anything else."

Then he clambered up the ladder to his topside vantage point to supervise the positioning of two "sea mules" for towing. Shortly, he returned to the flight deck, where about thirty passenger seats had been installed behind the cockpit area. Engine man Harry Kaiser was standing in the working part of the flight deck along with flight engineers Don Smith and Joe Petrali, electrical panel operator Merle Coffee, and others of the crew. Howard mentioned to the press that "Joe Petrali was six times American Grand National champion motorcycle racer."[26]

Howard took off his new snap-brim fedora and familiar two-tone sports jacket. "Hi, Dave," he greeted his "copilot," hydraulic engineer Dave Grant, as he jack-knifed his tall frame into the pilot's seat. Grant's excitement showed in his young, brown-eyed ruddy face. That he, a non-flier, should be copilot during the test program was an idea unique to Hughes. Hughes did not want a regular copilot; with himself in full control it could never be claimed that he himself had not actually flown the big plane. Moreover, Grant was the designer of the flight control hydraulic system, the most critical part of the airplane; in Hughes's mind it was fitting that Dave share a seat at the controls.

Chuck Jucker, the crew chief, positioned himself between the two pilots, belted himself to a stool secured to the deck, and adjusted his interphone headset. Jucker was to be Hughes's link with the rest of the crew throughout the ship. Chief engineer Rae Hopper and program manager Bill Berry were behind Hughes on the flight deck.

Flight engineers Joe Petrali and Don Smith were checking their controls and instruments just behind Grant, while Merle Coffee stood alongside the engineers and monitored the electrical panel. Across from them, just aft of the radioman's position, electrical engineer Jim Dallas monitored the control system strain gauges he had designed and installed.

Further aft on the flight deck, power plant mechanic John Glenn stood by the auxiliary electrical unit. Systems mechanic David Van Storm also was on the flight deck, but would be in the cargo compartment when the plane took off.

Electrical mechanic Jack Jacobsen manned his station forward on the cargo deck at the starboard hatch, while Ben Jiminez stood by on the port side. Hydraulic mechanic Bill Noggle moved about checking the operation of the hydraulic system and the flight controls. Power plant mechanic Al Geverink was in the right wing behind the engines and Phil Thibodeau in the left wing behind the number two engine.

Other crewmembers and observers on board were: Tom Dugdale, hydraulics mechanic (now deceased); Dave Evans, radio and electrical engineer (now deceased); Mel Glaser, power plant mechanic; George W. Haldeman, Chief, Aircraft and Components Section, CAA Region Six (who had been recently appointed by a committee of representatives of the Army, Navy, NACA, CAA, and the Reconstruction Finance Corporation to serve as technical observer of all tests of

During the last phases of pre-taxiing check-out, the Flying Boat still sits in dry dock on November 1, 1947 after moving out of the hangar.

Above: The beautiful airplane has moved away from land, and undergoes last minute preparations prior to taxiing. Below: Surrounded by a myriad of boats, including battle-ships, the Flying Boat lays at anchor in Long Beach harbor on the day before the big event.

As Howard Hughes had predicted, he taxied his Flying Boat on November 2nd. Here it is shown with downtown Long Beach in the background.

IT FLIES!

the Hughes flying boat); Warren Read, assistant chief engineer (now deceased); Vic Leonard, hydraulics mechanic; Chris Reising, electrical engineer; Dave Roe, power plant engineer; Don Shirey, power plant mechanic. (List prepared by crew chief Chuck Jucker.)[27]

Hughes had walkie-talkies on his lap for communicating with press boats, sea mules, and other craft in his fleet. Seeing that everyone was on board, he picked up one of them and instructed the sea mules to take the flying boat in tow. One took the nose line while the other tended a line to the tail to keep it from swinging with the wind. Mooring lines were cast off. At the last moment, Ben Jiminez at the port cargo door unhooked the ship-to-shore intercom line, and they were free to move.

On the way to the outer harbor test area they kept a sharp lookout for boats and other floating hazards. In the copilot's seat Dave Grant had no interphone headset. He had asked for one when he came aboard, but in the confusion his request had been forgotten.

As the two sea mules gingerly maneuvered the big plane toward the outer harbor Hughes could see Navy ships at the Long Beach Naval Base pier and a large number of small craft in the harbor. Spectators lined the breakwater at the opening to the outer harbor, waving and cheering them on. In the outer harbor an armada of water taxis and pleasure craft had gathered for the event. It was Sunday and the crowds were in a festive mood. Many of Howard's friends were watching from the yachts of the Hollywood great and near-great, and many a glass was raised in his direction. (Before boarding the flying boat, Hughes had put Nadine Henley and Jean Peters on one of those yachts.)

The skies were crowded too. Blandford, returning in a company BT-13 from delivering the XF-11 to the Air Force at Muroc, saw the flying boat in the outer harbor at Long Beach. But the sky was so full of airplanes going in all directions that he "got the hell out of there and landed at Culver City."[28]

As the big plane approached the test area, Dave Grant thought he recognized Howard Jucker, Chuck's younger brother, at the helm of one of Hughes's fleet of small craft. Howard Jucker's job was to check the test area for floaters and other debris. That was one thing they did not need: to hit a floating timber or railroad tie at a hundred knots. A Coast Guard cutter assisted in clearing the channel and in keeping the small craft out of the way.

When they arrived at the test area, Hughes and his engineers started the eight engines one by one until all eight props whirled and glistened in the bright sun. The sea mules cast off and retreated to one side.

When Hughes saw that the way ahead was clear, he advanced his four master throttles. Each of these controlled adjacent pairs of engines through two sets of vernier throttles that fine-tuned the engine readings. As the engine revved up to the power called for by Hughes, Petrali and Smith operated these vernier throttles to even out the readings across the board. But just as they had done so Hughes hauled his throttles back again. The plane slowed its forward charge and settled back, coasting in the water.

Hughes immediately noticed that not all engines had returned to idle. "What's wrong with the throttles?" he called. Petrali and Smith hastily reset their vernier throttles and the engines idled evenly again.

Dave Grant wanted to point out the problem to Howard, but he had no interphone. Since he did not want to yell across the cockpit in front of the reporters, he turned around and told Joe, "Tell Howard that if he's going to jockey the throttles, the vernier throttles are in series and shouldn't be used unless he intends to leave the power set long enough to make it worthwhile to even things off." But Joe was the kind of guy who was afraid to speak up, according to Grant, so he said nothing. Finally the reporters moved back and Grant leaned across and reminded Howard, "The verniers are in series." Howard understood immediately and avoided rapid throttle jockeying after that.[29]

Thus the first run down the bay was actually a series of about three short taxi runs in which Hughes accelerated to about forty knots and then decelerated as he felt the plane out while moving in one continuous line.

During this first slow-speed pass down the bay, Hughes had everyone in the cockpit peering through the windshield looking for logs and other floating hazards. He himself spotted one, but it was off to one side and easily avoided. At the far end of the bay he throttled back again and swung the aircraft around for the return trip. The plane handled very well on the water, responding quickly to rudder and engines.

Hughes made no effort to have his passengers strapped in during these runs. All of the reporters, including one woman, were free to move about the flight deck. "Everybody was yakking," remembers Chuck Jucker.

In position for the second run, Hughes's right hand advanced the four throttles once again while his left hand steadied the wheel on the control column. The eight R-4360 Wasp Majors roared as they drove the 17-foot 2-inch props. The plane surged ahead and climbed rapidly onto its step without wallowing or hunting. As the airspeed climbed past fifty, sixty, seventy to seventy-five knots, the hull spanked only the tops of the waves. Throughout the run, despite the chop which was just short of developing whitecaps, the hull spray fell away well below the propeller line. At the end of the bay where they had started, Hughes closed the throttles with satisfaction. The run had felt good.

As the plane weathercocked into the wind, engines idling, Hughes answered reporters' questions.

Yes, he was satisfied with the ship's performance.

Yes, according to plan, he would try one more taxi run.

Yes, he felt that the seven million dollars of his own money that he had ploughed into the airplane was well spent.

The United Press correspondent asked another question.

"Howard, are you going to fly the boat today?"

"Of course not," replied Hughes. "As I have explained, I estimate it will be March or April before we're really ready to fly this airplane."

"In that case," said the UP reporter, "is there a possibility of going ashore to file my story?"[30]

"Certainly," Hughes said. He picked up his walkie-talkie to call for a boat. Hughes never used standard voice procedures for his radio communications. This time he just said, "A few fellas want off. Have a boat come alongside."[31] Then, in an aside, he ordered Petrali and Smith to shut down everything but one engine to have minimum way on while maintaining a source of hydraulic and electrical power.

As the boat came charging into the test area, bow waves curling white and spray flying, Hughes eyed it narrowly.

"Come up alongside from the rear," he said. He was as protective of the flying boat as an old mother hen of one of her chicks, and he kept up a running stream of instructions and cautions. "Now don't let that boat touch this ship," he said. "Keep it well fended off. . . ."

The UP reporter triggered an exodus. No one wanted to be "scooped."[32] Hughes accompanied by mechanic Van Storm went down to the cargo deck to see them off. Van Storm lay on his belly at the left forward hatch to hold the boat clear of the aircraft while two reporters walked over his back to make the transfer. "Be careful," Hughes cautioned. They thought he was being solicitous of their welfare. Actually, he was thinking of the flying boat.[33]

Two or three magazine writers, who had no deadlines, about five other reporters, and a couple of photographers elected to stay aboard. James C. McNamara, news editor of independent Los Angeles radio station KLAC and the "broadcast pooler" for all the radio newsmen, had no alternative but to stay too. He had waited until the third run to wrap up his story because he thought he would gain a more intelligent approach after the on-the-spot education provided by the first two runs. By the time he could finish the third and last run and get his recording to radio-central via Long Beach station KFOX, the icing would be off the story. With a heavy heart he watched his colleagues leave.

About this time, Dave Grant sent Bill Noggle back to check the control system actuators, control valves, and plumbing in the tail. Hughes was unaware of this; neither did he make any check to see that crew and passengers were in their places and ready to go before the next and final run.

After the boat headed back to Terminal Island with the reporters, Hughes restarted all engines and taxied farther downwind to get in position. The final run would be westward toward San Pedro and roughly parallel the shoreline from Pier A in Long Beach to the western boundary of the Terminal Island Navy Base.

McNamara by this time had moved forward to stand just behind crew chief Chuck Jucker—a good vantage point from which to relay to the American public his view of what was about to happen.

In 1947, the reporting of special events away from the broadcasting studio was not easy. McNamara's equipment was portable, but ponderous: a storage battery for power, a heavy turntable recorder, a supply of 15-inch acetate discs, assorted cables, and a microphone—a back breaker. While McNamara told the story through his KLAC microphone, his engineer, Harold Huntzman, in a front row seat, monitored the recorder at his feet.

It Flies

McNamara began his famous broadcast, which later won the 1947 Sigma Delta Chi award for the best on-the-spot reporting. "This is James McNamara speaking to you from aboard the Howard Hughes two hundred-ton flying boat, the world's largest aircraft. At this moment as we speak to you from the spacious flight deck, this mighty monster of the skies is slowly cruising along a northwest course in the outer Los Angeles Harbor."

After considerable commentary about the ship, the setting, and "the Thin Man from Culver City," he leaned forward and spoke in Hughes's ear. "Howard, do you have time at this moment to explain for our radio listeners exactly what you're doing—the operation?"

"Yeah," said Hughes. "We're taxiing downwind very slowly to get into position for a run between the entrance to Long Beach Harbor and Myrtle Beach and San Pedro. It's about a three-mile stretch there and we're gonna make a high-speed run in that direction. The wind is changeable—it's been changing all day—but it's not too serious.

"The water is fairly rough for the outer harbor here. You see, there was quite a heavy wind last night, up to forty-five miles an hour, I believe, which created quite a sea here and that shortens the length of runway we have available because down toward the southeast end here there's effectively an open sea coming around the end of the breakwater and it's very, very rough. But I believe we have an area here that's sufficient and pretty soon we'll be ready to make a run."

"Howard, I didn't hear you," said McNamara. "There's so much noise here. But did you tell our listeners the speed you achieved on that last run?"

"That was right around ninety miles an hour. We were well up on the step and the airplane could have lifted off easily if I'd just pulled back on the control, I'm sure. But we have so many mechanical devices in this ship right now that I wanta check a few of 'em out a little bit before we try anything like that and as I say, I previously estimated it'd be March or April before we're really ready to fly this airplane. You have no idea how much machinery, how many electrical, hydraulical, and mechanical devices we have on here, all which should function right before we take the ship up in the air."[34]

With that, Hughes turned his attention back to the cockpit. Looking at Grant he said, "Lower fifteen degrees of flaps."

This was recommended takeoff setting for the giant, semi-fowler-type wing flaps. So as Grant's left hand grasped the cube-shaped knob of the flap control lever protruding from a diagonal slot in the top of the pedestal between the two pilots, he thought that Howard might just lift off on the next run! Grant clearly remembered the high-speed taxi tests of the XF-11 when Hughes had "taxied" into the air several times well before the official test program had ever started.

Grant moved the lever to takeoff flap position. Nothing happened! Feeling somewhat embarrassed, he looked back and caught the eye of hydraulicsman Tom Dugdale, who was standing at the rear of the flight deck near the wing's front spar. Dugdale was supposed to have wired a malfunctioning "hydrofuse" to the open position because this "leak protector" had previously shut off hydraulic actuating fluid when no leaks existed. Dugdale immediately knew what was wrong, quickly headed for the flap hydraulic units on the rear spar, yanked the manual override handle to "open." The flaps started down.[35]

Meanwhile, Hughes lined up in position. The fifteen to twenty knot wind had shifted. Now the channel that had been cleared of debris and pleasure craft by the Coast Guard cutter and Hughes's boats was no longer directly into the wind.

He picked up his mike and asked Petrali and Smith if the engines were ready for another run.

"All set," they replied.

Hughes hung up his mike and spoke over his shoulder to McNamara.

"Hang on." He made a quick visual check of cockpit instruments and control settings, looked ahead and saw that their intended path was clear. With the heel of his right hand he eased all four paired throttles forward in one smooth motion.

With a crescendo of sound, the giant plane surged forward, engine noise mingling with the out-of-sync beat note from props not turning at exactly the same speed. The noise reverberated through the wooden ship. The thump of the bow against the waves sounded like a speed boat's pounding in choppy water, but magnified and booming hollowly.

Just then, a power boat raced across their path from right to left, spray flying, passengers waving. Hughes swerved angrily, but the incident was more irritating than hazardous. The plane responded beautifully.

The nose of the plane came up slightly during initial acceleration until, smoothly and without effort, they were on the step. McNamara called out the speeds for the benefit of the radio audience. "It's fifty. It's fifty over a choppy sea. It's fifty-five; it's fifty-five. More throttle. It's sixty. It's about sixty-five. It's seventy." Suddenly, just before McNamara called "seventy-five," it was very quiet. They were airborne! The plane had left the water shortly after reading seventy mph. Hughes pulled the throttles back and then immediately pushed them forward again. In the sudden silence immediately after lift off, everyone heard Harry Kaiser yell, "It's off!"

The right wing started to drop in the blustery cross wind. Hughes immediately wracked his wheel to the left. He was not yet sure how fast the aileron would respond so he purposely overcontrolled. It was more than enough. The wing came right up and he returned the wheel to neutral.[36]

With his right hand he held the power steady for a moment. Then, bit by bit, he pulled the throttles back, easing the ship to a power-on landing. He must have been unsure of elevator response, because all the way down his left hand pumped the control column back and forth as much as plus-or-minus twenty degrees, according to copilot Grant.

"But you couldn't feel the airplane responding to that," said Grant, "because he was doing it fairly rapidly. He made probably the most perfect landing I've ever been involved with. You couldn't even feel it hit the water."[37]

The landing was so smooth, in fact, that the stylus of McNamara's recorder never even bounced.

The Flight from Aft

Before the flight, Grant had sent Bill Noggle to the tail. At first it was quite smooth and relatively quiet back there and he could hear the hiss of the hydraulic servo valves, which were designed to bypass about a gallon per minute when the controls were in neutral.

Noggle had no warning of the takeoff run and was halfway up the ladder to the elevator control units when it started. A tremendous weaving and shaking pinned him to the ladder. (Van Storm thinks that shaking was caused when Hughes inadvertently dipped a wing tip float in the water.)

"One and a half g's at the center of gravity is ten g's at the tail," says Dave Grant. "Noggle shouldn't have been there, but that was Howard's lack of procedure."

Jack Jacobsen, at his station in the fore part of the cargo deck, looked back and saw the long catwalk weaving and shaking.

"You could hear the wood creaking," said Jack. But once we were off the water, everything just smoothed out. I could tell the minute it left the water. When it settled in the water it started creaking again."[38]

Dave Van Storm, who was in the port bow entry area at this time, heard no wood creaking, only engine and water noise. To him the movement of the tail seemed a designed movement not out of line with a designed wing deflection of seventeen feet at the tip.[39]

Harry Kaiser was on the flight deck at lift-off, but he went down on the cargo deck after touchdown and saw the tail twisting around. Noggle came running out and said, "Look at that SB, Harry, it's about ready to leave us."[40]

Ben Jiminez also saw Noggle come out of the tail. "He came down out of that empennage like he was on fire."[41]

Noggle adds that "when the plane was airborne, everything smoothed out. So I scrambled up the rest of the ladder and was able to look out and see that we were in the air."[42]

Tom Dugdale, inspecting hydraulic units on the rear spar, told Grant that when he heard the engines rev up he figured that he was right over the center of gravity, so he just stayed there.

Phil Thibodeau was in the left wing behind the number two engine. "There are drain holes in the bottom of the nacelle about one-half inch big. Straight down was the only view I had. But I could sure tell when we left the water. It was very rough that day. On the water it swayed back and forth—a sidewise motion. After he lifted it, he throttled back and there was a glide. It was a real sensation."[43]

213

Power plant mechanic Al Geverink was in the right wing behind the engines. "They had air throttles at that time," he said. "We helped to start them . . . and made sure they operated properly. We took the lens out of the landing light so we could see when we were airborne."[44] Power plant mechanic Don Shirey shared the view with Geverink.[45]

Geverink said that he saw no indications that Hughes planned to fly and that he, Geverink, was very much surprised to be airborne. "I think he had intentions of just picking it up a bit. But once he got it up, he didn't know what to do with it. It got quieter when we got airborne. You could hear the sound of the water spanking the hull before that."

Ben Jiminez was surprised too. "I wasn't even thinking of going into the air. It's just my opinion that he got on the step there and it just took off. After it takes off, Hughes just rides it out."[46]

Flight engineer Don Smith agrees. "I'm sure it ballooned out of the water before he was ready for it. The thing that convinces me is that as soon as it came off the water he yanked the throttles clear back."[47]

Other crew members claimed they sensed that Hughes was going to take off. Jack Jacobsen said that before each run he cracked the forward door open enough to peek at the wing flap position. Before the last run the markings on the flap showed they were set to the takeoff position.

Kaiser sensed it too. "When he dumped the passengers off and taxied around a little bit," said Kaiser, "we knew we were going to fly. . . . He didn't tell us."

Glenn Odekirk, Carl Babberger, some photographers, a rescue team in fireproof suits, and a select group of other passengers saw the takeoff from the flagship of the Hughes fleet, a surplus three-engine Navy PT boat capable of about sixty-five knots. As the flying boat roared across the outer harbor, the PT boat paralleled its course on the seaward side, spray flying. The camera crew filmed the liftoff and the landing from the PT boat's stern.

After the giant flying boat had cleaved the water smoothly on touchdown, the regional chief of the Civil Aeronautics Authority who was on the PT boat put his arm on Odekirk's shoulder and said, "I knew the son of a bitch was going to do that."[48]

After the landing Hughes was elated. "Boy, those flaps really ballooned this thing," he told Grant.

"How were the controls?" Grant asked.

"That was a good landing wasn't it?"[49]

McNamara asked, "Howard, did you expect that?"

"Exactly," said Hughes. "I like to make surprises."

McNamara then summed up his impression for the radio audience. "At one time, Howard said that if this ship did not fly that he would leave the country. Well, it certainly looks at this moment that Howard Hughes will be around the United States for quite some time to come."

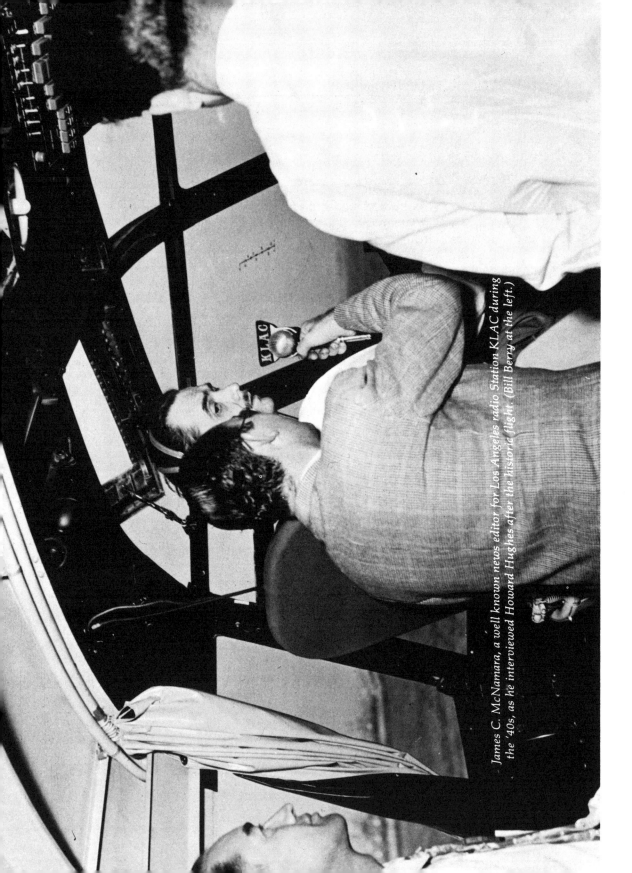

James C. McNamara, a well known news editor for Los Angeles radio Station KLAC during the '40s, as he interviewed Howard Hughes after the historic flight. (Bill Berry at the left.)

Then, McNamara spoke to Hughes again. "Howard, may I again offer my congratulations, sir?"

"Well, thank you very much."

As McNamara signed off with his radio audience, Hughes said, "Well, you got the first ride."[50]

"Do you want to taxi again?" Hopper asked Hughes.

"Hell no," said Hughes and headed the plane toward Terminal Island. This time he didn't bother with "sea mules." He taxied the plane in under its own power right up to the buoys as though he were maneuvering a yacht.

All the way, he talked animatedly about how great the airplane was. He was euphoric; the airplane performed "beautifully," and several times he mentioned how the flaps had "ballooned it."[51]

After the huge ship was fast to the buoys, Hughes left his seat and put on his jacket and new brown snap-brim hat, which he had apparently purchased for the occasion. As he left the flight deck, he pushed back his hat, rubbed his brow and remarked to no one in particular, "She sure jumped off easy."[52]

McNamara joined Hughes on the cargo deck ready to disembark. One of the small Hughes craft pulled up and Hughes got in first and sat in the stern. Mc-Namara followed, but as he stepped over the gunwale the two vessels separated. With one foot in the airplane and the other in the boat he had to strain to the utmost to keep from falling into the water. Hughes made no effort to help, just sat back and laughed and laughed. Somewhat discomfited, McNamara finally made the transfer.

Hughes and McNamara were the only passengers. As they headed for shore Hughes said, "You hungry? You had your lunch?"

"Of course I haven't had anything," said McNamara, still somewhat miffed. "I've been doing this shit."

"Yeah, I know," said Hughes. He opened a brown bag and offered McNamara a sandwich. McNamara bit into it: just plain peanut butter, nothing else at all.[53]

On shore Hughes could not keep from grinning, and he swaggered a bit as he walked along the jetty. He chewed a sandwich nonchalantly as spectators clustered around him offering congratulations.

"I think the airplane is going to be fairly successful," he said. "I sort of hoped it would fly but didn't want to predict it would and make people disappointed."

Hughes's description of the takeoff was somewhat less than truthful about the speed of the plane and the purposefulness of the maneuver. Dave Grant comments that "Howard himself was very reluctant to admit we were going that slow when we took off. I never could quite figure that out."[54] The *Hughes* version was that "when I got going with the flaps in takeoff position there was so much buoyancy and it felt so good I just pulled it off. The maximum speed during the flight was a little over a hundred. The takeoff speed was ninety-five miles an hour (about eighty-two knots). The takeoff distance was two-fifths of a mile.

"The landing was really gratifying. As soon as the ship was in the air I cut back the power because I didn't want to hit those small boats in San Pedro harbor.

"The controls operated well. We will follow the original testing schedule." That schedule called for a first flight in March 1948.

Hughes publicly congratulated members of his staff who helped him design the plane and work out its technical problems. Then he escorted a party of visitors aboard the plane via one of his small boats. They entered through a water-line cargo hatch.

Hughes explained that his plane was three times the size of the Martin Mars and seven times the size of the Douglas DC-6, the largest commercial airliner then operating. The Hughes boat could carry an estimated 700 passengers, he said. From the cargo deck to the flight deck there is a ladder with seventeen standard steps. The cockpit is more than thirty feet above the water line.[55]

By the time Grant got ashore he was being paged to line up for a photograph with Hughes and the rest of the crew. Did Hughes have any parting words for the crew? "It wasn't like Howard to make speeches," said Grant. Right after the pictures, Hughes left for Beverly Hills with the Odekirks. A piece of sand or something had lodged in his eye, so they stopped at a doctor's office on the way and had it removed. Then Odekirk drove Howard out in the San Fernando Valley to a girl-friend's house. Apparently, Jean Peters had been left to fend for herself.

A Flight Test All Along?

According to Odekirk, Hughes thought the flying boat felt "real good" during the test runs and flight. "He was very happy about it," said Odekirk.[56]

At one point after the flight, Hopper asked Hughes, "Did you mean to take off on that run?"

"What do you think?" asked Hughes.[57]

Dave Grant thinks the takeoff was both planned and inadvertent. "At the very beginning," said Grant, "I think he really did plan to just taxi the aircraft. But he wanted to fly it and in his mind that possibility was there. However, he probably didn't really commit himself to it until after those first two runs."

As to the inadvertent part, Grant says that while they were designing the controls, Howard wanted a lot more response than he needed. "He kept telling me how it was necessary to rock flying boats off the water and things of that type. But this particular hull was different from the others. It had absolutely no porpoising tendencies. It had excellent water handling characteristics.[58]

"On previous runs we'd been at higher airspeeds without taking off. I think what actually happened was he didn't expect the added lift . . . with only fifteen degrees of flaps. They're tremendous flaps—semi-fowler, in effect, because their hangers are way below the wing.

"With the flaps at fifteen degrees, the airplane took off as soon as it got on the step and I think he expected to have to pull it off. That's what I mean by both in-advertent and on purpose. The only thing he was surprised about was the airplane took off without him having to do it."[59]

Moreover, Grant says that he has the flying boat performance curves showing stall speed versus weight. At their test weight of about 280,000 pounds, the curves show that stall speed should be between seventy and seventy-five mph. "And that's about where we were when we took off." The flying boat performed just as designed.

Carl Babberger says that "all the factors were present for takeoff—a high head wind, the fifteen-degree flap setting, and a light load. It probably got airborne before he expected it to, but on the other hand it wouldn't surprise me that being under fire from Senator Brewster, he was prepared to gamble. If it took off, fine. If it didn't, fine."[60]

Final Considerations

It appears from accounts of Hughes's test flights—the Sikorsky test on Lake Mead, the XF-11, and the flying boat—that he was a rather undisciplined, seat-of-the-pants type of pilot. It was his habit not to use check lists, file flight plans, brief his crew and passengers, make communications checks, or coordinate with or effectively use any crew members other than his flight engineers. The departure from Terminal Island for the day's tests, for example, was strictly informal. He did not introduce the crew to the press and did not even brief them. "In fact, Howard hardly communicated with crew members. He left that up to us," said Dave Grant.

Except for his engineers, Howard made no checks with crew stations at all before taxiing or taking off, not even through his crew chief, according to Chuck Jucker.[61]

"After the second run," says Dave Grant, "he spent more time placing the press boat than he did anything else."

As for safety precautions, there were no life vests or life rafts readily available, nor did Hughes give safety briefings to passengers or crew. Passengers wandered around the flight deck during all phases of the test including the takeoff.[62]

When crew chief Chuck Jucker was asked if Hughes gave him any instructions regarding crew assignments and duties, he said, "There was one specific instruction that I remember very clearly—that nobody was to leave [an assigned] station unless he said so. I had left my station momentarily, and that's when he told me that."

12

Whatever Happened to the Spruce Goose?

IMMEDIATELY AFTER the successful flight of the flying boat everyone understood *Time* magazine's terse headline: "It Flies!" But after the first flush of publicity it seemed almost as Grover Loening had predicted: "I think it will fly . . . and that after a great many pictures have been taken of the crew and pilot, and Mr. Hughes looking very tired and very heroic . . . it would probably be run up on the beach and stay there, like any other movie set."[1]

The November hearing was an anticlimax. Senator Brewster had gone gunning for big game—Hughes and the Roosevelt connection. The committee instead bagged Brig. Gen. Bennett Meyers, whose financial misdeeds were uncovered during the Hughes investigation.

Partisan dissension delayed release of the Senate committee's report of the Hughes investigation until April 1948, and even then it was fully approved by only the Republican members of the committee: Owen Brewster of Maine, Homer Ferguson of Michigan, Joseph McCarthy of Wisconsin, John Williams of Delaware, George Malone of Nevada, and Harry Cain of Washington. The main conclusions of the report regarding the HK-1 flying boat were that the project, "which produced no planes during the war, was an unwise and unjustifiable expense as a wartime project. The manpower, facilities, and public funds devoted to it during the war were wasted at a time when military planes were urgently needed. . . . The conclusion is inescapable that the decision of the War Production Board was influenced because of the wide and favorable public acceptance of the proposal of Henry J. Kaiser for the mass production of huge cargo planes which Kaiser claimed would overcome the existing submarine menace to ocean transportation." But "the technical side of the war cannot be waged from day to day in a manner to accord with public opinion."

The failure to follow normal procurement channels was, the committee concluded, "a costly mistake. The Defense Plant Corporation did not have personnel qualified to supervise an aircraft construction program. Because of this inadequacy in personnel, the Civil Aeronautics Administration and the National Advisory Committee for Aeronautics, each were given some supervisory authority. . . . This divided authority . . . together with the inefficient management of the Hughes organization resulted in allowing Hughes Aircraft Company to carry on the project in an inefficient and wasteful manner."[2]

The following month, Democratic minority members of the committee, Carl Hatch of New Mexico, Claude Pepper of Florida, J. Howard McGrath of Rhode Island, and Herbert R. O'Conner of Maryland, issued a dissenting report. They declared that "Howard Hughes and his companies were entitled to a positive finding by the committee, especially so far as fraud, corruption, and willful wrong-doing are concerned. There is absolutely nothing in the evidence which discloses any fraud, corruption, or wrongdoing on the part of Howard Hughes or his associates."[3]

Was Senator Brewster really blackmailing Hughes, or did Hughes just think he was? Senator Pepper recalls that "Brewster might as well have been on the payroll of Pan American as a vice president. He rode their planes as if he were an executive of the company. He called on them for all sorts of favors, and in addition to that he passionately fought their cause. I was on the committee of commerce where the decision had to be made as to whether we were going to support the chosen instrumentality legislation (that would name Pan American sole U.S. air carrier), and Brewster had worked on me. He'd tried to get me to go along with it. I didn't have the slightest confidence in Brewster and I thought Hughes was telling the truth. Brewster was a strange kind of man. He had great energy, had a lot of ability, a lot of drive, but he never was regarded as a great man by his colleagues, or an outstanding man because he was always involved in petty causes like this, pursuing them with a passion that *suggested*, whether it was confirmed or not, that he had a personal interest in the matter."[4]

An after-effect of the investigation was that Hughes was confirmed in his passion for secrecy. Dietrich had been amused by Hughes driving through the night streets of Washington discussing strategy because he feared electronic eavesdropping. But as it turned out, both his room at the Carlton and Dietrich's at the Mayflower *had* been bugged!

In 1949, it came to light that police lieutenant Joe Shimon had done the job. No one accused Brewster, but this was Drew Pearson's immediate assumption. None of the appropriate Congressional committees was prepared to investigate a colleague. But Pearson persuaded the sometimes receptive Senator Pepper to convene a sub-committee of the District of Columbia Committee on the premise that it was probing the police department, not Brewster. The probe revealed that: "1) Brewster had requested the Washington Police Department to assign to him Lieutenant Shimon, the department's wiretap expert. 2) Shimon had received 'expense payments' from Brewster's secretary—a violation of police regulations. 3) In setting up the tapping and bugging operation, Shimon had instructed the three cops who manned the equipment to listen particularly for references to TWA or anything about airlines. 4) The eavesdropped information was transmitted to one Henry Grunewald. 5) Shimon was seen on one occasion receiving a $1,000 cash payment from a man fitting the description of Grunewald."[5]

Senator Pepper says that "Drew was a little unhappy that I wasn't more demanding and more exacting, but I told him that I went as far as I thought I could go on it. I didn't have any special ax to grind. I was simply trying to bring out the facts. And we brought out the facts. But what could I do with Brewster? I didn't want to bring a citation against him or anything. We'd shown him up before the public as engaged in that nefarious activity which the public had come to believe was par for the course for Brewster."[6]

Drew Pearson continued to hound Brewster during the five years leading up to reelection time in 1952. At that time he introduced a representative of Brewster's opponent, newspaper publisher Frederick Payne, to a representative of Howard Hughes. Hughes threw his support to Payne, with the instructions, according to Noah Dietrich, to "give Payne whatever he needs, and the hell with what it costs."[7] The Carl Byoir agency, Hughes's publicity agent whose primary job was to keep Howard's name out of print, twice transported $30,000 to Maine for Payne's candidacy and supplied Payne with information about Brewster's nefarious activities.[8] Payne won.

In 1948 Hughes spent $1.75 million for a specially built, humidity controlled hangar where he kept the plane under twenty-four-hour guard. Even Long Beach fire officials were not allowed inside. Some journalists have alleged that Hughes had a longstanding feud with Long Beach Harbor Department authorities as he fought them over the years to retain both his secrecy and his lease to the Terminal Island site. But Charles Vickers, who worked for the Long Beach Port and Harbor Department for forty-five years and held the top management position there from 1958 until his retirement, disagrees. "We never had any trouble with Hughes. . . . It was 1965 or '66 before it got to where we could have developed the area if he hadn't been there. But we raised the rent and got as much out of him as you could get for anything else that could be developed [at that site]. So if he wanted to stay and pay the rent, so what? . . . Hughes can afford to spend $100,000 to have his plaything. That's what it cost him a year for rent. . . . I don't give a goddamn what he does as long as he pays his rent. That's none of your business or mine."[9]

In 1953 a flood severely damaged the flying boat and Noah Dietrich urged Hughes to take advantage of the opportunity to junk it and get rid of the crushing expense. Over the years, the steady pumping of oil from under Terminal Island had caused the land to sink up to eighteen inches a year. The land surrounding the Hughes site had been built up by soil dredged from the channel; but the Hughes site had not been filled in, and only coffer dams and dikes kept the mud and water out.

Hughes came down the night of the flood and looked everything over. The plane was floating and had been lifted against the overhead, damaging the props and tail. Scaffolding was hanging from all the nacelles.

"It was a heck of a mess," said George Bromley, the general supervisor of plant engineering at the hangar. "Everybody was wading in the water and we were trying to get a diver down to get the debris out so we could get the plane back down in its cradle."

Hughes said, "Well, it's a hell of a mess. Let's get it cleaned up." That was all he said. Commander Garland "Jack" Suggs, the Navy diver who dove for the Sikorsky in Lake Mead, had been told by Odekirk that "when you get out of the service, you've got a job." So Suggs had taken charge of the Hughes fleet at Terminal Island in April 1948 and was available to do the diving.

Over Dietrich's urging to junk it, Hughes repaired the flying boat. Other expensive steps were taken to preclude damage from other such incidents. Originally, the airplane sat flat on the bottom of its drydock on blocks. But as the island sank, workmen built up the sides of the dock and raised the airplane on a cradle. Workmen raised the airplane in 1954, working around the clock on twelve-hour shifts. When the job was finished an earthquake hit. There was no damage, but it shook everyone up.

Air bags were installed under the nose of the aircraft as it rested on its cradle. They were hooked to a rack of compressed gas that would be triggered if accidental flooding of the dock were to occur. The inflation of the bags would lift the nose and depress the tail so that the tail would not hit the overhead. The very heavy and expensive-looking cradle that supported the airplane could be tilted six degress nose up and six degrees nose down by huge walking beams moved by heavy cables that ran through pulleys to connect to the pistons of very large hydraulic cylinders on the floor of the dry dock.[10]

Until 1960, Terminal Island sank about an inch a month. Then water was injected into the old oil wells to stop the subsidence.

Through the years, Hughes maintained the aircraft in mint condition. Operational maintenance was performed continuously. Engines were run weekly until devices to rotate the engines and circulate hot pickle oil were designed and installed.[11] The flight controls were exercised once a week. In fact, all systems were operated in accordance with an established schedule. Many modifications were designed and installed. For years the crew fully expected that it would fly again.

Al Geverink said, "We had a fly in July schedule. [For] six months we'd get it ready and then [for] six months we'd tear it down. It was frustrating. We'd go on 'fly in July' and 'a new crew in 52.' But . . . it was nice experimenting; you always had something different to look forward to. We tore the airplane completely apart and rebuilt it. We put new surfaces on and, God, we did everything to that airplane."[12]

An Unflown Giant

Yet Hughes never flew the airplane again. Why not? Noah Dietrich thinks that Hughes was afraid of it. This view is reflected in the relatively recent television dramatization of Hughes's life. However, Odekirk says that the conversation in the

TV dramatization that he was supposed to have had with Hughes in which Hughes said he was afraid to fly the plane again never took place, "absolutely not." Odekirk goes on to say, "When they did the TV movie, Dietrich wanted me to get with his producer and all. When I read the script I wouldn't let 'em use my name because he was trying to take credit for everything and it was all so incorrect. That fella in there running the plant, "Pete"—well, that was me. They had me in the script, but I wouldn't let 'em use my name."

Another close associate of Hughes who definitely disputes the TV version that he was afraid of the flying boat was his chief engineer Rae Hopper, who was standing behind Hughes during the flight. Although the boat was noisy and bouncy during the taxiing, Hopper says, it was very smooth and quiet in the air. When Hopper asked Hughes how the boat landed Hughes said, "Great! Just great!"

Evidently, however, the airplane did have its weaknesses. According to one of Hughes's mechanics, "Maybe one of the reasons why they didn't fly it [again] was there was a little fluctuation in the tail, and maybe it wasn't beefed up enough to suit him."

Another mechanic said, "There was a lot of little damage. I don't know whether I should say it or not, but there was. That's when they went out into the wing and put little metal stiffeners in there to hold the glue joints together. A lot of angles snapped loose. I guess the whipping of the wing is what did most of that."

The excerpts from a May 5, 1948 news article by *Chicago Tribune* reporter Wayne Thomis that follow indicate that Hughes was concerned about strength and control:

"Through a spokesman, Hughes said here today that preparations are under way to sheath the hull and the wing—at least the half which carries the eight 3,500 horsepower engines of the 200-ton craft—with corrugated aluminum.

"The metal is being applied, he said, to add stiffness and strength to the plywood structure. Need for this additional strength apparently showed up on the taxiing and 30-second flight last fall." Hughes was further quoted as saying, "We are devising entirely new methods for getting instant responses from our controls, both aerodynamic and power."

"It should be understood clearly," he added, "that the Hercules is considered only a research aircraft. It will never be used in competition with military or commercial machines, but will, in my estimation, be worthwhile because problems which will concern really big airplanes of the future will be solved here. The Hercules will point the way for really good big airplanes."[15]

Dave Grant says that after the flight, Hughes "spent a solid year with us going into all of the changes he wanted before going into the flight test program. Originally there was a six-month delay, and then he kept extending it. Basically, he was trying to make it crash-proof. His concern was that there was only one airplane and if something kooky happened like with the XF-11, where the prop went into reverse. . . . he didn't want to take that kind of chance on losing it. So he was really the inventor of what people call modern-day reliability. As far as I am concerned, he invented redundancy. He went into it to a much greater degree than anybody else had ever done before. It's kind of commonplace now."[16]

Haldeman said that Howard had ordered thirteen 1,000-gallon fuel tanks. "I'm sure he had in mind an around the world flight. But that never did come out as public information as far as the company was concerned."

As to why Hughes never flew the plane again, Haldeman ventured that "he had a physical problem at the time and I think it just got worse and worse."

Hughes also had discussed with his close friend Cary Grant plans for a movie featuring the flying boat in which a secret agent (a la James Bond) would battle for the right in exotic parts of the world. The flying boat would provide the agent's international mobility, just as Agent 007 makes use of advanced modes of transport. The idea was probably little more than conversation. When Senator Ferguson asked Hughes during the hearings, "Have you contemplated using this in your movie production business?" Hughes replied, "Senator, that is rather an absurd suggestion."[17]

Power plant mechanic Al Geverink said that Hughes "used to come around [to the flying boat site] until about 1952" and less and less from then on. "We had an awful lot of work to do. You know, change this, change that, and then engineering got a hold of it. It just seemed that they wanted to make a career out of just keeping it in the hangar. Of course, we mechanics were trying to get it ready to fly all the time.

"I was looking forward to flying it again," said Geverink. ". . . I thought it was one of the best aircraft I'd ever seen as far as workmanship was concerned. It was a beautiful piece of work. Like a fine piece of furniture. The only way to really appreciate it is to see it."[18]

Only Hughes knew why he never flew the boat again. Hopper believes that other interests took up too much of his time. New tests were scheduled, but Hughes always cancelled out at the last minute. "He just would not spend the time with us that was needed to get ready for the next flight," says Hopper. "I can't believe he was afraid. *I* wasn't."

Dave Grant also believes that other interests and demands on Hughes's time kept him from flying the boat again. "When he first left the flying boat he was mixed up with RKO. After that came TWA. He just never got unmixed up with other stuff to come back to us."

There was yet another factor: After World War II the expected need for and interest in large seaplanes simply dried up—giving Hughes no sense of urgency to proceed with further tests. Although water covers most of the globe and most key coastal cities have protected harbors, giant seaplanes require special shore-based handling facilities of some complexity. (Hughes himself had spent many months designing a floating dock.)

Meanwhile, the construction of military airfields in nearly every corner of the world during the war removed the incentive to develop such facilities. Landplanes could go more places than seaplanes, and support facilities were already in place and could be easily improved.

Equally important factors were the nearly universal switch from wood to metal construction and the coming of the jet age. Hughes's wooden, prop-driven flying boat was a tremendous achievement, but it was on the wrong side of a great watershed in aviation development.

In 1949 the General Services Administration took over the assets of the Reconstruction Finance Corporation including title to the flying boat. For the GSA the aircraft became "just a disposal problem." Not only did the GSA want to get rid of the monster but the City of Long Beach wanted to regain its valuable waterfront property to develop a major oil terminal. In addition, the Internal Revenue Service no longer agreed to Hughes's use of flying boat expenses as a tax writeoff. Hughes stood to lose millions if he did not get rid of it.

Although the General Services Administration had legal title to the flying boat and the right to sell it to anyone, the only people who wanted to buy it were promoters. Hughes said that if the boat were sold to "any of their ilk," he would sue. To him the flying boat was a great accomplishment and should be recognized as such.

According to Don Lopez, Chief of the Aeronautical section of the Air Space Museum at the Smithsonian Institution, "GSA wanted to give it to us. But we had no use for it. We don't have the budget to move it here—if that's possible at all. We can't set up a museum on the West Coast. It's just completely impractical. So finally it was agreed that we would accept the flying boat from the GSA. We in turn would give full title to it to the Summa Corporation (the umbrella corporation for Hughes enterprises) in exchange for the racer, which we wanted. The racer was a very important airplane and the right size for us. But in order for the government to come out at least even, we decided that a group of aircraft appraisers and a committee of experts picked by the American Institute of Astronautics and Aeronautics would appraise both airplanes and decide what would be a fair difference. It turned out that the basic trade was that we got the racer and $700,000 from Summa. They got clear title to the flying boat.[19]

At first it was planned that the flying boat would be donated to the Smithsonian and eight other museums around the country to be displayed in pieces. The Smithsonian would take the cockpit and a section of one wing and the remaining parts would be parceled out to the others. Hughes balked at this, and Nadine Henley wrote him a strongly worded memo saying that donating the airplane, even in pieces, would resolve his tax problems and assure the flying boat a dignified place in history. "We implore you," she wrote, "more for your sake and your name in history than for any other reason to take the ghost out of the hangar and allow the Smithsonian to make a shrine of it forever."[20]

There was a vigorous public protest on the West Coast when proposals to dismantle the huge flying boat were made public. Summa Corporation was picketed. On April 15, 1975, Carl Byoir & Associates issued a press release from Summa saying that the Smithsonian Institution and Summa had agreed to delay any dismantling of the craft. "Although it is contemplated that a non-profit museum might devise some method of preserving and displaying the HK-1 intact, there are clearly many uncertainties as to costs involved in moving such a large craft overland, providing a suitable building, and operations and maintenance."

Howard Hughes died April 5, 1976. In the fall of that year Summa telephoned Rear Adm. Carl Seiberlich who was managing an Advanced Naval Vehicle Concept Evaluation Project for the Deputy Chief of Naval Operations for Air Warfare. The Summa representative told the admiral that they wanted to do something useful with the airplane—something Mr. Hughes would have felt right about. Was the Navy interested?

"Well, we'll look into it," said Seiberlich. "Not only that, but I will coordinate with other government agencies."

In November, a government team inspected the airplane in Long Beach. They found it was not just big, it was a work of art put together by cabinetmakers. The laminated wood made by Fairchild's Duramold process had a finish as smooth as glass. There was a complete set of engines and several sets of spares preserved in cans.

"Everything's in perfect condition," Seiberlich said during an interview in his Pentagon office. "You could go fly that airplane."[21]

Seiberlich explained the Navy's interest by saying that as part of their evaluation of advanced naval vehicle concepts, the Navy was interested in the wing and ground effect phenomena—the extra lift provided when the wing's downwash cushions out against a ground or water surface. This effect extends to an altitude equal to about fifty per cent of the wingspan—one reason for the Navy interest in the 320-foot wing of the giant Hughes creation.

The Navy's idea was that if a plane were big enough, and designed to maximize the wing and ground effect, it would make possible transoceanic flights within the ground effect envelope at thirty per cent less power than would be required to fly comparable weights outside the ground effect range. Fuel savings would permit even greater loads to be carried.

Admiral Seiberlich explained this with the help of a framed photograph hanging on his office wall of the Hercules airborne on its first and only flight.

"It's flying in ground effect right there," said the admiral. "In this particular design, the hull and the solid struts to the tip floats act to fence in the main wing and engine areas and enhance the wing and ground effect. The propellers are all within this envelope. The wing flaps extend completely across it. Thus the flaps act to direct the prop blast and wing downwash trapped between these end plates downward towards the water surface. It would not take too much modification to make this an ideal wing and ground effect vehicle.

"I think that Hughes was quite surprised when it lifted off the water well below the design airspeed for that gross weight," Admiral Seiberlich said. "He suddenly found himself airborne and then spent the remaining part of the flight, which was a little over a mile, just in landing the airplane. That's my opinion and only my opinion."[22]

Hughes's chief aerodynamicist, Carl Babberger, thinks the admiral is wrong in thinking that the airplane took off well below the design takeoff speed. "Ground effect didn't have anything to do with takeoff speed," he said. "Classical ground effect occurs when the ground plane [surface] is near enough to the wing that it doesn't allow the air to be deflected downward as much as at altitude, and therefore the induced drag is less."[23] This affects power requirements, but has nothing to do with lift.

According to Dr. Harvey Chaplin, Director of the Aerodynamic Laboratory, David Taylor Model Basin, who is involved with wing and ground effect studies at the Pentagon, "Carl Babberger is quite right. The kind of benefit you'd realize in flying transatlantic within the ground effect altitude would be a drag reduction which would reduce fuel consumption, increase range, and increase payload. This other business about the lift being generated from the propwash: we've been doing research on airplanes that generate a hell of a lot of lift that way. Generally, it depends on the gap through which you allow the air to escape underneath the flaps. To be effective, this area has to be less than your slipstream area. In the case of the Spruce Goose, I'm pretty sure you wouldn't get much boost from the slipstream because there is too much gap between the surface [of the water] and the bottom of the flaps."[24] But, Chaplin agrees with Seiberlich that flying such a large aircraft within the ground effect envelope could result in very substantial increases in load-carrying ability and fuel economy.

Thus there were very real reasons for Navy interest. Furthermore, this is the only giant seaplane in existence; another like it will never be built. "So before we cut this one up," said Seiberlich, "we want to be sure that we know all we need to know about large seaplanes."

This is why the U.S. Navy in 1977 became seriously interested in a full flight test program for the 30-year-old Hughes flying boat. Seiberlich consulted a number of outside experts during the course of his investigation, including Grover Loening who at that time was still alive. He also consulted Ernie Stout, who designed the Pan American clippers and the Coronado flying boat, regarding the hull design.

Unfortunately, after a six-month study, the Armed Services, NASA, and other interested agencies reluctantly concluded in March, 1977 that even though the aircraft was flyable, a test program with the flying boat would take money from projects of greater current priority.

With that, Summa finally pulled the plug on the air conditioning system at Terminal Island. Now their efforts were concentrated on finding some group or organization that could maintain the aircraft as a permanent display in one piece. Arelo Sederberg, vice president of Carl Byoir & Associates, speaking for Summa Corporation in April 1977 said that preliminary discussions had been held with a group of aviation history buffs who had formed the Air Museum of the West. Long Beach Municipal Judge Gilbert Alsten, a museum organizer, was optimistic about raising the several million dollars required. "We're hoping we can save the airplane," he said. "Nothing like it has ever been built before, and nothing like it probably will ever be built again."[25] Their organization sparked a great deal of interest in the project, but in the end they lacked the necessary backing to consummate a deal.

In January 1980, the Summa Board of Directors met at corporate headquarters in Las Vegas and postponed a decision as to whether to put the Hughes Hercules on display next to the Queen Mary in Long Beach or at the Aero World theme park planned for Mira Mesa near San Diego, or at a theme park near Redwood City, California on San Francisco Bay called Marineland-Africa-USA.

Aero World developers would require that the airplane be disassembled and barged to San Diego. The Redwood City site was such that the airplane would not have to be disassembled, but could be moved intact by sea up the coast, under the Golden Gate and San Francisco-Oakland Bay Bridges to the bayside display site. The move to a site near the Queen Mary in Long Beach would be easiest of all. This, plus the attractions of a double bill, gave Long Beach an advantage if only the proper mix of money, organization, and management could be found.

There were problems. Long Beach had lost money on the Queen Mary project (a record $2.5 million in 1979—80) and there was a reluctance on the part of some of those involved to become over-committed. Bill Berry, former Summa program manager for the flying boat, told the author on January 29, 1980, that Long Beach did not want to put up any money. "They want us to pay for the advertising, for exhibits, carpeting, and so on. We feel that wasn't in our original bargain, that that is part of museum operation. Our offer was to provide a display building and pay for the delivery of the airplane."

In early April 1980, the Committee to Save the Flying Boat under Chairman Robert L. McCaffery held a press conference aboard the Queen Mary after Summa had announced that if $175,000 could be put up to move the flying boat, Summa would fund the rest. But by the time the Summa board met to consider the problem on May 21, the money had not been raised. Summa announced plans to dismantle the boat. McCaffery's committee continued its media blitz and contacted local Assemblyman Bob Dornan, an ex-fighter pilot. Dornan sparkplugged a resolution of the State of California declaring the aircraft to be of historic significance.

The efforts of the Committee to Save the Flying Boat attracted national attention which culminated in the appearance of Glenn Odekirk and Robert McCaffery on the July 16 "Good Morning America" show and with the listing of the flying boat in the National Register of Historic Places of the Department of the Interior.

In the meantime, Richard Stevens, an active member of the Aero Club of Southern California and president of Wrather Hotels, helped bring the Wrather Corporation and the Aero Club into the picture. (Wrather Hotels operates Disneyland Hotel, among other of its concerns, as part of Jack Wrather's Beverly Hills-based entertainment conglomerate.)[26]

The Flying Boat Finds a Home

In July 1980, the Aero Club developed a letter of intent, jointly signed by Summa, Wrather, and Nissen Davis, president of the Aero Club of Southern California and vice president for public relations of Flying Tiger Airline. The letter of intent stated that upon the satisfaction of certain conditions, Summa would donate the Hughes flying boat to the Aero Club, a nonprofit organization, which would enter into a management agreement with Wrather to move the airplane, design and erect a permanent building to display the boat, and operate a museum. The funds required for the move and the building will total more than $2.5 million and will be provided by loans to the Aero Club from Summa ($1.5 million), Wrather ($250,000), ARCO, and others. The money will be repaid from expected receipts from the operation of the museum and associated activities.[27]

At last it appeared that a viable combination of money, organization, personnel, connections, and experience had been found. On August 25, 1980, Wrather signed a forty-year lease to operate the Queen Mary and display the Hughes flying boat in Long Beach Harbor and began an aggressive program of development and promotion.

On October 31, William Rice Lummis, representing the Hughes family and Summa, officially turned the flying boat over to the Aero Club.

In building the world's largest airplane, Howard Hughes hoped to make a great leap forward, a major contribution to the progress of American aviation. That the aircraft did not live up to his dreams does not diminish the fact that its completion in the face of almost insuperable obstacles was in itself a tremendous achievement.

A 1948 letter to "The Men and Women of Hughes Aircraft Company," reassured his employees that although he had just bought RKO he was not turning his back on the flying boat or on Hughes Aircraft. He had high hopes for both:

"It is true that I have spent a good deal of time recently on the RKO deal. However, I am sure that you are also aware that I finished my design work in connection with the changes on the flying boat some time ago. There has intervened, by necessity, a period during which these changes are going through the process of final engineering, fabrication, assembly, and installation.

"I have tried to finish all phases of the RKO deal during this period, so that I will be free before the changes on the flying boat are completed.

"In view of the vicious political campaign which has been waged against me by certain competitive airline interests, together with their pal, Senator Brewster, and which attack has centered around the flying boat, it should hardly be necessary for me to say that nothing in this world means more to me than this airplane. . . .

"And if we do finally succeed in designing, building, and flying an airplane twice as large as anything else in the world, and overcoming the hundreds of serious obstacles which are a part of this tremendous step ahead in the world's progress in aviation, then I believe people will wake up to what we have accomplished and complete vindication will have to follow.

"What's more important, we ourselves will know what we have done for aviation. . . .

"And I believe that one of these days this company will be one of the leading aircraft organizations of the United States, second to none in research, and recognized as such.

"When that time comes we can all hold our head up, and the more so because the way hasn't been easy and there have been plenty of people shooting at us."[28]

It is fitting that the aircraft should go on display as a monument to that aspiration.

13

A New Nest

Jack Wrather, who owned the Disneyland Hotel, had leased the Queen Mary from the City of Long Beach as an exhibit and built the huge geodesic dome alongside for the Hughes Flying Boat in 1982. When Wrather died in 1988, the Walt Disney Company bought the Wrather Corporation, including Wrather Port Properties, and continued to operate the two exhibits. However, by 1990 Disney was heavily involved in two major foreign investments, EuroDisney and Disney Tokyo.

After two years of disappointing financial returns from the Queen Mary and Flying Boat exhibits, Disney decided to cancel the lease agreements with the City of Long Beach and to convert the Queen Mary and Flying Boat complex to a major sea park with "no provisions for the Spruce Goose."

Accordingly, on March 6, 1990, Disney formally notified the Aero Club of Southern California and its subsidiary Aero Exhibits, Inc., the owners of the Hughes Flying Boat, of their intention to discontinue the lease effective September 30.

Robert McCaffery, who in 1980 was deeply involved with the work of the "Committee to Save the Hughes Flying Boat" and in 1985 was president of the Aero Club of Southern California, again launched a media blitz. In slide lectures to hundreds of corporations, management associations, and service clubs, and in appearances on radio and television shows, he emphasized the importance of preserving this national historic monument.

Ronald Reagan had written McCaffrey saying that the Flying Boat "represents some of our people's best characteristics: imagination, ingenuity and daring. It is appropriate that we pay tribute to the American tradition by preserving the great legacy of this Flying Boat for many generations to come."

McCaffrey also quoted Senator Barry Goldwater who wrote: "It may never fly again, but it certainly stands as an example of what skilled hands can do under the direction of talented and dedicated brains."

As the search for a new home developed, Aero Exhibits, Inc. (AEI) received dozens of inquiries from locations across the U.S. In April of 1990, AEI selected eight organizations considered to be most worthy of consideration. Six responded with formal proposals. Among them, a proposal supported by a group of Las Vegas businessmen for a privately financed aviation exhibit hall and convention center in Las Vegas was eliminated.

By mid-May, AEI further narrowed the field to three: the Oceanside Tourism Foundation at Oceanside, California; Bissett McGrath & Co. of Tampa, Florida; and Evergreen International Aviation of McMinnville, Oregon. All bidders agreed to continue the annual donations to the Scholarship Fund of the Aero Club of Southern California.

On July 9, the Board of the Aero Club of Southern California voted unanimously for relocation of the Hughes HK-1 Flying Boat to a new aircraft museum to be built by Evergreen International Aviation at the Company's headquarters in McMinnville, Oregon. A spokesman for the Club called it "finding a good home for our child."

Who and what is Evergreen International Aviation and how did they become involved in the restoration, preservation and display of historic aircraft?

In 1960, thirty-year old Delford M. "Del" Smith, a graduate of the University of Washington and an Air Force veteran, launched Evergreen Helicopters with a vision of providing helicopters for humanitarian missions, fire fighting, agriculture and industry. Evergreen began operations with two Hiller 12E's. Today, Evergreen is a world leader in helicopter technology and its applications, employing more than 100 rotary-wing aircraft for agriculture, construction, forestry management, health, logging, petroleum and utilities.

The heavy lift division of the helicopter group has performed miracles in power line construction and in specialized support for other construction and industrial projects.

In the 1970's the United Nations World Health Organization contracted with Evergreen to provide helicopters, spray systems, crews and ground support to fight blindness in seven African countries where black fly-infested riverways were the problem. Upon completion of this 20-year program which Evergreen pioneered and launched, more than 20 million people will have been protected from the blindness-causing black fly and allowed to return to the fertile areas of Africa. The World Health Organization has identified these operations as the most successful health mission ever conducted.

Evergreen Helicopters, Inc. was the starting point for the development of the Evergreen International worldwide empire that now includes Evergreen International Airlines, Inc.; Evergreen Air Center, Inc. (located on a 2,080-acre airpark in the Sonoran Desert near Tucson, Arizona); Evergreen Aircraft Sales & Leasing Company, Inc.; Evergreen Aviation Ground Logistics Enterprises, Inc. (EAGLE); Evergreen Agricultural Enterprises, Inc. and EvergreenTours.

The largest division of the Evergreen family, Evergreen International Airlines (EIA), is known as the "airlines' airline." Many aircraft carrying the logos of better known airlines are actually owned and maintained by Evergreen and flown by Evergreen crews who wear the uniforms of the companies that hire their services.

Evergreen boasts the world's largest B747 operating fleet with 14 B747. The approximately 50 fixed-wing aircraft belonging to the company include the Boeing 747 and 727, the Lockheed L188, and the McDonnell Douglas DC-8 and DC-9. The company has flown under contract for Air France, Air India, Garuda Indonesia, Iberia, Japan Airlines, Quantas, Saudi, El-Al, Alitalia, South Africa Airlines, New Zealand Airlines, and Lufthansa.

Evergreen developed and managed operations for United Parcel Service, Emery, and the United States Postal Service. On January 11, 1993, the airline added to its role as the airlines' airline by becoming a common carrier in its own right, serving the Far East as the third American airline receiving authority to fly into China.

Under the direction of founder and owner Delford M. Smith, the Evergreen group has achieved an averaged growth rate of forty-five percent for each year of the past twenty years. A skilled pilot, a brilliant businessman and a dedicated humanitarian, Del Smith has parlayed a lifelong love of aviation into a thriving international business.

Now this same love of aviation and its history has led to the development of a world class aviation museum, the Evergreen AirVenture Museum.

The Evergreen collection of historic aircraft restored to flying condition is already one of the very best in the country. Particularly strong in warbirds, the aircraft complement the World War II era of the Hughes Flying Boat.

Once again a move of the giant boat required meticulous planning and organization. George Kruska, Evergreen's disassembly supervisor, had worked on the HK-1 assembly team as a young engineer. Now he recruited a cadre of Hughes veterans to assist in the disassembly. Ray Kirkpatrick, David Grant, Jack Real, Bill Berry, John Boseker, Stan Soderberg, and Van Storm were once again involved with the aircraft that had been the center of their professional lives for such a long time in the 1940s and beyond.

The planners, schedulers, mechanics, engineers, riggers and equipment operators operated under a demanding schedule that called for completion of the project in two months. Close coordination and daily project review were conducted from a control center in a cramped construction trailer. Meals were provided by the crews mess of the Queen Mary.

Propellers, engines and smaller parts were crated and shipped overland on Interstate 5. A 60 by 60 foot window was opened in the geodesic dome to allow removal of the fuselage, wings and tail. The parts were shrink-wrapped for protection from sunlight and moisture. Specially designed cradles braced the large sections to withstand the rigors of the sea and land transfers. On October 10, 1992, the rudder, ailerons, elevators, flaps and horizontal stabilizers departed Long Beach by barge and arrived at Portland Terminal 2 five days later.

The fuselage and wings, after disassembly and shrink-wrapping, were rolled out of the dome and onto the large Sause Brothers ocean-going barge NEHALEM.

Finally, on October 13, the ocean-going tug NATOMA took up the slack in the lines attached to the NEHALEM and departed Long Beach. For nearly five days, the two moved northward, 20 miles off the coasts of California and Oregon, at an average speed of 8 knots. As they berthed in Portland, the sun was just going down on October 18.

Portland Mayor Bud Clark proclaimed October 22nd "Spruce Goose Day" and thousands of spectators came to Waterfront Park to welcome the flying boat to Oregon. The 980 nautical mile sea voyage was history. Now came the hard part.

Throughout the next several months, weather and river levels wreaked havoc with the move schedule. A recurring obstacle was the Willamette River at levels either too high for the wings to clear the bridges, or too low to allow off-loading. Finally, the move up the Willamette River began. When the fuselage past through the historic Willamette Falls locks at West Linn, it set a record for the longest load ever to pass through. The wings set a record for the highest.

All sections were finally off-loaded on Oregon territory near the end of January. Now they faced a seven and one-half mile journey over narrow back roads of Yamhill County. Setting off from the Weston Bar off-load site, the caravan stretched more than 1,500 feet.

Three 475-horsepower prime movers, each with 104 forward gears, pulled the 181-foot Flying Boat fuselage cradled on a hydraulic transport dolly. This load needed at least 35 feet of overhead clearance. Each 158-foot wing was ensconed in a steel cradle. Tipped in vertical positions on their trailing edges, they reached a height of 62 feet.

The tail sections, also encased in steel cradles and tipped on their trailing edges, measured 39 feet in height and 62 feet in length.

As the convoy moved the final mile to its destination, a Spruce Goose Homecoming Parade of vintage military vehicles, classic automobiles, antique fire and farm equipment, equestiran groups, school bands, and Scout troops joined them. Members of the Evergreen air force, along with local vintage aircraft and hot air balloons, saluted the HK-1 from the sky. The arrival marked the end of the 1,055 mile, 138 day odyssey from Long Beach, California.

A short welcoming ceremony paid tribute to founder and chairman of Evergreen International Aviation, Delford M. Smith, who had acquired the Flying Boat for display at the new Evergreen AirVenture Museum. Ceremonial speakers included Oregon State Representative Marilyn Dell, community leader, Dan Corrigan, and a longtime friend and confidant of Howard Hughes, Jack Real, now President of the Evergreen AirVenture Museum.

There were letters of congratulation from Oregon Governor Barbara Roberts, U.S. Representative Mike Kopetski, U.S. Senator Mark O. Hatfield and Senator Robert Packwood, State Representative Patti Milne, and State Senator Stan Bunn.

It was fitting that the arrival of the Hughes Flying Boat to its final display site should be so saluted.

Appendix

Working for Howard Hughes

EACH OF THE FOLLOWING STORIES from Hughes associates and employees provides a revealing look at Hughes the man and what it was like to work for him. The first story indicates something of Hughes's secretiveness, his dislike of government regulations or of anyone telling him what he could or could not do, and the lengths to which he would go to prove a point or cling to a point of principle.

Jack Jacobsen, former Hughes electrical mechanic, tells of working on Hughes's Sikorsky at wartime Grand Central Airport, a military base at the time. Hughes had a hangar about a quarter of a mile from the main gate. For a reason known only to Hughes, he did not want the soldiers on the field to know that he had a huge four-engine Boeing Stratoliner and a new twin-engine Beechcraft in the hangar. So if Hughes employees wanted to use the hangar door on the airfield side, they had to peek out and make sure nobody was around, go out quickly, and close the door immediately behind them. Once out, they could not get back in from that side.

This secrecy was probably related to Hughes's later charge that the War Department was trying to take TWA's five Boeing Stratoliners away from the company and turn them over to Pan American to fly the Atlantic.[1] Obviously, Hughes would not want the Army to know that he had a Stratoliner that was not gainfully employed.

According to Glenn Odekirk, Hughes had originally planned to use the Boeing 307 Stratoliner for a goodwill tour of major world capitals in 1939, but this plan had been blocked by the war.

"We were working on Hughes's Sikorsky just outside the hangar on the airfield side," says Jack Jacobsen. "We'd load our tools and equipment in one of our three-wheeled motorcycles, go out on the main street, through the main gate, and back up to the airfield side of the hangar to work on the airplane.

"One day Hughes came out the back way to look things over and then couldn't get back in. So he said to me, 'Take me around front on a motorcycle. I want to make a phone call.'

"Okay," I said. So up the airstrip we went to the main gate.

"The colored sergeant MP said, 'Where's this man's ID?'

"Hughes wouldn't talk to him. He was sitting on the back of the three-wheeled motorcycle, and he tapped me on the shoulder. 'You tell him who I am.'

"So I explained to the guard, 'This is Mr. Hughes. We just want to go in and make a phone call.'

" 'Well,' the sergeant says, 'he has to have an ID, some identification like you have before he can come through the gate.'

"Now, Hughes wouldn't talk directly to the guard. He tapped me on the shoulder again and said, 'You tell him again who I am and that I left my ID in the hangar.'

"I tell this to the guard and he says, 'No, no. I can't let him through without an ID. I don't care where it is.'

"Hughes just sat there and tapped me on the shoulder (this went on about four times), 'Tell him who I am and where I left my ID.'

"Finally the guard said, 'I don't give a goddamn who he is. He isn't gettin' off this field without either an ID or going to the Provost Marshal to get off.'

"Well, Hughes said, 'Take me back to the airplane.' The Sikorsky was about ready to fly, so Hughes said, 'Now you stay here a minute. When I start to taxi down to get on the runway, you get on your motorcycle and go back to that guard. When you see me fly by, you tell that guard that I just flew over and got off this field without an ID.'

"And that's exactly what I had to do."[2]

During the construction of the H-1 racer, Hughes telephoned Dick Palmer and William Rockefeller one evening, after having worked with them all day, and said that he had an urgent matter he wanted to see them about. When they arrived they learned that the "urgent" matter was to drive him ninety miles to a dinner date in Santa Barbara. Hughes had neither car nor driver's license at the time and was always borrowing cars and then forgetting where he left them.

On the way to Santa Barbara, a stray dog dashed in front of them and was hit. Hughes picked up the bloody animal in his arms and insisted that they find a veterinarian although, in typical fashion, he was already two hours late for his date with a California socialite.

They were three hours late by the time they called for the girl, but Hughes offered no explanation, neither did he talk to the girl during dinner. Instead, he spent the evening talking shop with Palmer and Rockefeller, breaking away occasionally to call the animal hospital. The dog recovered, and Palmer kept it.[3]

Another instance of Hughes's concern for animals is provided by Jack Jacobsen. They were at the D-2 desert test facility at Harper's Lake. Ava Gardner was in Las Vegas getting a divorce, and Hughes wanted Jacobsen to drive him the eighteen miles or so to Barstow so he could telephone her. About ten of those eighteen miles were dirt roads meandering through the sagebrush. It was very dark as they returned, and Hughes said, "You're driving sort of reckless. There are a lot of rabbits along this road. Don't hit one of those. If one jumps up in front of the car, I want you to run off into the brush, but don't hit it. And you tell all the other fellas not to hit a rabbit."[4]

Food and Dress

Hughes scheduled his activities according to his own interests and biology, not by clock and calendar. He worked as long as interest and endurance prompted and only slept and ate when he felt like it. He never carried a watch. That other people, who lived according to time and schedule, might be inconvenienced was of no concern to him. His flight engineers and other close associates simply had to adjust to this.

Earl Martyn was twenty-five years old when he started work for Howard Hughes as a general aviation mechanic in 1935. His first job was to help build the tail section of the H-1. Hughes liked Earl, respected his abilities, and began using him as a flight mechanic. In the early 1940s, nearly everywhere Hughes went Earl went too.

Many times Hughes would go all day without eating, and then would eat three steak dinners at midnight. By that time Earl would feel so lousy that he didn't care whether he ate or not. He often told Hughes, "If you'd eat regularly and eat the right kind of food, you wouldn't have these headaches and whatnot you've been having."

Apparently, Hughes was aware that his lifestyle was hard on his flight engineer because he later autographed a photo of the F-11, "To Earl with my apologies for all the meals I made you miss." But he joked to everyone who flew with them that "Earl's the eatinest guy I ever knew."[5]

Hughes dressed for comfort and convenience and did not care what others might think. "He'd show up at the airport in his shirtsleeves and his valet would come out with a box of clean shirts, and that's all he'd take," says Earl Martyn. "Oh, he used to carry cookies with him once in awhile [Mrs. Martyn says they were usually the oatmeal cookies he liked so well which his housekeeper baked for him], but he didn't even do that all the time. He used to carry milk with him, but not in later years. He had ulcers for awhile, I think. He was drinking milk for that."[6]

John Glenn, former power plant mechanic for Hughes, recalls that a blue serge suit, white shirt, and no tie were standard. "Sometimes he'd wear kind of a cardigan sweater that he had for God I don't know how long—for years (laughs)."[7]

Sherman Fairchild said, "I've never seen all this business of going around in tennis sneakers. Any time Howard ever went out with me he always looked very well, blue suit on; extremely gracious to my aunt; he's a very charming person, very simple person. On the other hand, an extremely determined person. Once he'd decided that something was going to be done, nothing under the sun could alter it."[8]

Aerodynamicist Carl Babberger remembers a meeting with Lockheed president Robert Gross and chief engineer Kelly Johnson regarding modifications Hughes wanted in the tail design of the Constellation. "I remember him asking them to do this and their refusing—Kelly Johnson trying to justify it and me telling Kelly that we both knew better than that. And when they said no, they wouldn't modify the tail, Howard just said, 'Well, that's the end of the conference'—very quietly. Howard was presentable at the meeting. Probably didn't have a tie on. I can't recall him wearing a tie. His typical garb was a white shirt open at the neck. He didn't wear a coat very often."[9]

Hughes was a perfectionist, extremely fussy about the smallest details. When new engines for the flying boat had to be brought by rail from the Naval Air Station in Norfolk, Virginia, Hughes worried that the bumping across the country with the crankshafts in one position would harm the bearing surfaces. So he arranged for them to be shipped in a special car equipped with devices on each engine that slowly rotated their crankshafts during the entire trip and special instrumentation that recorded the speed of the train, the bumps, the starts, the stops, everything, all the way from Norfolk to California.

When the engines arrived in Long Beach they were torn down completely, inspected, and reassembled. "Then," says engine man Jack Jacobsen, "we would have to take them one at a time up to Culver City and run 'em through a special break-in procedure on the test stand there. But we could only run them from twelve o'clock at night to eight o'clock in the morning providing the wind was lower than three miles an hour (laughs). And by golly, he was out there to see that we did it."[10]

Hughes kept reasons to himself and made little effort to keep his employees informed. As John Glenn put it, "To work on something and not know what the heck is going on is frustrating and confusing. And this was his bag. He did this all the time. The Old Man bought a regular Connie after the war. We never could figure out what the hell he was going to do with it. It was full of ballast tanks. It had the damndest plumbing system. He'd fly it and shift the water around, move the ballast back and forth. He never did tell any of us what he was doing with it. We assumed he was checking performance with various center of gravity locations."[11]

Personal Habits and Hospitality

Hughes was rarely seen by most who worked for him. Carl Babberger, then chief of the Aerodynamics and Research Department, worked with Hughes on the D-2, the flying boat, the F-11, and other projects. When Babberger came with Hughes at $50 a week in 1939, they were just starting the D-2. At that time there were half a dozen engineers in the engineering department.

For about ten years Babberger had fairly close relations with his boss, but Hughes never came to the design office. "He never came in to be seen by anybody that I recall," says Babberger. "There may have been one or two times that he was generally seen, but I certainly didn't see him. He never came into my office. If he came to see what was cooking, such as when we were building the new plant, he came after everybody had gone home. He may have gone up to see Hopper a few times or somebody like that, but no, he was a recluse, basically. He was uncomfor-

238

table among people. The guy was very shy and very health conscious—6'4" and 165 pounds—so he wouldn't be in crowds. He didn't socialize worth a damn. His socialization was pretty much limited to a business meeting of some kind or sleeping with some broad."[12]

Yet some of the mechanics, technicians, and flight crew members at times saw Hughes fairly often and communicated on a first-name basis. When Babberger was reminded of this, he said, "Well, with those who worked on the airplane, Petrali, Bruce Burk, and one or two other guys he was a regular fella. Very quiet, though. I mean he wasn't an outgoing fella in any way, shape or form." He laughed. "Basically a recluse. He just got more so as time went on."[13]

In later years Hughes tried to get his flight crews to call him "Mr. Hughes" rather than the more familiar "Howard." Flight engineer Ray Kirkpatrick recalls one flight when Hughes said, "Now, fellas, when we get to Las Vegas, I want you to say, 'Now Mr. Hughes, this is what we're going to do.' " Obviously, this was an indirect way of saying, "Don't call me Howard."

"We'd already called him Howard for a couple of years," said Kirkpatrick," and we were a pretty small group. Somehow or other he thought he ought to have more dignity. We had a hard time learning to say Mr. Hughes, but we finally did. Most of us anyway."[14]

Most of Babberger's association with Hughes was at Hughes's house. "We got pretty close for awhile there." One day while Babberger was there Hughes got a call or two that evidently were from women. "He'd never talk over the phone in your presence. He went into another room. He came back and I had a smirk on my face and he said to me, 'Babberger, you sonofabitch, you.' He knew that I knew what the hell was going on.

"A week or two later I was up to his house and he gave me all the cigars he had. They were the driest cigars that I've ever seen in my life. He felt he was being very generous. He didn't smoke. So I said to Howard, 'Howard, you ought to take up cigar smoking. That's a lot of fun.' And he looked at me and smiled. What he thought was fun was women."

Although many engineering conferences were held at Hughes's house, he normally never offered his visitors so much as a glass of water while they were there. Babberger gives an example:

"He called me up after dinner, but when I came up there the power plant men were there and they were discussing something about the layout of the power plant. He had one of his handmaiden boys bring in his dinner—his usual meal was steak and peas. Well, . . . McElroy, who was head of power plants, remarked about they were getting hungry. That was apparently right after this F-11 accident. Howard was lying in bed and we were showing him our layouts and whatnot drawings right on the bed, and he'd look at them. He never got out of bed. And so he leaned over to the bedside stand and pulled out a twenty-dollar bill, which in those days was a lot of money, and sent three or four of them down to somewhere to get a meal.

"I was there in conference until they came back. . . . They went on and concluded their business, and about when they were ready to leave Howard said, 'Well, wasn't there any change?'

"And McElroy says, 'Well, yeh, if you gotta be precise, there were a few cents.' And he reached in and put out about twenty-five cents. Howard looked at him and drawled with emphasis, 'Well, you must be eatin' *pretty well.*' "[15]

Hydraulics engineer Dave Grant recalls that Hughes was businesslike, but he smiled often enough and once in awhile even told dirty jokes. "With me, he was always very pleasant. His usual greeting was, 'Hi, Dave,' and normally, if we'd been talking about any particular thing the previous time I'd seen him, he'd just go on from where we were. He seemed to associate people with exactly what he'd talked about. But as far as I was concerned in those days before he holed up at the Beverly Hills Hotel he didn't hesitate to shake hands or any of those normal things.

"He didn't, however, with the exception of one time, ever offer as much as a glass of water when you were at his house or anywhere else. That was a peculiarity, although right after he flew the second F-11 I bumped into him shortly after the flight when I was walking into the lab and that was the only time he ever took me to lunch."[16]

Hughes had no candy, magazines, ashtrays or anything around his house for visitors, but designer Roy Wendahl says that he saw a hospitable side of Hughes during meetings there. "He even sent out to the Gotham Restaurant for sandwiches and things if you were going to have a meeting of any length—or he'd send us down there to get something to eat. (The Gotham is no longer there. It was a fine late supper place near Highland and Hollywood Boulevard.) Howard was very considerate in those terms. But he never broke out the booze. He didn't drink himself, you know. He was very kind and considerate and friendly. No one ever treated me with more respect, was more kind—very apologetic if he called you at odd hours and that sort of thing. He was a loner, and yet you enjoyed your relationship with him because he was the big boss and yet he had a lot of respect for things you were able to do for him. He was very considerate in those terms; but when your job was finished you wouldn't hear from him for considerable periods of time."[17]

Another engineer states that Howard never mixed conversations. "If we were working on something, that's what we talked about. He didn't make any asides. Oh, once in awhile he'd tell a story. But he'd immediately put a stop to any further frivolity by saying, 'Let's get on with it.' "

Memory and Decision-Making

Rae Hopper said that Hughes sometimes had a convenient memory. He remembered a lot that they wanted him to forget, but he forgot a lot that he should not have. He had a knack for remembering technical detail.[18]

Part of Hughes's absent-mindedness was perhaps due to preoccupation with only those matters that interested him. His lack of concern for most people made it easy for him to forget people-related things. He could never remember where he had parked his car and this sometimes extended to people. He would say, "Where's

Bob?'' And someone would say, ''Don't you remember? You left him in Houston.'' But this kind of absent-mindedness was combined with a tenacious memory for legal precedents, principles of physics, aerodynamics, and electronics.

Earl Martin, former president of Hamilton Standard Propellers (not Earl Martyn the flight engineer), recalls sending a propeller serviceman to Canada at Hughes's insistent request when Hughes was there with a Constellation airplane. Hughes saw that the man was put up at the hotel, but then never contacted him. The man was there for a week; but Hughes never called him, never asked him to do anything. Finally the prop man called for instructions and Martin said, ''Well, come on home then.''[19]

Hughes could never tell the difference between movie producer Dore Schary's wife and Schary's secretary. He would peer cautiously at the person answering the door and say hopefully, ''Mrs. Schary?''[20]

Hughes had a poor memory for names and for people who were associated only briefly with certain events, while he could remember extremely well the technical details connected with those same events. His last major public interview illustrates this very well. On January 7, 1971, seven veteran newsmen gathered at the Sheraton Universal Hotel in North Hollywood to conduct an interview with Howard Hughes three thousand miles away in the Grand Britannia Beach Hotel on Paradise Island in the Bahamas. William R. (Dick) Hannah of Carl Byoir & Associates, Inc., lifted the receiver and direct-dialed a secret number.

During the two-and-a-half-hour interview, Gladwin Hill of the *New York Times* said, ''During your development of the Constellation airplane, you were assisted at some points by a professional pilot whose last name was Martin.''

Hughes could not remember the man. Step by step, Hill tried to refresh his memory until finally it was pinpointed that Martin had gone out to Lockheed with Hughes one day to discuss the design of the cockpit during the mock-up period. ''Well,'' said Hughes, ''I don't remember Mr. Martin, but I can tell you an awful lot about those mock-up discussions.'' And he proceeded to do so.[21]

Hughes was also notorious for indecision. Some have linked this with his desire for perfection—a willingness to wait for the latest developments before choosing a course of action. Carl Babberger has a different theory.

Design meetings at Hughes's house were held whenever he wanted someone to present what he had. He would look at the material but frequently would not make a decision on it. ''He'd either delay you by giving you other jobs,'' says Babberger, ''or wouldn't give a decision on such things as rib spacing, or whatever it was, for a considerable period of time. I think that I've got that figured out. Now this is purely Babberger's idea. He waited for the spirits to tell him. I think that's the reason for these damn delays in most cases. Some cases he may have been trying to swing a bargain of some kind or get special consideration or prices or something else, but I think that a genius and a madman are separated by a fine line. I think the guy had his nonlucid moments. His behavior, where he would sit in a room for a long time and look at the walls, the fasts, the delaying actions, all adds up to me to mysticism."[22]

Engineer Bruce Burk, who started working for Hughes in the spring of 1937 and stayed with him for thirty-nine years, agrees that Howard had trouble making up his mind. "We had to kick things around from pillar to post. We'd have forty different approaches to it before we'd finally sell it to Howard."[23]

Hughes's indecision sometimes caused serious delays. In 1943 a huge wooden hangar, 750 feet long, 250 feet wide, and 100 feet high was built with Defense Plant Corporation funds just north of Hughes's existing plant at Culver City. In August, the supervising engineer of the DPC complained that "we had plans out for a fire reservoir early in March and we now have a building costing in the neighborhood of $1,600,000 without adequate fire protection due to delay in construction. This delay had been brought about by neglect and indecision as to where the reservoir should be located, and to date, we have received no definite decision as to when construction of the reservoir will be started."[24]

Later, when Hughes lived in Las Vegas from 1953 to 1954, he became even more dilatory, routinely failing to respond to urgent appeals for action from Culver City. Two years passed before he authorized paving the 9,000-foot grass runway at Culver City. Meanwhile, each heavy rain turned the runway into a quagmire.

It has been mentioned that Hughes was adept at brain-picking and bringing out the best in people. Carl Babberger comments that "he didn't give us ideas and ask what to do with them. He asked us for ideas and told us what he thought about them."[25]

Lockheed's Kelly Johnson says, "Hughes liked to discuss engineering problems, but his way of discussing engineering problems was [that] Sunday morning he would call me and say—in terms of the [flying] boat, for instance—'Kelly, I'm going to make the nacelles look something like this and this and this, and what do you think of that?' And I'd tell him, spend a couple of hours on the phone. And then he'd call George Shirer up at Boeing immediately thereafter and he'd say, 'Kelly Johnson said that it should be something like this and this and this, what do you think?' And then he would end up calling Gene Root at Douglas and say, 'Kelly said that and George said that and what do you think?' "[26]

Bruce Burk says that Hughes was sharp: "He had a tremendous memory. He was nobody's fool. A brain picker? Oh, God, yeah. He'd call everybody. He was very thorough. He'd get involved in some particular project; it might be rather trivial, but God dang, he'd wear it out. He made a point to learn a lot, and that's one thing that held up the F-11; just [Hughes] learning a lot about engineering, really, and getting into structural engineering quite a bit, too."[27]

Flight mechanic Bill Grant thinks that Hughes was a much greater man than this country ever thought he was. "It'll be a hell of a long time before we get another guy that will devote his own personal interest and money in aviation like he did," says Grant. "And no glory for it afterward either."[28]

Babberger thinks that what was really important in Hughes's approach to design was reflected in what Hughes said to him sometime around 1950: "You know, Carl, we have to figure out, project, and prophesy where this industry is going to be ten or twenty years from now." Babberger feels that this consideration was reflected in everything Hughes did. "We were not a big enough company and we were in full competition with the giants. They could start out and do something and run like mad and not be too concerned about whether they were going to end up with an obsolescent airplane. But we went more conservatively and gave considerable thought to how long this thing was likely to be good for. I believe that this is one of the principal characteristics of his thinking and accounts for much of the slow progress that we made. . . . It amounted to watching the straws to see which way the wind was blowing. At the time I thought it was crazy, but since I had to do it to get along with him, I learned the trick and have been fairly successful in predicting way ahead. So I believe you want to make a point of that in discussing Howard's characteristics."

Some of the projects Babberger worked on with Hughes after the flying boat and the F-11 indicate Hughes's concern with future trends. These projects included a nuclear-powered airplane, a feasibility study of using hydrofoils to cross the Atlantic at 100 miles per hour, and the design of specialized submarines.[29]

Design meetings which he called were usually held at his home. During the design and construction of the flying boat this was a rented house at 619 Sarbonne Road in Bel Air, behind the tenth green of the Bel Air Country Club. Renting instead of buying reinforced Hughes's claim that he was a resident of Texas, in California on business, and thus not liable for California state income taxes. The meetings in the Bel Air house were usually at night, but as Babberger says, could be at any time, day or night. Some Sunday conferences were held at around ten a.m. One time Babberger received a phone call at two o'clock in the morning telling him to meet Hughes at a bungalow of the Beverly Hills Hotel. Babberger thought this was a little unusual because Hughes was normally on the phone until four a.m. and then slept until about noon.

Some have said that the reason Hughes used the phone so much was because it was easier for him to hear with an amplifier than face-to-face. Babberger thinks this was partially true. "He got a little harder of hearing all the time, but when I was with him he never had any trouble understanding me. I have a pretty good voice. I don't recall ever having to repeat except maybe over the phone on one or two occasions, possibly, when he might not have been at home with an amplifier. He did have an amplifier on his home phone."[30]

Hughes did not try to hide his deafness. At one point during the 1947 Senate Hearings, Senator Ferguson said, "Could you hear better if you held that earphone to your ear?"

"Yes," said Hughes, and did so. Flash bulbs popped.

Ferguson, disturbed, started to admonish the press, "Just a moment," he said.

But Hughes interrupted, "It's all right. I don't mind having my picture taken with it. Everybody knows I am deaf. I don't try to hide it."[31]

Christopher A. Reising, Jr., was an electrical engineer who left Lockheed to work for Hughes right after the war. He, too, remembers many nighttime meetings with Hughes: "I guess he had other things to do in the daytime. Usually, you were alerted ahead of time that you would probably have a meeting and to stay close to the phone so he could contact you."[32]

Designer Roy Wendahl says that occasionally meetings were held at Sam Goldwyn's lot in Hollywood on a sound stage or in a trailer, "but most of the time it was at night and mostly at home."[33]

Powerplant mechanic John Glenn, who started working for Hughes when there were only about 500 people at Hughes Aircraft, says that Hughes treated his employees well overall. "I attribute that to Rae Hopper and some of the other boys who were high-ups in the company. He never flinched about increases or anything like that. We had the best of machinery, machine shops, everything else. There was no scrimping on anything. When we went to do something, to build something, we had the best and we had it right now. So all in all it was an excellent company to work for. It still is, I understand."[34]

Of all his employees, Hughes was probably closest to those who flew with him. But, says John Glenn, "He'd take his flight engineer and fly to Houston and he'd say, 'Now you stay here and watch the plane and run it every day and take care of it.' And then he'd take off in another plane and, well, hell, maybe he'd be gone for two or three months. And there the guy would sit.

"The poor guy would start calling the plant and ask 'How long is he going to be gone?' As long as he had somebody there that's all [Hughes] cared about. In this respect he figured he paid us well, which he did, and we were supposed to do what he told us, which was only right, but he was not very considerate at times about those that were closest to him."

Hughes did not like to have to do anything. Government regulations and taxes galled him particularly. He did not seem to fit too well into the tightly-controlled new air space with radar traffic control. Flight engineer/mechanic Van Storm recalls that one time on departure out of the Los Angeles area, the controller noted that Hughes was deviating from his clearance routing and called him on it.[35]

Hughes the Pilot

He flew illegally during the last years of his flying career. John Glenn says, "He shouldn't have been flying due to his physical condition, be he did it anyway. Of course, he did a lot of things he wasn't supposed to do. But all in all, I had a lot of confidence in the man."[36]

Earl Martyn worked for Hughes for thirty-one years and probably flew with him as much or more than anyone else. "I got along with him fine," Earl recalls. "But he was a hard one to know. He's thinking about everything, you know, and he mixed his flying up with his business.

"When there weren't strangers around that I didn't know I called him Howard. But when there were strangers around that I didn't know I called him Mr. Hughes.

"He treated me fine except I never got any time off. Everyone else that ever flew with him got left someplace. He didn't leave me. I think the reason he didn't was because he knew that I would hop an airline and be right home. I was quite outspoken with him. If I didn't like something I told him. He'd listen to me. But most people, you know, kowtowed to him all the time and I don't think he liked that. If there was something I didn't like, why I told him about it, and he really liked that. He wasn't used to it.

"I went for, I don't know how many years [without a vacation], and he never let me have a vacation when my kids were out of school. I'd ask him and he'd say, 'Well, I'll let you know.' He'd keep putting me off. So finally I just decided, well, I'm going about it wrong.

"We had another fella who was supposed to be a stand-in in case I couldn't go sometimes, but he never did go with us. So one night we'd been out flying and we got home late at the airport at Culver City and I said, 'Well, look, Howard, I'm going to leave on my vacation, do you want me to get Charles to fly with us for awhile to get used to him and whatnot?' He says, 'Nope.' He didn't know what to do; I just told him I was going.

"So when the time came, he didn't try to talk me out of it but said, 'Well, what time are you leaving tomorrow?' That was on a Wednesday, I think, and I said, 'Well, I'm not leaving until Friday after work.'

"He got in his car, slammed the door and said, 'Well, go ahead and go.'

"I was gone a week. He called Odie and asked him when I was coming back, and [Odekirk] said, 'Well, he's got three weeks coming. He won't be back for three weeks.' And he had a fit.

"Well, when I got back he never said a word. He never mentioned it again. He was that way. If something would happen, you know, why the next day never another word about it.

"After I got back I ran across Rae Hopper walking across the yard at the plant and Rae says, 'I understand you've been on vacation?' And I said, 'Yeah.' And he said, 'How'd you ever work that?' I said, 'Well, I just decided asking didn't do any good so I just told him when I was leaving and I left.' And Rae said, 'Heck, I haven't had a vacation in years.' And I said, 'Well, now you know how to do it.' I still don't think he did it."[37]

Dave Grant, Hughes's hydraulic engineer, who designed the controls for the flying boat and flew in the copilot's seat on its one and only flight, recalls that Hughes had one peculiarity as a pilot. When he came in for a landing he kept the controls moving in a constant jitter, as if feeling the landing out all the way down. But Earl Martyn laughingly said, "Hah, he used to grease them on so you wouldn't even feel it." Martyn thought that Hughes was "a real good pilot and real good navigator" and that he handled in-flight emergencies well. "We took off from Palm Springs once and lost an engine on takeoff, so he just feathered the prop, shut that engine down, and we flew the rest of the way home to Los Angeles on one engine. We were in Mexico once and we lost an engine on takeoff and just turned around and came back in and landed. It had blown a hole in a piston." Asked if they were in Mexico on business, he laughed and said, "Monkey business, I think."

Because people had to speak loudly to him in airplanes, Howard was less conscious of his hearing deficiency while flying. Asked if being hard of hearing hindered Hughes's radio communications when he flew, Martyn thought not. "I think that he could hear better in an airplane than he could any place else. He called me his copilot and flight engineer. So I rode in the right seat and used to spell him sometimes so he could go to sleep or something. But Howard handled most of the radio communications."

Hughes was a good instrument pilot, says Martyn. "I know one trip we took to New York. We took off on instruments from Los Angeles and the only place we could get in for gas was Oklahoma City. There was a ground fog there so that you couldn't even see the runway, which was about two feet below the fog (laughs). We landed there and gassed. Then we took off and had to climb to about 15,000 feet to get above the first strata. There was another strata above us so we flew all the way to New York without ever seeing the ground or even the sky.

"We didn't have any oxygen. If you sat still you were all right. But I used to go back to the tail to do something, you know, and boy, I'd be puffing when I got back. I used to carry a pocketful of cube sugar with me and that helped."

According to Martyn Howard Hughes got his relaxation flying. He was a different person when he got up and away from everything. "There were times when we'd joke. I got him to laugh once in awhile. He was a little odd, but if I had that much money I'd be odd too."[38]

Hughes didn't follow the standardized rules and procedures that govern airline and service pilots. He was not a "book pilot," says one of his senior engineers. He developed his own techniques and peculiarities. One unusual technique was that when landing he would always trim for nose up so that he would have to push the nose down and fly it on to the runway. When asked why he did this he said, "That way, if anything happened to me we wouldn't crash into the ground, we'd pull up."[39]

Noah Dietrich thought that Howard bent the rules to suit himself. Dietrich was not a pilot himself, but he had his own airplane and was a close observer of what went on. He flew with Howard only once, but as he sat in the cockpit with him that one time he noticed that the power setting appeared excessive. "My pilot doesn't keep the manifold pressure that high," he remarked.

Howard put his finger to his lips. "Don't tell anybody about that," he said. According to Dietrich, Hughes was always pushing his airplanes to the limit of their capabilities.[40] Hughes's flight engineers disagree. Dietrich's airplane had different engines with different power settings and engine limits. Hughes was putting him on. All of Hughes's flight engineers agree that he babied his engines and never overboosted. Odekirk concurs. "That is absolutely correct," says Odekirk, "except when he broke the world's landplane speed record, of course."[41]

"Howard would no more abuse an engine or any piece of machinery than he would hit a baby," says mechanic Bill Grant. George Haldeman, a CAA Flight Standards test pilot, who checked Hughes out in the four-engine Boeing Stratoliner, the world's first pressurized airliner, called Hughes "a damn good pilot." As Haldeman recalls the 1939 flight check-out at the Boeing plant in Seattle, Hughes came to the field from his hotel wearing an open-necked shirt and rather soiled white duck pants. His first words on getting out of the taxi were: "I'm looking for a fella named Haldeman."

"That's me," said Haldeman.

"Have you got any money?" asked Hughes. "I didn't bring any with me. I wanta pay the cab."

Haldeman, who later was the CAA representative on the flying boat project, flew with Hughes four times during the check-out. Although the airplane was new to Hughes and he had not flown many four-engine airplanes, he was a quick student.

"I was impressed with how fast he caught on to the characteristics of the airplane," said Haldeman.[42]

A Dip of the Wings

Hughes asking Haldeman for money to pay the cab was typical of the man. Bill Grant gives another example. "We had the Sikorsky out at Palmdale one time during the war. We'd pump fuel in that thing during the day and he'd fly it all night making touch-and-goes. Afterward we'd always meet at the White House Cafe and have breakfast. One time he said to Dick Beatie—I think it was Dick—"Have you got any money?' And Dick said, 'Yeah, I've got three or four dollars.' (You didn't dare tell him how much money you had or he'd borrow it from you.) He asked us all how much we had and I guess maybe it totaled twenty dollars. Then he turned around to me and said, 'Goddamn it, fellas, we're broke.' He didn't have a goddamn nickle."[43]

Mrs. Earl Martyn, the former Bernadette Odekirk, provides some unique observations of Hughes based on her many years of observing his comings and goings with her husband. "Usually, he'd call and tell Earl they were going and to get on out to the plane and get it ready, you know. And then when he came, why he'd just say, 'Hi,' or maybe wouldn't say anything, just a little grin or something and climb in.

"Sometimes he'd have things he wanted me to do—phone calls to make or arrangements for cars where they were going—just very casual. I used to get a kick out of it. I knew by the greeting he gave me how many things he wanted me to do. Sometimes I was 'dear,' and sometimes I was 'honey,' and then I was 'sweetheart,' and then I was 'darling' if there was a lot of stuff. I could always tell. You know how they do with telephone operators and the waitresses. They put on that same kind of a deal. It meant nothing. Probably just trying to make me feel better. But I saw right through it. It didn't make any impression on me. I enjoyed doing it, because I enjoyed watching them fly. I watched all the time—testing the racer and starting on the around-the-world flight—well, I wasn't in New York, but I saw them depart Burbank—the cross countries, the world speed record, and all that. I was always at the airport.

"I enjoyed it. I'd go to the end of the runway at Lockheed when they went to taxi out to watch them go over, and he'd always dip his wings at me. He knew I was down there. He would arrange by phone calls so I would meet him. So I would be down by the end of the runway, you know, by the railroad tracks at Lockheed there."

They flew from three places: Los Angeles Airport, Lockheed Burbank, or Culver City. At Los Angeles he usually had the plane at the TWA hangar, so Earl could just park in the parking lot and go through that gate and go on the flight. When the weather was bad, they occasionally had to land at Palmdale just over the hills from the Los Angeles smog area. But usually they flew from the Lockheed Burbank field. Hughes would come and go in ordinary-looking Chevrolets without company markings. As Mrs. Martyn remembers, they were usually the same color—a cream color, very light.

"Most of the time he drove himself," said Mrs. Martyn. "He had some men at the Hollywood office that came and picked up cars and moved them around for him and things like that, but most of the time he drove himself. When he did have a driver he rode in front."

Mrs. Martyn adds that when Hughes arrived at the plane he would not look it over but go right to the pilot's seat. If his valet brought a box of fresh shirts, they were delivered separately before Hughes's arrival. She seemed to recall that Hughes usually left his hat on when he went to the pilot's seat. "He had it on his head most of the time."

Earl and Howard made two trips to the Senate Hearings in 1947. Mrs. Martyn met them on their return each time. "Earl called me to meet him at the plant. They knew I liked to see it come and go," she said.[44]

Al Vollmecke was a flight standards engineer for the Civil Aeronautics Authority who represented his agency at meetings at the War Production Board. Vollmecke said that he had heard Hughes was hard to get along with, but with them Hughes had always been most cooperative. The first time Vollmecke visited the Culver City plant he was not certain where the plant was. But that was no problem; Hughes had left nothing to chance. As he drove along the crowded highway, Vollmecke spotted the multi-millionaire standing beside the road in his shirt-sleeves directing him to the plant entrance.[45]

Steve Rolle was in the Civil Aeronautics Authority's Western Region office when he first met Hughes. "From time to time I wondered about his ability as an aircraft designer," Rolle said. "After all, he had virtually no formal education in the field. But one afternoon all my doubts were dispelled. We had been talking about the fuel system on a Boeing Stratoliner that he was modifying. After a while he asked me for a pencil and paper. He never carried anything with him, not even money.

"Then he sat down and on the spot drew the plans for a very well thought-out

248

dual fuel-flow system that in case of failure would adjust automatically without ever letting the engines know something had gone wrong. That's when I realized that he was a very capable engineer and a talented designer." Rolle added that it took a team of engineers three months to come up with blueprints which Hughes had drawn in an hour. "Even then, the job the slide-rule guys turned in wasn't as good as what Hughes had done!"[46]

John Parkinson, NACA hydrodynamicist who worked with Hughes on the flying boat's hull design, hadn't met him in person until the 1947 Senate hearings when he was called by Hughes as a technical witness. "Many times during the hearings," says Parkinson, "he actually brushed his lawyers aside and conducted his own defense. In the end he pinned more on the chairman of the committee than they did on him.

"He was probably arrogant—like all people with more money than the government—but [there was] no question about his abilities. He was one of those self-made technical people who could more than hold his own with his own people. He really was able to boss graduate engineers, you know.

"I developed a great admiration for the man. For several years I got a Christmas card from him; probably the most ornate Christmas card I've ever seen—a big, gaudy, triple-sized thing. I was very distressed, almost like it was a friend, when I heard of his very undignified, terrible ending."[47]

Flight engineer Earl Martyn had a ringside seat at the hearings, too. "Anytime Hughes was going to be on, I was there. In fact, I sat right next to Benny Meyers's wife. That was my seat," he said, laughing. "How did Hughes handle himself? Oh, he handled himself great, I thought. Ferguson would ask him the same question two or three times and Hughes would only answer it once. Whenever Hughes would say something a little out of the ordinary, the crowd would cheer like they were at a football game."[48]

Life as a Hughes Project Engineer

Edward West, Jr., the Hughes F-11 project engineer, told the author in June 1981, "Every decision Howard made was based on looking at least 10 years ahead. On the D-2, analysis showed that we needed eight-blade, 19-foot diameter propellers to get the best performance at 50-thousand feet. These propellers were not available. But Howard had us move the location of the booms out far enough so that the 19-foot diameter blades would clear the fuselage if they became available in the future."

Edward West, Jr., who like Carl Babberger was an aeronautical engineering graduate of Stanford University, was 31 years old when he went to work in the Duramold Division of Hughes Aircraft. A few days after starting work, he was invited to go with a group of engineers to Hughes's house to discuss D-2 problems. Aerodynamicist Dick Murrow coached him. "If Howard asks you anything, shout like hell at him because he's deaf."

At the meeting West's loud, clear voice made a good first impression. Little by little he fell into the job of modifying the D-2. "Nobody else wanted the job," said West. "They all wanted to work on the flying boat." This led to daily contacts with Hughes and West later became project engineer for the F-11, photo-reconnaissance airplane.

It was typical of Hughes that a new man like West should be given such an important position. According to West, "Howard never went through channels or observed seniority—never. You'll notice even in his movies he always got some actor or actress nobody'd ever heard of and made stars of them. That's the way he was. I was only a draftsman on the board when I first started talking to Howard. Of course, I had an engineering degree and was being coached and helped by Carl Babberger, Dick Murrow, Colonel Ginny Clark, and Stan Bell.

"For some reason, when I got into the act, Stan Bell, the chief engineer at the time, was in disfavor with Howard. But Stan was a fine engineer and a good organizer. He knew how to put an engineering group together—all the things that I didn't know. Without him I couldn't have handled the job at all."

West says that Howard seldom came to the plant. "Once in awhile he'd come down at 2 o'clock in the morning, but most of the meetings were at his house. Oh, one time when he was cutting film on the *Outlaw* in rented space at the old Goldwyn Studios he called and asked me to come up. It was 12:30 or 1 o'clock in the morning, something like that, and the fellas who were cutting film with him were *real* disgusted. He asked them to go have a coffee or something and he talked to me until two in the morning. Out in the back alley, where I parked, was a car with a young, gorgeous-looking chick sitting there with her hands folded. When I came out she was still there waiting for him.

"As the design proceeded on the F-11, I spent more and more time with Howard, seeing him daily, Saturday, Sunday and holidays I also travelled with him quite a bit.

"Noah Dietrich spent a month in my office on business one time. Howard wouldn't talk with him, but I went to Howard's house every night and Howard would send instructions down to Dietrich through me. Dietrich didn't like this very much. He was always polite to me, but I could see the smoke coming out of his ears when he was getting instructions from 'some office boy'."

"Fred Ayers, the general manager, didn't resent getting instructions through me. Fred, as far as I know, never met Howard. He was an experienced and capable manager who had come out of retirement to help in the war effort. He had more or less an advisory capacity in the early stages. Then Howard hired two or three new managers in succession. I remember one time Howard told me, "I can't seem to get a decent manager. Every time I hire another manager, he's worse than the one before."

"Because Howard took so long to make up his mind, the design of the F-11 progressed very slowly. Howard had to know everything about the design before he'd make a decision. Even then, he would stall and stall. One of Howard's weakness, was the excessive time he took to make decisions. He would stall and stall until everybody would grow crazy waiting. I can remember when someone came into my office and asked, Where's Ed?, my secretary answered, He's gone up to Howard's house to do some undesigning and get some indecision.

"Since we were short of engineers, Howard told me to get some from Rae Hopper. I had no desire to scuttle the boat project, so we worked out arrangements for sharing engineers. Later the staff engineers spent the morning at Culver City and then came up to Hollywood in the afternoon on my project.

"All the time I worked for Howard, he lived by himself in a leased 16-room house up in Bel Air. Well, not by himself. He lived with Faith Domergue at the time. But I only saw her once when she was getting out of the car that he bought her.

"He stayed very much to himself and only saw people when he had to and did as much business as he could on the phone. I believe this was because he had the amplifier on his house phone and could hear better.

"When I'd go up to see Howard, Faith Domergue would stay upstairs. We stayed downstairs in the library. Eddy, the red headed house man who was the only servant at that time, cooked his meals. I'd go up there in the middle of the afternoon and at meal time Eddy would bring Howard's dinner on a plate—the same thing every night, a small loin steak, some green peas, and a glass of milk—and Howard would sit there and eat right in front of me and never offer me anything.

"But there was another side of Howard. Dow Chemical sent a man out to the plant one time when Howard was considering building the airplane out of magnesium. Typically, the man sat around for four days waiting for Howard to see him. I finally called Howard and told him the man was going to have to go back, so he asked me to bring him up. I took him up to the house and we had about a three hour discussion. It was dinner time when we left, so I started to walk the Dow man over to the House of Murphy to eat, but couldn't remember how to get there. I turned around and walked back to Howard's and asked him how to go. Howard said, 'Would you just as soon eat at the Castle? I can make a reservation for you there.' That was fine with us.

"We were disgusted with having to sit through three hours of talk after four days of waiting, so at the restaurant we ordered everything in the place including champagne and drinks. When I asked for the bill, the waiter said, 'No bill. All taken care of. Mr. Hughes, when he called, he said, Mr. West, if he want the restaurant, you give it to him.'

"One night Howard called me at home just as we were getting ready to go out. 'If you aren't busy, I'd like you to come up,' he said.

"Well, Howard, I'll come if you want, but I was just going out to a musical."

" 'Oh, well, Ed,' he said, 'you've been working hard and you've been workin' long hours. You go ahead, and you go to your show and whatever you want to do after the show, but when you get all through come on up to the house.'

"Usually I'd go up there 10 or 11 o'clock at night, but this time it was probably 2:30 in the morning when I got to Howard's house in Bel Air and he had all the staff engineers, ten of them, sitting there. They had been there since 4 in the afternoon waiting for me. I didn't know they were there. I would have gone right on up there if I'd had any idea. They didn't hold it against me because they knew him, but it was inconsiderate of Howard. Then, he took us all to breakfast. We took off in automobiles and drove out to the desert camp, which was 28 miles northwest of Barstow and about 100 miles from where we were, and got there after sunup."

"Howard had a mind like an elephant," West said. "I was very careful what I told him. If I didn't know I said so. If you tried to bluff your way through he'd find out. If you told him something and six months later you told him something different, he'd say, 'Well, when you were up to my house on such and such a night you said so and so.' He remembered.

"Babberger says he thinks Hughes was a mystic. I don't agree on that. I think it was just in his nature it takes a long time to make up his mind on anything. Usually he wouldn't make a decision until he had talked to at least three or four different people whose opinions he respected. And he talked to them individually as though each was the only one. He would compare what they said, but he made up his own mind in the end. He made all the decisions. He would ask your opinion, but before he would use it he would double check with someone outside the company.

"Everything he did was very secretive. He insisted on people following his instructions to the letter. When he explained something to you he'd go over it about five times like he was talking to a five year old child. If you were driving him someplace, he wouldn't say where you were going. He'd say go left, go right, go straight and so on until you got there. It might be someplace that you knew very well and could have driven to undirected if only he had said where we were going."

It was a peculiarity of Hughes that he used other people's clothes, other people's money, and other people's cars. The money he paid back. Cars and clothes seemed to rate differently. West recalls an incident during the period they were working on the D-2 at the Harpers Lake desert camp. One day Hughes was about to shuttle back to LA in Odekirk's Waco. "Ed," he said, "we're going to town and I want you to come with us. I want to talk about the D-2."

"Well, Howard, my car's up here."

"Well, we're coming right back. We're coming right back."

When they landed back in the city, Hughes said, "Well, I want you to get started right away on that."

"Howard, I gotta go back and get my car."

"Well, I'm going back. I'll bring your car back."

"Well, I've gotta have something to drive."

So Hughes gave West a Cadillac out of the studio pool. According to West, "Howard had a girl friend stashed away up at Lake Arrowhead in the mountains and used a back road out of the desert. My car was a black Ford sedan which looked like a thousand other cars on the road and that's what he wanted. So I drove the Cadillac and he drove my Ford.

"Three weeks later I saw Howard walking toward my car in the gravelled parking lot at the desert camp and started toward it. Howard saw me, ran to the car, jumped in, and tore out of there with the wheels spinning and throwing gravel. Five minutes later I got a phone call.

" 'Ed, have you got any gas stamps? I'm out of gas.' I got some gasoline, found him just five minutes away, and traded cars with him. That's how I got my car back."

"I'd only been working for Howard a short time when he crashed that Sikorsky on Lake Mead. He wasn't badly hurt, but he had a big gash on his head. They put a patch on that and put him on an airplane to fly him back to Los Angeles. He'd lost all his clothes so Odie had bought him a pair of jeans and shirt at Sears. But it was chilly that morning so Howard said, "Odie, let me have your coat, I'm cold."

Odie said, "Howard, this is a new suit. This is only the second time I've worn it."

"Well, I'll mail it right back to you. I'll send it back on the next flight as soon as I get to town."

It was a beautiful coat—part of a tailor made suit. Howard wore that coat for the next two years. When I went to see him when I got back to Los Angeles he was sitting up in bed wearing this coat with a patch on his head. Everyplace he went he wore that jacket. Never went to the cleaners, never pressed or anything. And Odekirk never got it back."

"Howard was a brilliant and likable man," said West. "But he was a loner, and didn't like to meet people. I was with him an awful lot on trips where we were together for long hours and I found him friendly except that he couldn't talk about anything except the particular job that we were working on. Once in a while he would tell stories and he would laugh and joke, but you went right back to the subject. Howard had terrific concentration and he would point everything in one direction as long as he was interested in that one thing."

"One time we spent several weeks in Washington waiting for General Hap Arnold, among other things. Howard had no baggage, just his old blue serge suit that he carried over his arm—it was all thread bare—and some shirts. I went up to his room one day and he had these shirts spread out on his bed looking them over. 'You know, Ed,' he said, 'every morning I look over my shirts and put on the least dirty one.'

"I said, 'Well, hell, Howard, there's a Serve-a-Door right there in your door and when we come back tonight, five o'clock, they'll be laundered.'

" 'Well, we might not be here at five o'clock,' he said. Sure enough, he called one morning about 10 or 11 o'clock and said, 'Ed, we gotta go to Dayton. I'll meet you at the taxi ramp in five minutes."

"I kept my bag packed all the time so I got to the taxi before he did. There he came across the lobby with his five shirts, the blue serge suit over his arm, and two bell boys carrying bundles of blue prints.

"When we got to Dayton, we went down to the men's room at the Biltmore Hotel and Howard had his shoes shined. Something I'd never heard of him doing. I said, 'Howard, I don't know if we can get in the dining room. Usually you have to wear a tie.'

"Howard looked at me with this grin that he had and reached in his side pocket and starts wheelin' out a tie, all rumpled, and gave me this sly look and went over and put on the tie and we went up to dinner."

Appendix

Notes to Chapter 1

1. The Douglas B-23, Hughes's favorite airplane for personal transportation during the late 1940s, is a little-known type because only thirty-eight were built. First flown in 1939, the B-23 evolved from the B-18A and embodied greatly improved aerodynamic form and the latest U.S. ideas on defensive armament, including a tail gun. After serving briefly on coastal patrols, all aircraft of this type were relegated to training and transport roles. In 1945 they were declared surplus and a civil conversion was approved for licensing. The transport version carried a two-man crew, seated eleven to fourteen passengers, and cruised at 210 miles per hour with a normal range of 1,455 miles.

2. Earl Martyn, author's interview, January 13, 1978.

3. U.S. Congress. Senate. Special Committee to Investigate the National Defense Program. Hearings. 80th Congress, 1st session. Part 40, *Aircraft Contracts (Hughes Aircraft Co. and Kaiser-Hughes Corp.)* (Washington, D.C.: Goverent Printing Office, 1947). Part 43, *Aircraft Contracts, Hughes Aircraft Co.* (Washington, D.C.; Government Printing Office, 1948), p. 24361. (Hereinafter cited as *Hearings*.)

4. *Time* Magazine, August 4, 1947.

5. The use of the term "United Nations" in 1942 in a government memo is interesting. Although the international organization of that name was not formed until 1945, its use here refers to the coalition of twenty-six nations formed in 1942 to combat the Axis powers.

6. Memorandum, F.H. Hoge, Jr. to Chairman, Planning Committee, War Production Board, May 22, 1942. File 314.444, Aircraft, Cargo-Production, Record Group 179, "Records of the War Production Board, National Archives, Washington, D.C. The National Archives building in Washington is hereafter cited as NA.

7. *The Oregonian*, Portland, Ore., July 20, 1942, pp. 1, 4.

8. *New York Times*, July 30, 1942.

9. Ibid., July 31, 1942, p. 8.

10. "War Production," File 314.444, Record Group 179, Robert E. Gross to Brig. Gen. Charles E. Branshaw, August 12, 1942, with copy to Donald M. Nelson.

11. Hearings, p. 23514.

12. During the 1947 Senate hearings Hughes testified: "When I travel and go to hotels and I do not want to be disturbed, by people trying to sell me insurance policies and bonds and whatnot, I always use a different name. I generally take the name of somebody I know who will not be offended, because if I say my name is Jack Jones, there may be a Jack Jones where I am" (Hearings, p. 24375).

13. Glenn E. Odekirk, author's interview, Santa Ana, California, November 2, 1979. Note that during this period Kaiser's executive assistant, Chad Calhoun, received a telephone tip from Dick Jamison, a Portland, Oregon acquaintance of Odekirk. Jamison told Calhoun that he had read about the runaround Kaiser had been getting and thought Calhoun should know that Hughes had about two hundred aeronautical engineers who would soon be free of other work (Hearings, p. 23598).

255

Notes to Chapter 2

1. Charles J. Kelly, Jr., *The Sky's The Limit* (New York: Coward-McCann, Inc., 1963), p. 246.

2. Transcript of interview of Granville A. Humason, July 7, 1953, Oral History of the Texas Oil Industry, Barker Texas History Center, University of Texas.

3. John H. Glenn, Hughes powerplant mechanic and nephew of Dr. Scherer, author's interview, January 13, 1978.

4. John Keats, *Howard Hughes* (New York: Random House, 1972), p. 3.

5. *The American Heritage History of Flight* (New York: American Heritage Publishing Company, Inc., 1962), p. 278.

6. "The Reminiscences of Roscoe Turner," May 1960, p. 12, Aviation Project, Volume III, Part 3, Oral History Collection, Columbia University. Used by permission.

7. Don Dwiggins, "Howard Hughes," *Plane & Pilot*, May 1971, p. 34.

8. Account of Hughes-Odekirk meeting and their initial association is from Deposition of Glenn Edward Odekirk, #139,362, Hughes Estate, Harris County, Texas, September 7, 1977, and from author's interviews of Odekirk, fall 1979.

9. *New York Times*, November 16, 1936, p. 15.

10. Odekirk Deposition, p. 38.

11. Walt Boyne, "Speed Merchant," *Airpower*, September 1977, p. 12. According to Glenn Odekirk, Palmer was not a full-time Hughes employee but was concurrently chief engineer for Vultee Aircraft (Deposition).

12. No outsiders were allowed in the hangar, neither was any information given out. Hughes was extremely security-minded since Clarence Reed, a bright young engineer at Hughes Tool, had become disaffected, walked out one day with some Hughes blueprints, and set up a rival drill bit manufacturing company. During a subsequent lawsuit Reed claimed he used the blueprints to help him avoid infringing on the Hughes patents; but the judge did not agree. It cost Reed half a million dollars, plus fifteen percent of all future sales of the Reed bit as a royalty to Hughes Tool.

13. Glenn Odekirk, author's interview, November 2, 1979.

14. A previous day's attempt to break the record was aborted when the evening light became inadequate for the photocell-triggered cameras at each end of the surveyed 1.86-mile course. According to Odekirk, Earhart and Mantz were separately airborne during the tests to see that Hughes did not exceed 1,500 feet of altitude at any time during the speed runs. So Noah Dietrich's account, stating that on Hughes's last run of the day he "zoomed up to 12,000 feet, then nosed down and hurtled toward the earth," appears to be in error.

15. Jacqueline ("Jackie") Cochran was a much more accomplished aviator than Amelia Earhart. At one time Cochran held all the international speed and altitude records for both men and women. She headed the Women's Air Force Service Pilots during World War II, was the first woman to fly a jet, the first woman to break the sound barrier, and the first woman to land and take off from a carrier. Although she only had a second grade education, she rose to become the founder and president of Jacqueline Cochran Cosmetics and later married wealthy financier Floyd Odlum, who sold RKO to Hughes.

16. The extracts from Hughes's logbook showing his flights with TWA were sent to the author by Van Storm, one of Hughes's longtime flight engineer/mechanics.

17. "The Reminiscences of Jacqueline Cochran," May 1960, pp. 103-104, Aviation Project, Volume VI, Part 3, Oral History Collection, Columbia University. Used by permission.

18. Glenn Odekirk, October 10, 1979. The average speed figure is from Hughes's logbook.

19. "Jacqueline Cochran," pp. 104-105.

20. Clarence M. Selberg, Hughes aircraft inspector, author's interview, April 7, 1979.

21. Sherman Fairchild, interview by Anthony Brandt, summer 1964, Public Relations Office, Fairchild Industries, Hagerstown, Maryland. Brandt conducted a series of interviews of Fairchild from 1964 to 1970 before Fairchild died in 1971.

22. Hughes later set a cross-country transport record in the same Lockheed from California to Floyd Bennett Field, New York, in 10 hours, 34 minutes. The Model 14 was the largest plane yet built by Lockheed Company; it could carry twelve passengers and a crew of two. Lockheed design engineers had been working hard to perfect their aircraft, and the success of this new transport was welcome news. It possessed many aerodynamic improvements, including the perfection of a twin-tail design, the introduction of a single spar wing, and the successful use of integral tanks; and it was proof that a high wing loading was possible. From the original Model 14 design were to come three extremely successful modifications; the Hudson bomber, the Lockheed Lodestar, and the Navy PV-1 Ventura and PV-2 Harpoon patrol bombers.

23. Sherman Fairchild, summer 1964.

24. *Houston Post*, July 31, 1938, p. 1.

25. Odekirk Deposition, pp. 83-84.

26. I am indebted to Anthony Brandt for the insightful comparison of Hughes and Fairchild and to Theron Rinehart of Fairchild Industries for making the material available.

27. U.S. Congress. Senate. Special Committee to Investigate the National Defense Program. Hearings. 80th Congress, 1st session. Part 40, *Aircraft Contracts (Hughes Aircraft Co. and Kaiser-Hughes Corp.)* (Washington, D.C.: Government Printing Office, 1947). Part 43,

Aircraft Contracts, Hughes Aircraft Co. (Washington, D.C.: Government Printing Office, 1948). p. 24366. As a practical matter, the Hughes H-1 could probably never have been a fighter plane without a complete redesign to incorporate military equipment and to facilitate production. It was a racer and a research vehicle, and that was all it was supposed to be.

28. Hearings, p. 24366.

29. Ibid., p. 24367.

30. It was Alexander who first gave flight instruction to Hughes in 1925, according to Dietrich, and who later became Hughes Aircraft Company's representative at Wright Field.

31. Hearings, p. 24367.

32. Ibid., p. 24368.

33. Assistant Deputy Commanding General, Research & Development, Procurement & Industrial Mobilization to Chief of Staff United States Air Force, Director of Public Information, Legislative and Liaison Division, October 8, 1947. Record Group 18, "Records of the Army Air Force," Files of Assistant Chief of Air Staff, Materiel & Services, Research & Development Branch, Case Histories 1941-1946, D-2, D-5, F-11 Project, Vol. 11, NA.

34. Hearings, p. 24370.

35. Glenn Odekirk, author's interview, November 2, 1979.

Notes to Chapter 3

1. U.S. Congress. Senate. Special Committee to Investigate the National Defense Program. Hearings. 80th Congress, 1st session. Part 40, *Aircraft Contracts (Hughes Aircraft Co. and Kaiser-Hughes Corp.)* (Washington, ,D.C.: Government Printing Office, 1947). Part 43, *Aircraft Contracts, Hughes Aircraft Co.* (Washington, D.C.: Government Printing Office, 1948). p. 24285.

2. *New York Times*, July 11, 1942, p. 8.

3. Hearings, p. 24672-24673.

4. Ibid.

5. Sherman Fairchild, interview by Anthony Brandt, June 1964, Public Affairs Office, Fairchild Industries, Hagerstown, Maryland.

Fairchild was also on the board of directors of Pan American Airways.

6. Hearings, p. 23608.

7. Ibid., p. 23551.

8. Kaiser's two proposals, the mass production of the Martin Mars and the development of a larger flying boat, were being merged by Loening's recommendation. Loening and the War Production Board would emphasize the idea of production for the war. But Hughes was not interested in mass producing a Mars, he was interested in development: in creating the world's largest airplane. This would become an underlying source of misunderstanding between Hughes and the War Production Board.

9. Grover Loening to Donald M. Nelson, August 28, 1942, Record Group 179, "Records of the War Production Board," File 314.4442, National Archives Building, Washington, D.C.

10. James MacGregor Burns, *Roosevelt, The Soldier of Freedom* (New York: Harcourt Brace Jovanovich, 1970), p. 39.

11. Col. R.B. Lord, C.E., USA, to Chairman, War Production Board, August 31, 1942, "War Production Board" File 314.444, RG 179, NA.

12. E.A. Locke, Jr. to Donald M. Nelson, August 31, 1942, "War Production," File 314.444, RG 179, NA. Locke suggests that Maritime, Smaller War Plants, or Jesse Jones, in that order of preference, should put up the

money and not the Army or Navy. A handwritten afterthought said, "Lend-Lease through Cargoes, Inc. is also a possibility."

13. R. Adm. J.H. Towers to Donald Nelson, September 12, 1942, and Robert A. Lovett to Donald Nelson, September 12, 1942, "War Production," File 314.4442, RG 179, NA.

14. John W. Snyder, Executive Vice President Defense Plant Corporation to Henry J. Kaiser and Howard Hughes, September 17, 1942, "War Production" File 314.4442, RG 179, NA.

15. Hearings, p. 24283.

16. Glenn Odekirk, author's interview, November 2, 1979.

17. Hearings, p. 24439.

Notes to Chapter 4

1. From an interview of a senior Hughes engineer who prefers not to be quoted by name.

2. Ibid.

3. Ibid.

4. Carl Babberger, author's interview, February 21, 1979.

5. Earl Martin, retired president of Hamilton Standard Propellers, author's interview, February 21, 1979.

6. Clarence L. ("Kelly") Johnson, author's interview, October 22, 1980.

7. Senior Hughes engineer.

8. Carl Babberger, March 5, 1979.

9. Ibid.

10. Walt Boyne, "The Other Martin," *Airpower*, March 1975, p. 51.

11. Loening report of August 2, 1943 visit to Kaiser-Hughes Aircraft plant, August 21, 1943, Record Group 179, "Records of the War Production Board," File 314.4442, National Archives Building, Washington, D.C. (NA).

12. Carl Babberger February 21, 1979.

13. Minutes of Kaiser-Hughes Flying Boat Conference, NACA Conference Room, May 4, 1943, "War Production," File 314.444, RG 179.

14. Memorandum for the files on meeting in Donald Nelson's office, October 21, 1943, dated October 25, 1943, "War Production," File 314.4442, RG 179, NA.

15. Loening memo to Wilson, "Report on visit to Hughes Aircraft Company and recommendations on HK-1 project," September 29, 1943, "War Production," File 314.4442, RG 179, NA, p. 12.

16. Ibid., September 29, 1943. The final outcome of this recommendation was that Hughes bought Admiral King's PB2Y-5Z from the Navy as war surplus in 1946 for a reported $8,000. Ex-Navy pilot Bill Purcell and flight engineer Don Smith, who later was one of the two flight engineers on the only flight of Hughes's giant flying boat, flew the plane down from Alameda to Terminal Island. After that, the plane made one flight to Honolulu with Glenn Odekirk, his wife, and several company mechanics in connection with the purchase of some surplus aircraft there. Don Smith says that the plane was intended for flight crew training, "primarily to give Howard the feel of a larger boat, but he never actually flew it. We got it ready for Howard to fly, oh God, eight or ten times it seemed like during the months after that. We'd put it in the water, get it ready, and wait several hours until he'd finally call and say he couldn't make it" (Don Smith, author's interview, October 30, 1979).

17. Roy Wendahl, author's interview, October 29, 1980.

18. John B. Parkinson, author's interview, spring 1977.

19. Senior Hughes engineer.

20. Loening memo to Chairman, War Production Board, February 22, 1943, "War Production," File 314.444, RG 179, NA.

21. Carl Babberger, February 21, 1979.

22. John B. Parkinson, May 15, 1979.

23. Ibid., spring 1977.

24. Earl Martyn, author's interview, January 13, 1978.

25. Dick Murrow, author's interview, November 5, 1980.

26. Glenn Odekirk, October 10, 1979 and Charles E. ("Gene") Blandford, October 25, 1979.

27. John H. Glenn, Hughes powerplant mechanic, author's interview, January 13, 1978. Information on the June 1942 engine change was provided by Van Storm, September 9, 1980.

28. John Leyden, "Facing Death With Howard Hughes," *Horizons* (Washington, D.C.: Federal Aviation Administration), p. 8, and author's interview of Charles E. ("Gene") Blandford, October 25, 1979, Palos Verdes, California.

29. Earl Martyn, January 13, 1978.

30. Donald L. Bartlett and James B. Steele, *Empire—The Life, Legend, and Madness of Howard Hughes* (New York: W.W. Norton & Company, 1979) p. 121.

31. The account of this accident is based on Blandford, October 25, 1979, and on C. W. ("Ted") Von Rosenberg's account in John Leyden's "Facing Death With Howard Hughes."

32. For many years Hughes took care of Cline's wife, son, and mother-in-law, giving $250 per month each to Mrs. Cline and her son and $150 to her mother. When Mrs. Cline remarried, Jim Reed, the CAA man who handled these arrangements for Hughes, told him that he could discontinue the monthly payments now that she was fixed all right.

Hughes thought it over and said, "Let me think about it. We'll just leave it for the present. I'm a lot better off than she is" (George W. Haldeman, retired FAA engineering test pilot, author's interview, January 30, 1980).

33. Loening memo to Chairman, War Production Board, February 22, 1943, "War Production," 314.444, RG 179, NA.

34. Donald M. Nelson letter to Howard R. Hughes. February 8, 1943, 314.444, RG 179, NA.

35. *Newsweek*, August 4, 1947, p. 26.

36. Howard Hughes letter to Donald Nelson, March 18, 1943, "War Production," File 314.4442, RG 179, NA.

37. U.S. Congress. Senate. Special Committee to Investigate the National Defense Program. Hearings. 80th Congress, 1st session. Part 40, *Aircraft Contracts (Hughes Aircraft Co. and Kaiser-Hughes Corp.)* (Washington, D.C.: Government Printing Office, 1947). Part 43, *Aircraft Contracts, Hughes Aircraft Co.* (Washington, D.C.: Government Printing Office, 1948), P. 23730.

38. Supervising Engineer, Defense Plant Corporation, Culver City, California. Memo Re: Kaiser-Hughes—Plancor 1424, Management of Cargo Plane Project, August 27, 1943, "War Production," File 314.4442, RG 179, NA.

39. Ibid.

40. Hearings, p. 24448. Exhibit No. 2442, War Production Board Memorandum for the record regarding Bern telephone call to Donald Nelson, August 30, 1943.

41. Chief, Aircraft Engineering Division letter to Director, Safety Regulations, Civil Aircraft Authority, September 7, 1943, "War Production," File 314.4442, RG 179.

42. Carl Babberger, March 5, 1979.

43. Dick Murrow, November 5, 1980. Edward West, Jr., former Hughes F-11 project engineer, says that the "hometown boys" called the outsiders "torpedoes" because this was the common term for a "hit man" in the Chicago gangs at that time. "LeDuc would come through the plant with his hat on and a whole parade of six or eight fellas with him all walking in step with their hats on. It was

strange to us because we had quit wearing hats in California."—Author's interview, June 5, 1981.

44. Carl Babberger, March 5, 1979.

45. Noah Dietrich and Bob Thomas, *Howard, the Amazing Mr. Hughes* (New York: Fawcett, 1972). p. 69.

46. *Hearings*, Exhibit No. 2450. H.R. Edwards, Supervising Engineer, to William E. Joyce, Vice President Defense Plant Corporation, February 19, 1944.

47. John Glenn, author's interview January 13, 1978.

48. Cdr. Jack Suggs, USN (ret.), information obtained by Van Storm, September 2, 1980.

49. John H. Glenn, January 13, 1978.

50. Clarence L. ("Kelly") Johnson, then Lockheed's chief engineer, tells a different story of Hughes's involvement in the development of the Constellation: "Hughes gave us a requirement that he wanted to haul twenty sleeping passengers nonstop across the United States plus a certain number of pounds of bags and mail, like 6,000 pounds. And the sleeper, of course, could hardly pay its own way no matter what the hell you did with it. We met down at his home near Wilshire Boulevard and then came back with a proposal to him that, yeah, we could do the job and a lot more. We had been working for some time on an airplane about the size of a DC-4 called the *Excalibur* [Model 44] and we almost had a deal with Pan American. But that [the Excalibur] would not do the job Hughes wanted to do. So we threw that in the ash can and went for the larger airplane [the Constellation]. Hughes didn't have anything to do with that design. We made proposals to *him*. . . . Howard put us in business on the Connie" (Clarence L. Johnson, October 22, 1980).

51. Jim Dallas, author's interview, September 28, 1979.

52. Harry Kaiser, author's interview, April 9, 1979.

53. Chuck Jucker, author's interview, March 11, 1979.

54. David Grant, author's interview, November 21, 1977.

55. Al Geverink, author's interview, November 21, 1977.

56. Christopher A. Reising, Jr., author's interview, November 7, 1977.

57. Bill Noggle, author's interview, November 29, 1977.

58. Homer ("Dave") Roe, letter to the author, October 20, 1980.

59. Senior Hughes engineer.

60. Earl Martyn, January 13, 1978.

61. From comments by Van Storm, September 2, 1980.

62. Carl Babberger, March 5, 1979.

63. "Hughes Flying Boat—World's Largest Airplane," *Automotive and Aviation Industries*, August 15, 1945, p. 15.

64. Hearings, p. 24308. Nadine Henley, longtime secretary to Hughes and later a high executive of Summa Corporation, writes that she saw a number of patents under the name of chief engineer Stanley Bell and Howard Hughes, though not necessarily connected with the flying boat. "I know at one time he [Bell] and HRH [Howard Robard Hughes or His Royal Highness?] worked out a map to use in flight, lighted underneath, which moved as the plane flew so that a glance would show exactly what was below one at that time. It was too expensive to put into production" (Nadine Henley in written comments to the author, September 17, 1980).

65. Chief, Aircraft Engineering Division, letter to Director, Safety Regulations, Civil Aeronautics Authority, September 7, 1943, "War Production," File 314.4442, RG179, NA.

66. Sherman Fairchild, interviewed by Anthony Brandt, September 1970. Public Relations Office, Fairchild Industries, Hagerstown, Maryland. Brandt conducted a series of interviews of Fairchild between 1964 and 1970 before Fairchild died in 1971.

67. Ibid., May 20, 1964.

68. Ibid., July-August 1968. Fairchild also helped Hughes in many small ways. When Hughes was in New York, for example, Fairchild acted as a kind of message center for him. Fairchild had a fine eye for attractive women and he suggested several for parts in Hughes's films. Fairchild also provided Hughes with a great deal of aviation equipment. He helped Hughes obtain parts for the Hughes Special, for which Hughes wanted a

certain kind of light valve made by Pratt & Whitney for military engines only. These valves were obtainable only by military contractors. Fairchild, still under contract for the XC-31 at the time, bought them for Hughes.

69. Louis Tribbett, author's interview, April 1979.

70. Ibid.

71. Carl Babberger, February 21, 1979.

Notes to Chapter 5

1. John Parkinson, author's interview, spring 1977.

2. Grover Loening, "Comments on Preliminary General Specifications for Hughes-Kaiser Cargo Airplane Model HK-1," April 3, 1943, Record Group 179, "Records of the War Production Board," File 314.44463, RG 179, National Archives, Washington, D.C.

3. Minutes, Kaiser-Hughes Flying Boat Conference, NACA Conference Room, May 14, 1943, "War Production," File 314.444, RG 179, NA.

4. Carl Babberger, author's interview, March 11, 1979. Rae E. Hopper, in a June 1, 1977 letter to the author, wrote: "Never, to my recollection, was I ever informed that dural would be available as a construction material for the flying boat. By the time dural appeared to be available, we were too far down the line in the design and testing of birch. Also Howard sort of fancied the smooth wood surface of the wing for aerodynamic reasons."

5. Grover Loening memo to Donald Nelson, August 21, 1943, "War Production," File 314.4442, RG 179, NA.

6. Loening memo to Nelson, September 10, 1943, "War Production," File 314.4442, RG 179, NA.

7. Loening memo to C.E. Wilson, Executive Vice Chairman, War Production Board, September 29, 1943, "War Production," File 314.4442, RG 179, NA.

8. Ibid., p. 14.

9. Ibid., p. 5-6.

10. Clarence Selberg, letter to author, April 14, 1979.

11. Loening to Wilson, September 29, 1943, "War Production," File 314.4442, RG 179, NA.

12. Chiefs of Aircraft Engineering and Flight Engineering and Factory Inspection Divisions, letter to Director, Safety Regulations, Civil Aeronautics Authority, September 7, 1943. "War Production," File 314.4442, RG 179, NA.

13. Minutes, Aircraft Production Board meeting, October 4, 1943, "War Production," File 314.4442, RG 179, NA.

14. R.L. Horne memo to files regarding October 4, 1943 meeting in Nelson's office, "War Production," File 314.4442, RG 179, NA.

15. Ibid., October 25, 1943.

16. Minutes, Aircraft Production Board, October 25, 1943, "War Production," File 314.444, RG 179, NA.

17. Ibid., November 1, 1943.

18. Aircraft Engineering Division, Civil Aeronautics Authority, letter to Special Aviation Assistant to the Secretary of Commerce, January 20, 1944, "War Production," File 314.444, RG 179, NA.

19. Loening to Wilson, November 29, 1943, "War Production," File 314.444, RG 179, NA.

20. U.S. Congress. Senate. Special Committee to Investigate the National Defense Program. Hearings. 80th Congress, 1st session. Part 40, *Aircraft Contracts (Hughes Aircraft Co. and Kaiser-Hughes Corp.)* (Washington, D.C.: Government Printing Office, 1947). Part 43, *Aircraft Contracts, Hughes Aircraft Co.* (Washington, D.C.: Government Printing Office, 1948), p. 23562.

21. Minutes, Aircraft Production Board, November 29, 1943, File 314.4442, RG 179, NA.

22. Wilson to Loening, December 8, 1943, File 314.444, RG 179, NA.

23. Aircraft Engineering Division, Civil Aeronautics Authority, to . . . Commerce, January 20, 1944, File 314.444, RG 179, NA.

24. Loening memo to George W. Lewis,

January 27, 1944, "War Production," File 314.444, RG 179, NA.

25. George W. Lewis to Grover Loening, January 27, 1944, Record Group 255, "Records of the National Advisory Committee for Aeronautics," NA. Also in Hearings, Part 40, Exhibit 2399, p. 24414.

26. Untitled, unsigned memo, February 3, 1944, "War Production," File 314.4446, RG 179, NA.

27. Loening memo, January 19, 1944. Hearings, Part 40, Exhibit 2397, p. 24410.

28. During the Senate Hearings in 1947, Grover Loening replied to Kaiser's implication that there was a double-cross in the cargo plane deal by charging that Kaiser double-crossed him by originally saying the planes would be built in existing shipyard facilities and then planning to erect a new aircraft plant to build them (*Aviation Week*, August 4, 1947, p. 12).

29. Telecon, Chad Calhoun in Washington, Henry Kaiser in New York, and Donald Nelson, January 29, 1944, "War Production," File 314.4446, RG 179, NA.

30. Kaiser telegram to Donald Nelson, February 16, 1944, "War Production," File 314.4446, RG 179, NA.

31. Jesse Jones to Donald Nelson, February 16, 1944, "War Production," File 314.4446, RG 179, NA.

32. W. L. Clayton to Donald Nelson, February 17, 1944, "War Production," File 314.4446, RG 179, NA.

33. Telecon, Howard Hughes and Donald Nelson, February 17, 1944, "War Production," File 314.44463, RG 179, NA.

34. Loening to Nelson, summary report of meeting held February 18, 1944, dated February 19, 1944, "War Production," File 314.44463, RG 179, NA.

35. Telecon, Hughes and Nelson, February 18, 1944, "War Production," File 314.44463, RG 179, NA.

36. Hearings, p. 23704.

37. Ibid., pp. 23703-23704.

38. Telecon, Hughes and Nelson, February 19, 1944, "War Production," File 314.44463, RG 179, NA.

39. Loening memo to Nelson, "Notes on meeting February 29th with Howard Hughes." March 2, 1944, File 314.4446, RG 179, NA.

40. Harold E. Talbott letter to Donald M. Nelson, March 4, 1944, File 314.4442, RG 179, NA. Talbott, who headed the WPB's 1942 Cargo Plane Committee and later became Secretary of the Air Force, had impressive credentials. In 1916 Talbott's father and two others established the Dayton-Wright Company, successor to the Orville Wright Company, with the young 28-year old Talbott as president Orville Wright was vice-president and engineer. During the First World War the company built 38 planes a day. Later, Talbott invested his profits wisely in a variety of major corporations and became a man of great means and influence.

41. Hughes letter to Nelson, March 17, 1944, File 314.4446, RG 179, NA.

42. Hearings, p. 24361.

Notes to Chapter 6

1. U.S. Congress. Senate. Special Committee to Investigate the National Defense Program. Hearings. 80th Congress, 1st session. Part 40, *Aircraft Contracts (Hughes Aircraft Co. and Kaiser-Hughes Corp.)* (Washington, D.C.: Government Printing Office, 1947). Part 43, *Aircraft Contracts, Hughes Aircraft Co.* (Washington, D.C.: Government Printing Office, 1948), p. 26488.

2. Lt. Col. H.A. Freidlick, Chief, Contracts and Facilities Division, Memorandum for the File, July 2, 1944, Files of Assistant Chief of Air Staff Materiel and Services (A-4) Research and Development Branch, Case Histories 1941-1946, Airplane F-11, Record Group 18, "Records of the Army Air Forces," National Archives, Washington, D.C. Hereafter cited as "F-11 Case History."

3. H.H. Arnold, memorandum for the Under Secretary of War, July 17, 1944, "F-11 Case History."

4. Hearings, p. 26773.

5. Nadine Henley, written comments to

author, September 13, 1980.

6. Hearings, p. 26481.

7. Clarence ("Kelly") Johnson, author's interview, October 22, 1980.

8. Ibid.

9. Noah Dietrich and Bob Thomas, *Howard: The Amazing Mr. Hughes* (New York: Fawcett, 1972), p. 178.

10. Nadine Henley, September 13, 1980.

11. Joe Petrali, as told to Maury Green, "O.K., Howard," *True*, February-March, 1975.

12. Dick Beatie, author's interview, October 29, 1979.

13. Bill Grant, author's interview, October 9, 1979.

14. "O.K., Howard," Beatie, and Bob Martin, author's interview, October 30, 1979.

15. Bob Martin, October 30, 1979.

16. Nadine Henley, September 13, 1980.

17. The foregoing account of the Shreveport incident is based on Bob Martin, October 30, 1979.

18. Ray Kirkpatrick, November 10, 1979.

19. Mrs. Earl Martyn, the former Bernadine Odekirk, author's interview, February 1979.

Notes to Chapter 7

1. U.S. Congress Senate. Special Committee to Investigate the National Defense Program. Hearings. 80th Congress, 1st session. Part 43, *Aircraft Contracts, Hughes Aircraft Co.,* (Washington, D.C., Government Printing Office, 1947). Exhibit No. 2714, pp. 27172-27176. Perelle letter to Hughes, October 29, 1945. Reviewing the manuscript for this book, Aerodynamicist Carl Babberger stated that Perelle's paragraph on the poor quality of engineering is "B.S."

2. Ibid., Exhibit No. 2716, Perelle to Hughes, December 18, 1945, p. 27177.

3. *Time,* January 21, 1946, p. 90.

4. Don Smith, author's interview, October 30, 1979. Smith was flight engineer on the Consolidated PB2Y-5Z Hughes bought from the Navy after the war and was one of two flight engineers on the one and only flight of the Spruce Goose. Smith worked as flight mechanic on the blimp used to advertise *The Outlaw.*

5. Hughes Aircraft Company studies of site determination route locations, site improvements, drydock construction, and press releases on the move to Long Beach are in the Air and Space Museum Library, Smithsonian Institution, Washington, D.C. The name of John Stearns was provided by Nadine Henley September 13, 1980.

6. Ray Kirkpatrick, author's interview,

November 10, 1979. With regard to the D-2 aileron control problem, aerodynamicist Richard Murrow says that the wing section NACA recommended had a maximum thickness at the sixty degree chord point (three-fifths of the way back from the leading edge). This abrupt change in thickness at that point caused a flow separation ahead of the ailerons. After initial taxi tests, Hughes complained that the ailerons had no feel at all. "So we tufted the whole aft section of the wing in the vicinity of the ailerons," said Murrow, and mounted movie cameras to take pictures of things. The pictures showed that there was a complete reversed flow over the last forty percent of the chord. So we added ten percent to the chord, which essentially changed the whole contour of the wing section out there, and got the flow going properly. After that I guess it was all right, but I don't think Howard ever did like the way the airplane flew" (Richard Murrow, author's interview, November 5, 1980).

7. Frank J. Prinz, letter to the author, March 8, 1981.

8. Charles E. ("Gene") Blandford, author's interview, October 25, 1979.

9. Contract W-33-038 AC-1079, Model XF-11 Airplane, Safety Inspection, April 24, 1946, Files of the Assistant Chief of Air Staff Materiel and Services (A-4) Research and Development Branch, Case Histories 1941-

1946, Airplane F-11, Record Group 18, "Records of the Army Air Forces," National Archives, Washington, D.C.

10. Statement of William George Dickman, Hearings, p. 24521.

11. Glenn Odekirk, author's interview, October 10, 1979.

12. Progress Report, XF-11, July 3, 1946, "F-11 Case History."

13. Frank Prinz, XF-11 Accident, Hearings, p. 24518.

14. Report of the XF-11 Accident Investigation Board, Hearings, p. 24507.

15. Dave Grant, author's interview, April 26, 1979.

16. Statement of Charles E. Blandford, XF-11 Accident, Hearings, p. 24525.

17. Gene Blandford, author's interview, October 25, 1979.

18. Glenn Odekirk, author's interview, November 2, 1979.

19. Blandford Statement, Hearings, p. 24524.

20. Hughes's verbal account of the flight, XF-11 Accident, Hearings, p. 24505.

21. Blandford Statement, Hearings, p. 24523.

22. Louis Tribbett, author's interview, April 1979.

23. Gene Blandford, author's interview, October 25, 1979.

24. Hughes, XF-11 Accident, Hearings, p. 24505. When asked by the author why Hughes was so worried about the gear being down and locked when the trouble had been getting it to go into the up locks, Gene Blandford, Hughes's longtime flight test engineer, replied, "Well, who knows. That was typical of him. He would do that" (Gene Blandford, October 25, 1979).

25. XF-11 Accident, Hearings, p. 24505.

26. Glenn Odekirk, author's interview, November 2, 1979.

27. Statement of Dick Fischer, XF-11 Accident, Hearings, p. 24509.

28. Hughes's account as contained in a letter signed by Dr. Verne R. Mason to Col. E. T.

Kennedy, Chief Western Division, Air Corps, July 11, 1946. The text was telephoned to Western Division by Glenn Odekirk, then messaged to Air Materiel Command, July 12, 1946, "F-11 Case History."

29. Hughes, XF-11 Accident, Hearings, p. 24506.

30. Blandford Statement. Hearings, p. 24522, and Gene Blandford, October 25, 1979. After landing they taxied in to the ramp. Murphy and Cagney got out, but Odekirk and Blandford, hearing that Hughes had crashed in Santa Monica Bay, took off again to look for him. They returned immediately when they learned that the XF-11 had crashed in Beverly Hills. Meanwhile, according to Van Storm, Storm had to ask Jean Peters and Audie Murphy to get out of the only company car on the ramp so he and two others could head for the crash site.

31. Fischer, Hearings, p. 24509.

32. Report of XF-11 Accident Investigation Board, Hearings, pp. 24505-24507.

33. Capt. William Lloyd Durkin, USMC (Ret.) author's interview, November 19, 1979.

34. New York Times, July 8, 1946, p. 1.

35. Glenn Odekirk, November 2, 1979.

36. New York Times, July 8, 1946, p. 1.

37. Verne R. Mason, XF-11 Accident, Hearings, p. 24508.

38. New York Times, August 30, 1979.

39. Glenn Odekirk, November 2, 1979.

40. Van Storm, note to author, September 2, 1980.

41. Glenn Odekirk, November 2, 1979. The name of the receptionist was provided by Nadine Henley, September 17, 1980. (Henley was on leave in the east at the time of the accident.)

42. After Hughes's death in 1976, Van Storm accompanied lawyers and others who were searching for a Hughes will to the storage area at Culver City, where they opened all the items to which Hughes had access. The bed was still there (Van Storm, September 2, 1980).

43. Glenn Odekirk, November 2, 1979.

44. Verne R. Mason, XF-11 Accident, Hearings, p. 24508.

45. Unsigned memo from Propeller Laboratory to Chief, Aircraft Projects Section, Engineering Division (TSESA-5), Crash of Hughes XF-11 Airplane, dated "Aprox. 16 August 1946," "F-11 Case History."

46. Gene Blandford, October 25, 1979.

47. Report of the XF-11 Accident Investigation Board, Hearings, p. 24507.

48. Carl Babberger, March 5, 1979.

49. Dave Grant, April 26, 1979.

50. Earl Martin, retired president of Hamilton Standard Propellers, author's interview, September 27, 1979.

51. Col. George E. Price to Deputy Commanding General, Engineering, "Crash Investigation, XF-11, AAF No. 44-70155." August 28, 1946, "XF-11 Case History."

52. Hearings, p. 26516. In September 1947, Hughes hired Gen. Ira Eaker as vice president of Hughes Tool Company (Hearings, p. 26792).

53. Noah Dietrich and Bob Thomas, *Howard: The Amazing Mr. Hughes* (Greenwich, Conn.: Fawcett Publications, Inc., 1976), p. 197 (paper back).

54. William L. Durkin, November 19, 1979.

55. Ibid.

56. Glenn Odekirk, November 2, 1979.

Notes to Chapter 8

1. However, the Lockheed C5A is the bigger load-carrying airplane with an overall length nearly 28 feet longer than the Hughes flying boat and a design payload of 220,967 pounds compared to a design useful load of 201,526 pounds for the flying boat. Size comparisons of the HK-1 or H-4, the Boeing 747, and the Lockheed C5A are:

	Wing-span	Length	Height	Maximum Weight
HK-1	320'	220'	85'	440,000 lbs.
C5A	222'8''	247'8''	65'1''	769,000 lbs.
747	195'8''	231'4''	63'5''	710,000 lbs. (later models 775,000 lbs.)

2. Ben Jiminez, author's interview, April 24, 1979.

3. Christopher Reising, Jr., author's interview, November 7, 1977. Several technical papers that system designer Jim Dallas wrote influenced the British, who produced several airplanes with the 120-volt DC systems (Jim Dallas, author's interview, September 28, 1979).

4. Merle Coffee, Hughes electrical and electronic supervisor, author's interview, March 5, 1979.

5. Jim Dallas, September 28, 1979.

6. Copper bars used for the current limiters gradually oxidized at full load operating temperatures. This problem was solved by heavy silverplating of the limiters.

7. Ben Jiminez, April 24, 1979.

8. Clarence Selberg (Hughes Aircraft inspector), April 7, 1979.

9. Gilbert C. Close, "Finishing the World's Largest Airplane," *Industrial Finishing*, December 1945, p. 50.

10. Harry Kaiser, author's interview, November 1977.

11. "Howard Hughes, Airman Extraordinaire," *FAA World*, January 1977, p. 15.

12. Technical details on the flying boat were reported in the following articles: "Hughes Flying Boat, World's Largest Airplane," *Automotive and Aviation Industries*, August 15, 1945, p. 18; "Mammoth Hughes H-4 Nears Takeoff Line," *Aviation*, October, 1945; "The Hughes H-4, Biggest Wooden Airplane Ready," *Canadian Aviation*, October 1945, p. 4; "Design Aspects of the Hughes H-4," *Industrial Aviation*, October 1945, p. 24.

13. Al Geverink, author's interview, November 21, 1977.

14. David Grant, author's interview, November 1977 and April 26, 1979.

15. The Hughes staff engineer in charge of controls was Wressey Cocke, David Grant became responsible for the hydraulic system that powered the controls.

16. Christopher Reising, Jr., author's interview, November 7, 1977.

Notes to Chapter 9

1. Hugh Fulton to E.A. Locke, Jr., January 14, 1944, "Aircraft, Cargo—Production," Record Group 179, "Records of the War Production Board," File 314.444, National Archives, Washington, D.C.

2. U.S. Congress. Senate. Special Committee to Investigate the National Defense Program. Hearings. 80th Congress, 1st session. Part 40, *Aircraft Contracts (Hughes Aircraft Co. and Kaiser-Hughes Corp.)* (Washington, D.C.: Government Printing Office, 1947). Part 43, *Aircraft Contracts, Hughes Aircraft Co.* (Washington, D.C.: Government Printing Office, 1948), p. 24675.

3. *Aviation Week*, August 11, 1947, p. 11.

4. Ibid.

5. Dietrich and Thomas, *The Amazing Mr. Hughes*, p. 200.

6. *New York Times*, February 1, 1947, p.1.

7. Hearings, p. 24201.

8. Ibid., p. 24135.

9. Ibid., p. 24120.

10. Ibid., p. 24123.

11. Ibid., p. 24135.

12. Ibid., p. 24140.

13. Ibid., p. 24137.

14. Ibid., p. 24131.

15. Ibid., p. 24142.

16. Ibid., p. 24178.

17. *Washington Post*, August 8, 1947.

18. Hearings, p. 24122.

19. Francis D. Flanagan, author's interview, January 23, 1980.

20. Hearings, p. 23869.

21. Hearings, p. 24145.

22. Ibid., p. 24122.

23. Noah Dietrich and Bob Thomas, *Howard: The Amazing Mr. Hughes*, (Greenwich, Conn.: Fawcett Publications, Inc., 1976), p. 200.

24. Hearings, p. 24183.

25. Ibid., p. 24185.

26. David Grant, author's interview, April 26, 1979.

27. Charles E. ("Gene") Blandford, author's interview, Palos Verdes, California, October 25, 1979. Clarence A. Shoop, the chase pilot who witnessed Blandford's wild ride, also witnessed the last moments of flight before the near-fatal crash of the first F-11. His expert, eyewitness statement concerning the 1946 crash appears in Hearings, p. 24510.

28. Francis D. Flanagan, author's interview, January 23, 1980.

29. George Meader memorandum, "Hughes Aircraft Investigation," April 16, 1947, Hearings, Exhibit 2522, pp. 24683-24686.

30. Ibid., p. 24684.

31. Ibid.

32. Ibid., p. 24685.

33. Ibid.

34. Drew Pearson, *Diaries: 1949-1959*, ed. by Tyler Abell (New York: Holt Rinehart & Winston, 1974), p. 478.

35. Jack Anderson with James Boyd, *Confessions of a Muckraker* (New York: Random House, 1979), p. 69-74.

36. *New York Times*, July 29, 1947, p. 3.

37. Ibid., July 31, 1947.

38. Ibid., August 1, 1947, p. 36.

39. Ibid.

40. Ibid., p. 1.

41. Jack Anderson, Anderson and Boyd, *Confessions*, p. 58.

42. *Aviation Week*, August 11, 1947, p. 11.

43. Anderson and Boyd *Confessions*, p. 70.

44. *New York Times*, August 4, 1947, p. 1.

45. Glenn E. Odekirk, author's interview, November 2, 1979.

46. *New York Times*, August 6, 1947, p. 3.

Notes to Chapter 10

1. Earl Martyn, author's interview, October 9, 1979.

2. Paramount News, August 13, 1947, PN 6.100, Record Group 200, National Archives, Washington, D.C.

3. Earl Martyn, January 13, 1978.

4. Noah Dietrich and Bob Thomas, *Howard: The Amazing Mr. Hughes* (Greenwich, Conn.: Fawcett Publications, Inc.), p. 203.

5. U.S. Congress. Senate. Special Committee to Investigate the National Defense Program. Hearings. 80th Congress, 1st session. Part 40, *Aircraft Contracts (Hughes Aircraft Co. and Kaiser-Hughes Corp.)* (Washington, D.C.: Government Printing Office, 1947). Part 43, *Aircraft Contracts, Hughes Aircraft Co.* (Washington, D.C.: Government Printing Office, 1948), p. 24089.

6. This tardiness was unintended. According to Dietrich, Hughes had locked himself in his room at the Carlton, and the combination of exhaustion and his deafness prevented Dietrich from waking him until they had used a duplicate key to unlock the door and a twisted coat hanger to release the chain lock (Dietrich and Thomas, *The Amazing Mr. Hughes*, p. 203).

7. Hearings, p. 24113.

8. William P. Rogers, author's interview, December 17, 1979. Rogers, who later became secretary of state under President Nixon, commented that "Hughes used the hearings to his advantage. Whenever there was a penetrating question, he couldn't hear. Eccentric, but clever like a fox."

9. Hearings, p. 24113.

10. *Washington Post*, August 7, 1947.

11. Hearings, p. 24116.

12. Ibid., p. 24117.

13. Ibid., p. 24119.

14. Ibid., p. 24119.

15. Paramount News, August 13, 1947.

16. Hearings, p. 24125.

17. Ibid., p. 24127.

18. Francis D. Flanagan, author's interview, January 23, 1980.

19. Hearings, pp. 24153-24155.

20. Paramount News, August 13, 1947.

21. Hearings, pp. 24155-24156.

22. Jack Anderson with James Boyd, *Confessions of a Muckraker* (New York: Random House, 1979), p. 84.

23. Hearings, p. 24156.

24. Ibid., pp. 24158-24173.

25. Ibid., P. 24175.

26. Ibid., p. 24186.

27. Ibid., pp. 24187-24188.

28. Ibid., p. 24188. Sen. Claude Pepper was a New Dealer, a loyal Democrat, and very able— "one of the brightest minds in the Senate," in the opinion of Francis Flanagan, "and one of the quickest." In defending the interests of the Roosevelt administration he was "a regular defense counsel" for Hughes. However, Carl Byoir did closely advise Hughes throughout the course of the hearings.

29. Ibid., p. 24196.

30. Ibid., p. 24197.

31. Ibid., pp. 24198-24199.

32. Paramount News, August 13, 1947.

33. *Washington Post*, August 8, 1947.

34. Hearings, p. 24254.

35. *Time*, August 18, 1947, p. 18.

36. *Washington Post*, August 8, 1947.

37. *Newsweek*, August 18, 1947.

38. Ibid.

39. Hearings, p. 24256.

40. Ibid., p. 24269.

41. Edward R. Murrow, "I Can Hear It Now," Columbia Masterworks Recording, XLP 1774, Side 1.

42. Hearings, pp. 24272-24277.

43. Ibid., p. 24290.

44. Ibid., pp. 24345-24346.

45. Ibid., pp. 24356-24357.

46. Ibid., p. 24354.

47. Ibid., p. 24361.

48. Ibid., p. 24362.

49. Ibid., p. 24364.

50. Ibid., p. 24363.

51. Ibid., p. 24305.

52. Ibid., p. 24303.

53. Ibid., p. 24366.

54. Ibid., p. 24370.

55. Ibid., p. 24377.

56. Ibid., p. 24378.

57. *Washington Post*, August 12, 1947.

58. *New York Times*, Sunday, August 10, 1947, p. 3.

59. *New York Times*, August 12, 1947, p. 1.

60. Ibid.

61. *Washington Post*, Tuesday, August 12, 1947, p. 1.

62. *New York Times*, August 12, 1947, p. 15.

63. Anderson and Boyd, *Muckraker*, p. 89.

Notes to Chapter 11

1. *Washington Post*, August 12, 1947, p. 1.

2. Charles E. ("Gene") Blandford, author's interview, October 25, 1979.

3. Merle Coffee, author's interview, March 5, 1979.

4. John H. Glenn, author's interview, January 13, 1979.

5. Chuck Jucker, author's interview, March 11, 1979. Hughes had met Jean Peters the year before, but he was not to marry her until March 1957, the year he fired Noah Dietrich. Nadine Henley, Hughes's longtime secretary and administrative assistant, told Odekirk just before the marriage that Dietrich had planned a takeover in which he was going to have Hughes committed. Odekirk told the author on October 10, 1979 that part of the advice they subsequently gave Hughes was to get married because only a wife could commit a husband.

6. Don Smith (flight engineer), author's interview, October 30, 1979.

7. Ben Jiminez, author's interview, April 24, 1979.

8. David Grant, author's interview, July 15, 1979.

9. Harry Kaiser, author's interview, November 1977.

10. Al Geverink, author's interview, November 27, 1977.

11. Clarence Selberg (aircraft inspector), letter to author, April 14, 1979.

12. John Glenn, author's interview, January 13, 1978.

13. Phil Thibodeau, author's interview, November 1977.

14. Ben Jiminez, April 24, 1979.

15. David Grant, July 15, 1979.

16. Ibid., July 25, 1979.

17. John Parkinson, author's interview, spring 1977.

18. Scholer Bangs, "Hughes Answers Senate Probe With First Flying Boat Flight," *Aviation Week*, November 10, 1947.

19. Paramount News, November 8, 1947, PN 7.21, Record Group 200, National Archives, Washington, D.C.

20. Chuck Jucker, July 16, 1979.

21. George Bromley (General Supervisor, Plant Engineering, Pier E. Terminal Island), author's interview, October 26, 1979.

22. Jack Jacobsen, author's interview, November 27, 1977.

23. Glenn E. Odekirk, author's interview, October 10, 1979.

24. Rae E. Hopper, letter to the author, June 1, 1977.

25. Sheilah Graham, *How to Marry Super Rich* (New York: Grosset & Dunlap, 1974), p.

217. Two recent biographers of Hughes say that such stories of Hughes's anonymous kindnesses are only part of a contrived legend "woven from fantasy." "His charity was reserved for those who could return a favor, when the act itself would help him achieve some fleeting ambition, or when it was a legal necessity" (Donald L. Bartlett and James B. Steele, *Empire: The Life, Legend, and Madness of Howard Hughes*, New York: W.W. Norton & Co., 1979, p. 487). However, when Glenn Odekirk was asked if this assessment was true, he said, "No way! I was with him personally so I know the things he did for people" (Glenn Odekirk, October 2, 1980).

26. Harry Kaiser, author's interview, April 9, 1979.

27. From a crew list prepared by crew chief Chuck Jucker. Note that one of the reasons George Haldeman was on board as the official technical observer was his past experience with big boats. He had flown the big Dornier DO-X in Germany and the Boeing 314 flying clippers bought by Pan American and TWA.

28. Gene Blandford, October 25, 1979.

29. David Grant, July 15, 1979.

30. James C. McNamara, author's interview, October 31, 1979.

31. Chuck Jucker, July 19, 1979.

32. James McNamara, October 31, 1979.

33. David Van Storm, author's interview, October 4, 1979.

34. During the author's visit with James McNamara in Pasadena, California on October 31, 1979, McNamara invited the author to place his tape recorder next to his and make a copy of that famous broadcast and of his interview with Howard Hughes.

35. David Grant, October 1980.

36. Merle Coffee, July 19, 1979.

37. David Grant, November 21, 1977 and July 15, 1979.

38. Jack Jacobsen, author's interview, November 27, 1977.

39. David Van Storm, comments, September 2, 1980.

40. Harry Kaiser, November 29, 1977.

41. Ben Jiminez, April 24, 1979.

42. Bill Noggle, author's interview, November 29, 1977.

43. Phil Thibodeau, November 1977.

44. Al Geverink, November 21, 1977.

45. Don Shirey, author's interview, October 21, 1979.

46. Ben Jiminez, April 24, 1979.

47. Don Smith, author's interview, October 30, 1979.

48. Glenn E. Odekirk, October 10, 1979.

49. David Grant, November 21, 1977.

50. From James McNamara's recording of the broadcast.

51. David Grant, April 26, 1979.

52. Merle Coffee, March 5, 1979.

53. James C. McNamara, October 31, 1979.

54. David Grant, November 21, 1977.

55. William Flynn (aviation writer), *San Francisco Chronicle*, November 3, 1947, p. 7.

56. Glenn E. Odekirk, November 2, 1979.

57. Rae Hopper, letter to the author, June 1, 1977.

58. David Grant, November 21, 1977. Flight test engineer Blandford said that the HK-1 hull was designed to accelerate and climb out of the water with practically no change in angle of attack—quite unlike Hughes's old Sikorsky, which went through great excursions of angle of attack while climbing up on the step and then planing heavily before takeoff.

59. David Grant, November 21, 1977.

60. Carl Babberger, author's interview, May 15, 1979.

61. Chuck Jucker, July 19, 1979.

62. David Grant, July 19, 1979.

Notes to Chapter 12

1. U.S. Congress. Senate. Special Committee to Investigate the National Defense Program. Hearings. 80th Congress, 1st session. Part 40, *Aircraft Contracts (Hughes Aircraft Co. and*

Kaiser-Hughes Corp.) (Washington, D.C.: Government Printing Office, 1947). Part 42, *Aircraft Contracts, Hughes Aircraft Co.* (Washington, D.C.: Government Printing Office, 1948). p.23561.

2. *Aviation Week*, April 26, 1948, p. 14.

3. Ibid., May 24, 1948, p. 10.

4. Claude Pepper, author's interview, November 13, 1980.

5. Jack Anderson and James Boyd, *Confessions of a Muckraker*, (New York: Random House, 1979), p. 91.

6. Claude Pepper, November 13, 1980.

7. Anderson and Boyd, p. 96.

8. Noah Dietrich and Bob Thomas, *Howard: The Amazing Mr. Hughes* (Greenwich, Conn.: Fawcett Publications, Inc.), p. 208.

9. Charles Vickers (former manager, Port of Long Beach), author's interview, October 30, 1979.

10. Author's tour of the flying boat in its hangar at Terminal Island with George Bromley, general supervisor of plant engineering, October 26, 1979.

11. Nadine Henley, in written comments to the author, September 17, 1980.

12. Al Geverink, author's interview, November 21, 1979.

13. Rae Hopper, letter to the author, June 1, 1977.

14. Glenn Odekirk, author's interview, October 10, 1979.

15. Wayne Thomas, "Hughes Alters Plane to Strengthen It," *Chicago Tribune*, May 4, 1948.

16. David Grant, author's interview, November 27, 1977.

17. Hearings, p. 24329.

18. Al Geverink, November 27, 1977.

19. Don Lopez, author's interview, April 18, 1977.

20. Nadine Henley to Howard Hughes, January 17, 1975, Hughes Estate, Harris County, Texas. Nadine Henley told the author on November 12, 1980 that this memo turned up in what was called the "Mexican Papers" at the time of Hughes's death. "A tax lawyer from Andrews Kurth called me up and said he was very shocked to see the memo I had written Mr. Hughes about the flying boat. And I said, 'What were you shocked about?' And he said, 'I didn't know that you wrote to him so frankly.' (She laughed) That's the thing. We were very quiet with other people around us, but we always said what we thought, both of us, when we were together. We had a fine relationship. He was a gentleman. When I first went to work with Hughes Aircraft in 1940 [as secretary to chief engineer Stan Bell], I always referred to him as 'Father.' This was just sort of a joke between Stan Bell and me, because if Mr. Hughes would be in the engineering department he would be there very late. I would write Stan Bell a note: 'Father was here and Little Indian may be late this morning.' "

She went on to say that they were very formal with each other, he was always 'Mr. Hughes' to her. "He expected me to call him 'Howard,' but I never did. He would tell me to call somebody and say this and that, and during his statement of what he wanted me to say he'd say, 'Now you tell them I just talked to Howard and he said so-and-so and I said so-and-so,' but I always called the person and said I just talked to 'Mr. Hughes.' I was always formal about it and he always called me 'Miss Henley.' There were many other women who worked for him that he called Jean or Joan, whatever, but he always called me Miss Henley until I got married, and then he had trouble remembering my married name [and] started to call me 'Nadine'."

21. R. Adm. Carl Seiberlich, author's interview, March 15, 1977.

22. Ibid.

23. Carl Babberger, author's interview, May 15, 1979.

24. Dr. Harvey Chaplin, author's interview, October 2, 1979.

25. *Times Herald*, Newport News, Virginia, April 27, 1977.

26. Following Hughes's death Summa endowed the Howard Hughes Memorial Award, which has been presented annually by the Aero Club of Southern California and the Marina City Club where the Aero Club is headquartered.

27. Eddie Holohan (secretary of the Aero Club of Southern California, formerly with

Flying Tiger Airline and now with the Los Angeles Department of Airports), author's interview, November 13, 1980.

28. Howard Hughes, letter, "To the Men and Women of Hughes Aircraft Company," Deposition #13, in connection with Deposition of Glenn Edward Odekirk, #139,362, September 7, 1977 in Los Angeles, California, Hughes Estate, Harris County, Texas.

Notes to Appendix

1. *Aviation Week*, August 11, 1947, p. 11.

2. Jack Jacobsen, author's interview, November 27, 1977.

3. John Keats, *Howard Hughes* (New York: Random House, 1972), p. 69.

4. Jack Jacobsen, November 27, 1977.

5. Earl Martyn, author's interview, November 1977.

6. Ibid.

7. John Glenn, author's interview, January 13, 1978.

8. Sherman M. Fairchild, interview by Anthony Brandt, summer 1964, Public Relations Office, Fairchild Industries, Hagerstown, Maryland.

9. Carl Babberger, author's interview, March 5, 1979.

10. Jack Jacobsen, November 27, 1977.

11. John Glenn, January 13, 1978.

12. Carl Babberger, March 5, 1979.

13. Ibid.

14. Ray Kirkpatrick, author's interview, November 10, 1979.

15. Carl Babberger, March 5, 1979.

16. David Grant, author's interview, April 26, 1979.

17. Roy Wendahl, author's interview, October 29, 1980.

18. Rae Hopper, author's interview, spring 1977.

19. Earl Martin, author's interview, September 27, 1979.

20. Jill Schary Zimmer, *With a Cast of Thousands: A Hollywood Childhood* (New York: Stein and Day, 1963), p. 180.

21. Don Dwiggins, *Howard Hughes: The True Story* (Santa Monica, Calif.: Werner Book Corporation, 1972), p. 10.

22. Carl Babberger, March 5, 1979.

23. Bruce Burk, author's interview, May 15, 1979.

24. Supervising Engineer, Defense Plant Corporation, Culver City, California re Kaiser-Hughes, Plancor 1424, Management of the Cargo Plane Project, August 27, 1943, Record Group 179, "Records of the War Production Board," File 314.4442, National Archives, Washington, D.C.

25. Carl Babberger, February 21, 1979.

26. Clarence L. ("Kelly") Johnson, author's interview, October 22, 1980.

27. Bruce Burk, May 15, 1979.

28. Bill Grant, author's interview, October 9, 1979.

29. Carl Babberger, March 11, 1979.

30. Ibid., March 5, 1979.

31. U.S. Congress. Senate. Special Committee to Investigate the National Defense Program. Hearings. 80th Congress, 1st session. Part 40, *Aircraft Contracts (Hughes Aircraft Co. and Kaiser-Hughes Corp.)* (Washington, D.C.: Government Printing Office, 1947). Part 43, *Aircraft Contracts, Hughes Aircraft Co.* (Washington, D.C.: Government Printing Office, 1948), p. 24180.

32. Christopher A. Reising, Jr., author's interview, November 7, 1977.

33. Roy Wendahl, October 29, 1980.

34. John Glenn, January 13, 1978.

35. Van Storm, author's interview, October 4, 1979.

36. John Glenn, January 13, 1978.

37. Earl Martyn, November 1977.

38. Ibid., January 13, 1978.

39. A senior Hughes engineer who prefers not to be quoted by name.

40. Noah Dietrich and Bob Thomas, *Howard: The Amazing Mr. Hughes* (Greenwich, Conn.: Fawcett Publications, Inc.), p. 129.

41. Glenn Odekirk, author's interview, October 10, 1979.

42. George W. Haldeman, author's interview, January 30, 1980.

43. Bill Grant, October 9, 1979.

44. Mrs. Earl Martyn, author's interview, February 1979.

45. "Howard Hughes, Airman Extraordinaire," *FAA World*, January 1977, p. 12. Courtesy Ted Maher, FAA Public Affairs, Washington, D.C.

46. Ibid., p. 14.

47. John Parkinson, author's interview, spring 1977. Nadine Henley questions that the cards were gaudy and triple-sized. "I bought all of HRH's Christmas cards until he married Jean Peters, which was 1947 or 1948. I always had small *understated* cards on very fine stationery with plain greeting of 'Merry Christmas and a Happy New Year' in small print" (Nadine Henley, comments, September 17, 1980).

48. Earl Martyn, January 13, 1978.

49. Edward West, Jr., author's interviews in Arlington, Va. June 5 and 6, 1981, and West's marginal notes on the manuscript and comments mailed to the author July, 1981.

50. Wayne Thomis, "Plywood Flying Boat— Hughes' Last Great Triumph in Public," *Chicago Tribune*, 1971.

Index

Andy Witherspoon

February 11, 1982—Spruce Goose moves to her ultimate "home" adjacent to the Queen Mary.

Andy Witherspoon